Scotch Baronial

Architecture and National Identity in Scotland

*Miles Glendinning and
Aonghus MacKechnie*

BLOOMSBURY VISUAL ARTS
LONDON • NEW YORK • OXFORD • NEW DELHI • SYDNEY

BLOOMSBURY VISUAL ARTS
Bloomsbury Publishing Plc
50 Bedford Square, London, WC1B 3DP, UK
1385 Broadway, New York, NY 10018, USA

BLOOMSBURY, BLOOMSBURY VISUAL ARTS and the Diana logo are trademarks
of Bloomsbury Publishing Plc

First published in Great Britain 2019
Hardback edition reprinted 2019
Paperback edition first published in Great Britain, 2021

Copyright © Miles Glendinning and Aonghus MacKechnie, 2021

Miles Glendinning and Aonghus MacKechnie have asserted their right under the Copyright,
Designs and Patents Act, 1988, to be identified as Authors of this work.

For legal purposes the Acknowledgements on p. xi constitute an extension
of this copyright page.

Cover design: Eleanor Rose
Cover image: Winton House, © Historic Environment Scotland

All rights reserved. No part of this publication may be reproduced or
transmitted in any form or by any means, electronic or mechanical,
including photocopying, recording, or any information storage or retrieval
system, without prior permission in writing from the publishers.

Bloomsbury Publishing Plc does not have any control over, or responsibility for, any
third-party websites referred to or in this book. All internet addresses given in this
book were correct at the time of going to press. The author and publisher regret any
inconvenience caused if addresses have changed or sites have ceased to exist, but can
accept no responsibility for any such changes.

A catalogue record for this book is available from the British Library.

A catalog record for this book is available from the Library of Congress.

ISBN: HB: 978-1-4742-8347-2
PB: 978-1-3501-6616-5
ePDF: 978-1-4742-8349-6
eBook: 978-1-4742-8348-9

Typeset by Newgen KnowledgeWorks Pvt. Ltd., Chennai, India
Printed and bound in Great Britain

To find out more about our authors and books visit www.bloomsbury.com
and sign up for our newsletters.

CONTENTS

List of Figures vi
Acknowledgements xi
List of Abbreviations xii

Introduction 1

Part One The First Castle Age

1 Pre-1603: Castellated Architecture and 'Martial Independence' 9
2 1603–1660: Court Architecture under the Regnal Union 25
3 1660–1689: Sunset of the Stuarts – From Castellation to Classicism 49
4 1689–1750: The Architecture of Dynastic Struggle 69

Part Two The Second Castle Age

5 1750–1790: Enlightenment and Romanticism 93
6 1790–1820: National Architecture in the Age of Revolution 113
7 1820–1840: Scott, Abbotsford and 'Scotch' Romanticism 133
8 1840–1870: Billings and Bryce – Mid-Century Baronial 163
9 1870–1914: Scotch Traditionalism 203
10 1914 Onwards: Scottish Architectural Identity in the Age of Modernism 233

Notes 253
Index 285

FIGURES

1.1 Caerlaverock Castle – built c. 1260–70, reconstructed c. 1630 12
1.2 Bothwell Castle – aerial view of 1968 13
1.3 St Machar's, Aberdeen, west front – completed 1440 14
1.4 King's College, Aberdeen – chapel (dated 2 April 1500) 15
1.5 Stirling Castle – forework showing triumphal arch gateway built 1500–1510 for King James IV 17
1.6 Kellie Castle – built mostly sixteenth century 20
1.7 Elcho Castle – built in phases from c. 1560 21
1.8 Fyvie Castle – 1590s west front 22
2.1 Linlithgow Palace – north quarter, begun 1618 28
2.2 Huntly Castle – rebuilt from 1602 32
2.3 Craigievar Castle – rebuilt 1620s 34
2.4 Castle Fraser – heightened 1617–18 by I. Bell 35
2.5 Amisfield Tower – built 1600 37
2.6 Pitreavie Castle – built c. 1630 39
2.7 Winton House – rebuilt 1620s 40
2.8 George Heriot's Hospital, dated 1 July 1628 41
2.9 Parliament House, Edinburgh, 1632–8, and Parliament Close 42
3.1 Palace of Holyroodhouse – rebuilt 1671–8, incomplete until twentieth century 53
3.2 Thirlestane Castle – rebuilt by Sir William Bruce, 1670–77 56
3.3 Glamis Castle – rebuilt 1668–84; 1686 elevation of main front 58
3.4 Drumlanrig Castle – rebuilt c. 1675–97 59

3.5 Leslie Castle – foundation stone dated 17 June 1661, dormer head dated 1664 60

3.6 Neidpath Castle – late medieval tower modified pre-1686 with gateway added 61

3.7 Kinross House – built from late 1670s by and for Sir William Bruce 64

3.8 Balcaskie House – rebuilt 1668–74 as a near-symmetrical house 65

4.1 Traquair House – a classicizing scheme of c. 1700 included the forecourt 75

4.2 Kelburn Castle – view from north centred on 1720s house 76

4.3 Craighall Castle – the arcaded 1697–9 frontispiece linked the castle's tower (on the right) and western turret (on the left) 77

4.4 Midhope Castle – tower house, plus lower wing completed late seventeenth century 78

4.5 Taymouth House – William Adam's modernization scheme of c. 1739 80

4.6 Michael Chapel, Gordonstoun – neo-Gothic private chapel dated 1705 82

4.7 Inveraray Castle – view from south with Duniquaich / *Dùn na Cuaiche* in background, a skyline folly of 1747–8 84

4.8 Inveraray Castle – unexecuted project by Dougal Campbell, c. 1744 87

4.9 Inveraray Castle – plans as executed by Roger Morris, 1744/5 88

5.1 Castle Huntly – restored by James Playfair and John Paterson, 1777–95 99

5.2 Gordon Castle – view from south-east, facing the garden 101

5.3 Douglas Castle – plans by John and James Adam as partially executed from 1757 103

5.4 Melville Castle by James Playfair, 1786–91 104

5.5 Melville Castle – James Playfair's plans of the ground and bedroom floors of the east wing 105
5.6 Wedderburn by Robert and James Adam, 1771–5 107
5.7 Seton House by Robert Adam 1789 – view showing entrance beyond the 'barmkin' 109
5.8 Culzean Castle by Robert Adam 1777–92 – view from south-west 110
5.9 Raehills House – view from south-east showing Alexander Stevens's 1782 design 111
6.1 Nelson Monument by Robert Burn, 1806, celebrating naval victory at Trafalgar, 1805 116
6.2 Statue of Sir William Wallace, Guardian of Scotland, Dryburgh – erected 1814 119
6.3 Mauldslie Castle – watercolour by David Bryce, 1860 121
6.4 Monzie Castle by John Paterson, c. 1795–1800 122
6.5 Darnaway Castle by Alexander Laing, 1802–12 123
6.6 Taymouth Castle – main block largely by John Paterson, from 1801 124
6.7 Taymouth Castle – staircase plasterwork by Francis Bernasconi, c. 1809 125
6.8 Kinfauns Castle by Robert Smirke, 1802 128
7.1 Edinburgh Castle and Esplanade – view showing reception of George IV 137
7.2 Abbotsford House, completed for Sir Walter Scott by William Atkinson, 1824 141
7.3 Abbotsford House – entrance hall and armoury 144
7.4 Tyninghame House – rebuilt by William Burn, 1829 148
7.5 Bonaly Tower by William Playfair, 1836, left-hand wing by Sydney Mitchell, 1888 152
7.6 Floors Castle by William Playfair, 1837–45 153
7.7 Donaldson's Hospital by William Playfair – designed c. 1835 154
7.8 Lennox Castle by David Hamilton, 1837–41 156

7.9 Sir Walter Scott Monument, Edinburgh, designed by George Meikle Kemp, c. 1840 159

8.1 Taymouth Castle – Banner Hall by James Gillespie Graham and A. W. N. Pugin, c. 1840 170

8.2 Balmoral Castle by William Smith for Prince Albert and Queen Victoria, 1853–6 174

8.3 Dunrobin Castle – north entrance front as remodelled by Charles Barry and William Leslie after 1844 176

8.4 Blair Atholl Castle – perspective drawing by David Bryce, 1869 181

8.5 National Wallace Monument, Abbey Craig, Stirling, by John T. Rochead, 1859–69 186

8.6 Albert Memorial, Edinburgh – unexecuted project by David Bryce for Balmoral-type tower 187

8.7 Edinburgh Castle – unexecuted project by F. T. Dollman, 1859 189

8.8 Aberdeen County and Municipal Buildings by Peddie & Kinnear, built 1868–74 190

8.9 Stow Town Hall – built 1854–7, financed by local aristocrat and Liberal MP Alexander Mitchell-Innes 191

8.10 Fettes College, Edinburgh, by David Bryce, 1864–70 193

8.11 Cockburn Street, Edinburgh – engraving of c. 1860 196

9.1 Dalmeny House – unexecuted proposal by Sydney Mitchell & Wilson, 1889 211

9.2 Barnbougle Castle by Wardrop and Reid – completed 1881 212

9.3 The Long Croft, Helensburgh, by A. N. Paterson; drawing published 1903 215

9.4 Hill House, Helensburgh, by C. R. Mackintosh, 1902 217

9.5 Eilean Donan Castle – rebuilt from 1911 by George Mackie Watson 219

9.6 St Leonard's/Free St Leonard's Church, Perth, drawing by J. J. Stevenson, 1882 225

9.7 Thistle Chapel, St Giles, Edinburgh, by Robert Lorimer, 1909–11 227

9.8 Scottish National Portrait Gallery, Edinburgh, by Robert Rowand Anderson, 1885–9 229

9.9 Scottish National Portrait Gallery, Edinburgh 230

10.1 Broughton Place by Basil Spence, 1935–8 235

10.2 Scottish National War Memorial – interior view of Hall of Honour 236

10.3 Scottish National War Memorial by Lorimer and Matthew, 1924–7 237

10.4 Pitlochry Dam and Power Station by Sir Alexander Gibb and Partners, 1947–53 239

10.5 Chessel's Court, Canongate – redevelopment scheme by Robert Hurd and Ian Begg, 1957 240

10.6 Dunbar, Fishermen's Housing, by Basil Spence, 1949–52 242

10.7 Scandic Crown Hotel, Edinburgh, by Ian Begg, 1988 245

10.8 Hillslap Tower – view from north; photograph of c. 1940 247

10.9 Hillslap Tower – photograph of 2002 248

10.10 Edinburgh taxi advertising Holyroodhouse, 2017 249

10.11 Scottish Parliament, Edinburgh, by Enric Miralles, after 1998 250

The support of The Strathmartine Trust towards this publication is gratefully acknowledged.

ACKNOWLEDGEMENTS

We would like to thank our families, friends and colleagues for their unstinting help and support during the preparation of this book. Among the latter, special mention should go to Malcolm Bangor – Jones; David Brown and Tris Clarke and their front-of-house team at the National Records of Scotland; Ian Campbell; Neil Fraser, Ann MacSween and Joe Waterfield at Historic Environment Scotland; Ian Gow; John Lowrey; Florian Urban; and David M. Walker. We also gratefully acknowledge the influence of the late John Dunbar, John Gifford and Charles McKean on our ideas about this topic.

The support of the Strathmartine Trust towards publication is gratefully acknowledged, as is the generosity of the numerous families, individuals and organizations who have kindly made their archives available to public access. We want also to thank the team at Bloomsbury Publishing – Sophie Tann, James Thompson, James Tupper, Shyam Sunder – for their encouragement and efficiency.

ABBREVIATIONS

NLS	National Library of Scotland
NRHE	National Record of the Historic Environment
NRS	National Records of Scotland
ODNB	Oxford Dictionary of National Biography
PSAS	*Proceedings of the Society of Antiquaries of Scotland*
RIAS	Royal Incorporation of Architects in Scotland
RPC	John Hill Burton et al. (eds), *The Register of the Privy Council of Scotland*, 37 vols (Edinburgh: Register House, 1877–1970).
SHR	*Scottish Historical Review*

Introduction

This book tells the story of a prominent and enduring strand within Scottish architecture and Scottish culture – the history of the Scottish castle and of castellated architecture in Scotland. It traces all their diverse phases of architectural expression and sociocultural meaning, including, above all, the pursuit of an architecture of 'national identity' in the 'homes' of the Scottish elites.

This core narrative links in all directions and constantly mutates in its character and concerns, in response to a range of external constraints, political and economic. Some of these had relatively slow trajectories, such as the changes in the nature of elite power stemming from the gradual supersession of feudal society by modern industrial capitalism, the long-standing dynastic tension between Stuart/Jacobite and Hanoverian factions, or the consequences of the development of the British Empire. Some impacts were more sudden, such as the shift to an absentee monarchy after the Union of the Crowns in 1603, or perhaps more dramatic, such as the abolition of heritable jurisdictions in 1747 which diminished the autonomous power and prestige of the landed aristocracy, a situation only partly reversed in the mid-nineteenth century in the eager embrace of Scotland by Queen Victoria.

Equally significant, however, were the constant shifts in cultural values and discourses, including movements such as Romanticism – an international ideology that was significantly shaped in Scotland by Sir Walter Scott, and within which the castle played a crucial role – or the linked ideology of Highlandism, a transformation of martial Gaeldom from an outcast threat to a symbolically central bulwark of 'British Scotland'. Perhaps surprisingly, many of the most emotive meanings of the castle were concerned with the issue of Scotland's place in Britain. Here, by the mid- nineteenth century, a range of cultural and political values had begun a mutually reinforcing interaction, to produce a potentially strong sense of Scottish national identity within Britain and the British Empire – the concept of 'Unionist nationalism', a world-outlook which provided a fertile context for the emergence of the climactic episode in our architectural story – the mid-nineteenth-century Scotch Baronial of David Bryce and his followers.

Within our story, architecture was not just an offshoot or reflection of politics of culture, but it had its own strong internal narrative of national identity, which evolved from the diverse but diffuse patterns of castellated architecture in the fifteenth to seventeenth centuries to the more precisely articulated historic styles of the nineteenth century – styles among which one of the most strongly defined was the Scotch Baronial. But these shifts in the specifically architectural concept of national identity were of even more crucial importance in the emergence of Scotch Baronial. The emergence and flourishing of the 'Scottish castle' from the twelfth or thirteenth to the seventeenth centuries, its eighteenth-century retreat in the face of an increasingly triumphal classicism, and its return as a more self-consciously 'Scotch', Romantic architectural ideology is the central theme of this book. That architectural narrative came to an end once more in the twentieth century, with its dominating architectural and cultural ideology of modernism and its growing tendency towards an international or even global economy and society. Within the Scottish context, the twentieth-century end of castle-building of any kind seemed to reflect the gradual decline in the power and prestige of the old landed elites, and more generally the withering away of the monarchical culture of unionist nationalism that they had championed. But that did not mean that the castle disappeared from Scottish architectural discourse – far from it. Instead, as we will see in the final chapter, the built legacy of both episodes of the castle story, the original thirteenth- to seventeenth-century castellated epoch and the eighteenth to early twentieth-century Scotch era, shifted from the arena of new architectural production and design into the linked but parallel field of heritage preservation.

To help structure this long and potentially confusing narrative, the chronological chapters have been divided into two broad epochs or 'ages', reflecting the profound political/cultural and architectural rupture in castle-building that occurred during the eighteenth century. In Part One of the book, comprising Chapters 1–3, we trace the 'First Castle Age' – the period from the late Middle Ages to the late seventeenth century, within which castellated architecture, in all its very broad diversity, flourished under the prestige of Scotland's feudal elites, with the Stewart monarchy initially playing a leading role in patronage, but the landed classes largely taking their place as patrons after the transformation of the monarchy to absentee status following the Union of the Crowns in 1603. This was a time when the international, universal ideology of classicism began to gain ground, in the process assuming an almost limitless variety of individual forms across Europe – including Scotland. But at all stages, early classicism during the 'Scottish Renaissance' was inextricably entangled with the castellated tradition, which only seemed to gain associative power during the seventeenth-century era of absentee monarchy.

The final rejection of the direct Stuart line in 1689, and its replacement by the aggressively modernizing Whig world-outlook that followed, brought the extended First Castle Age to a decisive and relatively rapid end. The immediate result, as we will see in Chapter 4 – an 'interregnum' chapter between Part One and Part Two – was a half-century of disorientation and uncertainty, architectural as much as political, within which the cause of classical architecture seemed suddenly to sweep all before it. But after that brief interlude, as we will see in Chapter 5, the birth pangs of a Second Castle Age began with astonishing speed – immediately following the final defeat of the Jacobite insurrections in 1746. From the start, this new ethos demonstrated fundamental differences from its predecessor, not least in its far more intellectually calculated relationship to the forces of modernity and improvement that were sweeping the country ever more violently as the eighteenth century proceeded.

As we will see in Chapters 5–10, the Second Castle Age would be shorter than the First – lasting only two centuries. It served as a kind of mirror of modernity, helping to offset the disruptive impacts of rampant urbanization and industrialization by celebrating the continuing prestige of Scotland's cultural traditions and landed elites. Steered now by named, celebrated architects, such as Robert Adam or William Burn, it exploited the powerful Scottish, or (as it was then called) 'Scotch' branch of the Romantic Movement, shaped by the writings of Walter Scott, as a symbolic bulwark of the new, passionately unionist Scottish identity that flourished under the British Empire – an ideology within which the position and status of the Highlands had changed fundamentally, from a wilderness of savagery to a redoubt of martial valour. These ideas initially found a range of architectural expressions alongside that of the new castle, including permutations of Gothic and Tudor styles. But the undisputed architectural climax of the Second Castle Age was the Scotch Baronial movement of the mid- and late nineteenth century – an architectural episode that coincided with the heyday of British imperial power, and of Scottish commitment to the colonial adventure in all its manifold aspects. Sanctified by Queen Victoria's embrace of the Highlands in her mountain 'home' of Balmoral, and invested with architectural power and panache by David Bryce and his contemporaries, Scotch Baronial expanded from its original stronghold of country-house architecture to take in a range of modern building types, urban as well as rural – including, of course, all manner of 'national monuments', as exemplified by the National Wallace Monument near Stirling.

At the end of the nineteenth and the beginning of the twentieth centuries, Scotch Baronial successfully navigated the transition from the architecture of laissez-faire individualism and ornate eclecticism to a new spirit of 'monumental simplicity', celebrated architecturally in the 'Scotch traditionalism' of architects such as Rowand Anderson or Sydney Mitchell. The end of the Second Castle Age followed almost immediately, after the upheaval of the Great War ushered in an era of far more radically egalitarian modernism, within which the traditional landed classes and their towered, turreted homes, old or new, seemed an anachronism if not an outright embarrassment – appropriately enough, the last really significant project of a significantly Baronial character was the 1920s' Scottish National War Memorial in Edinburgh Castle.

In recent decades, as we will see in Chapter 10, Scotland has once again entered an era of accentuated concern for symbols of national identity – but as demonstrated in the lavish new Scottish parliament project at Holyrood, the architectural means available for expressing that concern within the built environment now involve obliquely metaphoric or 'iconic' gestures rather than explicit historical styles or ornate details such as turrets or crowsteps. Instead, the architectural legacies of both the First and Second Castle Ages have now been appropriated by the world of heritage conservation, a homogenizing setting within which the originally sharp differences between the two Ages have begun to seem less and less important – even as the relationship between Scottish and British identities becomes more and more polarized, and the relationship between national identity of any kind and the forces of globalization becomes ever more problematic.

Overall, the chief focus of this book, not least in terms of chapter length, is the Second Castle Age. It sets out to explain how and why it was Scotland that produced Europe's first and longest sustained age of castle revivalism; and why the fashion continued when places elsewhere adopted different architectural aims. But while the main part of this book concerns the age of castle revival, this analysis has had to be grounded in an understanding of the First Castle Age up to the eighteenth century, because that period provided the cultural paradigms, ideologies, resource material and models adopted by the revivalists.

In following this protracted narrative, in tracing the ever-changing connotations and imagery of the castle and of castellated architecture, we have had to systematically correlate documentary history with architectural history, in a way not often attempted in previous Scottish histories of the built environment – with notable exceptions such as documentary historian Ronald Cant and architectural historians John Dunbar and Charles McKean. This book is straightforwardly intended to bridge that gap, combining both disciplines in an attempt to arrive at a more nuanced definition of one of the most enduringly significant strands of Scottish architecture.

In this sense, the book differs significantly from previous 'castle' or 'Baronial' studies, and also from more general architectural histories of Scotland, as pioneered by John Dunbar's *The Historic Architecture of Scotland* (1966). Dunbar, in his official role at the Royal Commission on the Ancient and Historical Monuments of Scotland, was one of several contributors to the topographical *Inventory* series, which documented rather than narrated historic castles; the similarly arranged *Buildings of Scotland* series, from 1978, led by Colin McWilliam and John Gifford, likewise described castles one by one within a guidebook format.

Publications by individual authors on the First Castle Age include those by William Douglas Simpson (for whom the National Library of Scotland catalogue lists 171 entries!), Stewart Cruden, Nigel Tranter, Chris Tabraham, Deborah Howard and Harry Gordon Slade. A recent work by a documentary specialist is Michael Brown's *Scottish Baronial Castles 1250–1450* (2009), Fiona Watson has also published on medieval castles, and Richard Oram has published more generally on the topic of Scottish medieval architecture. For the sixteenth to seventeenth centuries, Alan MacDonald has provided a fresh understanding of the architectural setting of the Scottish parliament, while Ian Campbell has argued that Scotland was a contributor and sometimes even a leader in wider Renaissance-age fashion. This book makes a similar point, but more forcefully regarding the international significance of the Second Castle Age – an epoch that has stimulated rather fewer dedicated books, one exception being Michael Davis's *Scots Baronial* (1996). Many, however, have contributed to studies on the period, most notably David Walker, whose work while in charge of the national 'historic buildings lists', and his more recent online *Dictionary of Scottish Architects*, also significantly enhanced scholarly knowledge of the topic.

In evaluating both Castle Ages, we have constantly sought to pinpoint the political or cultural significance or symbolism of architectural choices or decisions, as opposed to restricted stylistic analyses. Firm evidence for these connotations of course becomes scarcer in the case of earlier buildings, but even here, research in recent decades by historians including Roger Mason and Michael Lynch has begun to contextualize motifs such as the imperial crown spire motif, or the 'Solomonic' proportion system of Stirling's Chapel Royal. In purely stylistic or formal terms, the core concern of the book is castellated architecture of all kinds, whether battlemented, turreted or crowstepped in appearance, and whether asymmetrical or symmetrical in planform, but its dual focus on built form and concepts of national identity broadens its potential architectural scope to include, for example, the widespread early nineteenth-century introduction of elements from English Tudor and Jacobean models such as bay windows and flattened arches. Overall, the central theme of the book is the relationship between architecture and the concept of the 'heritage of Scotland' – the persistent concern among elite patrons for their buildings to appear clearly Scottish – and to draw on Scotland's past in order to show the continuing vigour of Scottish culture – yet built for clients who, from the seventeenth century onwards, were no less clearly unionist Britons. These were castle-builders who accepted unquestioningly the value of the union with England that had brought Britain into existence – Scots who regarded themselves as both Scottish and, more importantly, British. This was the architecture of unionist nationalism.

PART ONE

The First Castle Age

1

Pre-1603: Castellated Architecture and 'Martial Independence'

Amid the Meid, repleit with sweit odouris,
A palice stude with many Royal Towris . . .[1]
– GAVIN DOUGLAS, C. 1501

. . . ful jurisdicioune and fre impire within his realme[2]
– 1469 PARLIAMENTARY ACT

Truly, the Scots are an antidote to the English![3]
– POPE MARTIN V (PONTIFF 1417–31), FOLLOWING THE BATTLE OF BAUGÉ, 1421

Introduction

Scotland's First Castle Age took shape in the centuries after the Wars of Independence, as a built outcome of the overriding concern of the country's feudal ruling elites to assert their autonomous status and power. Medieval Scotland developed a national ideology based on martial success in repelling a succession of attempted English conquests – as celebrated most extravagantly in the triumphalist national history of the *Scotichronicon*. The martial values which, it was claimed, had secured the country's independence were also reflected within architecture, in the emergence of an appropriately showy, military style – the castellated architecture that was employed for almost all secular buildings and even some churches. This trenchantly militarized protonationalism intentionally contrasted with the contemporary architecture of England, while making frequent references to that of England's main enemy – France. At first, especially under the Stewart kings, it was the monarchy that made most of the running in the development of Scottish castellated architecture. After the Reformation in 1560, the political context became more complicated, as Scotland began to find common cause with Protestant northern Europe, and power began to shift from the monarchs to the nobility. Yet the First Castle Age continued without significant interruption, and the place of the 'castle' within the symbolic architecture of Scottish national identity became even more secure than before.

Castles and Palaces: The Architecture of the Kingdom of Scotland

Following the end of Roman power in the former province of 'Britannia', south of Hadrian's Wall, in the fifth century CE, a succession of little kingdoms gradually amalgamated into two powerful groups, each expansionist, and each a rival to the other. To the north was the territory, approximately, that we now call 'Scotland', while the bigger, southern element, 'England', annexed Wales from the 1270s. David I (reigned 1124–53) temporarily annexed part of what today is northern England, while regional Norse incursions ended in the ceding to Scotland of the Hebrides and Man in 1266; the Northern Isles would follow in 1470–72 as a dowry. In the thirteenth century, an accepted boundary and a general 'truce' between the two other countries appears to have been in place. This all changed with the commencement of the Wars of Independence with England from 1296, when England sought to annex Scotland, bolstered by the origin-myth of King Arthur – the supposed early ruler of the whole island – from whom their monarchy claimed entitlement and descent. What all this shows is that there was a distinctive Scottish kingdom by the beginning of the period we discuss in this book.[4]

With the failure of English strategy at the battle of Bannockburn in 1314, mainland Britain became more clearly established as a two-kingdom entity, and an elaborate Scottish counter-ideology emerged, claiming that Scotland had enjoyed (since 330 BCE) an uninterrupted monarchy, which both Romans and English had failed to conquer, and which was thus far more ancient and legitimate than that of its southern neighbour. All this was packed into Walter Bower's 1440s *Scotichronicon*, which was itself an augmentation of John of Fordun's fourteenth-century *Chronica Gentis Scotorum*; the story was supplemented in the next century by Hector Boece's history. From the rhetoric of the period came a growing emphasis upon the two figures of Sir William Wallace – the 'Guardian of Scotland', whose death in 1305 was portrayed as a martyrdom, and King Robert I, 'the Bruce' (1274–1329), the victor of Bannockburn.⁵ As we will see in the following chapters, the meanings attributed to these 'national heroes' across the following centuries would repeatedly shift – in the same way that the architecture of Scottish national identity would mutate frequently and radically. In natural reaction to the increasingly entrenched attitudes towards England from 1296, Scotland allied itself with France, where English expansionism had been similarly unwelcome, and Scots fought alongside the French against the English during the Hundred Years War – victorious at Baugé in 1421, defeated at Verneuil in 1424. As in the case of sibling rivalry, national tension turned to mutual insult – for example, the Scots (and French) claimed that the English had tails, as God's punishment for the treatment of St Augustine, while the English coined the verb 'scotch', meaning to frustrate or obstruct.⁶ Opposing interpretations developed into a mutual incomprehension and, as we will see in due course, would colour psychological, political and architectural developments over the centuries.

Just as the initial expressions or articulations of the nascent Scottish national identity were somewhat inchoate, the same applied in the field of architecture. Two themes that would later become all-consuming – building in stone rather than brick or timber, and a love of 'castellated' architecture – began gradually to emerge, in the former case perhaps as early as the ninth century,⁷ and certainly by the eleventh century, when large-scale religious complexes began to be built in Scotland by European monastic orders whose stereotyped designs demanded use of stone. Not until the thirteenth century, however, when it was prescribed that parish churches should be built of stone⁸ was there evidence of a concerted programme of stone castle-building, and early examples were more or less similar to those in other countries, especially France. Prominent cases included the triangular-plan Caerlaverock (c. 1260–70) (Figure 1.1), or Bothwell (pre-1296) (Figure 1.2), whose circular donjon-tower affirmed its builders' connections with France, deriving apparently (via family links) from the royal castle of Coucy.⁹ These and other castles were seized by the English from the 1290s, but during the 1300s–1310s counter-attacks, they proved vulnerable to surprise capture and were dismantled by the Scots to prevent them from once again becoming occupation bases.¹⁰ England's annexation from 1296 of Scotland's commercial capital, Berwick, was followed by centuries of physical and economic warfare.¹¹ Consequently, many tower-houses were necessarily rebuilt in the more settled post-Reformation era, while continuing economic damage by repeated English invasions meant that construction on the scale of the thirteenth-century castles and religious houses could not be meanwhile repeated.

The decisive step in the beginning of the First Castle Age in Scotland would prove to be the supersession of the 'donjon', in its turn, by the residential tower, as already seen elsewhere at castles such as Vincennes. The leading Scottish example of this new fashion was David II's Tower (c. 1368–72) at Edinburgh Castle, dominating the town and thereby

FIGURE 1.1 *Caerlaverock Castle – built c. 1260–70, reconstructed c. 1630; view from south showing part of the c. 1630 courtyard front.* © *Historic Environment Scotland. HES Scan: mb240506017_o1*

proclaiming royal authority.[12] Royal continuity was signalled there by prominent reuse of ashlars from a predecessor castle destroyed by Robert Bruce, David's father; and in its turn, David's Tower would later fall victim to military bombardment, in 1573 – its remnants today encapsulated within the Half-Moon Battery. At Edinburgh Castle, castellated architecture was paralleled by more explicit martial display, notably in 1454, when Philip 'the Good', Duke of Burgundy, gifted to his great-nephew-in-law, James II Mons Meg, one of the biggest guns the world had seen. England had nothing that could compete with it, and it was accordingly long commemorated, as a symbol rather than as a weapon: images of it were even sculpted on seventeenth-century panels now reset in the castle's gatehouse. David's Tower was the beginning of that most dominant and resilient Scottish building type – the castellated 'tower-house', an image that became so entrenched that it began to spread to other building types, as in the case of the fourteenth-century St Machar's Cathedral in Old Aberdeen (Figure 1.3), or the Holyrood royal palace built for James V in the early sixteenth century. Such residential towers – today, better known as 'tower-houses' – were built by elites from the fourteenth century onwards, with a heightened burst of activity in the late fifteenth century. Even before Scotland's Reformation in 1560, funds officially due to the papacy were being siphoned off to facilitate a new castle-building era.

FIGURE 1.2 *Bothwell Castle – aerial view of 1968. Turret bases (top left of the castle in this view) show the castle's original thirteenth-century extent.* © Historic Environment Scotland. *https://canmore.org.uk/collection/1543405*

Castellation, however, was only the foremost of a range of architectural responses to political concerns. Most noticeably in the ecclesiastical field, for example, there developed a fifteenth-century Romanesque revival, referencing the idealized national past (that of the royal dynasty which ended with Alexander III's death in 1286 and that of his granddaughter, the 'Maid of Norway', in 1290), as would the Florentine Renaissance and equivalent revivals elsewhere.[13] Here there was no question of a French inspiration, as this was a time dominated elsewhere not by the Romanesque but by Gothic pointed arches and slender constructions – in France as much as in England. More specific national identity-motifs also began to emerge in these centuries, for example, in reflection of the 'Roman' imperial symbolism adopted by a

FIGURE 1.3 *St Machar's, Aberdeen, west front – completed 1440; photograph of 1940.* © Historic Environment Scotland. https://canmore.org.uk/collection/536304

range of consolidating European monarchies from around the mid-fifteenth century. To help reinforce the message that the monarch was emperor within his or her domain, architecture most often had recourse to two stereotypical images – the 'closed' or imperial architectural crown, and the triumphal arch. Both these motifs were enthusiastically embraced in Scotland, both at a micro-scale and architecturally. In 1469, parliament proclaimed King

James III (who reigned 1460–88) as having 'ful jurisdicioune and fre impire within his realme', and coinage represented him with an imperial crown. In 1528, and to avoid any doubt in the matter, Hector Boece said of Aberdeen's King's College that its steeple had 'a stone arch in the shape of an imperial crown'[14] (Figure 1.4). The best known architectural crown spire is that of

FIGURE 1.4 *King's College, Aberdeen – chapel (dated 2 April 1500) with imperial crown spire; on the right, part of John Smith's neo-Tudor quadrangle west front, 1822–6; photograph of 1999.* © Historic Environment Scotland. https://canmore.org.uk/collection/447202

St Giles, Edinburgh. Another example was St Michael's church, Linlithgow. Crown spire arch-plinths at the towers of St Mary's Dundee and St Mary's Haddington may represent crowns dismantled as a safeguard to artillerymen when the towers were used as gun platforms during 1540s warfare. Slightly confusingly, the fashion was revived a century later in Charles I's time, for example, at Glasgow's Tolbooth (1626). Triumphal arches were a feature of temporary royal processional decorations throughout Renaissance Europe, but they soon migrated to formal architecture as well. Scotland's earliest stone-built triple-arched version was at Stirling Castle. There the castle was reorientated 1500–1510 by James IV so as to face south, towards the site of the Battle of Bannockburn. A monumental, near-symmetrical, castellated ashlar 'forework' proclaimed the change, underlining the message of Scottish independence by a massive, triumphal arch entrance bristling with tall turrets (later truncated) (Figure 1.5).

Imperial symbolism conveyed a message that Scotland's monarchy was independent in character, as well as au fait with the latest European fashions. It also signalled that the monarch was, and would continue to be, firmly in charge of the kingdom – something not to be taken for granted in Renaissance Europe, as witnessed by the centuries-long chaos and rivalry of countless power centres within the Holy Roman Empire, culminating in the carnage of the Thirty Years War (1618–48). The chief architectural outcome of royal power was the building of grand royal palaces – a campaign that reached its culmination in the half-century prior to James V's death in 1542. Linlithgow Palace had been rebuilt by James I over a century previously, after 1424, along Italian seigniorial palace lines, with a colossal hall hoisted high above the then-principal eastern approach, and had been extended by James III, whose work at Stirling may have included commencement of the Great Hall.

But Scotland's principal palace builders were James IV and James V, who created a series of rich and impressive castellated complexes within and around the Forth valley – an area that served as a focus of monarchical building in the same way as the Loire or Thames. Linlithgow, Falkland, Dunfermline, Stirling and Edinburgh were all reconstructed in the by-now-standard castellated national manner, variously including tall turrets, great halls and lodging blocks. Architecturally, the most noticeable trend was an increasingly explicit French influence during the reign of James V, who had visited the French court and took two French brides in succession – Madeline, Francois I's daughter, who died prematurely, followed by Marie de Guise. Unsurprisingly, he imported French masons to work on his palaces, including Nicholas Roy and Moses Marten, who reconstructed Falkland – work that derived straightforwardly from the Loire school, as, for example, at St Eustache in Paris, which James would probably have seen during construction, or the royal palace of Villers-Côtterets. At Falkland, the differences between James IV's and James V's interpretations of the Renaissance are seen at their clearest. Both employed roundels to articulate

FIGURE 1.5 *Stirling Castle – forework showing triumphal arch gateway built 1500–1510 for King James IV as part of his realignment of the castle to face south, towards Bannockburn; conjectural restoration by David M. Walker, 1994.*

the window bays, but those of James IV (the east quarter), flanking orthodox hood-moulded windows, were emphasized by Loire-school bay divisions added in 1537, whereas the south quarter's courtyard front (1539) was built in a single campaign.

A French-looking castellated royal palace in Scotland underlined the alliance between the two kingdoms and hinted that France's military power might be available in defence of Scottish sovereignty if necessary. But the English royal marriage alliance concluded by James IV meant that English connections, and power, were never altogether absent, even at this stage – an ambiguity hinted at in James V's additions to the palace agglomeration south-west of the abbey cloisters at Holyrood, just east of Edinburgh;

these comprised the slightly incongruous combination of a tower-house and a large-windowed, symmetrical, somewhat Tudor façade; a matching southern tower to balance the whole composition remained unbuilt until the late seventeenth century, by which time, as we will see shortly, changed royal priorities had left Holyroodhouse as the last functioning Scottish royal palace.

Kings and Lairds: The Post-Reformation 'Dispersion' of Castellated Architecture

James V died in 1542, leaving a six-day-old successor – Mary I, or 'Mary Queen of Scots'. His widow, Mary of Guise, acted as regent from 1554, succeeding the Regent Arran, and presiding uneasily over a country divided between Catholic traditionalists who looked to France, and Protestant reformers who might even be hostile towards the pro-French alliance. A proposed royal marriage to the English king's son was abandoned, resulting in another English attempt to annex Scotland. Instead, Mary was sent to the French royal court where, in 1558, she married the Dauphin, the future Francis II, briefly becoming queen of France from 1559 until Francis's death in 1560. But by then, religious-political developments within Scotland were tilting the balance of influence decisively away from France and towards England, which from 1558 had a new Protestant Queen – Elizabeth I. A group of nobles took control of parliament, introduced the Reformation in its most extreme, Calvinist form, and aligned Scotland with anti-Catholic northern Europe. When Mary returned, very possibly seeking a degree of religious tolerance, she was eventually forced in 1567 to abdicate in favour of her infant son, James VI, and was imprisoned and ultimately (in 1587) executed in England – a tragic saga that, as we shall see, would be repeatedly evoked and celebrated over the following centuries.

During all of these twists and turns, however, Scotland still successfully avoided English annexation – an achievement that further fuelled the national narrative of sturdy independence, even as the Reformation's diminution of royal power shifted and broadened its focus away from kings and queens towards the Protestant aristocracy and the Calvinistic clerical and intellectual elite, in the process consigning to the background the earlier contributions of Catholic humanists such as John Mair (1467–1550). By 1600, Scotland could pride itself that it had five universities (two in Aberdeen), while England had only two, and Scots boasted that their Reformation had produced the most 'godly' faith possible – again in comparison with England, which had supposedly retained a backdoor link to Rome as shown by the liturgy and norms of its episcopal system.

This dispersion of power outwards from monarchs to aristocracy did not diminish the impact of Scotland's First Castle Age – the very opposite, in fact. Its architectural outcome was a broadening-out of castellation: simply, many more castellated tower-houses were now being built and rebuilt as the dwelling-houses of the wealthy elite – a class today referred to in shorthand as 'lairds'.[15] Reflecting the generally stable society of Scotland, these were essentially peacetime residences (as the thirteenth-century castles had been),[16] although they were often described at the time in an interchangeable mixture of domestic and martial terminology. For example, in 1572, reference was made to the 'house and fortalice of Lochwood' and to the 'castle and house of the Chan[on]rie of Ross'.[17] Between 1601 and 1609, Sir Duncan Campbell, Seventh Laird of Glenorchy, built the 'castell' of Finlarig, the 'toure' of Achallader, the 'houss' of Lochdochart, and Barcaldine, 'ane greit hous' – all of which would today be called castles or tower-houses.[18]

In architectural terms, a 'castle' was any laird's house which used the language of castellation. Castles were almost invariably characterized by a tall and dominant residential tower with an enclosure, or close, called a barmkin. The barmkin typically incorporated the outer walls of courtyard buildings and had a large, round-arched decorative gateway like a mini-triumphal arch and set either beside the tower (Rowallan) or opposite to it (Toward). Towers were rectangular-shaped blocks, supplemented – except in the most modest versions – by any of a wide range of projections, turrets or wings ('jambs'), resulting in a correspondingly wide range of forms. In doubtless intentional contrast to the large rectangular fenestration and ground-floor main rooms of Tudor England, the ground floor contained service and storage vaults with a hall on the *piano nobile* above, all with rather small windows – all in all a rather similar pattern to large houses in Mediterranean Europe. One of the most popular plan-forms comprised an L-plan front with a smaller set-forward jamb, the door set not in the long 'front' wall but in the re-entering angle of the jamb: the latter contained an inviting stair which delivered visitors to the 'lower' end of the hall, which was a place of assembly, authority and entertainment. In larger castles, a chamber of dais might lie beyond, and often a bedchamber, perhaps with a closet in a space or turret beyond that. This was the original arrangement at Castle Menzies, built for James Menzies in 1571–7.[19] Frequently the stair to the upper floor(s) was corbelled outwards from where the hall and chamber met, while the jamb typically contained rooms above the stair, the top level often externally enriched – as at Maybole (c. 1600?), which was faced in dressed ashlar with an oriel, suggesting that an important room (possibly a study or library) lay within. In some cases, towers were straightforwardly rectangular in plan, as in the case of one of the few examples built abroad – the Erik Rosenkrantz Tower in Bergen, Norway, built in 1563 by Scottish masons ('muremestre og stenhuggere af Skotland').[20]

External ornament was generally concentrated at the upper levels, in features such as 'crowsteps' (stepped gables) and corbelling, the latter being often used to carry corner 'rounds' or what here we call 'bartizans', as well as semiextruded staircases and corbel-tables (stretches of projecting

FIGURE 1.6 *Kellie Castle – built mostly sixteenth century; drawing by Robert Lorimer, 1888.* © *Historic Environment Scotland. https://canmore.org.uk/collection/802292*

walling) (Figure 1.6). In some cases, round towers were corbelled out into square upper stages, as at multiphase Elcho (begun c. 1560) (Figure 1.7) or the diagonal-towered Claypotts, built c. 1569–88 by owner John Strachan to celebrate his post-Reformation emancipation from tenant status.[21] Doorways were always enriched, and top-floor rooms were lit by pedimented dormers set above the eaves. Distinctive regional styles developed, including the heavy cable-moulded ornament common in the south-west, as at Haggs and Kenmure in the 1570s–80s, or the prominent chequer-corbelling of the north-east, continuing into the next century.

From 'Court Style' to Classicism in the Late Sixteenth Century

Despite the spread of castellated architecture throughout the entire landed class, the patronage power of the monarchy, both direct and indirect, was by no means at an end. From around 1570, a new fashion began to establish itself in the houses of influential courtiers such as the Regent Earl of Mar

FIGURE 1.7 *Elcho Castle – built in phases from c. 1560; view from south-east; photograph of 2011.* © *Historic Environment Scotland. HES Scan: elc.1-000066_o1*

in Stirling. It was characterized by a stylized interpretation of the classical orders, including tiered, slender, vertical shafts with complex mouldings set intermittently between base and capital. Other prominent examples of this style include the post-1573 Regent Morton gateway at Edinburgh Castle, and 1570s Carnasserie, built for Bishop John Carsewell.[22] From the 1580s, a more overtly classical architecture developed, having more formalized principles of monumental symmetry and regular interrelationship of parts – as opposed to the applied classical detailing of buildings such as Mar's Wark. This was seen at the remarkable diamond-studded courtyard range of c. 1590 at Crichton Castle for Francis, Earl of Bothwell, or more clearly at Newark (Renfrewshire) of c. 1597, whose pediments referenced Michelangelo's Porta Pia. Combining castellation and symmetry in a more idiosyncratic way, Fyvie Castle, built by the cosmopolitan politician Alexander Seton, had a massive façade like a compacted Stirling forework and a giant triumphal-arch centre (Figure 1.8).

Some works commissioned by the monarchy itself had a similarly hybrid character, such as Queen Anna's House at Dunfermline Palace, built from the 1590s by James VI and his Danish wife in a castellated style with classical elements, as a reconstruction of a gateway beside the abbey. Here

FIGURE 1.8 *Fyvie Castle – 1590s west front; 1905 photograph by Henry Bedford Lemere.* © *Historic Environment Scotland. https://canmore.org.uk/collection/695340*

an inscription proclaimed that 'this porch, and the house built above it, having through age and the injuries of time fallen down and come to ruin, have been restored from the foundation, and built on a larger scale by Queen Anna, daughter of Frederick . . . prince of Denmark . . . in 1600'.[23] The outer face featured an overdoor oriel, as was common in Tudor buildings, but also at King Frederick's Kronborg, where James and Anna had spent a long honeymoon. Towards the close was a crowstepped jamb with regular fenestration and string courses dividing the floors (a detail typical of 1610s palaces), and a corbelled turret in one angle.[24] The new work almost resembled a tower-house, except that it straddled a roadway (as would Anna's Queen's House at Greenwich, begun 1616), and, significantly, it represented a clear decision to adopt the castellated style.

But a far more decisive shift towards a more regular, classical interpretation of stone-built monumentality was presaged in James's small but emblematic Chapel Royal project of 1594 at Stirling. Here the client was, of course, King James VI, and the designer was presumably William Schaw (d. 1602), King's Master of Work and Chamberlain to the Queen (and founder of modern freemasonry): the royal Masters of Work were the first and only formally identified 'architects' in the country, up until the seventeenth century. James VI had inherited a range of palaces and had little need for more, even supposing the resources had been available to build them, but his Chapel Royal was an exception. In 1594, James's queen, Anna, gave birth to a son, diplomatically named Henry Frederick (in commemoration of both the English king Henry VIII, James's own father-in-law, and Anna's father; and of James's own father too, Henry, Lord Darnley). A chapel royal was built within months for the baptism, whose guest-list was drawn from across Europe. The aim was to highlight the prince's claim as a potential successor to the childless Elizabeth as English monarch, in effect reversing the longstanding English royal claim to overlordship over Scotland. Architecture provided a potent vehicle for this dynastic propaganda. First, the new chapel was designed in an advanced, somewhat Florentine classical style, without any contemporary northern European parallel for its time; and second because the building was proportioned in accordance with Solomon's Temple, as described in the Book of Kings. Showcased in this way as a modern Solomon, who ruled by wisdom and by peace,[25] James duly succeeded to the English throne in 1603, whereupon he emigrated to London as King James I of England and Ireland. Although the chapel project, having served its purpose, had no direct architectural progeny because the mainstream castellated tradition still signalled the required martial imagery, the classicizing seeds had already been laid within Scottish architecture, forefronted in the first instance by Schaw, and by his successor, Sir David Cunningham of Robertland (d. 1607), whom James took to England as royal surveyor. From this point onwards, the grand projects of the landed elite would balance castellated tradition with efforts at symmetry and regularity – with very diverse results.

Conclusion

The official ideology within late medieval and Renaissance Scotland was that of a distinct ethnic community, in support of which it laid claim to an unmatched antiquity of pedigree, an imperial monarchy and an assertive religious and intellectual tradition. All this translated indirectly into the field of architecture, through symbolic references to imperial status through crown spires and triumphal royal palace architecture, as well as through the more general spread of castellated architecture among elite groups after the Reformation in 1560. Overall, there was no significant pattern of emulation of the architectural features of the royal palaces in lairds' own houses, except that James V's Holyrood tower revalidated the residential tower formula in the 1520s. The palaces' impact was different from that of David's Tower, which, as we saw above, was a clear model. Twin-towered gateways such as Tolquhon (1584–9) were built, and the sculptural and triumphal-arch façade of Mar's Wark indicates references to the palace complex nearby, but this was rare. After all, the client at Mar's Wark was the Regent Earl of Mar; the architectural prestige of the palaces was of a more general kind. The period's close witnessed an increasingly classical architectural orientation, exemplified by the construction of Scotland's first classical building, the Chapel Royal of 1594, created to help demonstrate the Stuart dynasty's appropriateness to inherit the thrones of Scotland's neighbours. This process of dynastic and national assimilation, beginning in earnest in 1603, would have increasingly far-reaching consequences in both the political and architectural fields – yet Scotland's First Castle Age would continue, and the fashion for castellation would flourish.

2

1603–1660: Court Architecture under the Regnal Union

Nobis haec invicta miserunt 106 proavi [106 royal forefathers have left these to us, unconquered].[1]

– 1617 LATIN INSCRIPTION AT HOLYROODHOUSE AND EDINBURGH (REFERRING TO THE ROYAL PALACES)

By any meanes do not take away the battelment . . . for that is the grace of the house, and makes it look lyk a castle, and henc so nobleste.[2]

– SIR ROBERT KERR, 1632

Introduction

The regnal union with England in 1603 was arguably a more significant milestone in the emergence of the political culture of unionism in Scotland than the parliamentary union of 1707. Almost overnight, political and cultural trends in England became the chief reference point for Scotland, not least because of the physical absence of the king in London, and the repeated efforts by James and his son Charles I to encourage political and religious convergence between the two countries.

The most immediate architectural repercussion of the absentee monarchy was in connection with the royal palaces, which now became more-or-less redundant. They were maintained, and sometimes rebuilt, to continue the connection between crown and nation, and James and his supporters decorated them with (Scottish) thistles and (English) roses to signal alignment. In the wider field of 'court architecture', including the houses of great noblemen of state, a new, hybrid architectural unionism began to evolve, making selective references to English architecture, in features like squared-off rooflines, mullioned-and-transomed windows, or 'Anglo-Dutch' ornament, while at the same time remaining more fundamentally dependent on the castellated traditions of Scottish architecture.

The mid-seventeenth century, with its upsurge in civil and religious conflict, brought a temporary pause in this royal architectural and cultural unionism, but no let-up in the ever-greater political intertwining of Scotland and England, with the interlinked revolts against Stuart divine-right monarchy on both sides of the border, and the consequent war and English military occupation lasting until 1660. Although the age of the 'Covenanters' was seminal in the development of Scottish cultural nationalism, the architectural consequences (save for forts) tended more towards destruction than new construction.

Regnal Union: The Political Context

For the Stuart dynasty, 1603 was the ultimate triumph: a Scot had occupied England's throne. What English kings had over centuries failed to impose through war, James had achieved in reverse through his 'Solomonic peace'. Surely this final, ironical twist to the Wars of Independence was God's will? On that basis, James began to plan to amalgamate the two kingdoms altogether, a cause for which his supporters also claimed Biblical authority, referencing, for example, Ezechiel regarding the divided kingdoms of Israel and Judah: 'I will (saieth the Lord) make them one people in the land and one king shall be king of them all, and they shal be no more two peoples, neither be devided any more hence forth in two kingdoms.'[3] English laws alienating Scots were repealed, and James summoned his parliaments in 1604 to discuss political union.[4] In Scotland, although a fully operational administration continued, the king's rule was mostly now delivered via politicians who presented themselves personally at court or via a newly upgraded postal system, to be implemented by the Privy Council. Scotland had now a satellite status; its international visibility and relevance declined, while pressure increased to simply acquiesce in royal priorities formulated in and perhaps for England.

But although the royal heritage of martial independence trumpeted by the *Scotichronicon* now became irrelevant – perhaps something of an embarrassment, even – to Scotland's monarchy, Scottish society and its intelligentsia continued more generally to esteem martial virtue and achievement, and consequently, Scots continued translating these ideologies into architectural form: the First Castle Age continued unabated. This was a society which produced no architectural books, but many on soldiering and martial prowess. In these, the foundations were being laid for a distinctive role for Scotland within Britain, that of a 'soldier race' that could ultimately help build a global empire. In 1627, for example, Thomas Kelly, laird of

Easter Barns, wrote in *Pallas Armata* that warfare was the only way for Scotland 'to maintain our Credite, Honour, and Libertie', and in his *History*, the historian-poet William Drummond of Hawthornden, owner of a pretty castle, evoked the Scottish monarchy of old: 'Remember ye Govern not the soft effeminate people of the *South*, but a fierce Warlike Nation of the *North*.'[5]

Royal Architecture under Regnal Union: The Palaces and Masters of Work

Scottish architecture now underwent two main changes. A new, hybrid architectural unionism began to evolve within court/courtier architecture, reflecting James's wish for general conformity to an English norm. No longer striving to be different, elites now instead made selective references to English architecture, with Anglo-Dutch ornament referencing contemporary English innovation, while continuing to maintain the now entrenched castellated tradition. The contrast between castellated 1590s Fyvie and bay-windowed Pinkie (enlarged 1613), for the same client, demonstrates this trajectory. Second, in a more bluntly propagandist trend, key buildings were now adorned with (Scottish) thistle and (English) rose symbols, set in parity, in a reference to the new royal union. In England, however, James's initial plans for union were blocked by concerns about a 'Scottish takeover', and there were few explicit architectural projects there that showed any preoccupation with union with Scotland. A rare exception was King's Manor, York – a royal property, and seat of the Council of the North, which in 1609 James rebuilt for his intended Scottish visits – while Rubens's 1636 Banqueting House painted ceiling celebrated Stuart 'Britain'.

The royal palaces modelled the architectural change most clearly. James's chief concern was that his new English palaces would be suitable for him, for which purpose he took David Cunningham of Robertland, his master of works, with him to London. Back home in Scotland, although Linlithgow's north quarter collapsed in 1607, it was soon rebuilt, and the other palaces – Holyroodhouse, Edinburgh Castle, Stirling, Falkland and Dunfermline – were overhauled for the royal visit of 1617, and again in 1633, for the reception of Charles I, with Holyrood Abbey Kirk remodelled for the coronation ceremonial. Where James V had deliberately adopted a French-accented palace architecture, the political somersault that followed meant that James VI now, equally deliberately, preferred English-accented work. The only newly constructed palace buildings of the period were at Linlithgow (the north quarter) and Edinburgh (on which see below). Each had its entrance in a half-engaged octagonal stair turret midway along its courtyard front, and each was ornamented with pediments crammed with symbols of monarchy and of union: crowns, thistles, roses, harps denoting Ireland, and fleurs-de-lis representing the continuing English claim to France. At Linlithgow the courtyard façade was ordered in a grid-like, classical arrangement with pedimented windows and strips of small openings flanking the stair (Figure 2.1).

A 1617 Latin inscription at Holyroodhouse translated as '106 royal forefathers have left these to us, unconquered'.[6] The message was that martial and ancient Scotland's unbroken line of monarchs had delivered Holyrood and other royal palaces securely, and through martial entitlement, to James. In this mixture of Scottish nationalist assertion and royal British unionism at the palaces, we already see an embryonic unionist nationalism. Scotland's national dignity was respected and national achievement lauded;

FIGURE 2.1 *Linlithgow Palace – begun 1618; view of north quarter; photograph of 2000.* © *Historic Environment Scotland. https://canmore.org.uk/collection/800009*

but its architecture began to be reflective of England – for example in the use of enormous leaded platforms rather than crowsteps and slate, although the elevations, being designed by the Scottish master of work, continued the formula of castellated symmetry in stonework, evident as we saw from the 1580s, and rejected the big-windowed and often brick-built English norms, while adding mullioned and transomed windows (notably on Linlithgow's north façade) which probably alluded to England. The establishment message was that the future lay in a British Scotland. James's political allies, many of whom received lucrative jobs in England, naturally promoted this ideology. The reconstruction of the palaces for royal visits was intended to present a positive image of the country to the visiting delegations, but also to remind Scotland of the monarchy, in the face of its physical absence. The palaces were unwanted for royal residence, but James wanted a continuing pretence of occupation, directing in 1617 'that thairfoir cair were tane that some face of a courte myght be keepit [at Holyrood]'.[7]

The central figure in the royal building programme, broadly defined, was the Master of Work. The office-holder since Robertland's death in 1607 was James Murray of Kilbaberton, who, in 1628, was conjoined in post with Sir Anthony Alexander, a son of Scottish Secretary Sir William Alexander who had 'by his learning and travellis abroad . . . acquired skill in architectorie'.[8] It was under Murray's oversight that Edinburgh Castle's palace block, overlooking the town, was rebuilt from 1615. Flat-roofed with square-bartizaned ends, the similarity to near-contemporary Bolsover Little Castle suggests Murray knew of it (although Murray added greater sophistication to his façade by articulating the parapet and omitting preclassical angle strips). Flat-roofed palace-like buildings had been previously built for two of James's prounion courtiers, who both became naturalized Englishmen after 1603: Edward Bruce, Lord Kinloss, England's Master of the Rolls, at Culross Abbey House (1608); and Sir George Home, Earl of Dunbar and Chancellor of England – a linchpin figure in James's union programme – at Berwick-upon-Tweed, a project that was abandoned when incomplete, on Dunbar's death in 1611. These houses helped inspire the new fashion of rectilinear, classical palace architecture to Scots and Scotland.

The Dunbar house, where Murray was 'surveyor and builder' (i.e. designer and contractor) had a strongly English character. Perhaps Murray, who moved within elite circles, had by that date encountered the work of key English designers such as the Smythsons. It was also bluntly unionist – perhaps because Berwick had previously symbolized Scottish-English warfare, having changed hands numerous times over the centuries and it had been latterly fortified by the Tudors. Now, it symbolized peace, as did the nearby new bridge, stone-built and thus permanent – just like James wished his union to be. The symbolism was underlined in time for James's journey to Scotland, Murray having been ordered to set the royal image on the new bridge's gate with the inscription: 'Duo regna hoc ponte junxi, tuetur unita Deus' [I have joined two kingdoms with this bridge/God looks after them together].⁹ The inscription indicated that James and God were aligned on the issue of union, and the bridge, although not completed until the 1620s, gave the message physical form. That the national border lay further north was irrelevant. The River Tweed symbolized the border. Of course flat roofs were far from being exclusively English; Culross, as we saw, was flat-roofed, but was also innovative in a different way, having an aedicule-windowed and linear gridded façade, reminiscent rather more of European houses such as the Villa d'Este, whose proximity to Rome had made it a popular attraction for visitors. Culross, which fronted a terraced garden, also dispensed with the traditional barmkin, whose obsolescence had already been signalled by courtyard-plan Fyvie and John Seton's Barnes, which fronted an open court. Seton (c. 1553–94) was Chancellor Seton's brother. He had been made a Knight of the Royal Order of Santiago by Philip II, and was afterwards James VI's ambassador to Spain. Barnes might have shown Spanish influences had it not been left unfinished after Seton's death.

The 'Golden Century' of the Scottish Castle

In strong contrast to the uncertainties of royal architecture, the building of castles for the Scottish landed class went from strength to strength in the wake of 1603 – symbolizing the burgeoning strength of the aristocracy under an absentee monarchy. Many of these have vanished without trace in the centuries since – giving us, today, a misleading picture of the number and distribution of castles in this, their 'golden century'. Around 1650, for example, there were reportedly fifty-two 'principal houses' in Lanarkshire, twenty-eight in Renfrewshire, whereas today only about a third of these survive in some form or other.¹⁰ In the many peaceful decades during the seventeenth century, local outbreaks of castle-building, fuelled by highly personal motives of kinship or emulation, could erupt anywhere, as vividly illustrated in a cluster of castles near Inverness – including Castle Stuart, Bunchrew House and Dalcross Castle – built within five years of each other. Here (as recalled in a 1674 account), Sir Simon Fraser, Lord Lovat, commissioned 'masons and wrights to build the houses of Bunchrive and Dalcross; his lady very anxious and impatient untill they were perfected' ... 'The great motive that induced Dame Jean Stewart to build at Dalcrosse was to be near her cousin, the Earle of Murray, in Castle Stewart, who was building that statly house, and were all finisht at once, for my Lord Lovat began the worke of these two brave houses of Dalcross and Bunchrive in 1619, and had them both perfected ... in 1621.'¹¹ Some owners had several houses, each assigned particular functions, such as those of the Earl of Annandale (as described post-1660) whose 'houses are Lochwood and Newbie; the one desireable for strength the other for pleasure; that for pasture, Moss or fire and Wood this for Fish and plenty of Coneys [rabbits]'.¹²

Architecturally, the overwhelmingly dominant theme within this continuing First Castle Age was now that of continuity with the centuries-old tradition of the castellated laird's house, whose plan, as we saw in Chapter 1, typically comprised a residential tower and a walled enclosure ('barmkin') of satellite buildings, as seen for instance at Castle Fraser (1631–3) and Skelmorlie (1636). But this continuity went hand-in-hand with constant adaptation. Tower designs continued to vary enormously, yet most were still one room deep, either rectangular in plan overall, or with a rectangular nucleus structure.[13] The L-plan frontage (that is, with a wing, or jamb, projecting forward at one end) typical of late sixteenth-century towers, as for example at Elcho or Castle Menzies, now tended to develop into a more compact arrangement with an entrance stair turret in the angle, instead of within the jamb, which now almost equalled the nucleus itself, and at Braemar (1628), the door was set on the splay, thereby creating a symmetrical, 'splay-plan' house – a layout that would become more common during the seventeenth century. Common alternative plan-forms included a 'T'-like arrangement, where the jamb was nearly centrally placed on a long-wall; or arrangements featuring two jambs, arranged to form either a 'U' or (if placed diagonally opposite one another, as at Menzies or Elcho) a zig-zag plan a little like a 'Z'. Gradually, the U-layout became more and more popular, owing to its symmetry (Barnes being the first symmetrical version), and as we will see in Chapter 3, after the restoration of the monarchy in 1660 it merged into the increasingly dominant movement of architectural classicism. In the later nineteenth-century Scotch Baronial revival of castellated architecture, it would instead be the L-shaped layout that would be especially favoured, precisely because of its more picturesque asymmetry.

But during the seventeenth century, most castles of any ambition attempted to balance classical symmetry and picturesquely castellated tradition, as is illustrated clearly by the case of Castle Stuart. Its overall 'footprint' was a symmetrical U-plan, but in elevation, the jambs were carried upwards and given intentionally different superstructures. Its 'rear' elevation was more symmetrical in profile, with diagonally set square bartizans (like those at Castle Grant), and asymmetrical fenestration, responding to the accommodation within. Here, a clear decision was taken to avoid the image of a symmetrical classicizing house even when the ground-plan was symmetrical: the requirement to maintain continuity with the castellated tradition was paramount.

In castles' materials and details, the same mixture of continuity and incremental adaptation prevailed. Walls were, of course, always of stone, with the usual tiny ground floor windows and larger openings on the *piano nobile*. But the roofs usually, by this period, were slated, in preference to heavy stone slabs, thatch, or (as at Canongate Tolbooth in 1591) wooden shingles. The barmkin contained a big gateway, meaning that there were two lockable gates before the tower could be accessed, rendering the house immensely safe from everyday intruders. The 'baronial' status broadcast by the mere existence of the castle (i.e. that the owner was a tenant-in-chief of the crown, and therefore a member of the nobility) was amplified by armorials and other imagery. Frequently the landed builders were commemorated, an extreme of ostentation being represented by the giant strip of names at Huntly (Figure 2.2). The emergent Scottish discourse of martial tradition, combined with lairdly authority, could be highlighted by inclusion of gunholes, often as part of elegant ensembles, as at Treasurer-Depute Sir Gideon Murray's Ballencrieff (c. 1625), where the gunholes are integral with the window sills of the big-windowed principal rooms. As an example of the concern for such symbolism, the 1639 building contract between owner Colin Campbell and masons Robert and George Nicholson for enlarging Cawdor Castle (completed by 1643) stipulated the provision of 'four storme windocks in the northe luiking to the garden, with armes names and siferis upon the said windockis weill and sufficientlie wrocht to the said Coleine Campbell his contentment'.[14] While the interior of Cawdor would feature the most modern domestic equipment, with each chamber served by its own 'easement' (toilet), the external style would be uncompromisingly traditional, including such castellated and symbolic features as 'ane sufficient squair crinell [crowning feature?] . . . [topped by "ane pawilion reiff"] . . . with corbellis . . . with thrie lichtis of heweine stonn therin, and archer hollis under the said windockis'.[15]

FIGURE 2.2 *Huntly Castle – rebuilt from 1602; view from south; photograph of 2013.* © *Historic Environment Scotland. HES Scan: DPHC170513011.*

Throughout the seventeenth century, castles continued to be enlarged or (as at Castle Fraser) heightened and decorated with neo-medievalizing castellation, gunholes and martial symbolism. Their high, near-blank walls and enclosed barmkins conveyed a sense of might, of authority, and invited respect. Castles denoted lairdly status, power and authority within the locality – they were the venue for local baron courts, as at Lickleyhead in 1626, 'for doing justice to . . . [the laird's] . . . tennents'.[16] Castles, the houses of the rich, were not built for warfare – forts fulfilled that purpose. The biggest security risk that castle builders had to address was not war but feuds with neighbours. For example, during the English invasions of the 1540s, the castles tended to be quickly abandoned. But when pressed into military service during the relatively rare periods of warfare or local rebellion, they could serve that function well.[17]

In contrast to the prevailing external continuity, the interior decoration of castles now changed quite sharply. Sixteenth-century ceilings, as in France, had frequently been painted and timbered, with narratives, instruction, and decoration (as at Crathes, for example, or at the 1610s Pinkie). Now, the English-type flat plaster ceiling became the fashion. These are first known from 1615, when they were introduced to Kellie Castle in Fife by Thomas Viscount Fentoun. Because their moulds could be reused easily, they quickly became popular. Plasterwork frequently combined Scottish national symbolism and unionist symbolism within the same designs, and was thus a means of normalizing unionism by bringing it into the everyday domestic environment of the landed elite. However, more narrowly English ideological motifs, such as the 'dragon and St George' plasterwork installed in Edinburgh Castle's new palace by the English carver Ralph Rawlinson for the 1617 visit, were not imitated by castle-building lairds, suggesting that there were distinct limits of acceptability in the field of unionist iconography.[18]

While it would not be accurate to speak of 'regional traditions' in the architecture of seventeenth-century castles, there were clusters of highly distinctive houses within certain areas, above all in the north-east, where the castellated tradition reached an extreme of highly decorated verticality, in a series of set-pieces that would later serve disproportionately strongly as inspiration to the nineteenth-century Scotch Baronial revivalists. The distinctiveness of the 'north-east castle style' was chiefly a matter of ornamentation, rather than plan-form. The most famous of these houses is Craigievar (Figure 2.3), said to have been completed in 1626 for maritime trader William Forbes, nicknamed 'Danzig Willie' (Danzig is modern Gdansk), whose initials are inscribed on the building. Craigievar is a compact and vertical L-shaped castle with a square turret in its angle, topped by a classical balustraded viewing platform, which forms only part of an extraordinary and eclectic superstructure of turrets, bartizans, cannon-shaped water spouts, balustrades, and stepped chequer-corbelling.[19]

FIGURE 2.3 *Craigievar Castle – rebuilt 1620s; view from south; photograph dated 1963.* © *Historic Environment Scotland. https://canmore.org.uk/collection/1579565*

Several castles within this north-eastern group, including Crathes, are attributed or connected to a local dynasty of mason-architects, the Bel family. Castle Fraser was heightened in 1617–18 by 'I. Bel' (i.e. 'John Bell'); its distinctive seven-storeyed circular angle tower was later beloved by the nineteenth-century revivalists, as we shall see (Figure 2.4). At Drum Castle, an old tower was retained as the dominant element within an otherwise radical reconstruction, commissioned by Alexander Irvine (who inherited the property in 1603) and completed around 1619. Drum referenced the new and more overtly classicizing ideas that were emerging further south: it comprised a regular courtyard grouping, with a new mansion on the south side quarter, flat-fronted and with square end pavilions, all reminiscent of Culross Abbey House.[20] Other principal castles in the region sometimes followed more idiosyncratic patterns. Craigston (1604–7) was given a U-shaped front whose wings are connected at a high level by a giant Fyvie-like arch, painted on its underside, and carrying a gallery above. Huntly Castle, which had been partly blown up in 1594 by Master of Work William Schaw (d. 1602) during a punitive expedition, and reconstructed around 1602–6 by its Catholic owner, the First Marquess of Huntly, included a monumental array of top-level oriels and, as we have already noted, an inscribed frieze visible from afar. Its main entrance,

FIGURE 2.4 *Castle Fraser – heightened 1617–18 by I. Bell; low wings added 1631–3; gateway and lodges by John Smith, 1836–9; view from north; photograph dated 2008.* © *Historic Environment Scotland. HES Scan: mb230908013_o1*

in lieu of a Fyvie-style arch, was instead ornamented with a lofty and imposing armorial panel, featuring royalist and dynastic motifs, plus illicit Catholic symbolism.[21]

In other regions of the country, equally ingenious solutions to the challenge of reconciling classical and traditional castellated elements were attempted. In the south-west, for example, an ambitious project for the reinhabitation of the ruined thirteenth-century Caerlaverock Castle and reconstruction of its north-east 'quarter' (the Nithsdale apartment) for Robert, Lord Maxwell, Earl of Nithsdale began in 1620. The reconstruction, completed around 1634, imitated the new palace formula exemplified at Linlithgow, with its gridded courtyard façade with pedimented fenestration, embedding the new structure in the massive old castle fabric, whose curtain wall was punched through and another grid of pedimented windows installed. But the castle was wrecked once again by Covenanter iconoclasts in 1640, as Maxwell was a Catholic and his castle signalled the fact. At nearby Amisfield, a radically different permutation was adopted, involving separation rather than integration of the classical and the castellated. The original, slender tower-house of 1600 features an ornate castellated superstructure of asymmetrically stacked elements jostling one above the other. Only three decades later, directly alongside it was built a new classical house, flat fronted and gable-roofed with pedimented *piano nobile* windows. The new house, with its horizontal intercommunication between rooms, met all conceivable requirements for modernity, while the tower was retained both as badge of status and as a security measure, in case of feuds with neighbours. The Fyvie-like drive for castellated symmetry also made itself felt in the south-west, for instance at Spedlins (dated 1605), reconstructed and heightened as part of a border 'policing' programme inaugurated in 1600.[22] The Scottish 'plantation' in Ulster gave an early opportunity for the use of martial castellated imagery in a colonial context: at Monea Castle, Co. Fermanagh, built by Revd Malcolm Hamilton from 1616 onwards, one end was formed of a pair of diagonally set round towers corbelled out to square, with an archway between, in a symmetrical, linear variant on the Claypotts formula.

In cases such as Amisfield, or Drum for that matter, the functional tension between the tower and its wings was highlighted (Figure 2.5). The general landed yearning for a more convenient lifestyle within modern, interconnecting rooms – achievable only in the larger towers – prompted an inexorable expansion of elite daily living space beyond the confines of the tower, and the refashioning of the barmkin wings as elite accommodation. Increasingly, the wings became larger, and were even elevated into the main living space, as for instance at Ancrum, where a gallery, low hall and stand-alone apartment were planned in 1632.[23] Castle Fraser's barmkin, as we saw, was reconstructed 1631–3 in the form of twinned long, low, parallel domestic wings; while the tower built at Scotstarvit by Latinist and philanthropist Sir James Scott in 1627 or earlier originally had adjoining wings – although, in a common pattern, these have since vanished and the

FIGURE 2.5 *Amisfield Tower – built 1600, with reconstructed 1631 successor house in background, to south; undated photograph.* © Historic Environment Scotland. https://canmore.org.uk/collection/1166416

tower now stands alone. The direction of flow was not, of course, absolute, and some towers were heightened rather than expanded laterally, as in the case of Preston Tower, heightened by another two storeys in 1626, with a then-fashionable curved parapet profile.

The 'Court Style': Houses and Civic Projects

The first significant departure from these patterns of landed castle-building – an initiative that enriched the First Castle Age with an enhanced element of classical sophistication, was launched, appropriately, by the royal Master of Work, James Murray (d. 1634). It is likely that some of his predecessors may have had a hand in some of the castle projects touched on above, but Murray's own contribution, in a group of three houses not far from Edinburgh, was altogether more innovative. With Berwick's onetime role as commercial capital gone, Edinburgh had been developing as a national capital since at least the fifteenth century, and numerous castles or castellated villas were built near, and sometimes facing, the burgh, with more orthodox castles including the L-plan Castle Gogar (1625), with its balustraded angle stair-turret,[24] or Craigcrook Castle with its pediment-dormered, flat-fronted wing added (c. 1626) to a pre-existing tower.

These three houses were strikingly different. In a mansion built in 1622–3 for himself at Kilbaberton (now Baberton), south of Edinburgh, Murray developed the symmetrical U-layout into an altogether more horizontal (compared, say, with Craigston) and reposeful 'Court Style', with angle turrets and little blocks over the angles in lieu of bartizans. Here for the first time we encounter decorative buckle-quoins, also used at George Heriot's – an elite contemporary feature that was later sometimes replicated in nineteenth-century revivalist buildings, particularly in Edinburgh. Significantly, Kilbaberton's chamber/drawing room window was aligned directly towards Edinburgh Castle. Pitreavie (c. 1630) (Figure 2.6), built for a friend of Murray's and relative of Alexander's, Sir Henry Wardlaw, is an enlarged version of Baberton, but more simply detailed (and now part-engulfed by Peddie and Kinnear's Scotch Baronial extensions of 1884–6). At the third of this group, Winton House (1620s), the U-plan was made carefully asymmetrical, with wings unequal in form, height, and mass, one of which is crowned by a viewing platform, with a parapet like that of Exton in England (Figure 2.7). Winton's decoration – which includes unionist thistle and rose motifs – is Anglo-Dutch in appearance, reflecting the stylistic developments of the late 1620s–30s as inaugurated at the Dunbar house, where Dutchman John Gospoole was carver.[25] All three of these houses share the classical details typical of the Court Style, such as pedimented and regularly positioned windows, string courses, and distinctive doorway/window mouldings shaped around a recessed flat strip. Common to all three houses, as one would expect with the royal Master

FIGURE 2.6 *Pitreavie Castle – built c. 1630; view from north-west showing early castellated Classicism; photograph of c. 1890.* © *Historic Environment Scotland.*
https://canmore.org.uk/file/image/1106518

of Work in charge, is a superlative quality of masoncraft. Other examples of Court Style landed houses included the long-gone Seton Palace, 'with its magnificent Samson's Hall', where around 1630 George, Third Earl of Winton built two quarters connecting with 'Jacob's tower, on the north side of the house'.[26]

Urban houses were also well suited to the new sophistication of the Court Style, a pioneering role here being played by joint Master of Work Alexander's father, Scottish Secretary Sir William Alexander, who in 1632 remodelled his Stirling town house (the Argyll Lodging) in the manner of a *hôtel* in contemporary Paris, combining some elements of the castellated tradition, such as a U-plan, high roofs and spired angle turrets, with regular classical fenestration and Court Style detailing. With its gable to the street, Moray House, begun c. 1625 for the Dowager Countess of Home, seems more like an orthodox north European town house; yet it has a semiextruded stair on its flank alluding to the castellated tradition and the recent palace works by Murray. Each of these houses acted as a pioneer of an entire new generation of town houses, including smaller examples such as the U-planned Acheson House, Canongate (1634), where the degree of castellation was reduced, by deleting parapets, for example. Rather more unorthodox was Lamb's House in Leith, a four-storeyed merchant's house of possibly c. 1610; like

FIGURE 2.7 *Winton House – rebuilt 1620s; engraving of drawing by Robert Billings published 1854.* © *Historic Environment Scotland. https://canmore.org.uk/ collection/1318190*

Linlithgow, it had a façade composed around a central stair projection, but here made more 'traditional' by applying asymmetrical corbelling and adding crowstepped but unequal frontal wall-head gables either side, on an otherwise symmetrical facade. But as we have seen, all this continued in parallel with unabated building of more orthodox castles by country lairds.

But the chief urban set-pieces of the Court Style were not houses, but large public buildings in Edinburgh and other burghs. Among these, as we have seen, new palace-building for the absentee monarchy played only a limited role. Instead, the most monumental new public building in Edinburgh had only an indirect royal connection. George Heriot's Hospital, a charitable school for fatherless burgesses' sons, was built from 1628 with a legacy from George Heriot, jeweller to James VI and Queen Anna (Figure 2.8). Here we see both the enduring power of the castellated tradition, and its adaptability to the new classical ethos. In its four-square courtyard plan, it echoes the precedent of Linlithgow Palace, whose new north quarter became the model for Heriot's flanks, but with each of the corner blocks now becoming a separately articulated tower-house, or castle. William Wallace, the King's Master Mason, worked there from the outset, emphasizing the prestige commanded by the project, and his mason's mark is still visible on some of

FIGURE 2.8 *George Heriot's Hospital, dated 1 July 1628 – view showing north front; 1950s(?); photograph by George Hay.* © *Historic Environment Scotland.*
https://canmore.org.uk/collection/710871

the building's fine ashlar blocks. Although no designers' names are known for sure, the connection with the royal architects and designers is clear.

The same applied in the case of Parliament House, built in 1632–8 by Edinburgh Town Council to the designs of Murray as both a civic enhancement and to secure Edinburgh as the parliament's home (Figure 2.9). This building had the plan of a castle, with an L-plan front, a hall filling its main body, bartizans and an entrance stair turret tucked into its internal angle, and lesser functions contained within partly vaulted spaces beneath. Unlike an orthodox castle, however, where leaded platforms within an otherwise gabled roofscape served both as outlook vantage-points and as astronomical towers,[27] its main roofs were flat. The rejection of steep roofs and gables also marked a clear rejection of the orthodox steep-gabled architecture of the tolbooths (traditional municipal buildings) across the country where the previously itinerant parliament had often met. Flat roofs were partly just a matter of fashion, popular in England, and so copied. But they were also increasingly used across Europe to symbolize authority, not just in London, in buildings such as Inigo Jones's Queen's House (from 1616) and the Banqueting House (1619–22), but also in Michelangelo's Capitoline in Rome – which would later be explicitly echoed in Linlithgow's 1660s tolbooth (on which see Chapter 3). Parliament House

FIGURE 2.9 *Parliament House, Edinburgh, 1632–8, and Parliament Close – post-1746 view by John Elphinstone, engraved by A. Bell. 1685 statue of Charles II is seen central, its presence and positioning making the Close into a Place Royale.* © Historic Environment Scotland. https://canmore.org.uk/collection/426674

was dotted with symbols of royalty and municipality, and also of union – including inscriptions such as '*Unio unionum*', the union of unions. These were messages, as we saw above, that would hardly have occurred to contemporary English architects or clients as worthy of special display. To broadcast this Scottish discourse of union, therefore, a modernized variant of that most traditionally Scottish building form, the castle, seemed the most appropriate choice. However, in contrast to printed or two-dimensional propaganda, the multifaceted solidity of buildings means that they are very unreliable vehicles for any specific political movement, and can all too easily be 'captured' by the opposing party – which precisely is what happened here. Although the project had commenced under the rule of Charles I, once completed it immediately became a focus of opposition to his rule, and of the insurrection that followed.[28]

Rather less political in character were the first large-scale Court Style buildings erected in the burgh of Glasgow. Glasgow's original university complex, Glasgow College (begun 1632) copied some specific features from Heriot's (such as the oriel), but unlike Heriot's, it had no angle 'tower-houses'. Rather it resembled a European collegiate institution, here with a regularly windowed tenemental street front and crowsteps. In contrast to its prevailing horizontality, the nearby tolbooth, built in 1626–7 by John Boyd, comprised a massive, five-storeyed block with a taller steeple. The main front was gridded, with pedimented windows, string courses and a parapet – very like the new palaces – as well as buckle quoins. It had a forestair whose platt was supported by a classical triumphal arch. At the time of its construction, King Charles was expected in Scotland for his coronation, and, as an expression of loyalty, the steeple was given an Imperial crown spire. Inside, the grandest space was a King's Hall, over forty feet long, a room which, in the event, no monarch ever set eyes on.[29] The interplay between castellation and classicism in the civic realm was so pervasive that it even shaped Scotland's 'mercat crosses', ornamental columns that marked a burgh's main public space for assembly, commerce, government, and authority. Edinburgh's cross was rebuilt for the 1617 royal visit in a strikingly castellated form, its shaft set within a drum-like base with a platform and parapet, with corbelling and bartizans. The cross in nearby Preston (c. 1619?) was similarly castellated, but far more sculptural in character, and in the style of Heriot's.

Castellated Churches and the Drive for Episcopacy

A somewhat different architectural interpretation of the new unionist values, incorporating a distinctive combination of traditional elements, applied in the case of religion. Even prior to the regnal union, James, who preferred the hierarchical episcopal system, with the king at its head, to the decentralized organization of the Scottish Calvinist Reformation, had begun to press for re-establishment of an episcopalian system in Scotland, inevitably bringing him into growing conflict with the country's presbyterian establishment. After 1603, the episcopal character of the Church of England, coupled with James's unionist agenda, massively bolstered this strategy, whose intransigent pursuit, especially by his son Charles, would, in due course, very significantly contribute to the outbreak of the Wars of the Three Kingdoms.

The first built outcome of this campaign stemmed from his 1617 visit, when James instructed that the chapel royal in Holyrood should be rebuilt as an episcopal chapel, which could also be used by his privy council; for this project, craftsmen were drawn from the royal works both in England and Scotland, and prefabricated classical fittings were transported north. This was only a remodelling project, however, and once the episcopal agenda progressed on to the commissioning of a complete new 'model church', it should be no surprise – given the rival claims of Episcopalians and Presbyterians of descent from the ancient Columban church – that its architectural expression should make significant references to Scotland's accepted traditional architecture – the castellated style. In 1621, Archbishop Spottiswood, who fronted James's episcopal campaign in Scotland, built a model parish church at Dairsie in Fife, intended to exemplify episcopal worship in its processional plan and big east windows. Externally, like St Machar's in Aberdeen, the primary expression of 'antiquity' was through castellation. Accordingly, the church was given crenellations and a daringly corbelled, oversized 'bartizan' as its belfry; it had also massive, somewhat primitive-looking tracery to reference antiquity. Although it was originally flat-roofed, the eclecticism of its design suggests that it might have been a creation of local masons rather than of the royal Master of Work.[30] However, those years also witnessed a more general, national resurgence of a 'primitive' loop-traceried (like Heriot's) or Y-traceried Gothic, which may align more generally with the drive for episcopacy – as built, for instance, at South Queensferry in 1633, the year of Charles I's visit.

Descent into Chaos: The Wars of the Three Kingdoms

The 'high' period of the Mastership of Works ended with war. Under Murray, it was a highly structured bureaucracy within which he himself (later, with Alexander) was in charge of design, controlled the key appointments (such as King's Master Mason), sourced materials, and oversaw budgets. The Mastership became less relevant following Murray's and Alexander's deaths, as royal interest in Scottish palaces rapidly waned. A more pressing influence, however, was the destructive effects of mounting civil unrest and war. Captain John Carmichael, whose appointment to the Mastership stemmed from his command of the surveying skills essential in warfare, was killed at Marston Moor in 1642. The craft skills of the early seventeenth century's greatest castle builders, people who had made an exceptional contribution in the 1610s–30s, would not be available to the successor generation.

The immediate background to the outbreak of conflict was the growing alienation of Scotland's Presbyterian ruling classes from royal authority, culminating in the signing of the National Covenant (1638). After Scottish Covenanters and English Parliamentarians found common cause and aligned themselves for war, a Scottish army captured Newcastle, and wars raged on either side of the Tweed, with the Scottish government army under the Marquis of Argyll defeated in a series of encounters in 1644–5 by a royalist army headed by the Marquis of Montrose and Alasdair MacColla. In a further sequence of vicissitudes, the Scots Covenanters captured King Charles and handed him over to the English parliamentarians, who executed him (1649), but although his son was crowned Charles II King of Scots in Scone two years later, nine years of English occupation, under Oliver Cromwell, were to come before the eventual 'Restoration' in 1660. By this stage, in diametric contrast to the previous position, Scottish and English affairs had become so entwined together that disentangling them would now be extremely difficult.

Although the destructive effects of these Wars of the Three Kingdoms were considerably less than the vast casualties and mass starvation inflicted by the contemporary Thirty Years War in Central Europe, the conflict (just as during the Wars of Independence) had a drastic impact on building activity in Scotland. By the mid-1640s, castle-building had slowed to a halt, and instead, many existing castles were garrisoned. What were built in great abundance were forts or sconces, designed by military men in conformity with all the criteria of modern warfare: low in height, with ditches, and every external wall capable of being covered by flanking fire from inside the fort. The movements of armies provoked frenzied building activity. In the area around Inverness, where we traced energetic castle construction around 1620, twenty years later, with Montrose's army in the area, the town was 'sconced round with an earthen wall, a deep trensh, rampards, and pillasads . . . and Inverness was made a considerable strength'.[31] Meanwhile,

> in the country, [William Fraser, laird of] Culboky made a sconce on the Carse off Kingily [Kirkhill]; Major Fraser, his brother, coming home, *anno* 1642 . . . drew this draught in the frame we see it, corners and bastians, a very pretty fensible strength.[32] Lovat was also fortified with a deep trench and ditch, a strong bulwark of earth within that, and a garrishon put there . . . The house of Beuly was also fortified, and John Fraser of Clunvacky, captain there . . . also built a neat sconce eastward from the orchyard upon the edge of the plain carse.[33]

For protection during wartime, people fled to garrisoned fortifications, not to castles. Facing an army, 'onely the garrishones were safe and preserved men's lives'. Outside Inverness, forts drew in thousands of 'soules, men, women and children, who had recourse for safety to these fortes to preserve their lives, otherwayes all had perished in the fury'.[34] These forts were built by society's elites, essentially the same social category of individual who built castles.

During the 1650s decade of English Cromwellian invasion, occupation and fort-building, however, castles once again found a martial role. Some were defended against the English – one being Redhall, whose defenders defied a detachment from Cromwell's army.[35] Soon, most castles were allotted the same tasks as their predecessors during the Wars of Independence – as English military bases in hostile territory. And just as Robert the Bruce, knowing that large castles in Wales had facilitated English conquest there, had systematically slighted as many as possible, so now a similar scorched-earth pattern was sometimes played out. Castles like Kilsyth were burnt, whether by Scots to diminish their value to invaders, or as punitive actions by English soldiers, while places like Finlarig and Braemar became important English garrisons. The English General Monck systematically evaluated the potential occupation role of domestic castles, in a report of 1657 advising Cromwell where garrisons should be, or already were, placed. A single company (seventy men) was placed in each of a string of bases along and beyond the Highlands fringe, including Duart, Aberdeen, Dunnottar, Blair, Finlarig, Sinclair, Scalloway, Bog-of-Gight (Gordon castle); two companies were placed in Kirkwall, a half-company in Dunstaffnage, Braemar and Cardross. 'These garrisons', wrote Monck, 'being soe laid will not only keepe footing for us in the hills northwards beyond [Perth], in case wee should have occacion to come in againe, but those places being not to bee taken without cannon (if the officers bee carefull) will be able to destroy any clan.' Monck's advice was that domestic castles, once garrisoned by around seventy men, provided secure bases for both garrisoning and launching assaults.[36]

Each of these military bases was a Renaissance castle. Not until the soldiers went back home in 1660 did normality return, once the castles were reoccupied as residences. And now a new generation of castle builders began work – a generation of lairds and masons that had some radically new architectural ideas.

Conclusion

As we saw in the case of Stirling's Chapel Royal in the previous chapter, James VI both understood and exploited the propagandist potential of architecture for his own ends. After 1603, his loyal Scottish lairds quickly adopted – or humoured – his unionism, and that of his successor, so far as architectural symbols and even influences were concerned; but that tolerance had become exhausted by the time they assembled in parliament in the late 1630s. In a feudal, largely Presbyterian society ruled by an absentee monarchy, the vigorous and diverse development of Scotland's First Castle Age in the seventeenth century largely resulted from the efforts of those landed classes, anxious to protect and nurture their own elite culture now that the king had largely given up his role as its leader and guarantor.

But alongside this mainstream 'castle culture', with its strong preoccupation with images of martial prowess, a new court style, formed out of a hybrid of Scots and English references, now began to coalesce. It combined castellated elements with an increasingly explicit classical regularity and unionist decorative iconography, in a range of domestic and public buildings from Edinburgh Castle's palace block to George Heriot's Hospital and Parliament House. Even here, though, the asymmetrical planning principles of the Scottish castle remained pervasively present – in contrast to the full-blooded symmetrical classicism of projects such as Amsterdam's Town Hall, built only a decade or so later.

On the outside of all these buildings, tradition seemed as all-important as ever. But on the inside of the new castles, things were increasingly on the move, with the expansion of the main apartment down from the tower, and the creation of horizontally planned new apartments in new extensions – as a result of which the tower was evolving into a sort of domestic and protective annex, combined with display of the vital lairdly images of status, continuity, legitimacy and authority. As we will see in Chapter 3, those trends would develop much further after 1660, in the last active phase of the First Castle Age, under the even more pronounced and normalized absenteeism of Charles II and James VII in the 'Restoration' years.

3

1660–1689: Sunset of the Stuarts – From Castellation to Classicism

Certain of our palaces and castles in our kingdom of Scotland, which lately by the injuries of a calamitous time are altogether fallen down, or become unfit for dwelling in, should be built and restored, particularly our Royal Palace of Holyrudhous.[1]

– KING CHARLES II'S GRANT TO SIR WILLIAM BRUCE AS OVERSEER/MASTER OF WORKS, 1671

This Palace, as you approach it, strikes you with Awe and Admiration, by the many Turrets and gilded Ballustrades at top ... The House is the highest I ever saw, consisting of a high Tower in the middle, with two Wings and a Tower at each end.[2]

– JOHN MACKY, OF GLAMIS CASTLE, 1723

Introduction

On the return home of the occupying English army in 1660, Scotland was once again independent in name, but in reality remained a satellite nation, as shown by the royal requirement that it should simply side with England in the Dutch wars. The hopes of an enduring return to peace proved short-lived, as the restored Stuarts reverted with a vengeance to their old religious agenda of promoting episcopacy and suppressing Presbyterianism.[3] By August 1660, the newly reconstituted Privy Council was already acting on royal orders to crush the 'conventicles' (informal Presbyterian congregations).[4]

And in 1661, Charles, who had sworn at his coronation (1651) to adhere to the Covenanting principles, instructed the Privy Council to proclaim the restoration of episcopacy, 'from our pious care and princelie zeale for the order, unity, peace and stability of that church, and its better harmony with the governement of the churches of England and Ireland'.[5] The result, in contrast with the many peaceful years of 1573–1625 during James VI's reign, was a society that was as divided as before, and which exploded into intermittent open strife, leading in 1689 to the forfeiture of the Catholic James VII.

Architecturally, the Stuart return of 1660 galvanized the First Castle Age back into vigorous life, but at the cost of politicizing its symbols in a way that would ultimately prove fatal to it after the dynasty's overthrow following the events of 1688–9. The post-1660 upsurge of architectural activity by the royalist elite was spearheaded by the rebuilding of Holyrood as the chief Scottish royal palace, and by the building of grand country and town mansions by landed grandees – all in a style whose bones were still castellated, but whose facades were often laid out to a greater or lesser extent in a 'balanced', sometimes explicitly classical manner. Holyrood exemplified this trend, its balanced plan-form including the conservation of a castellated ancient tower and creation of a new, duplicate tower. Some of the foremost crown officials built similar projects, at times on a monumental scale, in cases such as Drumlanrig. But after 1689, everything associated with the image of the castle would increasingly be rejected by the new ascendancy as being tainted with the values of the outgoing 'Jacobite' dynastic succession.

The 'Restitution' of Absolute Monarchy: Holyroodhouse and the Cult of Mary, 'Queen of Scots'

It was a bruised and changed Scotland which emerged from the English occupation in 1660. For royalists, the king at least was now fully in charge, the old order had returned, and Scots courtiers again haunted London, where the power was; in their view, it was not England that was to blame for the military occupation and Scottish humiliation, but the regicidal republicans. The royal will, as before, was for a London-controlled union, and the post of Secretary of State for Scotland was established on a more powerful basis and entrusted to a series of individuals who could be relied upon to implement royal orders. In England, the so-called *restoration* meant that the monarchy was restored, parliamentary powers were upheld and internal stability guaranteed. In Scotland, the equivalent 'restitution',[6] or reinstatement of Charles II as king, involved the surrender of all political progress back to the monarchy, and consequential instability caused by dictatorial and remote royal demands resulting in intermittent civil warfare from 1666 onwards.[7] The demand for episcopacy sparked a renewed Covenanting movement, which the government crushed in a series of confrontations from 1666 onwards, notably at the Battle of Bothwell Bridge (1679), and in the so-called *Killing Time* of 1681–5 – a campaign of repression far in excess of anything experienced before, and which generated a crop of martyrs whose legendary exploits later helped shape Scotland's reputation as a land of Romanticism, above all in the writings of Sir Walter Scott.

The architectural consequences of the previous quarter-century of strife were initially, unsurprisingly, negative. In 1661 the Privy Council read the royal order for the destruction of citadels 'for removing all seids of jealousie betuixt our kingdoms',[8] but although the soldiers were now gone, many major secular buildings had fared badly, as barracks, or worse: Glasgow's College was among the small group of buildings whose construction had continued during the occupation. Falkland and Holyrood Palaces had been partly burned, and Holyrood remodelled. Even the wealthiest families, such as the Hamiltons and Queensberrys, were so burdened by the combination of financing the 1640s war and 1650s taxation that they could not immediately build anew. With the continued religious unrest, church building activity was largely confined to conservatively styled minor works: for example, in 1687–8 at Gifford's parish kirk (now Yester Chapel) the choir vault was plastered by Alexander Eizat with 'Springs of plaister . . . after the Gothick maner' and a new Gothic arch was installed by mason John Petticrew.[9]

It was overwhelmingly in secular architecture where the great turnaround in building activity eventually began, as the economy began to recover and building activity resumed. As part of that, Scotland's elites once more began to rebuild or replace their castles, which returned to being prestigious residences as before. The monarchy was naturally in the vanguard of those efforts – with the lead being taken first by Charles II, in the 1670s, and then between 1679 and 1688, by the Duke of Albany and York, who between 1679–82 held a 'satellite' royal court at Holyrood, and who reigned from 1685–9 as James VII. Scottish Secretary John Maitland, Earl and (from 1672) Duke of Lauderdale, reporting his successful 'management' to Charles in 1669, added that 'never was king more absolute than you in poor old Scotland'.[10] In support of that agenda, the post of master of royal works was filled once again. However, only after another failed union attempt in 1670 was it charged with an active palace-building campaign, as distinct from merely overseeing repairs to a still largely unusable Holyroodhouse. Charles's union scheme of 1668–70 might have meant no Scottish parliament, and perhaps no need for Holyroodhouse anymore. The plan failed, and instead the reverse happened: Holyrood was reconstructed, the main quadrangle hugely enlarged, subordinate structures incrementally demolished. On Lauderdale's recommendation, Sir William Bruce – a union negotiator in 1670[11] – was appointed to the Mastership in 1671 as 'general overseer and superintendent' and 'general superintendent' of the royal works;[12] the king's master mason was Robert Mylne (d. 1710). Charles's intention, in agreeing to this plan, was that 'certain of our palaces and castles in Scotland, which lately by the injuries of a calamitous time are altogether fallen down, or become unfit for dwelling in, should be built and restored, particularly our Royal Palace of Holyrudhous'.[13]

Holyrood's reconstruction was not as a working, 'everyday' palace, but for display, addressing the ideological need to project a distinctively Scottish monarchy, and showcasing symbolic royal presence rather than physical royal occupation. In the process, it acted as the spearhead of a national movement for castle revitalization, as well as a rather more distant harbinger of Scottish 'proto-Romanticism'.[14] Intensely bound up with Holyrood was the first 'romantic' (as opposed to martial) historical cult in Scotland: that of Mary, 'Queen of Scots', possibly the first ever Scot with a strong international profile. Francis Osborne noticed in 1673 how insistently present Mary was in people's imaginations – not just in Scotland but also in England, where 'recollections' and souvenirs of her circulated among the wealthy.[15] But as a former Queen of France as well as Scotland, Mary also inspired fictional, historical and propagandist accounts throughout seventeenth-century Europe. English public opinion was mobilized by Anglican Stuart royalists, connecting Mary's story to that of her executed grandson, Charles, 'consolidating a culture of passion and pity that would become the grounding for sentimental Restoration royalism'.[16] In Scotland, over the following centuries, her legend would be appropriated by a succession of royalist political and cultural movements, in a burgeoning associative cult that left the whole country, from Jedburgh to Inverness, dotted with 'Queen Mary's Houses'. Its consequences within new architecture were subtle but pervasive. For example, Bruce's Kinross House, a mainstream classical mansion (see below) whose site was decided in the 1670s, was aligned directly upon Lochleven Castle, where Mary was imprisoned in 1567–8 and where she abdicated. This was partly a celebration of Stuart monarchy, and the new Kinross House would be diminished without the associative 'monument'. The arrangement followed the Renaissance-period fondness for alignment, as seen at Balcaskie (begun 1629), which faces the Bass Rock; but it also anticipated the eighteenth-century Romantic idea that an old castle was a thing to view, rather than occupy; artist John Alexander (d. 1757) left unfinished the first known history painting of Mary, a scene of her daring escape from Lochleven.[17]

All these considerations applied with special intensity in the case of Holyrood (Figure 3.1), where the royal apartment within James V's tower, scene of the renowned 1566 murder of Mary's private secretary, David Rizzio, was arguably the focus of her growing cult. Designed by Bruce, this was Scotland's most substantial palace project since James V's time. Between 1671–8, the previous untidy agglomeration of structures was demolished except for the main courtyard, which was reconfigured by Bruce as a lofty and symmetrical standalone quadrangular block, with the pre-existing Abbey Kirk at its north-east matched by a new, neo-Gothic-windowed

FIGURE 3.1 *Palace of Holyroodhouse – rebuilt 1671–8, incomplete until twentieth century; bird's eye view published 1753.* © Historic Environment Scotland. https://canmore.org.uk/collection/891890

kitchen block at its south-east. To the west, the James V tower was made into the north wing of a new, strikingly hybrid façade with a classical gateway at the centre – its central aedicule framed by paired classical columns – and another, identical castellated tower built to the south. The other courtyard facades alluded to rather stereotyped European (Dutch) classicism,[18] while its interiors resembled contemporary work in England, with ceilings by plasterers (John Houlbert and George Dunsterfield) from the English royal works. The remodelled Holyrood set out to signal the antiquity of the monarchy in Scotland, not least through its reverent showcasing of the traces of Mary: the royal apartment was modernized by Bruce, but her monogrammed ceiling ornament was retained. Lauderdale and Bruce's reconstruction of the palace set out to underline the sense that she was symbolically 'present', as her bed chamber faced the town, and soon an expensive bed was installed to signify her 'residency'. The legend could touch anything at Holyrood, old or new: when Defoe visited Holyrood shortly after the 1707 parliamentary union, he was shown the so-called Queen Mary's Dial – an extraordinarily impressive, complex sundial, made in 1633 by the elder John Mylne for Charles I's coronation visit to show him what Scotland's scientific community could achieve, subsequently appropriated by the Marian cult.[19]

Overall, the reconstruction of Holyroodhouse set out the key parameters for the balance of castellated and classical architecture, between tradition and modernity, that would become generalized in post-1660 Stuart Scotland. Its design, driven from the core of governmental power, combined up-to-date classicism with history-focused castle conservation and revitalization, with its southwest tower duplicating the old Stewart tower. For now, all these served as visible expressions of royal and national antiquity on a modern classical building. Within a century or so, this formula, somewhat modified, would have become explicitly linked to the modern cultural movement of Romanticism (see Chapter 5) – in the process becoming interconnected with a growing admiration for the image of the 'heroic Highlander', and the romantic Highlands: as early as 1680, courtiers at the 'satellite' Stuart court of James Duke of Albany and York envied the Highland dress for its allegedly powerful, manly associations.[20] Within a century, in the Second Castle Age, after an interlude when it was vilified as a 'primitive' hive of sedition, the Highlands would be enlisted by the unionist establishment, and would join Mary in the hierarchy of Scottish Romantic iconography.

Courtier Castles: The Architecture of Theatre

The crown was not alone among society's elite strata in embarking on ambitious projects for dramatically 'balanced' residences created by the expansion of older castles. In a continuation of the long-established pattern of autonomous landed aristocratic power, key establishment figures commissioned castle projects that were sometimes modest but, in some cases, of comparable scale and monumentality to that of Holyrood. Figures of this standing could call on the services of government designers, such as the King's Master Mason, John Mylne, who had been one of the Scots involved in the union discussions of 1652 in London and then a commissioner (elected representative) to the Scottish parliament in 1662. He was, for example, commissioned in 1666 by John Leslie, Seventh Earl of Rothes to improve Balgonie Castle for Margaret, Countess of Leven, adding a crowstepped stair turret connecting the tower and a wing: Rothes had been captured at Worcester and imprisoned until 1658, and until eclipsed by Lauderdale, was one of Charles's foremost politicians, being president of the Privy Council from 1660 and chancellor from 1667.

Arguably the most emblematic of these courtier castles was the work of Charles's right-hand man in Scotland, John Maitland, the First Duke of Lauderdale (d. 1682). Prominent politically since the 1640s, Lauderdale was appointed Secretary of State for Scotland in 1660, on his return from exile with Charles. Until 1679, when he was blamed for the insurrection that culminated in the Battle of Bothwell Bridge, Lauderdale was trusted by Charles, who created him a Knight of the Garter in 1672, raised him to the English peerage in 1674 and appointed him to the English Privy Council.[21] Lauderdale set out to build projects that would reflect his new importance while reflecting his landed antiquity. The focus of his work was Thirlestane Castle, south-east of Edinburgh, a corner-turreted, rectangular block originally built in the late sixteenth century within the remains of a 1540s English fort. It was regularized in 1670–77, while retaining and indeed intensifying its dramatic, castellar silhouette (Figure 3.2). Being based on the existing castle, with its narrow but deep plan, the result was hardly an orthodox 'classical' layout. The west short-wall became the centrepiece of a grand, multitowered and pedimented entrance facade, massed with mountainously pyramidal drama. This in some ways harked back to James IV's Stirling forework (prior to the latter's truncation), but here with steps to a terrace on the level of the *piano nobile*, and a grand new entrance door. Stretching back inside were superimposed apartments, one made a 'state apartment', using the craftsmen from the royal works. Here, we see Scotland's most prestigious aristocratic patron at work reconstructing and dramaticizing his family seat to create, in effect, a new castle. Lauderdale engaged Bruce to remodel two other properties, Brunstane House, an L-plan Edinburgh suburban villa which he extended (1672–5), and Lethington (now called Lennoxlove) (1673–7): these less elaborate projects also illustrated the process of clearing the functions of the barmkin structures away from the main house. Ultimately, however, Lauderdale made his main residence at Ham House, near London.

FIGURE 3.2 Thirlestane Castle – rebuilt by Sir William Bruce, 1670–77; view by John Slezer, published 1693. © Historic Environment Scotland. https://canmore.org.uk/collection/695492

Other noblemen at the top of late Stuart society set about extending their castles in an equally theatrical way, each following its own individual pattern, and stressing 'balance' rather than exact symmetry. At Glamis Castle, for example, the existing L-shaped tower house layout was intensified by Patrick, Earl of Strathmore, in 1668–84, into an almost Baroque 'splay plan' composition of interplaying diagonals and verticals (Figure 3.3). Strathmore explained that 'tho it be an old house and consequentlie was the more difficult to reduce the place to any uniformitie yet I did covet extremely to order my building so that my frontispiece might have a resemblance on both syds'.[22] Nearly half a century later, Macky observed of Glamis, 'This Palace, as you approach it, strikes you with Awe and Admiration, by the many Turrets and gilded Ballustrades at top . . . The House is the highest I ever saw, consisting of a high Tower in the middle, with two Wings and a Tower at each end.'[23] Altogether more rectilinear, but equally monumental and Baroque, was Drumlanrig Castle, rebuilt in 1679–89 for William Douglas, Duke of Queensberry, with the architect Master James Smith closely involved in its design. Smith (c. 1645–1731), a former trainee priest who returned from Rome to Scotland in 1678 as an architect, was appointed royal overseer in 1683 on Queensberry's recommendation. Here the castellated tradition referred to is not that of orthodox castles but that of the corner-towered quadrangle, as at Linlithgow Palace and George Heriot's Hospital, here with Murray-type string courses and stair turrets tucked into the internal angles. The north show-front references Heriot's, with regular window bays and a central tower-cum-turret – here, carried upwards as a lantern topped by a ducal coronet, copying the arrangement at Holyrood (Figure 3.4). The upper window pediments collide dynamically with a giant-pilastered Corinthian order. There are no traditional crowsteps because the roofs are flat, but the Heriot's references continue, the towers being flat-roofed with leaded bartizans and decorated corners, with rustic rather than buckle quoins. The Heriot's courtyard arcade was likewise replicated here, with a Roman cryptoporticus below, set behind a horseshoe stair resembling that at Fontainebleau or Anet. The ancient structure was disguised, while the new structure gestured powerfully both towards the past, with its jaggedly towered skyline almost recalling the north-eastern castles, and towards the classical European present in its vast frontal avenue and the regimented balustrades dotting its wall-heads.

In other cases, the castles of leading Stuart government figures were reconstructed in a more practical manner. At Craigmillar Castle, Sir John Gilmour, Lord President of the Session from 1661, member of the Privy Council and commissioner to parliament for Edinburghshire (Midlothian) carried out a remodelling scheme from 1661, in which the two-storeyed west courtyard block, containing prestigious spaces (perhaps a suite containing kitchen/dining room/drawing room), was reconstructed and connected to the main tower, with decorative pediments and chimneys added over the west curtain.[24]

FIGURE 3.3 *Glamis Castle – rebuilt 1668–84; 1686 elevation of main front; copper plate engraving by R. White after drawing by John Slezer.* © Historic Environment Scotland. https://canmore.org.uk/collection/1069808

FIGURE 3.4 *Drumlanrig Castle – rebuilt c. 1675–97; view from north; photograph of 1999.* © *Historic Environment Scotland. https://canmore.org.uk/collection/1137507*

Late Stuart Towers: Revived and New

The individuality of these often grandiose, palace-like complexes was echoed in that of projects lower down the social scale. There were now three main options for the new generation of landed builder-patrons. They could revitalize an existing castle, such as Neidpath; build or rebuild a castle anew, as at Leslie (Aberdeenshire) (Figure 3.5); or build a classical mansion in the more mainstream style of northern Europe. All three options could be used to stress loyalty to 'national tradition', albeit much more indirectly in the third case. In almost all cases, not just sentiment but the sheer solidity of existing tower houses ensured that they tended to be retained in reconstructions, sometimes in concealed form but more often publicly on display, to protect

FIGURE 3.5 *Leslie Castle – foundation stone dated 17 June 1661, dormer head dated 1664; built to a pattern resembling that of the 1630s pre-war period; photograph by Angus Graham, 1942, prior to restoration of 1979–89.* © Historic Environment Scotland. *https://canmore.org.uk/collection/1200085*

and intensify the sense of history and lineal entitlement. Old L-plan houses such as Balcaskie (1668–76) could be symmetricized by converting them to a 'double L' or U-plan, possibly with pavilions added – which, just as at Holyrood, meant castle conservation and castle duplication or 'revival'. Classicizing, however, frequently meant concealing or disguising the tower.

The revitalization of existing castles itself covered a wide range of approaches. Because of their value to, and treatment by, the occupying soldiers, some 'slighted' castles, such as Invergarry, required to be substantially rebuilt, while others, such as Neidpath, only needed straightforward overhaul. Invergarry Castle, seat of the MacDonells of Glengarry, had been another wartime casualty: General Monck, who led the English army in Scotland, informed Cromwell on 29 July 1654 that Colonel Morgan's brigade had burnt 'Glengaries new House' the day before, and 'the remayning structure I order'd to bee defaced by the pyoneers'.[25] It was rebuilt from 1670 for Aeneas, Lord MacDonell (d. 1680) as what he regarded a 'newe hous', but now with a full-height scale and platt stair jamb.[26] It was once again a castle – a visual and cultural asset, and a place of entertainment and community gathering, duly celebrated by bard Iain Lom as a 'picturesque tower [house]' ('tùr dealbhach').[27] By contrast, the alterations required at Neidpath Castle were far more modest: it was modernized, for the Tweeddales, with a timber-panelled interior by king's master wright James Bayne (1668–71), and a restructured barmkin by James and John Nichol, masons[28] (Figure 3.6). A new gateway and approach were built c. 1670, an archway composed of alternately rusticated/ plain blocks, like that at Glasgow College, Arniston, and elsewhere. A new entrance doorway was cut into the main tower – signalling that a more settled society was envisaged – and in 1682, Robert Inglis and Thomas Boyd modernized the garden with terrace walks and a summerhouse. The result was similar to numerous others such as Inveraray which were likewise relatively straightforwardly returned to normal everyday use.[29] Neidpath was purchased in 1686 by the Duke of Queensberry, for his second son, the Earl of March – who likewise appears to have changed it little, confirming its continuing appropriateness.

In some cases, castellated rebuilding schemes were largely confined to refacing or embellishment, sometimes including classical features as in the case of Kinneil House, which comprised a tall rectangular tower, aligned approximately east-west, its orientation and setting dictated by the Roman wall it was set beside, with an L-plan, crowstepped largely sixteenth-century palace complex adjoining to the north; around 1677, the Duke of

FIGURE 3.6 *Neidpath Castle – late medieval tower modified pre-1686 with gateway added; view from east; photograph of 1912.* © Historic Environment Scotland. https://canmore.org.uk/collection/1174652

Hamilton upgraded the tower, with a dressed ashlar grid-windowed façade, balustraded flat roof, and end pavilions, each with a traditional looking turnpike tucked into its rear angle.[30] In other cases, the embellishments were calculated to enhance the house's castle-like appearance, as in 1689, when Sir Thomas Kirkpatrick of Closeburn contracted tradesmen 'to build, putt up an[d] perfite ane square battelment round the old tower of Closeburne, conforme to . . . [that] . . . of the tower of Glencairn', and 'to raise the stoneworke of the turnpeick head or jamb'.[31] The Kirkpatrick family was steeped in martial renown from the Wars of Independence and a castellated image doubtless helped dramatize this reputation.

Frequently, the remodelling work involved substantial new castellated extensions, or even the construction of completely new 'castles', some of which were unvaulted at ground floor level, indicating a change in fashion and the continuing flow downwards of the important living spaces. Hatton Castle, for example, although poorly documented and long gone, is known to have been rebuilt sometime around 1680 for Lauderdale's brother Charles, Lord Hatton, with Holyrood-like interiors. It comprised a tower-house nucleus, clasped by two lower and near-symmetrical ranges in an L-plan, and circular corner turrets. The east entrance front had outer gables part-overlaid by the turrets, and a long balustrade between: even the tower-house was given a balustraded platform roof. Hatton was set within a massively reconstructed garden, complete with pretty casement-windowed French-looking pavilions. At Woolmet Castle, in 1685–6, 'Normand Bruce . . . masone in E[dinbu]rgh' (who had worked with Bruce and Smith at Holyrood) connected the north and south ranges with a big three-storeyed block, with pedimented top-floor windows, all 'according to the draught [therof] . . . drawen by the said Normand'. On the outer, east wall, a new square turret was added containing a scale-and-platt stair, a turnpike in its angle leading to a balustraded roof platform. The interior was to be timber-panelled, the windows casements, the adjoining work remodelled to match.[32] And at Kilravock Castle, Hugh Rose added in 1665–7 an enormous new block adjoining the old tower, designed in traditional form – a rectangle with a turret, and a corbelled stair on the garden front. The masons were local: Robert Nicolson, whom we encountered at Cawdor Castle in 1639–43, and James Smith, father of Smith the architect (discussed below).[33] For new castles, the most popular option was a modernized L-plan. William Forbes of Leslie was quick off the mark, building or rebuilding Leslie Castle ('Funded: Jun[e]: 17: 1661', an inscription proclaimed). Leslie followed closely the pre-war angle-turreted L-plan formula, although the house's diamond-set chimneys, like those at Glasgow College and Moray House, were an innovation for the north-east. Auchenbowie House (c. 1666) was plainer, three-storeyed, with a polygonal stair turret in the angle,[34] while Crichton House (late seventeenth century; undated) is similar, but with one window bay on either side of the stair against Auchenbowie's two; each of these houses has the door on the angle, creating a near-symmetrical splay in the manner of Braemar, and with turrets rising above the eaves, as at Heriot's; Ford House (1680) is a miniaturized version. Cluny Crichton (dated 1666) was a rare, symmetrical variant of this plan, with equal-sized matching rooms in either jamb. Like Leslie, though, its angle turret was square, making it impossible to achieve a symmetrical splay-plan. Symmetry was not here the aim: that was mostly reserved for some public buildings and churches. Instead, as in the sixteenth century, builders sought a 'correspondence' and 'balance', a regularized revitalization of the castellated tradition.

Kinross House and the Drift to the Classical

Within both the commissioning of new houses and the rejuvenation of old, the drift towards a more overtly classical approach was becoming ever stronger. Still overshadowed for the moment by the prestige of the castle tradition, this mostly expressed itself relatively subtly, in the remodelling of houses in a regularized form, although Bruce's design of his own house, Kinross, in a completely mainstream northern European classical style, not dissimilar to examples like the royal pavilions at Vincennes (1650s) or England's Coleshill (completed 1662), acted as a harbinger of developments to come in later years. It was, rather ironically, the classicism promoted by Bruce, a noted Stuart loyalist, that would become associated with the revolutionaries of 1689 (Figure 3.7).

More usual than building classical set-pieces was a solution like that adopted by Bruce in 1667–72 at Leslie, in Fife, working probably with both John and Robert Mylne as masons, for one of the country's foremost politicians, the Seventh Earl and First Duke of Rothes, whom we mentioned above. Built around a square quadrangle incorporating an L-plan house, with polygonal stair turrets in the eastern angles, its courtyard interior may have resembled Drumlanrig. Each external face was made symmetrical, and each differed from the others. On the three-gabled classical (west) front, instead of Holyrood-like balustrades it had dormer heads reaching through the eaves and cornice in a traditional 'castle' manner. Unlike Leslie, Panmure House (built 1666 by John Mylne for the Earl of Panmure) was a completely new house on a new site, but its design approach was similarly classical, with a triple-gabled front, creating an E- rather than a U-plan roof, here with balustrades, skews rather than crowsteps, and square angle pavilions overlaying the outer gables as on a castle, and like Balcaskie, or Hatton (Figure 3.8).

Other variants of the symmetrical U-plan included Methven (1678–82), four- or five-storeyed, more compact and castle-like with its circular pavilions and crowstepped gables; its gables crowstepped, its flanks expressed as gable-plus-wing elevations,[35] or Prestonfield House, completed in 1689 by Edinburgh's Lord Provost, Sir James Dick, a merchant and friend of James VII/II,[36] to replace a house burned by anti-Catholic rioters in 1681.

FIGURE 3.7 *Kinross House – built from late 1670s by and for Sir William Bruce. This aerial view from the west shows the alignment on Lochleven Castle, the prison of Mary Queen of Scots in 1567–8; photograph of 1997.* © Historic Environment Scotland. *https://canmore.org.uk/collection/704832*

The rebuilt Prestonfield was flat-fronted and symmetrical, but with twinned curvilinear and ball-finialled gables separated by a balustraded centre bay. It also had buckle quoins, referencing the likewise twin-gabled Kilbaberton House of the Murray period; its windows had Bruce-type classical architraves, its south view aligned with Craigmillar Castle (associated with Queen Mary) and the interior was expensively finished, with plasterwork in imitation of 1670s work, and embossed leather hangings. Gallery (1672–80) and Wallyford (1677) each comprised a symmetrical rectangular block with twinned south-facing outer pavilions or wings, with a relatively high wall-to-window ratio. Gallery, 'ane double house' (i.e. spine-walled), was flat-fronted, its jambs square and individually roofed, and it had a gallery above

FIGURE 3.8 *Balcaskie House – rebuilt 1668–74 as a near-symmetrical house, central part altered in the nineteenth century; 2013 photograph of north front.* © *Historic Environment Scotland. https://canmore.org.uk/collection/1343552*

the piano nobile,[37] whereas Wallyford's jambs were proportionately larger, and its roofs integrated, like the earlier Kilbaberton or Pitreavie. Wallyford had a little three-room enfilade plus corridor access to these rooms, and a scale-and-platt stone stair with a solid newel with half-shaft ends – the formula first seen at 1580s Crichton and still favoured in eighteenth-century tenements. Wallyford's main apartment was well lit; but its north face was regular rather than symmetrical, responding to interior lighting requirements.[38]

From 'Urban Castles' to 'Place Royale'

The shift away from castellated to classical solutions was rather more pronounced in an urban context, where the weight of tradition was not so symbolically heavy. Scotland's greatest town house of this period, Hatton Lodging, later renamed Queensberry House, was, essentially, a classical design, built by Smith in two main stages, but with traditional ogee-domed corner pavilions – which also referenced France, whose seventeenth-century architecture was almost characterized by individually roofed elements. In alterations to existing structures, a more conservative approach prevailed, as in the case of Stirling's Argyll Lodging, the onetime Alexander town house which now served as the town-house of the Ninth Earl of Argyll (whose main seat was Inveraray Castle). In 1674, the Argyll Lodging was modernized, with a classical interior paintwork scheme, and its French hotel frontage was subtly classicized with a deep-rusticated external gateway surround (derived from a publication by Alessandro Francini), designed evidently by architects or craftsmen connected to the royal works; however, a castellated-style polygonal stair turret and crowsteps were also added.

In Edinburgh's Parliament Close, where Parliament House's 1630s design had rejected symmetry in favour of an L-shaped castle plan, there seems to have been no concern that the buildings added later in the century to complete the Close should follow a programme of symmetry, and instead, the structural concerns were restricted to factors such as building lines/heights, fire safety, and materials. In January 1685, however, a statue of Charles II on horseback arrived in Edinburgh, and was set up in Parliament Close. At a single stroke, this modernized the Close as a 'Place Royale', following the precedent of contemporary France, where a public *place* was normally focussed upon a statue of the king; the Edinburgh statue was reputedly a reaction following an abortive 1650s plan to erect a statue of Oliver Cromwell in the Close, for which purpose a rough-hewn ashlar block, eight feet high, had arrived in Edinburgh for completion by a sculptor.[39] Through this equestrian statue, Parliament Close became, in a way, Edinburgh's first 'classical square' – but a square that, for the moment, lacked classical buildings. On the other hand, in a clear bid to dignify a public space near Linlithgow's royal palace, its new 1660s tolbooth was modelled closely on Michelangelo's Palazzo Senatorio on Rome's Capitoline hill. It was, however, given a Scots-type steeple.

The Fall of the Stuarts: 1688–9 and 'the Alteratione of the Government'

Charles's brother and heir, who reigned as James VII between 1685 and 1689, was more interested than Charles in Holyrood and in Scotland. He built no castles, although his Chancellor, the Earl of Perth, built a new mansion (completed c. 1686) at Drummond Castle, probably by Smith, beside the ancient tower there.[40] But by now unrest was once again on the upsurge, following the confrontations over the signing of the Test Act of 1681, leading to the 1685 Protestant crusading invasion by the Earl of Argyll. Once again several castles, including Dunstaffnage, Tarbert and Skipness, were garrisoned; Carnasserie was besieged, captured and partly wrecked by explosion. Argyll's invasion, and in England 'Monmouth's Rebellion', were easily crushed, but the castles had served military duties well. However, in December 1688, following the outbreak of England's anti-Catholic 'Glorious Revolution', anti-Catholic riots broke out, and the following year a 'Convention' parliament deposed James and in his place installed

William and Mary, now monarchs of England and Ireland – ushering in a fresh cycle of dynastic and religious polarization.[41] For the second time in the century, parliament had seized control. Scotland now had the Protestant monarchy her elites had sought, as well as an aggressively anti-Catholic administration – which, in turn, would trigger fresh civil wars and give birth to Jacobitism.

Conclusion

As we will see in the next chapter, the architectural implications of this political 'alteratione'[42] would prove to be not only rapid but far-reaching, as international northern European classicism established a total hegemony. After 1660, castles had continued being built in Scotland as prestigious residences for the country's landed elite until the century's closing decades, but their image had become more and more bound up with the values of the outgoing regime. With this conjunction of political and architectural revolution in 1689, the Scottish castellated tradition was finally running out of time.

In the 1580s–90s, as we saw at places like Crichton and Newark, a hybrid and confident-looking castellated style with classical elements had developed – a style strikingly different from the more Renaissance-style loose application of classical references, typical of the 1570s, as at Carnasserie. English influence had made its mark after the royal emigration of 1603, but now, nearly a century later, the ever-stronger prestige and ideological coherence of international classicism had become too overwhelming to resist. In that, Scotland was only one offshoot of a northern European trend which (should we discount Stirling's Chapel Royal) had begun earlier, in places like Holland, where the vernacular was more resoundingly rejected in the early seventeenth century; or France, where the Renaissance morphed gently into the classical. What was arguably most remarkable about the Scottish case was the 'Golden Century' that had followed the 1603 regnal union – an Indian summer of castle-building, sharply divergent from the course of architecture elsewhere in the Stuart kingdoms, and which was only brought to an end by the shock of the fall of their dynasty, with its centuries-long Scottish roots. In the next chapter, we will trace the new architectural currents that flowed into the void left by the downfall of the Jacobite Stuarts, during a hiatus of roughly half a century. But only after the violent conclusion of dynastic conflict in 1745/6 could Scotland's 'castle culture' achieve a decisive break from the 'dangerous past', allowing it to become the foundation of a richly creative 'Second Castle Age'.

4

1689–1750: The Architecture of Dynastic Struggle

I am bound in duty to informe that unless some serious settled measure be laide doune for keeping Her Ma[jes]t[y']s palace Castles and forths in repair they'l infallibly go all to ruine.[1]
– MASTER JAMES SMITH TO LORD MAR, 1707

When I make any designe I have no regard to . . . any old matter wch. are oblique & not agreeable to a modish and regular designe.[2]
– SIR WILLIAM BRUCE, 1694

Old houses and Touers are, I think, the Honour and pride of a Country.[3]
– SIR JOHN CLERK OF PENICUIK, 1741

[Sir John] Vanburgh's vision of a turreted castle entitles us to regard him as the grandfather, if not the actual parent, of the Scottish baronial style which found birth at Inveraray.[4]
– HOWARD COLVIN, 1964

Introduction

Following a brief interval of semi-independence, the drive towards further Scottish–English integration continued apace after 1689, this time under the aegis of the militantly Protestant successor monarchies. This period witnessed revolution and intermittent civil war from 1689 to 1746, and parliamentary union with England in 1707. Over these years, successive waves of propaganda converted 'Jacobite Scotland' from a rational alternative politics, forefronted by improvers and intellectuals, into a menacing evil, and then, eventually, into a harmless Romantic legend. This was the age of Scotland's formal exodus from the international scene, but the age, too, in which Scotland gained access to England's commercial empire, plunging voraciously into ever-more acquisitive territorial conquests.

This half-century of unrest was dominated in Scotland, architecturally, not so much by grandiose monuments as by the building of fortresses, for the purposes of policing society against 'sedition'. Now that the First Castle Age was drawing to a close, no more royal palaces were commissioned or even enlarged in Scotland, as the country acclimatized to being British. Within the new architecture that was built – for example, in the country houses of the Hanoverian ruling elite – this assimilation was at first expressed through the homogenized spread of the northern European classicism that was now well established both in England and in King William's native Low Countries, with 'local' differences reduced to subtle nuances. The foundations for this radical change had already been laid by Bruce and Smith, and after 1689 their groundwork was rapidly and radically exploited, in a wave of mainstream classical houses such as Smith's Melville House (1697–1700) and the even more Dutch-looking Dalkeith Palace (1702–10): the only obvious castle feature to continue was the ogee-domed pavilion-turret. From the 1720s, the classical architecture of Scotland was dominated by William Adam, whose style followed that of James Gibbs and his English clients. But once the post-1689 discontent was finally crushed militarily in the 1740s, the architectural consolidation of the new Britain – perhaps unexpectedly – started to diverge towards a revival of castle-building – a Second Castle Age that was inaugurated by the new castle commissioned in 1743 by the Duke of Argyll at Inveraray.

The Organization of Government Architecture

Following the 'alteratione of the government' in 1689,[5] conflict and warfare continued to be a significant preoccupation. Parliament was again rather more liberated, able to pursue its own agendas, but many were appalled at the deposing of the king, leading to fresh civil war. The 'rebel' leader, John Graham of Claverhouse, was killed, and the Highlands became a militarized landscape. King William's primary interest in Scotland was as a military resource for his wars, to the point that in 1694 Chancellor Tweeddale complained that 'now yow may consider this Kingdome as sufficiently emptied of train'd men, and in place of two Regiments of ye best dragoons ever I saw we have on[e] to levie'.[6]

The regime change had an inevitable impact on the organization of government architecture. Perhaps unexpectedly, the new establishment had supported James's architect James Smith when he appealed for help to finish the Canongate Kirk – notwithstanding its being conceived as a counter-Reformation structure. However, although Smith was not officially dismissed, the post of Master of Works was among those eventually filled by a 'new man', Sir Archibald Murray of Blackbarony, one of those who looked for employment as a concrete reward for supporting the 'alteratione'. He aimed at first for the lucrative Chancery, but on discovering that 'it seames that is sticked so I most steare to some other shore, I have now thought upon the maister of works place which I think is [in] no bodyes view, it is ane imployment very honorable';[7] 'being upon the mater now vacant in so farre that theire was only ane ordinaire worke man [i.e., Smith] imployed, tho it formerly has beine always in considerable gentlemans hands'.[8] Blackbarony's bid suffered from his lack of experience in architecture and building, and in a brief tussle in London in 1693–4, Smith strenuously defended his position, lobbying the king with the support of the Duke of Hamilton. Blackbarony reported to Tweeddale that Hamilton might 'gett a letter to the tresaurie to roupe [=sell] his Ma[jesty's] palace & casteles which will cutt of my gifte';[9] and that 'Smith . . . gave in a memoriale to the King concerning my place what is in it I know not, he makes such a noyce about it that I am lyke even w[i]t[h] all ye freindshipe I can make to have a hard pull for it, I may expect all ye myscheife from the M[aste]r of Staires'.[10] Given the king's lack of interest in Scottish affairs – as Blackbarony politely put it, 'I beleive His Maj[esty] gets hardly tyme to reflect upon the Condition of our Co[u]ntry'[11] – politics eventually trumped professional specialism, and Blackbarony was successful.

As Master of Works, however, his effective sphere of action was very limited, as he relied largely on his assistant and cousin, Walter Murray of Halmyre, and Smith's expertise could always be called on in important cases, as especially in the case of Holyroodhouse. There could, of course, be no question any longer of significant new works here or in any other palace, as there was no longer even the pretence of royal residence; a possible coronation was postponed 'both because the Queen is not coming, and that the circumstances of the nation is such, that it cannot reasonablie be expected, ther will be such ane appearance as is proper for such ocations'.[12] The king was, though, expected to present himself, crowned, at parliament.[13] At Holyroodhouse, from now on, select aristocratic elites were allocated apartments within the palace: the Bruce scheme remained incomplete, but money was once more being spent there, on the rehabilitation of the apartments allocated to the wealthy. The windows began to feature new English (and Dutch) inspired sash windows in place of Bruce's casements, and dormer windows to service new-made garret rooms.[14] In 1690, the Treasurer, John Kennedy, Seventh Earl of Cassilis, wrote to Secretary of State George Leslie, Fourth Lord and First Earl of Melville, that

By a letter from his Majesty, [Leven] and I were appointed . . . to visit the Palace of Hallirudhouse. A considerable part . . . is taken up by D[uke].H[amilton]. his lodgings, and his son E[arl]. of Arran, with that which Marquis of Athole is yet in possession of. Wee went thorough all the King's own apartment, which is in pretty good order, but the other lodgings will need considerable reparation, a particular accompt whereof wee ordained James Smith to draw up and give in to the Tresaury.[15]

Thus although Blackbarony was officially the master of works, for important advice, Smith was still available. After Blackbarony's death in 1700, however, the Mastership of Works rapidly declined into architectural irrelevance. In 1705, it was given to another Borderer from Blackbarony's kin group, Sir Francis Scott of Thirlestane, who oversaw a cosmetic refitting of Holyrood in time for the 1706 parliament. Instead of winning applause, however, Scott was dismissed by Argyll, who had the mastership gifted to his uncle, Campbell of Mamore (conjoined with Urquhart of Meldrum). Thirlestane appealed to the government over unpaid salary, arguing that 'I had served as Master of Work within [a few] days of a whole yeare by which . . . I had right to expect a whole years salary . . . I conceave it my duty to address myself to your Lo/ in this matter, so I hope you will have the goodness to favour my just protestations . . . [and lay these] . . . before the Queen'.[16] From 1706, the post of master of works was, effectively, a sinecure for government supporters with little or no knowledge of architecture. In the specific case of Holyroodhouse, Halmyre continued to oversee works, in default of any input from the masters of work: Smith pressed for repairs to be made, but with minimal success, and the palace survived as a block of increasingly ill-maintained aristocratic town lodgings.

Overall, the leadership within Scottish architecture which had stemmed from the active input of the monarchs and their masters of works during the First Castle Age, had now run its course, along with the rhetorical unbroken line of kings, but the associated ideology of a martial nation-in-arms simply needed to be slightly adjusted. England's wars were now Britain's wars, and the market for Scottish soldiers was only beginning: a martial imagery sometimes continued in landscape design, in cases where houses were sometimes enfolded by 'fortified' garden walls, as at Loudoun, Hopetoun and Newliston. It was, however, the internal threat of civil war that spurred the main thrust of the new government's building policy, which was now not concerned with palaces but with fortifications – in this case, of a modern and utilitarian rather than symbolic kind. Numbers of castles, such as Braemar, became anti-Jacobite fortifications to consolidate the regime change, and in response, some Jacobites fortified their castles, encouraged by William's military setbacks: in 1691 Lord Melville was informed that '[MacDonell of] Glengary [was] fortifieing his house with an earth work and pallisados . . . M'Lean was, of rendring Dowart Castle . . . but the news of taking Mons, and the storyes of great assistance comeing to them from France or Ireland

... hath b[u]oyed them up again'.[17] A fortress – named Fort William, in honour of the king – was built in Lochaber. Its governor, Colonel John Hill, explained, 'this being the center off the Highlands, and neer to which all the men of actione are'.[18] His tactics included psychological warfare – and more extreme measures.[19] On St Valentine's Day 1692, Hill reported to Tweeddale on the Massacre of Glencoe by soldiers from Fort William:

> I have also ruined Glencoe, old Glencoe and Achatriaton (the two Cheifs off the two familyes off the Clanean in Glencoe) being Killed, with 36 more, the rest by reason off an Extraordinary storme escaped, but their goods are a prey to the souldrs, & their houses to the fire . . . They Come from all partes to submit to the Kings Mercy, & take the oath of allegeance & soe (according to my orders) save their lifes, I hope this Example of justice & severity upon Glencoe will be enough.[20]

MacIan of Glencoe's residence was not a castle, with the result that he was more vulnerable than others who resisted the changes such as Glengarry, with his heavily fortified Invergarry Castle.

Parliamentary Union and 'British Classicism'

Following the failure of the Darien colonial venture in 1700, a parliamentary union was finally enacted in 1707.[21] A financial recompense from England for Darien, 'The Equivalent', doubtless helped sponsor new architecture. Queensberry's 1710s expenditure at Durisdeer, which included monuments and an overscaled ducal aisle, all (save for a monument by Jan van Nost) designed by Smith, almost suggests a client having difficulty in spending money fast enough; while a 1709–10 classicizing project of Smith and McGill for Cullen House would have transformed Chancellor Seafield's country seat to a post-castle. On the whole, however, the post-1707 system left government even more remote, despite the creation in 1727 of the Board of Manufactures, intended to promote linen and fishing. Frustrated that it was 'extremely difficult to bring [government] with any degree of attention or concern to think of Scotch matters',[22] Lord President Duncan Forbes wrote gloomily in 1743 that 'if nothing is to be done [for Scottish matters in this session of parliament], there is an end to very flattering hopes; and those manufactures, from which I looked for a sort of resurrection to this dead country, must infallibly die'.[23]

Architecturally, the decades that followed the parliamentary union seemed to mark both the lowest point in the fortunes of castellated architecture in Scotland, and also the dominance of the fashion for a purer classicism in both Scotland and England – a phase associated with a significant upsurge in the migration of classically orientated Scottish architects to England – including James Gibbs, Robert Mylne and Colen Campbell. Traditionally, the latter trend has been interpreted as an implicitly or explicitly 'political' phenomenon, stemming from burgeoning Whig British nationalism – an interpretation based chiefly on the longstanding impact of Campbell's *Vitruvius Britannicus*, published in 1715, which advocated a 'neo-Palladianism' as a national style for the new 'Great Britain'. Celebrating England's Inigo Jones, and claiming that he, by adding 'Beauty and Majesty', had surpassed the master, Campbell presented England's supposed triumph as all Britain's – a line of argument that would every so often crop up again, as we shall see.[24] At the architectural 'coal-face' in Scotland, however, the increasing hegemony of classicism was not so much a reflection of the impact of British nationalist tracts as of the longstanding architectural impact of Bruce, and even more of Smith, who – rather like James Gibbs in England – had brought back from Rome a more sophisticated knowledge of Italian architecture. Around the turn of the century Smith, the former royal architect, was still highly regarded and the wealthy preferred him (or, sometimes Bruce) to design their new buildings, whatever the apparent political or ideological inconsistencies: Smith's clients included 'Williamites' such as Hamilton, Melville, and Queensberry. He built some of Scotland's greatest buildings of the age, including Hamilton Palace (whose giant portico had columns in scooped-out recesses in the Roman manner), and as we saw, Melville House and Dalkeith Palace (the last two seemingly referencing Dutch classicism such as William's palace of Het Loo). There were few castle-builders in that clientele.

The First Castle Age might have been coming to an end, but castle-building was not yet quite defunct, even within the works of 'classical masters' such as Bruce or Smith. It was, ironically, within the previously rather subordinate civic realm that one of the most obvious continuing generic relics of the castle tradition remained embedded: the massive towers that were the trademark of the civic tolbooth, and which were combined with scholarly façade architecture as early as Bruce's studiously classical Stirling Town House of 1703–5. Where the castle tradition persisted most strongly was in the old agenda of adapting existing castles to create 'balance', a practice prevalent especially of course among those opposed to the new order – as was seen, for example, in Smith's reconstruction of Traquair (Figure 4.1), a castle in Peeblesshire, around 1700–1705 for its militantly Catholic Jacobite laird, Charles Stewart, Fourth Earl of Traquair. Smith planned to duplicate the asymmetrical L-plan and bartizans, with the projections linked by a porch rather like the one he had added to Queensberry House, and dormers cut through the eaves.[25] This plan was simplified and cut down in execution – perhaps owing to the fact that Lord Traquair, along with Sir William Bruce and Lord Nairne (a client of Bruce's at the time), was listed in 1708 among those 'who are nou under confynement by order of the Earle of Leven' as Jacobite sympathizers.[26] Although the balancing wing was not built, classical interiors were created, together with a symmetrical forecourt with wings and wrought ironwork, and twinned terminal pavilions in the terraced garden.

FIGURE 4.1 *Traquair House – a classicizing scheme of c. 1700 included the forecourt, though was largely internal as executed; view from south-west; photograph of 1963.* © Historic Environment Scotland. https://canmore.org.uk/collection/1203284

In later decades, a formula of decastellation would become prevalent, but at this early stage the lairds' priority was usually to maintain the castle formula, while securing interior opulence and a balanced viewing 'frame'. Traquair House even survived a more thoroughgoing classicizing scheme of around 1740 by architect John Douglas, which remained unimplemented with the exception of a heavily rusticated gateway, the so-called Bear Gates of 1737–8, which, according to family tradition, are to be unlocked only when the Stuart line returns to the throne.[27]

A similar approach was followed by one of the leading Jacobites of the 1715 'Rising', John Erskine, Sixth and Eleventh Earl of Mar (1675–1732), politician, amateur architect, and friend of Scotland's top architects of the time, Smith, Alexander McGill and Alexander Edward. Having originally campaigned in favour of the 1707 parliamentary union, Mar subsequently changed his mind and led an army in opposition to it in 1715, being exiled thereafter: his story is told by Margaret Stewart.[28] At his own seat of Alloa House, around 1706, he recast the main massive tower-house in a similar manner to the 1677 scheme at Kinneil mentioned in the previous chapter, with a determinedly classical window-grid hammered through the ancient thick walls and a grand new interior stair installed. Mar had also laid out the landscape at Alloa in an expansively classical manner, with views aligned on significant historic buildings, including Stirling Castle, where he was hereditary governor.

But a continuing willingness to retain and adapt castles, within the longstanding architectural formula of 'balance', was far from being confined to Jacobites – as was demonstrated by the programme of alterations to the Ayrshire Castle of Kelburn (Figure 4.2) implemented between around 1692 and 1722 by David Boyle. Boyle had been created Lord Glasgow in 1703 and was an active proponent of the 1707 parliamentary union. Like Traquair at his castle, Lord Glasgow created a big, formal and symmetrical forecourt with the retained tower-house as the dominant element. His interventions provided a new series of state rooms in a near-detached and carefully symmetrical crowstepped block. The new work had necessitated demolition of a predecessor structure, and the new block comprised a long rectangle, one room deep. Its great dining room/saloon was centrally positioned and set crosswise, thus projecting outwards on both fronts with big-windowed twin-gabled elevations; the plain 'castellar' exterior contrasted with the sumptuous extremely elaborate interior, groaning with elaborate timber

FIGURE 4.2 *Kelburn Castle – view from north centred on 1720s house; photograph of 1942.* © *Historic Environment Scotland. https://canmore.org.uk/collection/1451415*

FIGURE 4.3 *Craighall Castle – the arcaded 1697–9 frontispiece linked the castle's tower (on the right) and western turret (on the left) – demolished prior to this photograph being taken) which were retained for display; 1889 photograph by Erskine Beveridge prior to demolition.* © Historic Environment Scotland. https://canmore.org.uk/collection/739304

panelling and Corinthian pilasters. If Lord Glasgow profited from The Equivalent, then there can be little doubt that some of this was spent on Kelburn!

Similar examples of castle adaptation included Craighall (Figure 4.3), which had two unequal-sized towers in 1697 when Bruce designed a new, classical façade: this new work was primarily a corridor fronting the connecting range with balustraded end pavilions, and it largely absorbed the lesser tower's façade, while the castle's residential tower on the opposite (east) side was ostentatiously retained. Equally, the stripped L-plan-with-angle-turret formula continued elsewhere, with Dunnikier House (renamed Path House), for instance, built in 1692. Here there were skewputts but no crowsteps.[29] By the early eighteenth century, a landed castle might comprise a retained tower; a close, formed by a barmkin wall with a big round-arched gateway; and a classical, grid-windowed and gabled wing adjoining the tower, reflecting the wish both to expand, and to move main spaces down from the tower, into suites of rooms. A typical example is Midhope (Figure 4.4), where the tower-and-wing arrangement was supplemented at the end of the seventeenth century by both heightening and extending the wing.[30] In the south-west, Sir James Douglas of Kelhead contracted with James Lockhart and Robert Hastie in 1692 to build a two-storeyed wing

FIGURE 4.4 *Midhope Castle – tower house, plus lower wing completed late seventeenth century; view from south-east; photograph of 1928.* © *Historic Environment Scotland. https://canmore.org.uk/collection/1216216*

('ane house of Tuo house high'), to adjoin the existing tower and extend to its full width. This was to contain a new kitchen and Brewhouse, evidencing the focus on changing culinary requirements, with rooms above.[31] Lady Tweeddale's 1721 reference to 'the Mansion House, and Mannor House of Auchans' underlines the dignity that was still attributed to castles, even in the heyday of Scottish assimilation into the 'new Britain'.[32]

Other outwardly classical buildings retained castellar elements in a behind-the-scenes manner. North of Edinburgh, Royston (renamed Caroline Park), for example, had an expensive new south front made for Sir George MacKenzie, Viscount Tarbat, in 1693, with ogee-domed square end pavilions, one of which was reshaped from a pre-existing angle turret. Similarly, Blackbarony was reconstructed for the late Master of Works' son before 1715 as a classical house, concealing the old castle, but with large, ogee-domed angle pavilions.[33] Where Smith and McGill had included pavilions, these were also ogee-domed, but preferably recessed on the flanks to show the full width of the façade – in contrast to the more overtly vertical-looking Gallery, or Methven, of the 1660s–70s. One of the most resilient components of the castle style was the crowstepped gable, used often in combination with decorative skewputts: the use of these was, arguably, continuous, meeting up with the Adam brothers' revivalist designs of the later eighteenth century. Thus while classicism was further strengthening its grip in the first half of the eighteenth century, new houses often combined crowsteps with a flat-fronted, five-bay centre-doored front. Sometimes such houses had a centre wallhead gable room – a combination also popular in Venice, although the Scottish version probably derived from the idea of a stilted gable (like Stenhouse) without bartizans. The early eighteenth-century Brisbane House, for example, had three such gables atop a gridded three-storeyed flat front.

1720s–40s: The Rise of Gothic

Over the three decades from 1720 to 1750, a yet more decisive break from the First Castle Age took place. In these years, Scotland's foremost architect was William Adam (1689–1748). He built for a pro-union landed clientele who wanted houses that looked less Scottish and more classically mainstream. For them, he devised an architecture characterized by heavy-rusticated detailing, sash windows, and sometimes by its similarity to some of the work of the Scottish architect James Gibbs, one of the leading architects in contemporary England – thereby further intensifying and complicating the Scottish–English interconnections in architecture. Paradoxically, Gibbs was a Catholic, and yet it was his classical architecture and not Campbell's nationalist 'Palladianism' that Adam's work most closely resembled: indeed, Adam went so far as to compile from the 1720s a riposte to Campbell's *Vitruvius Britannicus*, entitled *Vitruvius Scoticus* – a collection of architectural drawings, largely his own, but including work by others (and only eventually published around 1812). Adam's affiliations were firmly with the new Hanoverian, unionist establishment, but his architectural approach was very much his own.

What was missing from *Vitruvius Scoticus* was any highlighting of castles – as these were now inexorably on the way out of the mainstream architectural scene. Occasionally, lairds still commissioned large-scale remodelling exercises following the principles of 'balance', as in the case of Adam's rebuilding of Taymouth Castle in Perthshire from 1739 for John Campbell, Second Earl of Breadalbane, Lord Lieutenant of Perthshire and (from 1747) a representative peer at Westminster (Figure 4.5). Here the castle had already been regularized on the Balcaskie model, the old L-plan jamb having been duplicated to create a symmetrical and bartizaned modern castle. Adam added classical pavilions and screen walls to this ensemble.[34] Here, the entrance was central, as seen both at Prestonfield, and in the design envisaged for Castle Grant, in Richard Waitt's 1714 painting of the Piper of the Laird of Grant.[35] Castle Grant had a Thirlestane-like platformed forecourt, bounded by close-spaced flanking wings, with the main block bartizaned as at Taymouth. More indicative of the shift in values that was now underway, however, was Adam's work for another gentleman

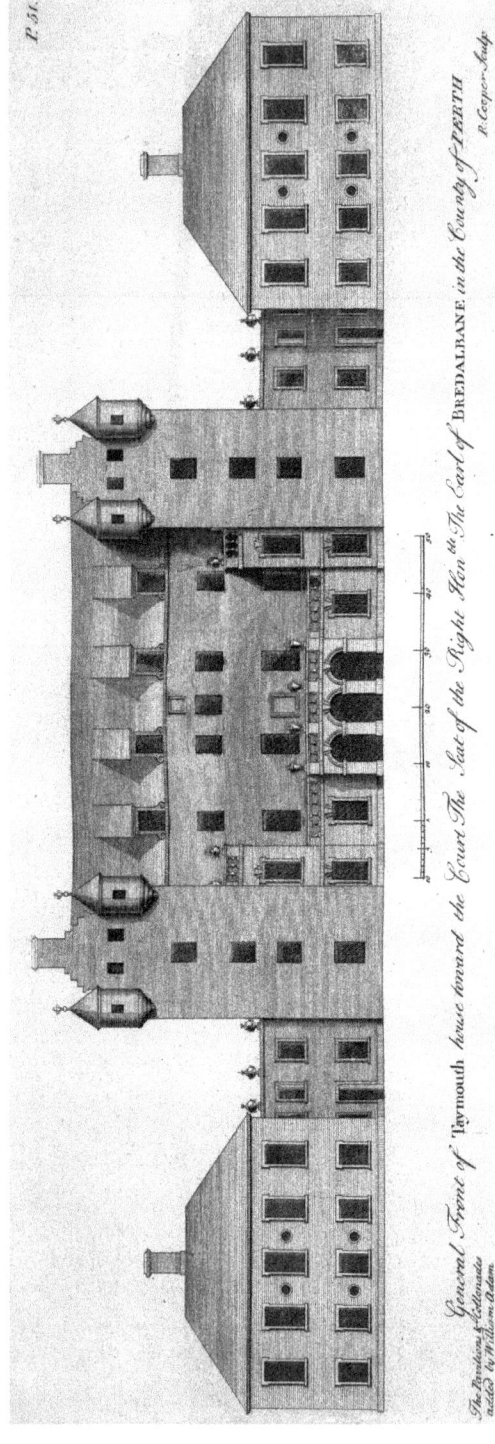

FIGURE 4.5 Taymouth House – William Adam's modernization scheme of c. 1739; engraving by R. Cooper for *Vitruvius Scoticus*. © Historic Environment Scotland. https://canmore.org.uk/collection/761027

architect-cum-unionist-politician, Sir John Clerk of Penicuik. Clark's best known architectural enterprise was Mavisbank, a miniature classical villa which he built with William Adam on a picturesque Midlothian site, adjoining an archaeological site that he believed to be Roman. For Clerk, an energetic antiquary, Scotland's castles were no longer part of an active building continuum but something unambiguously of the past, whose treatment was to be conditioned by a balance of practical and emotional criteria. In the design of his classical villa, Clerk had prevented Adam from adding an extra storey, by which it 'wou'd have lookt like a Touer and been quite spoiled'.[36] But his attitude changed when considering 'real' castles. He had said of Ravensneuk tower, a family property, that 'it was against my inclination that it was pulled down; but as my father . . . wanted stones for the park dyke . . . I submitted. The touer of Pennicuik was pulled down on the same account, but if I had the stones in readiness I would repair them both. Old houses and Touers are, I think, the Honour and pride of a Country'.[37]

In most cases, new houses were designed by Adam and his contemporaries in an unambiguously classical manner, with symmetrical, 'rational modern' plans and horizontal room arrangements – even if their design specifics differed significantly from the formulaic 'neo-Palladian' approach proselytized by Campbell and others in England. But from the mid-eighteenth century onwards, the first twinges of the Romantic Movement began to inspire a different form of external architecture, evoking the 'national past' in a more calculated, and yet ambiguous way, which partly reflected the hegemonic status of English culture within the 'new Britain' in its symbolic use of both Gothic and castellated architectural features.

Hitherto in Scotland, as we saw in previous chapters, the use of Gothic or 'pointed' architecture had been relatively marginal, both prior to the Reformation when it was sidelined by 'neo-Romanesque' (in churches) and castellated (secular) features, and since the Reformation when it was seen by many as tainted with Episcopalian if not Catholic leanings, and its use accordingly was kept occasional and small scale. The single, spectacular exception during this period was the Michael Chapel (1705) (Figure 4.6), a mausoleum at Gordonstoun. It was centre-doored and symmetrical, rather like the Chapel Royal, but designed in a 'spiky'-traceried Gothic – a choice that linked it to some buildings connected with James Smith, notably Durisdeer's Queensberry Aisle (1695–c. 1716), while Durisdeer's belfry has tracery rather more like the massive, chunky West Greyfriars' Church in Edinburgh (1718). In England, however, the place of Gothic was rather more complex and entrenched, in the first instance because of the pervasive role of 'Perpendicular' within late medieval secular and religious architecture, and its protracted afterlife in the seventeenth century – an English equivalent to the centuries-long hegemony of castellated architecture in Scotland. By the 1730s and 1740s, and partly inspired by earlier work by Sir Christopher Wren,

FIGURE 4.6 *Michael Chapel, Gordonstoun – neo-Gothic private chapel dated 1705; view from south-east; photograph dated 2013.* © *Historic Environment Scotland. https://canmore.org.uk/file/image/1350333*

Gothic survival was increasingly becoming Gothic revival – a shift from instinctive, unintellectualized practices towards conceptual discourses or ideologies, whose close interconnections with the beginnings of the Romantic movement, through the medium of aesthetic-cum-ethical concepts such as the 'Picturesque' and the 'Sublime', have been extensively documented by many historians.

Although the early built outcomes of this shift in values were mostly of a rather frivolous and small-scale character, including landscape follies, garden pavilions or internal house decoration, it was also increasingly bound up with an earnest ethical discourse focused especially on the assertion and definition of English national identity. Although it would not be accurate to talk of an explicit nationalist discourse in the manner authoritatively defined in the 1760s and 1770s by Johann Gottfried Herder – who argued that cultural traditions, including music, dance and art, were among the strongest of the ties that create a modern 'nation' – what we are dealing with here are at least early pointers towards this idea.

In the vanguard of this movement was the landscapist and designer Batty Langley (c. 1696–1751).[38] His writings applied a patriotic filter to all architectural styles, including the classical, where he protested at the 'foreign' origins of the orders[39] and instead devised an 'English Order of my own Composition', featuring a star and garter representing honour, palm branches symbolizing peace and plenty; and oak leaves representing 'the Blessing and Strength of the Nation: By the Blessing, I mean his present Majesty . . . By the Strength of the Nation, I mean our naval Forces and Trade . . . which no Nation in *Europe* can parallel for Strength and Duration.'[40] As suggested by the reference to the (British) navy, the hegemonic role of England within Great Britain ensured that any discourses of 'Englishness' developed during the eighteenth century would inevitably conflate the 'English' and the 'British' – a tendency that would leave unionist Scots in a distinctly uncomfortable position, exacerbated in the early eighteenth century by more general prejudices, as evinced in Langley's disparagement of James Gibbs's '*Scotch* Mode of Speech', and of the expressions Gibbs used 'in his Low language'.[41] The medieval heritage was even more central to Langley's campaign of design patriotism, and prompted much anxiety over the question of nomenclature: in 1742, he denounced the term 'Gothic' as an alien misnomer, and insisted that the correct 'English' name was 'Saxon';[42] the patrons of his *Ancient Architecture* of 1742, the Second Duke of Argyll among them, were hailed as 'Encouragers to the Restoring of the Saxon Architecture', but by 1763 Langley was happy to advertise 'a great variety of *Gothick* Mouldings . . . Which being entirely new, I hope will be favourably received'.[43]

Despite Langley's own xenophobic attitudes,[44] the discourse of architectural 'Britishness' exerted a considerable influence among influential London-based Scots. At the didactic landscape garden of Stowe, developed after 1735 in an Anglo-Scottish partnership between William Kent and James Gibbs, the ambiguity of 'British-English' architectural symbolism was pervasive: Kent's classical Temple of British Worthies (1734) featured statues and inscriptions commemorating exclusively English historical set-pieces, while Gibbs's nearby Temple of Liberty (1741–8) was flamboyantly Gothic, its spiky silhouette exploiting a specifically English architectural trope as a way of dramatizing the Whig British national paradigm of liberty, or freedom from external domination. Here was a recipe that was calculated, despite its elision of the 'British' and the 'English', to appeal to a unionist Scottish elite increasingly anxious that militarized Jacobitism might succeed in destabilizing the union and even in reintroducing Catholicism.

Eventually, as we will see in the next chapters, the associations of the 'Gothic' would shift significantly under the influence of the burgeoning Romantic Movement, to the point where the castellated heritage of the First Castle Age could begin to inspire a fresh era of castle architecture: a Second Castle Age, whose main elements were adumbrated in a remarkable project in the heart of the West Highlands, at Inveraray Castle.

Inveraray Castle: Fortress or Fantasy?

Within the unionist elite, those who arguably had cause to be most worried were the aristocrats who retained great estates in the Highlands but had themselves become assimilated into London society and the Whig Hanoverian establishment. Two of the most emblematic examples of this transcultural landed class were the brothers John and Archibald Campbell, successively the Second and Third Dukes of Argyll. Both were born in their grandmother's Ham House and reared in England; both were military men who fought at Sheriffmuir against Mar's Jacobite insurrection in 1715, John eventually being promoted to field-marshal, created Duke of Greenwich and buried in Westminster Abbey,[45] and both developed estates in England with new classical houses – John, at Sudbrook (1715–19, by Gibbs), Archibald, at Whitton Place (c. 1732–9, by Roger Morris). Between them, the two brothers were responsible for initiating and carrying through to completion, at their Argyllshire seat of Inveraray (Figure 4.7), the single most decisive project in the transition to a new type of castle architecture, a new architecture that

FIGURE 4.7 *Inveraray Castle – view from south with Duniquaich / Dùn na Cuaiche in background, a skyline folly of 1747–8; photograph by J. Valentine and Son prior to fire of 1877.* © *Historic Environment Scotland. https://canmore.org.uk/file/image/1233617*

could lend historical authority and symbolic *gravitas* to the shift from the old Stuart Scotland to the new, Hanoverian 'North Britain'.

The Inveraray project represented, from its first beginnings, a sharp break from the First Castle Age's orthodoxy of castle adaptation and enhancement: both the Second Duke and his father had originally explored c. 1720 a project to enframe the old Inveraray Castle as a processional climax to a massive and otherwise wholly classical design by Smith and McGill. Directly afterwards, presumably, all this was jettisoned when the Second Duke commissioned a startlingly different design from Sir John Vanbrugh, the leading English Baroque architect and Whig activist, whose own house in Greenwich (1717) had precociously explored the associative potential of round-arched, castellated, asymmetrical architecture as a picturesque neo-medieval alternative to the Gothic. For Inveraray, Vanbrugh proposed a substantial expansion of the same round-arched, quadrangular, corner-towered formula – composed around a square centre with a full-width gallery opposite the entrance.[46] Possibly because the family saw little of the place, and most expenditure was therefore channelled to the English properties, Vanbrugh's plan remained unbuilt and little was actually done at all beyond construction of modest pavilions – but it clearly had fundamental influence on the castle that was eventually constructed.

Archibald, the Third Duke,[47] was in many ways 'the personification of unionist Scotland in the first half century after union',[48] having (as Lord Ilay) served as one of Scotland's sixteen representative peers in the post-union House of Lords, and having significantly furthered the Scottish Enlightenment in the 1720s as co-founder of the Faculty of Medicine and the pro-Hanoverian Royal Bank of Scotland. It was left to him to develop and carry through to implementation this innovative concept for a new castle at Inveraray. On inheriting the dukedom on John's death in 1743, he immediately began rebuilding both the town and the castle of Inveraray – the former naturally on a regular classical layout symbolic of the modernity of Whig Hanoverian 'improvement', but the latter as a new castle, set alongside its ancient castellated predecessor. In paradoxical contrast to the largely symbolic martial features of the Scottish castles of the Stewart/Stuart centuries, here the decision to build a new castle appears to have been influenced not just by cultural symbolism but by very real and urgent security concerns. By the 1730s, there were moves at the exiled Jacobite court at St Germain towards launching a pro-Jacobite invasion or insurrection within Britain – probably, as before, beginning in the Highlands.[49] Archibald Campbell was all too aware of the danger: his associate Lord President Forbes, according to Fraser, 'saw the insecure foundation on which public tranquillity was based'.[50] The new Duke knew, too, that Argyllshire had been specifically targeted barely a century earlier, during the civil wars; that when he was aged three, his father had narrowly escaped being hanged outside his castle when Argyll was again ravaged in 1685; and that his militantly Whig and Hanoverian family had subsequently become even more unpopular among Jacobites, having seen off first the MacDonalds, and more recently the MacLeans. The Argyll political and military record at both the 1707 union and Sheriffmuir made him, personally, a prime focus for the hostility of Jacobite-sympathizing neighbours.

Thus Archibald's natural anxiety, on inheriting the dukedom in 1743, to renew and 'improve' his Scottish country seat, was tempered by an unusual concern with security – even although British army units were stationed nearby, constructing a road via Loch Lomond-side which would pass his front door. Conceivably, his brother's involvement with Vanbrugh had reflected similar preoccupations in the wake of the 1715 war, given that the latter was himself a military specialist, and architect to Marlborough, who was the Second Duke's rival as the leading British general. The Third Duke now took the process a stage further, by obtaining a design from a military engineer (and kinsman), Dougal Campbell. He designed 'a HOUSE ... in the Castle Stile, Defended with a Fosseé' (Figure 4.8), which, although undated, must have been prepared between 1743 and 1745. Star-shaped in plan, this envisaged a symmetrical splay-plan house with forecourt, all contained within a deep fosse which, in turn, had outer walling and sloped embankments beyond. Campbell highlighted 'the Court which covers the *Entrance* of the *House*, the *Draw Bridge, Fosseé* and *Covered Way*, projected to defend the *House*'. Here the word 'defend' was meant not metaphorically but literally. The outer perimeter had a single small entrance covered by a gun-hole and beyond, the main entrance was reached via confined spaces. The design certainly had a picturesque profile, and corner turrets, but the plan abounded in square and odd-shaped rooms, with no scope for a big reception space or gallery. All in all, this was more of a defensible fortress than a domestic castle, and its sheer massiveness was comparable even with modern military complexes such as Dumbarton. Perhaps Argyll hoped for government assistance in its construction because of his political prominence; but eventually Campbell's design was shelved.

What was eventually built at Inveraray, under the oversight of Archibald's English architect and old friend, Roger Morris, was a hybrid between Campbell's design and that of Vanbrugh (Figure 4.9). On plan, Morris's building was very similar in its square plan to Vanbrugh's. Both schemes proposed castellation and symmetry; but more precisely drawn from Campbell's scheme was the fact that the house would be flat-roofed and composed around a taller centre tower, and – vitally, with insurrection now brewing – would all be set within a deep defensive fosse. By early 1745 the fosse was begun; but by the time of the foundation-laying ceremony of 1 October 1746, with William Adam (here overseeing construction) present, the Jacobite Rising was already crushed, and the foundation stone inscription duly celebrated Cumberland, the victor.[51] The fosse would have presented a real barrier to potential assailants, but now, by the time of its completion, it already seemed an expensive unnecessity. Almost overnight, the 'castellated' form of the house shifted into the field of romantic symbolism, its external

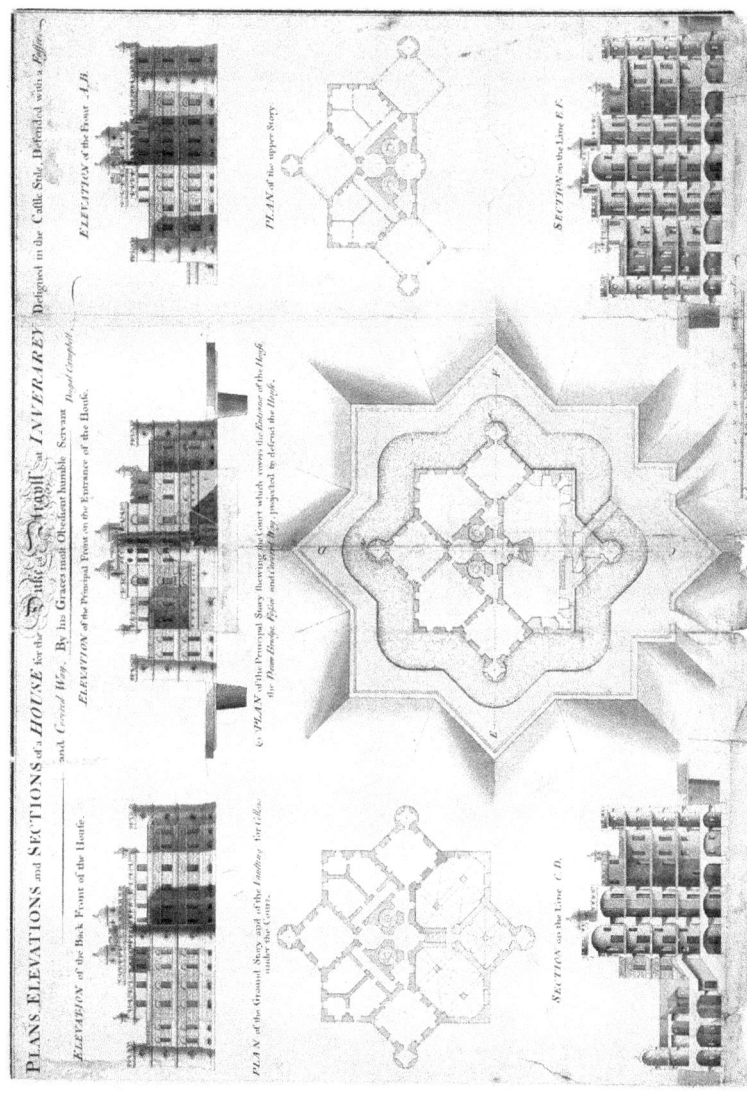

FIGURE 4.8 *Inveraray Castle – unexecuted project by Dougal Campbell, c. 1744, for a 'House . . . in the Castle Stile, Defended with a Fosseé*. © Duke of Argyll. https://canmore.org.uk/search/collection?SIMPLE_KEYWORD=SC1233583

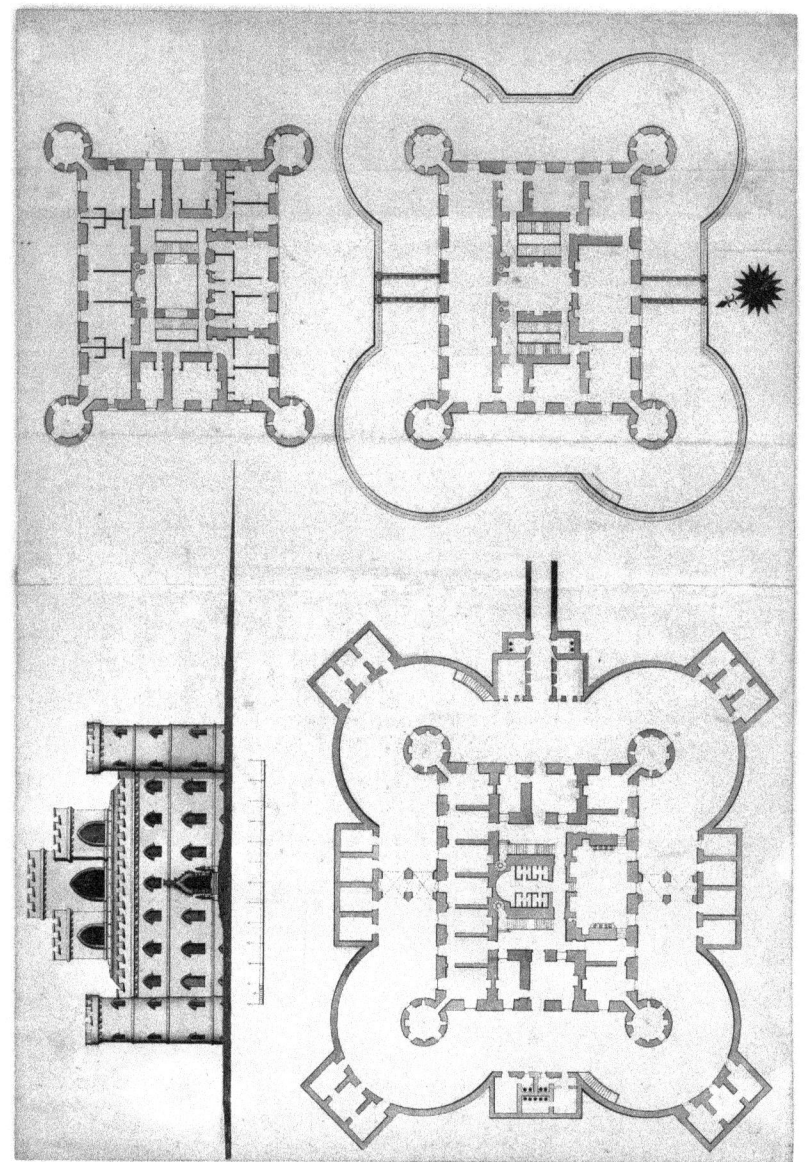

FIGURE 4.9 *Inveraray Castle – plans as executed by Roger Morris, 1744/5.* © *Historic Environment Scotland. https://canmore.org.uk/collection/1233622*

features eclectically mixing crenellation and turrets with Batty Langley-style Gothic (or 'Saxon') fenestration.[52] Crowsteps, bartizans, ostentatious gunholes, high roofs and asymmetry were all absent in this castle revival, distinguishing it clearly from the continuity that still intermittently flared, for example, at contemporary Taymouth.

Conclusion

Overall, Inveraray Castle, a project whose own evolution from fortress to fantasy castle was a direct representation of the final defeat of Jacobitism,[53] went on to provide, almost single-handedly, an architectural foundation on which the post-1707 and Hanoverian union could be invested in imagery of ancient territorial legitimacy. In the hybrid Scottish–English genesis of its design process as much as in its hybrid castellated-Gothic style, it celebrated the 'historical roots' of the new Britain. For the moment, the hegemony of England and English values within Hanoverian Britain, and the transcultural, anglicized lifestyle of the London–Scottish elite, left this agenda burdened for a time with significant associative anomalies – as would be seen in subsequent developments like the popularity of Tudor or English Gothic in early nineteenth-century Scotland. But equally, the scene was now set for the future reinvigoration of the Scottish castle, in a Second Castle Age that would span two centuries, initially through the impact of Robert and James Adam, as a monumental symbol of a new and increasingly confident unionist nationalism.

PART TWO

The Second Castle Age

5

1750–1790: Enlightenment and Romanticism

I have repaired an old castle and by the help of Bob Adams have really made it much older than it was . . . it would suit you, who are an Antiquary, perfectly.

– SIR JOHN DALRYMPLE, 1784 (OF OXENFOORD CASTLE)[1]

An old house, Gothic, & expressive of the dignity of a highland Laird.[2]

– ANONYMOUS DIARIST, DESCRIBING CRAIGIEVAR, 1771

Yon palace too, deserted and forlorn,
No Court attends her fast-decaying walls! Those Royal Mansions, with vacation torn, Loudly to Scotia's Lords for reparation calls.
. . .
But shall that ancient place yet shine anew? Shall yet in Scotland Majesty be seen?
Ye hidden fates! 'tis only known to You,
Who knows what is – to come – and what has been![3]

– EXTRACT FROM PUBLISHER JOHN MURRAY'S HOLYROOD-HOUSE: AN ELEGY. ADDRESSED TO THE NOBILITY OF SCOTLAND, 1781

Introduction

Following 1746, the militarized challenge to the Hanoverian order was ended, and Scotland was now fully committed to the new Britain. In economic and political terms, the focus was now on a combination of Whig capitalist 'Improvement' and colonial expansionism. Coupled with this was a broad upsurge of intellectual development, subsequently dubbed the 'Scottish Enlightenment' – a movement which, paradoxically, was attracted not just to rationality but also to Romanticism, a movement whose beginnings we touched on in previous chapters, but which was now approaching full maturity. Here the literary cult of Ossian made Scotland, for the first time, a focus of international elite cultural fashion, and the country's own culture came to respond to this Romantic myth. Architecturally, this response took the form of a full-blown Second Castle Age, very different in architectural character to its predecessor, with classical designs and plans for country houses often clad in castellated garb, developing the precedent set by Inveraray along new and innovative lines. Here, Robert Adam was a dominant and innovative force – as exemplified in his work at Culzean. Behind this increasingly dominant imagery, castles and classicism still co-existed, but in a complex and multifaceted form: towers referencing tower-houses were introduced, while tower-houses which had been abandoned as old-fashioned were now sometimes reoccupied. Talented architects such as John Paterson followed in the wake of Robert Adam, with new castles now built for a clientele increasingly interested in the fashion.

The Years of Transition: From 'Scotophobia' to Romantic Celebration

Jacobitism was resoundingly defeated in 1746, and the monarchy celebrated by erecting the Culloden Pillar at Windsor Great Park, thereby claiming 'ownership' of the victory. In Scotland, atrocities and executions ensued, Jacobite castles were wrecked and Highland dress was banned except for the military.[4] In England, the distinctions between Highland and Lowland, Jacobite and Covenanter, were muddied together and the conflict briefly provoked a more general climate of 'Scotophobia';[5] in 1754, for example, Mons Meg was taken to London, its stone cannonballs destroyed, to highlight the break with the Scottish past.[6] Some aspects of this persisted for many years, notably the disparagement of the Scottish accent:[7] late eighteenth-century philosopher David Hume 'de-Scoticized' his speech, and writer James Beattie published remedies for 'Scotticisms'.[8] But the wider prejudice proved short-lived, and within a few years, the neutralizing of the Jacobite military threat allowed its threatening 'wildness' to be subtly appropriated by Romanticism: its 'backwardness' and 'barbarism' became transformed into a paradigm of Sublime exoticism, which could act as a foil to the furious transformations of the Age of Improvement – an era of Enlightenment and Progress that was supported not just by industrialization and commerce but by empire and slavery.

Gauging popular opinion, or inactive dissent is difficult, but by mid-century, most literary Scots appear to have regarded themselves both Scottish and British.[9] There was still some nostalgia in the Highlands, and one eighty-nine-year-old recalled in 1864 of his childhood that 'Prince Charles and his cause was the universal talk in the evenings, and all the country people were for him'.[10] Sometimes lairds, too, were still unconvinced, but this remained at conversational level. Bishop Forbes highlighted the exceptional character of the laird of Cadboll's views in 1762, 'he being so keen a Scotsman, that he would have nothing to do with England at all; insomuch that he is for disuniting the two Kingdoms altogether in every Respect, and for having a King over Scotland alone independent of England, and let the English have a King for themselves'.[11] A vehicle for dissenters such as John Howie to express political dissatisfaction was religion: it was difficult to object to references to religious authority.[12] However, the Kirk establishment strongly supported the new monarchy and the mutually reassuring anti-Jacobite guarantee which the union provided; ministers enjoyed a comfortable lifestyle and high social status, and their political support in the pulpits, with prayers for the monarch, could normally be expected, meaning that the Kirk's impact on public opinion could be pervasive.

Within the built environment, the radical rural transformation, with the first large-scale population 'clearances' opening the way to new farms created on 'scientific' principles, underpinned rampant urbanization, and fuelled the emergence of new landed and middle classes, with their increasingly multifaceted building demands. From the 1770s onwards, Edinburgh's New Town began to take shape as a British nationalist landscape, celebrating the monarchy in its street names, as well as the 'thistle and rose' theme common in seventeenth-century plasterwork: a wealthy, ordered vantage-point from which the unionist elite – including author Sir Walter Scott – could view the muddled, picturesque, frequently timber-built, pre-Union 'old Scotland'.

At the same time, the suburbs and countryside were becoming dotted with new classical mansions and villas – and new castles. For the castle remained as entrenched as ever in the cultural imagination of Scotland. But the form that the Scottish castle could, and should take, was now changing radically, under the influence of the Romantic movement in general, and the beginnings of the Gothic Revival in England in particular. In England, like France or Germany, but unlike Scotland, 'Gothic' was widely seen as a mark of national identity, and a focus of competing claims of antiquity, with terms such as 'Early English' later coined to underline its 'national' character and 'ownership'. To antiquarian John Carter, for example,[13] 'Gothic architecture had been ages back the taste of Englishmen . . . [Grecian was] . . . the invention of foreigners.'[14] England looked nostalgically to ecclesiastical Gothic as a golden era, and connected Gothic with nationalistic pride. To Scotland, the castle was the primary authority: for Presbyterians, at least, elaborate Gothic detailing could be seen as evocative of pre-Reformation Catholicism and Episcopacy.

But by the mid-eighteenth century, those distinctions between the 'Scottish' and 'English' pasts were beginning to lose their sharpness. For example, the old Scottish cult of Mary Queen of Scots, of using historic buildings to commemorate 'the unfortunate Mary', now spread to England. Women might dress up as Mary, and Romantics visit places associated with her.[15] On visiting Hardwick Hall, where she had been confined, Thomas Gray, author in 1757 of 'The Bard', remarked: 'One would think that Mary, Queen of Scots, was but just walk'd down into the Park ... [all was] ... just as she left them. A little tatter'd indeed, but the more venerable; & all preserved with religious care.'[16] Wallace and Bruce were already being dislodged by historians who foregrounded the Romantic Mary. Validated by Mary as British heritage, Holyrood became all the more attractive to visitors, her architecture valuable to revivalists.

For architecture, the more significant Romantic influences came in the other direction, from England to Scotland. In 1750, only a few years after the commencement of Inveraray, the writer and antiquarian Horace Walpole, author of arguably the first 'Gothic novel', *The Castle of Otranto* (1764 – renamed as '*a Gothic Story*' for the 1765 edition),[17] announced, 'I am going to build a little Gothic castle.'[18] For this suburban villa just outside London, Strawberry Hill, he engaged a 'committee of taste' (including Robert Adam) and crammed the house with antiquities, drawing on scholarship in an attempt to replicate 'Gothic' features. The new was to seem old: for example, the house's Beauclerk Tower 'look[ed] very ancient'.[19] In due course, Walpole's asymmetrical, organic-looking Strawberry Hill would inspire a new strand of asymmetrical Gothic houses, notably Richard Payne Knight's own Downton Castle (1772) – characterized by asymmetrically bunched crenellated towers referencing ancient castles such as Warwick – and, as we shall see, Scott's Abbotsford.

This new, explicitly Romantic and Picturesque conception of the castle would find many echoes in Scotland, as in 1784, when Sir John Dalrymple said of Oxenfoord Castle that Robert Adam had 'really made it much older than it was'.[20] And it was, above all, the architect sons of William Adam – John (1721–92), Robert (1728–92) and James (1732–94) – who would play the most decisive role in setting the context within which the Second Castle Age could flourish. Robert Adam's renowned years of overseas study, in 1754–8, were, of course, focused above all on the classical ruins of Rome. But he was equally sensitive to the medieval heritage, returning from Italy via the Rhineland,[21] where numerous hill-slope castles survived as picturesque ruins. He set up practice in London, and in 1763 was joined in partnership by his brother, James, on his return from Italy, while John stayed at home as the improving laird of Blair Adam: Robert and James were, successively, architects of the King's Works from 1761 to 1782, and Robert was briefly the MP for Kinross-shire.

In their classical architecture, the Adam brothers showed an acute sensitivity to British nationalism and its symbols: Robert made a design for a new British Parliament House in 1762–3, and James invented for it a 'Britannic Order' and a thistle-detailed 'Chapiteau Ecossais'.[22] James envisaged Scottish iconography for the intended new building: 'I have taken care that North Britain shall bear its own share in all decorations – so that I will venture to say that posterity would even guess at the architect's being from beyond the Tweed.'[23] But they also had an instinctive grasp of the symbolic potential of castellated architecture in Scotland, especially in the hybrid Scottish-English form influenced by Vanbrugh and Walpole, merging 'Gothic' and 'castle' in a picturesque whole – not least because in their earlier years, both father and sons had worked at Fort George and Inveraray, giving them a privileged grasp of the latest trends of new 'castle architecture'. It seems certain that at Inveraray the brothers saw Dougal Campbell's unbuilt design, described as being in 'the castle stile'. This was precisely the term that they later adopted in their own work. For during the 1770s, 1780s and 1790s, while Robert was refining his new classical style, the brothers were also busy devising a new 'Scotch castle revival' – a cousin of England's Gothic Revival. One of the earliest coherent Romantic national revivalisms, its emergence reflected Robert Adam's own antiquarian enthusiasms, which by 1781, when he became an honorary fellow of the Society of Antiquaries of Scotland, had expanded beyond classical antiquity to embrace the Scottish past.[24]

Ossian and the Revival of the Highland Castle

This period also saw the full, post-Jacobite rehabilitation of the Highlands, on the basis of its martial commitment to Britain, and of the absorption of its culture within the realms of Romanticism. The Highland Society of London, for example, was founded in 1778 to promote Gaeldom and seek rescinding of the proscription of tartan, which was achieved in 1782.[25] Bagpiping was co-opted by unionism: the prize-winners at the Falkirk Tryst in 1783, for instance, marched around the tombs both of government generals killed during the 1745–6 Jacobite Rising and Scottish heroes from the 'fallen' of Wallace's army at the Battle of Falkirk in 1298, while 'playing the celebrated MacCrummens [sic] Lament'.[26]

A crucial role here was played by the writer James MacPherson. Opposed to the government's systematic post-1746 assault on his own Gaelic culture and history,[27] he set out to publicize its worth, in an inventive and unconventional way. From 1760, he published poetry which he claimed to be the work of 'Ossian', a legendary third-century bard, but which was in fact an amalgam of genuine salvaged pieces and his own composition.[28] In a demonstration of the fashion-driven internationalism of the Romantic movement, the cult of Ossian inspired Germany's *Sturm und Drang* Romanticism and its leaders such as Johann Wolfgang von Goethe, and Napoleon carried a copy with him on his campaigns. News of it travelled quickly, reaching James Adam in Rome who in 1761 speculated, 'I have been thinking who this is, that is now call'd the highland Bard, has wrote an Epick poem & has been more than once in the highlands finding poems.'[29] MacPherson became wealthy, with assets rumoured to be worth £100,000 when he died.[30] Ann Grant of Laggan joked that the 'bard . . . is as great a favourite of fortune as of fame, and has got more by the old harp of Ossian than most of his predecessors could draw out of the silver strings of Apollo'.[31] His intellectual talents found him lucrative government employment, he became MP for an English constituency, and he commissioned a new country seat from Robert Adam, Balavil, or Belleville (1790–96),[32] near his childhood home. No longer a Jacobite-inclined youth nor a Romanticist but a Highland laird, a classical design in accordance with English norms was what Macpherson chose; although German enthusiasm for *Ossian* meant its design was nonetheless published by architectural writer Christian Ludwig Stieglitz in 1801.[33] Macpherson was buried in Westminster Abbey, establishment Britain's Valhalla.[34] By its enshrinement of the Highlands as a place of long-lost heroes, Ossian securely embedded it within the 'new Britain' and helped give birth to Scotland's 'heritage' tourism.[35] It also almost single-handedly placed Scotland at the heart of Romantic Europe – and helped inspire many Scottish patrons to build themselves neo-medievalizing Romantic castles.

During the late eighteenth century, it had become increasingly common for replacement houses for destroyed castles to be completely classical – even when the patrons were the descendants of Jacobites, as in the cases of Shewglie (1762)[36] and Invergarry (pre-1800).[37] Although previously well repaired by Henry, Third Duke of Buccleuch, from the 1770s Langholm Castle was left to fall into ruin,[38] and was replaced in 1786–7 by a James Playfair-designed classical mansion, Langholm Lodge.[39] And Moy Castle (following despoliation by soldiers in 1745–6) was superseded first by a modest house of 1750–52 'near Castel-moy' and then by the present centre-pedimented Lochbuie House of 1793[40] (the old castle being used as, among other things, a prison in 1773).[41] A more urban setting might offer a redundant castle an alternative future: in Hawick, the Buccleuch town house of Hawick Tower (today known as Drumlanrig Tower) was repaired and converted into an inn in 1768–9, complete with new sash windows, while the local ducal presence was consolidated at Branxholm Tower.[42]

Especially in the Highlands, a laird's castle could still provide an unparalleled way to signal ancient lineage, status, entitlement, and patriotic support for the monarchy – as was evidenced in the c. 1772 portrait of Sir Alexander MacDonald, ninth baronet of Sleat and first baron MacDonald.[43] MacDonald, an Eton-educated clan chief, British soldier and Royal Archer, was represented wearing full martial Highland dress with the ruin of ancient Duntulm Castle behind him,[44] while standing on Cnoc an Eireachd (Hill of Pleas), his clan's former place of justice and assembly prior to the abolition of heritable jurisdictions in 1747.[45] In response, the old practice of adaptation of ancestral castles continued on a relatively modest scale. In the case of Invergarry Castle, a specific target of government reprisals in 1746, the MacDonell family, as we saw, built a replacement classical house; it was in turn replaced by the present David Bryce-designed Glengarry Castle of 1866–9. The Clan MacPherson's classical mansion was similarly targeted during these reprisals; it was reconstructed to a castellated design in 1805 and re-named Cluny Castle.

Exceptionally, disused castles were reoccupied and restored, as occurred in 1776, when George Paterson, a nabob newly returned from India, married Anne, daughter of Lord Gray, and acquired and reoccupied Castle Huntly, near Dundee, employing Playfair and John Paterson to restore it in 1777–95;[46] the castle, built by the first Lord Gray, had been abandoned during the seventeenth century. In 1795, it was claimed by the anonymous *Statistical Account* author (according to Bruce Lenman, possibly Paterson himself) that 'the castle . . . although completely modernised within, has assumed even a more castellated appearance outwardly than formerly. The wings, embattled walls, round tower, and corner turrets, have been given it by the present proprietor'[47] (Figure 5.1). In other cases, the established practice of adding classical blocks or wings continued, as in the case of Castle Grant, whose anti-Jacobite laird (from 1747),[48] Sir Ludovick Grant MP, added a classical show front (by John Adam, 1753–6), retaining the castle aspect as viewed from the south – the resulting ensemble being described as 'the Old modernizd castle' by one observer in 1754.[49] In 1774, at Nisbet, the

FIGURE 5.1 *Castle Huntly – restored by James Playfair and John Paterson, 1777–95; view from south-east; undated 'Valentine' series postcard.* © Historic Environment Scotland. https://canmore.org.uk/search/image?SIMPLE_KEYWORD=sc1233625

old 'tower and wing' formula was reversed,[50] when an already classicized, near-symmetrical castle was extended by a taller, square, tower-like block modelled on Robert Adam's Mellerstain end towers (as well as Mellerstain's William Adam wings); this was added asymmetrically to one side, giving the external impression almost of an ancient nucleus, while internally containing a drawing room, with a guest apartment and library on the floors above. The same castellated classicism was the model chosen for Fyvie Castle's Gordon Tower, added to the north-west corner of the main L-plan structure in 1793.[51] There, the object was not that the new tower should dominate, as at Nisbet, but that it should be unobtrusive: again, it had neat symmetrical facades and a castellated superstructure matching the other towers, and contained single stacked rooms. Increasingly, such tower-like additions were conceived in overtly Romantic terms: in 1789, for example, James Playfair's addition of a new tower for Inchmurrin which would give 'the effect of an old gothic tower of strength', while containing a new dining room with a drawing room above; the offices would be disguised behind ruined-looking arches, and the whole would have a 'delightful prospect over the lake'.[52]

In the complex case of Huntly and Gordon Castles, a composite ensemble of this kind was employed as the direct replacement for a ruined castle. Huntly had been part demolished in 1731,[53] possibly already abandoned when garrisoned around the time of Culloden, and abandoned finally thereafter. Its owner, the Eton-educated Fourth Duke of Gordon, instead rebuilt another nearby castellated house, Bog of Gight, from 1769, and renamed it Gordon Castle.[54] With his architect, the Rome-trained John Baxter the younger, he visited Huntly in 1770, but no action followed that,[55] and it was temporarily converted into a meal store in 1773;[56] restoration was considered again in 1813, and, again, nothing was done.[57] All effort was now focused on Gordon Castle, which was made into an enormous building, with a big centre block flanked by extremely long wings (Figure 5.2). What marked it out as a castle was its crenellation, and its prominently retained tower. The garden front appeared symmetrical at first sight but the staged recessing of the wall planes from left to right gave Gordon a suggestion of the L-plan advance and recess pattern of older castles. Gordon's significance as the centrepiece of a new dynastic landscape was clearly uppermost in the duke's mind in 1774 when his new town of Fochabers was at conception stage, as he attempted to align it axially with the town layout.[58]

From Inveraray to Adam: 'New Castles' of the Late Eighteenth Century

Far more significant for the course of future Scottish architecture, however, was the trend that the Duke of Argyll had first set at Inveraray, and which the Adam family thereafter took the lead in promoting: that of celebrating

FIGURE 5.2 Gordon Castle – view from south-east, facing the garden. The predecessor castle's turret was retained as the centrepiece of John Baxter's design of 1769; photograph of c. 1950 prior to demolition. © Historic Environment Scotland. https://canmore.org.uk/collection/1483236

both landed prestige and British patriotism not by adapting an old castle but by building a completely new one. The brothers realized from the outset that Inveraray was a vital foundation for further success. Robert's European journey began from there with a helpful send off from Argyll: he reported that 'the Duke has at last settled affairs with us, & We are to receive Three Hundred pounds . . . it is so much that we never expected, & The Duke was extreamly pleased with the settling it . . . The Duke say'd that we had behaved vastly genteely & that he was obliged to us'.[59] Having won the favour of Scotland's foremost political figure, the connection duly continued, as seen in 1758, when Robert, in London, wrote to John that 'I have fast hold of His Gr[ace] at present as I have [Agostino] Brunias busy making out a large view of Inveraray in Oil Colours which if it Succeeds well, will surely lay him under obligation to me, on a favourite subject . . . I intend not to take any thing for it.'[60] The Duke's own patronage and castle enthusiasm continued, and in 1758–60 he commissioned John to build the castellated Aray Bridge.[61]

Meanwhile John Adam, probably working with James, was building Scotland's next major castle – a new Douglas Castle for Archibald, First Duke of Douglas, who, like the Duke of Argyll, was a Hanoverian veteran of the battle of Sheriffmuir. It was begun in 1757 while Robert was in Italy, but was incomplete when halted on the Duke's death in 1761.[62] Clearly inspired by Inveraray, Douglas was U-planned and larger, with wing-ends resembling Holyrood's towers (Figure 5.3). The Douglases were a family whose ancestral heroes were not mere regional magnates but the warrior-victors of the Wars of Independence; yet the pro-establishment, Hanoverian connotations of their house design were essentially the same as those of Inveraray. In 1791 James Playfair proposed a design for completing the castle. The new quarter would be lower, though its external façade would be full-height, and it would feature an enormous (thirty-five feet diameter) domed circular stair tower, classically styled internally, but Gothic externally. Playfair's presentation perspective was contrived to make his Douglas design resemble Inveraray very closely.[63] And an Inveraray affiliation continued to be prominent, as we shall see next, in a further succession of prestigious designs.

The role earlier played by Argyll as Scotland's 'manager' for the Hanoverian state was filled from the mid-1780s by Henry Dundas (1742–1811), First Viscount Melville – a Tory and extraordinarily successful political manipulator, holding such power that he was nicknamed 'King Harry the Ninth'. He showcased his ambition and status in a project for a new house near Edinburgh, Melville Castle – which closely resembled Inveraray.[64] Melville was designed by James Playfair in 1786[65] (Figure 5.4). Like Inveraray, it was four-square and crenellated with higher lancet-windowed corner turrets, and pointed basement windows. But there was one significant divergence: whereas Inveraray's tower occupied the heart of a broader and more horizontally proportioned complex, at Melville the tower was itself the mansion. Dundas thus reintroduced the concept of the

FIGURE 5.3 *Douglas Castle – plans by John and James Adam as partially executed from 1757; engraving by R. Cooper for Vitruvius Scoticus.* © Historic Environment Scotland. https://canmore.org.uk/collection/1242528

FIGURE 5.4 *Melville Castle by James Playfair, 1786–91 – view from south-east; photograph by George Hay 1950.* © *Historic Environment Scotland. https:// canmore.org.uk/collection/1233614*

tower-house as an elite residence, but, as an outspoken loyalist, co-opted it to the British Hanoverian cause.[66] Melville's east wing, containing a waiting room and library, together with his bedchamber and dressing room, was Dundas's personal 'command centre', from where he controlled the affairs of Scotland[67] (Figure 5.5). The main house was otherwise fairly orthodox, but with a stupendously decorative staircase on the east, emphasizing, for visitors, the owner's viceroy-like standing. Just as in the cases of Inveraray and Douglas, an adjacent predecessor tower-house was demolished, even although in this case it was traditionally associated with David Rizzio and thus connected to Mary Queen of Scots. Until Melville, new towers had normally been added to existing mansions (or created as pleasure features); but from now on, new mansions frequently took a tower-like form in their entirety.

It was very largely Robert and James Adam who now developed this post-Inveraray agenda into a fully fledged 'castle style', exploiting and reinterpreting the key elements of both Campbell's unexecuted design and the finished house, so as to combine the symmetrical plans that were now thought essential with an irregular-looking skyline, to create the picturesque dynamism vital for Robert Adam's concept of 'movement'.[68] Thus their castellation often featured a central square tower, sometimes with wide-angle strips dotted with narrow openings: the overall impression was

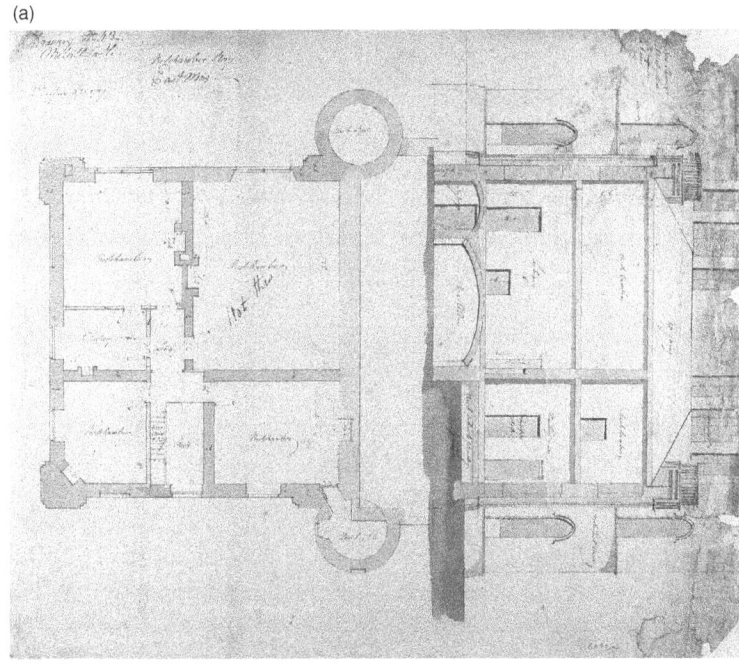
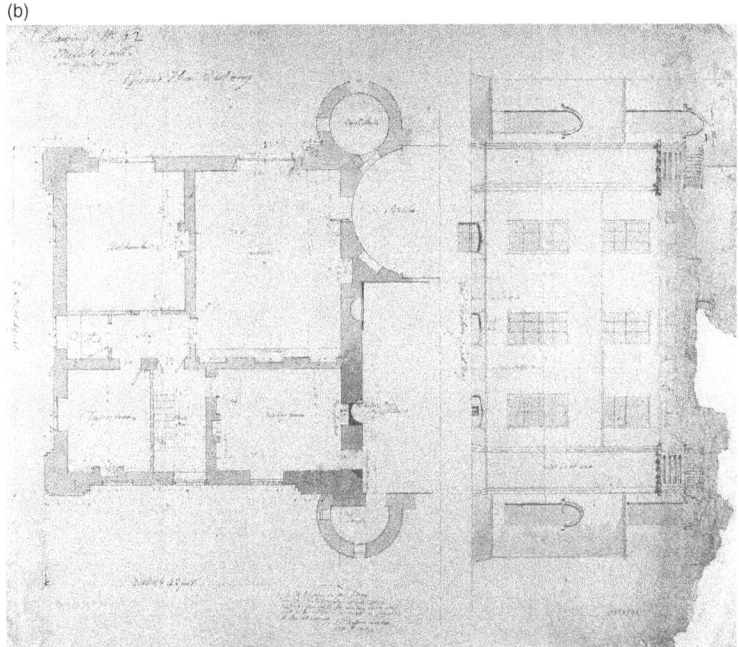

FIGURE 5.5 *Melville Castle – James Playfair's plans of the ground and bedroom floors of the east wing, Lord Melville's 'command centre' for the management of Scotland.* © National Records of Scotland.

sometimes rather like an Anglo-Norman castle such as Rochester, but with classical cornices. Sometimes the Adams' turrets were splayfooted, their enhanced depth seeming to emphasize the fortified imagery (as Gillespie Graham was later to do at Taymouth). Frequently added to these were twinned towers in the style of Holyroodhouse, similarly corner-turreted and proportioned approximately 3:2, the turrets sometimes with pointed roofs and on occasion square-shaped (at Mauldslie). Other castellated details were drawn freely from both Scottish and English precedents, mixing together crowsteps, Tudor-type hood-moulds, cross-shaped 'arrow-slits', corbelling/ machicolation and circular angle bartizans or 'pepper-pots'. Crosses, referencing the pre-Reformation past, appeared as both finials and recessed 'archer-hole' panels.

Appropriately, one of the first proposed examples of this hybrid style would have been located not in Scotland but just over the border, in Cumberland. In 1766, Robert wrote that 'Sir James [Lowther] seems resolved to impose upon me the arduous task of placing a castle upon this his principality'.[69] Castellated projects of 1767 and 1771 for Lowther, first by James and then by Robert, remained unexecuted, but they foreshadowed much of the later Adam repertoire, including twin-turreted Holyrood towers.[70] Meanwhile, the Adams built several projects of a somewhat more hybrid character, both 'classical' and 'castellated' in character. Mellerstain, built around 1770–78 for George Baillie of Jerviswood – whose wife, Eliza, was the daughter of an English MP – was essentially an infill set between two 1720s classical blocks: it featured a 'tower-house' central section and towered ends. Robert's intention had been to also castellate his father's flanking wings which the new house was squeezed between, but this was not done.[71] Demonstrating that new 'castle ruins' could also be designed as effective landscape features, a 1774 design for 'the Top of the Hill at Mellerstain', proposed a tower-house with Holyrood-like turret.[72] A similar concept of designed ruin was seen at Hume Castle, whose ruins were rebuilt before 1789 by a 'clansman', the Third Earl of Marchmont, as an eyecatcher, proclaiming the family's importance.[73]

The Adams' Wedderburn (1771–5) almost resembled an Edinburgh New Town classical terrace, with its rusticated ground floor, while at the same time perhaps referencing Campbell's Inveraray project (Figure 5.6). The formula, like Mellerstain, was that of a long block emphasized at the centre and ends. The centre was, though, more like a tower-house, complete with octagonal corner turrets that seemed to answer Inveraray's circular ones.[74] Progress at Wedderburn was recorded in a series of letters to the client, Patrick Home of Billie, in Italy, from his cousin George Home. He concluded, following a 1774 visit to England, including a visit to Stowe, that

> I saw nothing equal to . . . [Wedderburn] . . . either in beauty or convenience – some of the old buildings in the Gothick Stile are to be sure very magnificent and I can imagine nothing of the kind more agreeable

FIGURE 5.6 *Wedderburn by Robert and James Adam, 1771–5 – view from west; photograph of 2018 by Aonghus MacKechnie.*

than to contemplate one of them on a Still moon light evening, but they cannot bear an examination at noon day ... There is an elegant simplicity about ... Wedderburn which I saw nowhere else, and which accords remarkably with the situation.[75]

Somewhat classical, too, were the designs by Robert Adam for Caldwell (1773–4), whose client, William Mure, was of an ancient family lineage – reflected in the castle's spiky bartizans connected by crenellations, while it at the same time featured a central shallow triumphal-arch panel like that of Kedleston (c. 1760).

More directly evocative of Campbell's Inveraray project were two unexecuted Adam projects that combined low elements with a higher splayed main block, answering Campbell's deficiency of grand spaces by adding prominent Holyrood towers flanking the entrances: Barnbougle Castle, designed in 1774 for the Earl of Rosebery; and Beauly (Bewley) Castle (later renamed Beaufort), designed in 1777 for General Simon Fraser of Lovat, a 'reformed' Jacobite soldier whose father was the highest-profile Jacobite to be publicly executed in London during government reprisals.[76] The Beauly design featured a 'barmkin' and an encircling outer turreted wall, as if in answer to Inveraray's martial-looking fosse.[77] Neither design was implemented. Robert Burn later redesigned Barnbougle in 1788 as a classical mansion with a new west wing duplicating the 'L' to create a 'perfectly uniform' U-planned south front. Burn advised that the reconstructed building would have 'a very Capital Kitchen' – using the same informal expressions as English elites to communicate with his Anglo-Scottish clientele.[78] In the event, Barnbougle Castle was part blown-up to create a folly, and – as we shall see – was thereafter rebuilt.

The mature series of new Adam castles, however, began with Dalquharran, built in 1789–90 by a client (Thomas Kennedy of Dunure) who was married into the Adam family. Schemes for modernizing or replacing the castle had been under development since 1782.[79] Its spiralled plan, containing a dining room, drawing room, bedroom and closet, replicated a formula that had been popularized since the 1680s, while the entrance front had a high triumphal-arched panel set between strong turrets, recalling Fyvie.[80] At Seton House, built in 1789 for Lt. Col. Alexander MacKenzie[81] in replacement of the old Seton Palace – one of Renaissance Scotland's superlatives – the 'clerk' (of works) was John Paterson, who became the chief exponent of the Adam castle style[82] (Figure 5.7). Here the tower-and-barmkin formula (designed, but unexecuted, at Dalquharran) was revived, and a close was built – small-windowed and castellated, with lofty round-arched blind recesses that seem almost to reference Fyvie. The imagery of hospitality began once within the close, where a crowstepped tower-house contained the entrance. The exaggerated elevational complexity, which included polygonal ends, belied Seton's orthodox tripartite plan.

FIGURE 5.7 *Seton House by Robert Adam 1789 – view showing entrance beyond the 'barmkin'; photograph of 2002.* © *Historic Environment Scotland. https:// canmore.org.uk/collection/823359*

The series culminated with Culzean Castle, which was one of Robert Adam's greatest works[83] (Figure 5.8). Built between 1777 and 1792 for the Tenth Earl of Cassillis, it illustrates (along with Seton) the climax of the developed phase of the 'castle style', venturing far beyond the comparatively cautious Wedderburn or Mellerstain. Culzean's spectacular seaside cliff-edge location provided a Romantic drama which Adam exploited eagerly. As was

FIGURE 5.8 *Culzean Castle by Robert Adam 1777–92 – view from south-west; photograph of 2009.* © *Historic Environment Scotland. https://canmore.org.uk/ collection/1142605*

normal for castle style proposals of this period, the interior was classical. Externally, the seaward face had tower-house ends, and a dominating central turret, arcaded, cavernous and mysterious at its lowest level, supporting a balconied terrace. The front face was very different and was set above a castellated terraced base. It had Holyrood end towers, the low link between them (arcaded, reminiscent of Bruce's Craighall) being set in front of an overscaled tower, as if to echo Inveraray. The whole was enclosed by a big barmkin or close, with gateways including a 'ruined' arch, designed to look ancient. The stables block at the northeast continued the same theme: it faintly resembled Holyrood, but with single-turreted end towers, while a bartizaned tower-house or steeple was set centrally in the group.

A range of other architects now began to develop similar themes. We have already met John Baxter the younger: his other castellated projects included extensions and alterations at both Ellon Castle (1781–7) for the Third Earl of Aberdeen, where his interventions included adding castellated bows; and Duns Castle for Robert Hay (1791), where castellated proposals for the main house envisaged a new wing balancing the pre-existing 'tower-and-wing' south front, and including a mammoth 'Picture Gallery, Library and Billiard room' (measuring 67'×25' in area by 21' in height). These proposals were unrealized, but Baxter did build the Duns stables block and Pavilion Lodge.[84] Both of these derived directly from Inveraray: the stables (1792) had uniform long facades with ranks of Inveraray-type hood-moulded pointed windows. The Pavilion Lodge comprised twinned Gothic towers resembling Inveraray's turrets, on flared bases, each standing in turn on a little house, with a simple Gothic archway of 1791 connecting the two. Alexander Nasmyth (1758–1840), rather like Schinkel in Germany, delighted in Romanticism in both painting and architectural design; castellated projects included a lighthouse like an Inveraray corner turret – an idea that reappeared in Robert Burn's design for Edinburgh's Nelson Monument after Nasmyth's 1806 design was rejected as too expensive. Alexander Stevens the younger built the crenellated and bartizaned Raehills (1782–6) for George, Third Marquess of Annandale, with two centre-towered 'quarters' in an L-plan with an entrance turret in the angle (Figure 5.9). A domed hall was even considered here, as part of its classical interior, similar to the one designed by Playfair for Douglas.[85] The cliff-top east quarter of Raehills had a bow-fronted centre tower, and an arcaded terrace which extended beyond the main block carried a full-width colonnade, supporting in turn a centre colonnade, creating a pyramidal effect. The drum tower idea followed the precedent of Robert Adam, but here the dramatic effect anticipated Adam's Culzean.

FIGURE 5.9 *Raehills House – view from south-east showing Alexander Stevens's 1782 design, plus William Burn's towered 1829–34 addition on the left; photograph dated 1958.* © *Historic Environment Scotland. https://canmore.org.uk/collection/1233577*

Conclusion

Castles, rather like tartan, would soon become paramount symbols of the landed elites of unionist Scotland, underpinned by the ancient high status of Scotland's nobility and lairds. Propelled by the global impact of *Ossian*, by the Adams's invention of a new castellated national architecture, and by the pan-British adoption of the cult of Mary Queen of Scots, castles were now increasingly helping highlight Scotland as the archetypal land of Romanticism – at precisely the period most commonly associated with Enlightenment Edinburgh's claimed classical 'Hotbed of Genius'. The chief models were Inveraray, partly due to the connection between the Duke of Argyll and the Adams; and Holyroodhouse, which recalled Mary Queen of Scots; while the generic tower-house once again re-emerged as a lairdly residence, above all at Melville Castle. Attitudes towards new castellation were still a little ambiguous, as evinced in a 1765 reference to Aray Bridge (at Inveraray) as featuring 'five arches wh[ich] are beautiful but spoilt entirely by semicircular turrets wh[ich] gives it a very heavy appearance'.[86] But overall, the built legacy of the First Castle Age was increasingly respected for its romantic antiquity, as in 1771 when Craigievar was hailed as 'an old house, Gothic, & expressive of the dignity of a highland Laird'.[87] Increasingly, that respect was reflected in the proliferation of new castles. Referencing Scotland's past in this emphatic way seemed to underline that the 'old Scotland' was irretrievably gone – whether for good or bad. Just as in the seventeenth century, the 'Scotch' castle was still the nest of the establishment laird: 'Your castle is so much resorted to by the great and the rich', remarked advocate David Morice to James Ross, the Duke of Gordon's cashier, in 1771.[88] But the establishment itself had transmogrified during the transition from the First Castle Age to its successor, and the 1650s Scots who had defied English Roundhead armies had changed into loyal eighteenth-century Britons. Within the new British Empire, Scots played an increasingly pervasive role: by the 1780s, half of the staff of the East India Company's staff were Scottish. In this colonial context, too, an urge to build new castles began to make itself felt, for example in Jamaica, where the late eighteenth century saw the building of two castellated houses by Scottish colonists: Stewart Castle, Trelawny (c. 1780, for James Stewart), and the diagonal-towered Edinburgh Castle, St Ann's (c. 1773, for Lewis Hutchinson). In Scotland itself, this period was pivotal above all in the fruitful way in which the talents of Robert and James Adam interfaced with a Scottish elite uncertain about its competing national identities, by formulating a wholly new architecture nourished by Ossianic Romanticism. Sidestepping the general international prevalence of neoclassicism, Scottish architects had begun to develop a fruitful architectural dialogue between Scottish and English castellation, and in the process had started to help steer international architectural Romanticism into significantly new territory.

6

1790–1820: National Architecture in the Age of Revolution

In the name of my brave and worthy Country, I dedicate this Monument as sacred to the memory of Wallace.[1]

– LORD BUCHAN, AT INAUGURATION OF STATUE TO SIR WILLIAM WALLACE AT DRYBURGH, 1814

A spacious, massy and lofty structure, uniting the idea of the power ... and grandeur associated with an ancient castle and that of the conveniency, comfort and brilliancy of modern refinement.[2]

– ANONYMOUS TRAVELLER, OF THE NEW TAYMOUTH CASTLE, 1819

Introduction: From the French Revolution to the 'Radical War'

The period between the French Revolution of 1789 and the 'Radical War' of 1820 was no longer dominated by the semi-militarized conditions of post-Jacobite society, but by war with France, allied victory at Waterloo and domestic pressure for the right to vote ('Radicalism'). Political continuity was assured through the continuing hegemony of the Dundas family, after the vice-regal powers of Henry Dundas passed in 1811 to his son Robert, Second Viscount Melville. The overall domestic cohesion of Scotland, and Britain, was unprecedentedly high: in these years, significantly, for the first time since James VI's reign, middle-aged Scots had never witnessed civil warfare. Yet the establishment viewed the French Revolution of 1789 with growing concern, in case something similar could happen in Britain. To nip in the bud any revolutionary tendencies, it went on the offensive in face of the threat of democracy, with sedition laws passed, transportations, and, following the '1820 Rising', executions. Establishment Scotland's two most powerful weapons were the law and the church. Lord Aberdeen in 1802 opined that 'of all Tyrannies a Monarchical Government is the best, an Aristocratical the worst, and a Democratical the worst possible'.[3] Popular interest in politics increased, and alongside celebrations for the King's birthday in 1792, rioting took place, with effigies burned of Dundas.[4] Walter Scott feared civil war in 1819: 'In Glasgow the Volunteers drill by day and the Radicals by night . . . [and in Edinburgh] . . . the Volunteer regiment . . . [is ready] . . . to garrison the Castle . . . The Highland Chiefs have offered their clans.'[5] 'Pulpit power', perhaps invigorated by the fact that many manses were rebuilt or improved by the lairds from around 1790, promoted conservatism and anti-Radicalism. The King's chaplain, Alexander Carlyle, modified scripture by adapting *Proverbs* 24.21: '*Fear thou the Lord, and honour the king; and meddle not with them that are given to change*'.[6] (He inserted the word '*honour*' before 'king'.)

In this period, the ambiguities of post-1745 Scottish national identity initially continued to prevail. In general, 'Western' nationalism was dynamic,[7] including integrationist and disintegrationist tendencies. The British monarchy sought an integrationist nationalism, externally perceived as a continuing England,[8] but incorporating aspects of 'Scottishness', and reorientating them as British, in the process creating what Smout denoted 'concentric loyalties'.[9] The legacy of Robert Burns shows this very clearly. He was too significant to ignore, so the establishment adopted him as theirs, deflecting his politics from view: he bade 'fareweel even . . . [to] . . . the Scottish name'.[10]

With the increasing success in maintaining a pacified society from the late eighteenth century, the way had now opened to an intensified exploration of the cultural-historical aspects of national identity. Within the burgeoning European Romantic Movement, it was above all the antiquarians of England who led the way, in the mid-eighteenth century, in the rediscovery and ideological valorization of the Middle Ages as national tradition. Scotland followed, now regarding the English past as a heritage of all Britain. In the course of the nineteenth century, as we will see in Chapter 7, Scotland would intensify this movement into a far more highly charged Romantic recipe, by adding into the mix the emotionalism of the heroic lost Jacobite cause, and the Sublime of the Highland landscape – along with the specifically architectural contribution of the castellated heritage. But in the earlier, less colourful stages of national antiquarianism, the initiative came from English antiquarians, who focused on Gothic (which they labelled as the 'truly English' style). For the moment (succeeding, where *Vitruvius Britannicus* had failed), many Scottish architects and clients were content to adopt

English styles as a shared British heritage – but that disorientation would dissipate almost immediately.

The Commemoration of 'National Heroes': Walter Scott and the Rehabilitation of Scottish History

The Napoleonic wars, and their victorious outcome, bound Scotland ever closer in with the emergent discourse of British unionist nationalism. In the battle of Trafalgar in 1805, five of Nelson's twenty-seven ships were commanded by Scots, and sixty Scots served on his own ship, 'Victory'. In Edinburgh, 'Trafalgar Day' is still officially commemorated at the Nelson Monument with the words 'England expects every man this day will do his duty', which was Nelson's signal to his men prior to engaging in battle (Figure 6.1). Visiting the Waterloo battle site in 1816, Edinburgh advocate James Simpson boasted that although the Old Guard, Napoleon's elite regiment of veterans, 'had never before failed', here it had yielded to onrushing troops shouting 'Scotland forever!'[11] He 'left the field, prouder of the name of Briton, than on any moment of self gratulation on the same score, during my life',[12] and he added that 'the mind has scarcely buoyancy sufficient to allot to England a pinnacle of glory high enough'.[13] In the post-1815 era, a patriotic Scot such as Simpson now, in effect, had three nationalities, and took pride in all of them.

This complex new layering of affiliations was reflected, architecturally, in a range of commemorative monuments – some reflecting the still prevalent European preference for the projection of national grandeur through classical (especially Grecian) monumentality, but others choosing instead to express national identity in Gothic or castellated garb. A post-Waterloo national monument to Scotland's 'fallen', modelled classically on the Parthenon, was planned for Calton Hill in Edinburgh: we will return to the later history of this project in Chapter 7.[14] Doubtless the conception of a national monument in this form was most directly inspired by King Ludwig of Bavaria's Walhalla, near Regensburg, by Leo von Klenze – a hall of heroes that celebrated triumph over Napoleon at Leipzig (1813) contextualizing it with a classical array of past Germanic heroes, including Arminius, mythical victor against the Romans. But as we saw, several years previously, Calton Hill had seen the building of another national monument in castellated form, commemorating Lord Nelson. An initial design of 1806 by Alexander Nasmyth for a 160-foot-high rostral column had been rejected,[15] together with its designer, on grounds of cost,[16] and a thriftier version was built instead, in the form of a circular castellated tower to Robert Burn's design, with a crenellated perimeter added in 1814–15: an overdoor inscription enjoined Edinburgh's 'sons to emulate . . . [Nelson] . . . and, like him,

FIGURE 6.1 *Nelson Monument by Robert Burn, 1806, celebrating naval victory at Trafalgar, 1805, where many Scots were involved. Here the monument is decorated to celebrate 'Trafalgar Day', signalling Nelson's eve of battle message 'England expects every man this day will do his duty'; photograph of 2017 by Aonghus MacKechnie.*

when duty requires it, to die for their country'. Another castellated Gothic hilltop Nelson monument tower, designed by Charles Stewart, was built at Forres, also in 1806. Other Romantic-themed commemorative monuments of Waterloo included some on hilltop sites, to maximize the message's visibility. That on Ben Alvie, Kinrara, was erected by the Marquis of Huntly, memorializing two officers and the 'fallen' of two Highland regiments. It was an east-facing seat, or summerhouse, like a tomb entrance but otherwise covered with a cairn of stones, like a prehistoric monument, thereby binding the 'fallen' to the land (rather as the National War Memorial in Edinburgh Castle was to attempt to do a century later).

This new, post-Waterloo upsurge in unionist nationalism was, however, far more sophisticated than the old Hanoverian triumphalism, as it began to attempt, with growing success, to appropriate and enlist the old symbols and heroes of preunion Scotland, exploiting the imagery of the Romantic movement. The first two decades of the nineteenth century witnessed a pronounced movement for the cultural rehabilitation of 'old Scotland'. Although 'the prejudices against North Britons among [England's] country people are so strong', as Loudon put it in 1812,[17] now Scotland was coming on show in a new way – loyal, exotic; Romantic. In the wider cultural arena it was above all Walter Scott, empowered by the success of *Ossian*, whose historical novels now 'moved Scotland squarely to the centre of the romantic map of Europe';[18] and in the architectural field, it was Scott and William Burn, in tandem, who were primarily responsible for the rehabilitation of Scotland's preclassical buildings. Because the British nation-building process now seemed more or less complete, Scots could now, paradoxically, address the 'ancient honours and constitution of their independent Monarchy'.[19]

Scott's own novels spoke subtly of union. They presented Scotland's Romantic past as vanished and, thus, politically irrelevant, no threat to the union. For his English audience, his characters included the chivalric heroes of *Ivanhoe*, while for his Scottish audience, he subtly concealed the 'real' historical narrative of the repeated devastation of the border region by English armies, and wrote instead of the dashing exploits of the Scots Border Reivers at the expense of their English counterparts. One catalyst for rehabilitation was the Highland soldier; no longer a ragged 'vermin' needing to be punished,[20] but now the kilted military hero in what Cookson called 'the warfare state'.[21] Cookson identified 'a strong . . . relationship between Highlandism in the early nineteenth century and Tory militarism . . . [as] patrons and promoters articulated a common purpose of strengthening and safeguarding the state by promoting the martial mores of the Scottish population'.[22] George III dressed his sons in kilts as early as 1789;[23] and as Prince Regent, the future George IV became chief of the Highland Society in 1817. In parallel with the onward march of Romanticism, a new age of historical scholarship could also commence:[24] the Society of Antiquaries of Scotland published its first volume in 1792.

But the boldest rehabilitation, and greatest paradox, of all concerned Sir William Wallace (c. 1270–1305), Guardian of Scotland, the patriotic 'martyr' who had defied English invasions. Now, he was reshaped as a triumphant, Romantic hero of Union. Jane Porter's 1810 historical novel, *The Scottish Chiefs*, argued that Wallace's achievement was in making Scotland fit for participation in a union of equals;[25] the foes of Scotland, and those of Britain, were now identical;[26] and an 1814 French translation of Porter's book was banned by the Ossian enthusiast, Napoleon, on grounds that it constituted pro-British propaganda.[27] Opinion about Wallace was not, however, unanimous, and in 1814 (500 years after the Scottish victory at Bannockburn) the pro-Republican Earl of Buchan,[28] on (what he believed to be) 'the Anniversary of the Victory obtained by the brave Sir Wm. Wallace, at Stirling-Bridge, in 1297, . . . dedicated the Colossal Statue of that Hero, on a rock at Dryburg[h] . . . [saying]: "In the name of my brave and worthy Country, I dedicate this Monument as sacred to the memory of Wallace"'[29] (Figure 6.2). Being a clear Scottish response to the British martial nationalism of the Nelson monuments, the radically unionist Scott was of course horrified. James Hogg, who 'liked and admired' the statue, recalled Scott saying: 'I'll . . . blow up the statue of Wallace with gunpowder . . . that there shall not be one fragment of it left – the horrible monster!'[30] A series of Wallace monuments followed, however, including Lanark (1822), and two in Ayr: paradoxically, these shifted commemoration of Wallace ever more strongly towards a unionist agenda, culminating subsequently in the National Wallace Memorial – as we will see in Chapter 8.

In the years after Waterloo, with the upsurge in popular and radical discontent, attention turned to address a national enigma. Did Scotland's royal crown and regalia, the 'Honours of Scotland', still survive? Sealed up in Edinburgh Castle in 1707, and stipulated in the Treaty of Union to remain in Scotland, rumour had it that the Honours had been removed[31] – a rumour that threatened to undermine popular support for the union. The advocate and writer Robert Forsyth argued in 1805 that 'if it was ever seriously thought the preservation of these relics of ancient royalty, in a place now become a province of a great empire, could have served any valuable purpose . . . [they] . . . ought not to be locked up from the eyes of the public, but to be produced occasionally'.[32] Scott organized the granting of consent for an investigation, and on 4 February 1818 the storage room was opened.[33] He argued that, first, they would be a valuable museum tool, illustrating the contrast between the lost 'old Scotland' and the modernity of Britain; and second, by proving popular anti-English fears of their removal to be groundless, the common benefits of Britishness would be further underlined. Once they were duly retrieved, the new confidence in the stability of the Union allowed these most powerful symbols of Scotland's former existence

FIGURE 6.2 *Statue of Sir William Wallace, Guardian of Scotland, Dryburgh – erected 1814 by David Steuart Erskine, Eleventh Earl of Buchan, a half-millennium after the Battle of Bannockburn in 1314; photograph of 2018 by Aonghus MacKechnie.*

as an independent state to be displayed for public enjoyment and edification, without fear of instability.

A fortnight after the retrieval of the Honours, workmen building Dunfermline's new Abbey Kirk found a grave which was declared to be that of King Robert Bruce, the hero, together with Wallace, of Scotland's Wars of Independence, victor against England of the Battle of Bannockburn.[34] How to handle this new discovery was a further, unexpected test for the establishment. In this instance, the response was to downplay the episode.

Penman argued that 'the paramount concern of the Scottish establishment must have been that the remains of this king, the hero of wars against royal England and famed ruler of Scotland as an independent kingdom, might become associated with violent agitation, or anti-Union and anti-Hanoverian sentiment, or worse, lingering Jacobitism and other forms of radical dissent'.[35] Instead, Bruce was hailed along with Wallace as co-deliverer of Scotland's equal status within the Union and his narrative was converted from a concern for Unionists into an opportunity: providing another substantial foundation stone for unionist nationalism.[36] Architecturally, it was left to Burn, as the architect of the Abbey Kirk, to decide how to celebrate the discovery. Reflecting the new, Unionist status of Bruce, he designed a tower parapet in Tudor-type silhouette lettering, reading 'KING ROBERT THE BRUCE'.[37] On the 1822 royal visit, as we will see in the next chapter, it was repeatedly emphasized that Bruce's blood flowed in the veins of George IV.

Continuing Castellation and Gothic Revival

Within this emergent Second Castle Age, the 'bread-and-butter' area of castellated building, just as under its predecessor, remained the country houses of the landed classes; but the 'new castle' movement developed by the Adams continued to evolve significantly. However, in line with the perceptions of shared British identity, a fresh enthusiasm for English heritage, Gothic, Tudor and Jacobean, was increasingly making its influence felt. Whereas thirty new castles had been built between 1746 and 1800; now no fewer than thirty more were begun in the single decade of 1800–1810.[38] Robert Adam developed his castellated style, with castles at Airthrey, Stobs, Mauldslie and Barnton (Figure 6.3). Stobs (1792–4) was a simplified version of Seton and became a model for houses such as Gillespie Graham's Kilmaron Castle (c. 1820) built for Admiral Sir Frederick Lewis Maitland, to whom Napoleon surrendered in 1815. Robert Adam also showed the potential for extending the castle style outwith the domestic architectural field at Edinburgh's Bridewell (1791–5), whose 'Bastile order of Architecture'[39] established the idea of dramatic castellation being appropriate to civic architecture – a concept that would significantly influence the Scotch Baronial movement of the mid-nineteenth century.

John Paterson (–1832), Adam's onetime employee, built Monzie (c. 1795–1800) for General Alexander Campbell, resembling Inveraray with corner turrets, the tower brought forward and shallow-bowed (Figure 6.4). It was followed by Eglinton (1797–1803), for Hugh Montgomerie, Twelfth Earl of Eglinton, politician, Improver and soldier. His portrait by John Singleton Copley shows him in Highland dress, leading the seventy-seventh Highlanders against the Cherokees in South Carolina. A new castle matched that image. Here, the place of Inveraray's tower was referenced with a circular one.[40] Then around 1805, Paterson enlarged Winton, the new work being carefully

THE AGE OF REVOLUTION

FIGURE 6.3 *Mauldslie Castle – watercolour by David Bryce, 1860, showing his proposed additions (nearest the viewer) to Robert Adam's house of 1792–6 (shown on the right).* © Historic Environment Scotland. *https://canmore.org.uk/file/image/1570216*

FIGURE 6.4 *Monzie Castle by John Paterson, c. 1795–1800 – view from south; photograph of c. 1920.* © *Historic Environment Scotland. https://canmore.org.uk/collection/1209184*

subservient.[41] Mellerstain echoes included James Playfair's Kinnaird for Sir David Carnegie, Earl of Southesk (1789);[42] and Darnaway, 1802–12, by Alexander Laing, which largely retained the medieval Randolph's Hall[43] (Figure 6.5). The long legacy of Inveraray continued, in examples including Bo-ness's 1770s Town Hall, described in 1796 as 'an exact model of Inveraray House'.[44] Inveraray's greatest derivative, however, was Taymouth, built for the Marquess of Breadalbane, a Campbell[45] (Figure 6.6). Nasmyth was involved in the project,[46] but Paterson initially took the lead in designing the new Taymouth (1801), 'in the stile of a Castle'.[47] Lord Breadalbane replaced Paterson with James Elliot,[48] and contracted in 1806 to dismantle the superstructure for an added storey: 'The ornaments and mouldings & Battlements . . . of the Great Centre Tower to be in the Monastic style . . . The Great Staircase . . . in the Gothic stile with . . . ornaments appropriate to that Stile of Architecture.'[49] The similarity to Inveraray would have been stronger in Paterson's design. 'Gothic cloisters' were added by Elliot in 1809,[50] perhaps echoing Strawberry Hill (and reproduced at Saltoun, Abbotsford, and elsewhere). On 11 December 1807 James Elliot wrote to Breadalbane, 'Now that the great center tower is finished the building has a nobel effect aproach it from what direction you please the appearance is

FIGURE 6.5 *Darnaway Castle by Alexander Laing, 1802–12 – view from northeast; photograph dated 2013. © Historic Environment Scotland. https://canmore.org.uk/collection/1350410*

truely grand.'[51] Taymouth was also, partly, an expanded version of Melville Castle, but its staircase plasterwork, by Francis Bernasconi was the richest of its time in Scotland (Figure 6.7). There was a 'Baron's Hall',[52] and a room intended to have Ossian-themed decoration.[53]

Arguably more important at this stage, however, was a fresh wave of English influence – Gothic, Tudor, castellated – with the former continuing to lead the way. The Gothic Revival, as always in Britain, was centred in England, where the overriding issue, as in France and Germany, was the 'ownership', and the consequent interpretation, of Gothic.[54] The claim was that Gothic was invented and reached its perfection in England, where 'English' and 'Norman' meant 'Gothic'.[55] A succession of antiquarians codified it from the late eighteenth century, enabling increasingly learned reproductions. The English antiquarian Rev. George Whittington, however, was the first to suggest that Gothic's origins lay not in England, but in France.[56] His book was published after his death in 1807, and seen through the press by his Cambridge friend Lord Aberdeen, the two having toured France together. With Tudor and Jacobean, the English antiquarians seemed to be on surer ground: from 1805 John Britton documented the buildings of a Tudor-Jacobean 'golden age' – a context within which the place of Scotland was still uncertain. Was Scotland to be included in this triumph as part of England, or excluded? Britton, unable to categorize Roslin Chapel,

FIGURE 6.6 *Taymouth Castle – main block largely by John Paterson, from 1801, followed by Archibald and James Elliot, 1806–10; tower on left by James Gillespie Graham and A. W. N. Pugin, 1837–42; wing on right by William Atkinson, 1818–21; view from south-east; photograph dated 1997.* © *Historic Environment Scotland. https://canmore.org.uk/collection/639036*

concluded in 1812 that it 'has . . . been called Scottish: but . . . this adjective . . . is unmeaning and useless'.[57] Rickman proposed an answer: Roslin was 'foreign'.[58] From this perspective, English medieval and sixteenth- to seventeenth-century architecture (and antiquarian culture) was now seen as commanding a more general, shared prestige, extending even to Scotland.

This validation of English revivalism in Scottish contexts[59] provoked a variety of responses, one of the most unusual being the 'scientific' quest for the origins of Gothic in 1797 by the Edinburgh Enlightenment figure, Sir James Hall of Dunglass.[60] Dunglass, a chemist, geologist, democrat and atheist, who befriended Napoleon at Brienne's military academy,[61] hailed Gothic as a British cultural trophy, which, 'with great truth, has been compared to the genius of Shakespeare'.[62] Inspired by watching French peasants with rods for supporting vines, he argued that the Gothic arch had originated in nature, and tested his theory 'by the construction of a wicker fabric now standing in my garden . . . In it all the . . . forms of Gothic architecture have been restored to their alleged original state'.[63] This, 'my willow Cathedral',[64] was

FIGURE 6.7 *Taymouth Castle – staircase plasterwork by Francis Bernasconi, c. 1809; photograph dated 1997.* © Historic Environment Scotland. https://canmore.org.uk/collection/408999

the book's frontispiece, and the location was evidently Dunglass: possibly Edward Blore, who drew some of the plates, helped design it. Its references were largely English: its crown spire was modelled on St Nicholas Church, Newcastle, which 'admits of an easy construction in wicker-work, as I have found in practice'.[65]

Unsurprisingly, within this context, prominent turn-of-century English architects found themselves increasingly in demand among landed Scottish patrons, and imitated by up-and-coming Scottish designers. Some projects were predominantly Gothic or Tudor in style: the innovative scholarship of Wilkins's Dalmeny (1814–17, for the Fourth Earl of Rosebery) found a ready response in the early work of William Burn, notably at Garscube (1826–7), while Smirke's Erskine House (1828, for the Napoleonic war veteran, the Eleventh Lord Blantyre) possibly influenced David Hamilton's Tudor designs.

Others mixed Gothic and castellated elements, now increasingly disposed in picturesque and asymmetrical arrangements, as in the case of Robert Lugar's Tullichewan (1808) and Balloch Castle (1809; then named 'Ardoch'), each facing Loch Lomond. Lugar explained:

In a well-wooded country, abounding with grand and romantic scenery, a house in the castle style is peculiarly suitable . . . the exterior character should be strength, the interior may possess all the . . . usage . . . modern times require . . . ornaments of the ancient or Gothic style may . . . be . . . suitable to the principal apartments of such a house as . . . Tillicheun.[66]

And another English architect, George Saunders, proposed a castellated redesign of Scone in 1802 for David Murray, the Third Earl of Mansfield. Saunders had altered Kenwood House, north of London, for Murray's uncle, the Second Earl. If executed, Scone would have been the earliest castellated project in a relatively scholarly Scotch style,[67] but in the event, William Atkinson's more orthodox English castle design of 1803 was chosen instead.[68] The reconstructed house concealed all trace of the substantial pre-existing fabric, while inside, Gothic ornament referenced its ecclesiastical and royal associations: the entrance aligned with an ancient twin-turreted gateway, made or kept deliberately ruinous.[69] The landscape specialist, Loudon, was also involved at Scone, which he acclaimed as potentially 'the first place in the British empire'.[70] Indeed, Scone was one of the largest building projects of those years in the UK.

The first decade or so of the nineteenth century saw incessant debate among landed patrons and their architects as to the most appropriate style in any specific case. In 1806, Loudon attacked Adam's castellated architecture, which he regarded as an incongruous mixing of Grecian with Gothic: 'Some of the best situations and finest scenery in Scotland were some years ago disgraced by [Adam's] buildings.'[71] Loudon's criticism was driven partly by '*amor patriae*'. These designs could be improved by adding 'Saxon' turrets, rather like Scone. Loudon advocated several new variants of Scottish revivalism, including the 'Tower Style', whose general characteristic was 'that high-roofed towers prevail in the outline';[72] or the 'turret style', which he characterized as having: 'projecting turrets . . . very high roofs . . . triangular pediments . . . The ground plan of the whole is commonly in the form of an L. A square tower, containing the staircase, is generally placed in the angle . . . In several cases an I was added to the L, forming an open square.'[73]

In the selection of the optimum style for a house in any particular location, the setting was all-important. In 1814, Gillespie Graham advised Campbell of Barcaldine on a (seemingly unexecuted) project, arguing that 'notwithstanding the Features of the Sublime Scenery of Barcaldine being in favour of the Baronial or Castelated style of Building . . . I think the site is much more appropriated to that of the Priory.'[74] And at Balloch, Lugar had originally hoped to build not Balloch Castle, but 'Balloch Abbey': a house designed like a massive church with a traceried great 'east' window, and Tudor arches, but the patron (Lugar grumbled) preferred to alter the existing house 'to give it the effect of a castle'.[75] At Duns, by contrast, Gillespie Graham was engaged by owner William Hay in 1818–22,[76] and the house was recomposed asymmetrically around a centre tower referencing Tudor gatehouses such as Eton – all somewhat 'English'-looking save that the left hand tower was treated like a Scots tower-house. A bastioned dummy fortification amplified the idea of a militarized castle.[77] In the far north-west, Armadale Castle, Skye, was rebuilt in 1815–20 by Gillespie Graham for the Second Lord MacDonald, and was admired by Neale as being 'admirably adapted to the romantic wildness of the adjacent country . . . A house, however elegant . . . if constructed upon the principles of classical architecture, must have lost its due effect in such a situation, backed by mountains whose lofty summits are covered in snow.'[78] This early phase of neocastellated architecture saw a constant circulation of ideas between English and Scottish architects and vice versa. For instance, Archibald Simpson's earliest castle design was Castle Forbes (1814) for Lord Forbes – a project completed by John Smith in 1821.[79] It has a square tower at one end of its south-west-facing entrance front, answered by a round tower opposite. This arrangement was copied by Smirke at Kinfauns – his only asymmetrical castle – and by Burn at Inverness Castle (Figure 6.8). A third tower was also planned for Castle Forbes, at its north-east, which was intended to have a lofty crowstepped superstructure, underlining the fact that the house had an 'authentic' tower house pedigree.[80]

A significant offshoot of the neo-Gothic movement was a so-called *priory style*, noticed above, and derived from English ecclesiastical rather than secular Gothic:[81] an early example was Rossie Priory, built in 1807–15 by William Atkinson for Charles, Eighth Lord Kinnaird (1780–1826). The Scottish architect James Gillespie Graham designed several houses in the 'Priory' style, notably Crawford Priory (1811–13, extending David Hamilton's 1809 house)[82] and Ross Priory (1812). In the building of 'real' churches, where the eighteenth-century experiments with crowstepped designs, such as Barony, had failed to establish a new castellated ecclesiastical architecture, but where classicism remained generally unacceptable, the favoured successor style tended to be uncomplicated post-Reformation

FIGURE 6.8 *Kinfauns Castle by Robert Smirke, 1802; view from south; photograph dated 2004. https://canmore.org.uk/collection/1440451*

Gothic, soon to give ground to Tudor, but sometimes crowstepped. Farnell, however, by James Playfair (1788–1806),[83] had crosslets and Rosslyn-like gable profiles, the crowsteps rendered as parapets. And Saltoun Parish Church was remodelled c. 1805 with a parapet enwrapping the gables, like a tower-house. John Paterson's St Paul's, Perth (c. 1800–1807) has little bartizans, while his Fetteresso Church (1810–12) has polygonal turrets and a castellated formula that hints at Inveraray, although here shaped to fit a D-plan interior. The Adams's narrow castle-turrets, resembling pilasters pierced by arrow slits, translated fairly straightforwardly into ecclesiastical work, notably at Edinburgh's Albany Street Chapel of 1816 by David Skae. Its pilasters resemble turrets, making the church appear rather castle-like.[84]

'Slighting' and Reuse

Within this new climate, empty castles often tended to be enjoyed as ruins, as at Toward, but the old reoccupation idea also reared its head intermittently. In 1796, for example, the wealthy slave-owner Neil Malcolm of Poltalloch acquired Duntrune Castle for reoccupation.[85] To Leyden in 1800, it was 'a clumsy, inelegant structure . . . modernised . . . to very little advantage, as the walls . . . resist every attempt to alleviate the prison-like gloom'.[86] But by 1815, Duntrune was considered a 'very comfortable residence'.[87]

In this light, the continuing official lack of interest in the royal palaces seemed increasingly objectionable. In 1817, an anonymous author complained that 'there are few subjects on which it is more difficult for a Scotchman to write with any sort of temper, than the manner in which the ancient palaces of our Kings have been treated since the union with England'.[88] Each palace followed its own trajectory of decay or appropriation. Both Edinburgh and Stirling, enclosed within castles, were converted for soldiers. A new battery was added at Edinburgh in 1690;[89] Stirling's defences were enhanced in 1708, and by 1725 a north battery was made 'to flank the bridge', that being the anticipated approach of any Jacobite army.[90] Stirling's Great Hall had been subdivided in the 1790s for barracks. The forework gateway was tidied up (1810) with 'dispiritingly mean crenellations',[91] its six lofty towers reduced to two plain stumps. An 1817 complaint concerning one ceiling at Stirling explained that

> the great weight of these ornaments [the 'Stirling Heads'] occasioned the fall of one or two compartments of the roof about the year 1777; and, as the idea of repairing the whole (a business which might have been accomplished at a very trifling expense) was altogether inconsistent with the spirit of the times, the roof was immediately pulled down, and the room itself converted into a supplemental barrack.[92]

At Dunfermline, repairs were carried out in 1812 by a neighbour named Hunt, who believed he had acquired a right to the ruins, but lost his claim in the House of Lords;[93] the palace's decline continued. Linlithgow Palace's decline was at first slower because its hereditary keepers, the Earls of Linlithgow, had lodgings there; while Falkland's decline (accelerated by war damage in the 1650s) led to the removal of the roof over the surviving south quarter being contemplated in 1820,[94] although in the event the palace was instead part-repaired from around 1822.[95]

The limits of the acceptable 'slighting' of the palaces were sharply highlighted in the case of Linlithgow. Having been burnt in the 1746 conflict, it was thereafter ignored until the French wars; it was held by mutinying Highland soldiers in 1794,[96] following which Robert Reid explored its conversion for French prisoners, a notion that aroused establishment concern among people such as Lord Aberdeen.[97] Henry Dundas cautioned in 1811 that 'I should have thought that our monarchical and aristocratical pride was much blunted and impaired if one of the palaces of our ancient Sovereigns, one of the few Badges of our monarchical pride had been . . . converted into a den for the execrable vermin destined to be its future inhabitants'.[98] The plan was abandoned. Local interest inspired a petition to the Remembrancer of the Exchequer to build a wall within the palace for public meetings, but this seems to have come to nothing.[99] Thereafter Linlithgow fell into extended neglect once again, until it was eventually declared an ancient monument 1874. Holyrood, of course, was different, as it still housed some governmental and royal activities, but by now the Romantic cult of Mary Queen of Scots was becoming of overriding significance: in 1806, it was remarked in an account of Edinburgh that 'strangers visiting the palace are usually led to Queen Mary's apartments'.[100]

Ireland

Following Ireland's union with Britain in 1801 (celebrated in street names such as Edinburgh's Union Street), suitable new architecture was needed to signal the ruling Protestant 'Britishness'. The foremost requirement was for a new Chapel Royal, within Dublin Castle, sufficiently opulent and rhetorical to symbolize royal power. The project was discussed from 1801, and government architect Francis Johnston's 'Oxbridge'-Gothic design was built 1807–14, the foundation stone having been laid by the Duke of Bedford. A forest of emblematic stone and timber sculptures included Brian Boru and St Patrick, and English Reformation heroes such as Henry VIII and Queen Elizabeth, plus a little Celtic cross finial:[101] blending Ireland's past with England's, precisely the process that would happen shortly in Scotland, and similarly manufacturing an imagined common 'British' Protestant heritage. The chapel 'projected both unionist and imperialist gestures, and . . . , culturally, . . . was an expression of Britishness'.[102] And of course (as in Scotland) British heroes would now be celebrated in the capital by monuments to martial Englishmen Nelson (by Wilkins, 1808–9; blown up 1966) and Wellington (the 'Wellington Testimonial' by Smirke, 1817–61).

In rural Ireland, Charleville Castle (1801–12)[103] referenced the Inveraray/Melville Castle model as signalling British authority 'provincially' (in other words, not in England) – being four-square and crenellated, with a central tower. Its unequal-sized corner turrets included an improbably lofty turret which hinted at Ireland's medieval round towers, while contemporary English fashion was echoed in Charleville's asymmetry (probably Ireland's first asymmetrical new-built neocastle). It was also given Tudor hood-moulds and fan vaulting, plus Irish-type two-stepped crenellations. This combination of English, Scottish and Irish elements made Charleville 'British', reflecting the client's politics. He was Charles William Bury, from 1806, Earl of Charleville. As Colonel of the Tullamore True Blue Rangers he had helped crush the rising of United Irishmen in 1798,[104] and in 1801 he was made an Irish representative peer in the House of Lords. The castle's design is ostensibly by Francis Johnston, but Charleville was a gentleman architect, and therefore he knew precisely the signals his house would convey.[105] Tullynally was reconstructed from c. 1801 as another post-union Inveraray-Melville derivative, for another Anglo-Irish peer, the Earl of Longford, the Duke of Wellington's brother-in-law.[106] Markree Castle (rebuilt 1802 by Francis Johnston, Wardrop and Francis Goodwin)[107] instead followed the Adam/Paterson castle formula, further indicating that Ireland could allude to Scottish architecture as a patriotic statement of Britishness. By including clearly Scottish references, these castles contrasted with the Chapel Royal, and their correspondent divergence from English norms would help feed the idea of what later would be denoted 'the Celtic fringe'.

Conclusion

Wealth from industrialism, Improvement, empire, and slavery meant that the status quo now commanded strong support, while the popular unrest of democratizing 'radicals' seeking a fairer society was successfully seen off, the French Revolution having prompted the establishment to devise a range of defences. From now on, Scotland's overriding political ideology was a proud unionist nationalism, a collective self-regard focused on a combination of Improvement, progress and martial prowess. 'Military service had done more than anything previously from the time of the Union to promote a sense of Scottish nationhood . . . England's dependence on Scottish manpower, never greater, declared Scotland's equal status within the union.'[108] Scotland's rehabilitation as an honoured partner within the British union was now so complete that Wallace and Bruce could be claimed as repatriated Britons.

The prevailing architectural expression for this emergent unionist nationalism still mingled Gothic, Tudor and castellated elements in a very eclectic mix, but in the second quarter of the century, the Second Castle Age took several major steps forward, as Scottish architecture and architects, led by Scott and that 'zealous Tory',[109] William Burn, responded to the burgeoning cult of 'tartanry' and the post-Waterloo pride in martial Scotland through a coherent and effective recipe, increasingly widely known at the time as the 'Scotch Baronial', or simply 'Scotch', style.[110] The starting point in this campaign was the reconstruction from 1816 by Scott of his own house, Abbotsford – whose extended development process we will examine in detail in the next chapter. As we will see, Abbotsford exemplified Tory unionist-nationalism, setting out to celebrate all that was great in Scottish history within the fullest spirit of unionism, both architecturally and in the eclectic antiquarianism of its contents and furnishings.

7

1820–1840: Scott, Abbotsford and 'Scotch' Romanticism

The king himself is a Jacobite.[1]
– CAPTAIN STUART OF INVERNAHYLE, ON GEORGE III, 1819

An old-fashioned Scotch residence, full of rusty iron coats and jingling jackets . . . in the old-fashioned Scotch style which delighted in notch'd gable ends and all manner of bartizans.[2]
– WALTER SCOTT, ON HIS PROPOSED HOUSE, ABBOTSFORD, 1816

The last purely Scotch age that Scotland was destined to see.[3]
LORD COCKBURN, C. 1830, ON THE EARLY NINETEENTH CENTURY

Introduction

The most significant foundations for the Scotch Baronial movement were laid in the early nineteenth century, when a fully fledged international cult of Romantic Scotland was elaborated in the novels of Sir Walter Scott. Scott's work inspired countless copycat works in many media: on the same evening in 1827, for example, a Paris theatre-goer could have chosen between four different Scott plays. Cleverly, Scott framed the lost past of Baronial Scotland as a poignant counterpoint to the thrusting modernity of Improvement, which seemed to pose a ceaseless threat to all authentic national identity: 'The last purely Scotch age', was how lawyer and conservationist Lord Cockburn described the earlier nineteenth century – a claim that could equally have been made fifty or a hundred years previously.[4] This richly complex ideology formed a key building block of Scotland's increasingly fervent unionist nationalism, which was inspired by a practical recognition of the unrivalled power and status of Britain in the decades following the 1814–15 Council of Vienna.

Within this politics of symbolic display, architecture played a central role in the reappropriation and valorization of 'Scottish heritage'. The key exemplar in the search for a distinctly and proudly Scottish architectural past was, however, largely new: Scott's own house of Abbotsford. This decisively rejected the symmetry of the 'Palladian plan' and freely replicated specific elements of historic Scottish buildings, in the first serious attempt to develop a new architectural style based on antiquarian study of 'original' (i.e. pre-eighteenth century) Scottish castellated buildings. Abbotsford was a key point of transition: it extended what had been begun by others, and set a precedent for what would follow. From the 1820s, William Burn fronted the decisive move towards generalization of the new Scotch Baronial idiom.

Scott's *Waverley* developed the establishment line of tension between the 'head' (Hanoverian unionist progressivism) and the 'heart'.[5] Romanticism was promoted by an increasingly broad range of establishment opinion, including the royal family, who encouraged the publication of Hogg's *Jacobite Relics of Scotland* 1819–21, under the aegis of the Highland Society of London,[6] which recommended that Scots should maintain and revive 'Celtic garb, Celtic music, and Celtic toasts' as a 'gratifying sight to a Foreigner, or even a native of England . . . giving him some idea of the manners and usages of times so remote'.[7] The *Jacobite minstrelsy* (1829) presented old Scotland as undisciplined, awaiting governance, and yet stirringly romantic: 'Jacobites . . . warred against common sense and the natural liberty of mankind; . . . We forget their mistaken views . . . and only think of their romantic courage . . . However much they erred . . . in religion and politics'.[8] The Highland Games 'revival' created an outlet for Highlandism and displaying hierarchy.[9] These pageants were promoted by elites, who attended as tartan-clad celebrities. Campbell of Islay displayed 'unwearied efforts to revive the Highland games and athletic sports',[10] and the 1821 St Fillans games featured the old 'baronial' style of entertainment.[11] Supposedly historical poems (such as Scott's 'Lochinvar') and Jacobite songs were composed.[12] The same romantic sensibility would underpin architectural Baronialism.

At the same time, the high estimation of English precedents also continued, with complex connotations attaching to the use of the terms 'Saxon' and 'Norman'. With the emergent racial pseudoscience of 'Teutonism', for instance, there were some in nineteenth century Scotland who began to argue that 'race mattered much more than nationhood'.[13] Teutonism created a hierarchy that conflicted somewhat with Highlandism. Within Britain, 'Anglo-Saxons' were considered 'superior' to 'Celts'. Was Scotland Teutonic or Celtic?[14] The question implicitly set Lowlanders against Highlanders.[15] In 1889, the future Conservative prime minister Arthur Balfour argued that 'the Highlands . . . are more unlike the Lowlands . . . than the Lowlands are unlike the North of England ... the line of division is not the division between England and Scotland, but ... far north of that'.[16] But the Norman invasion of England in 1066 had created even more tangled complexities. As Kidd puts it, 'some ... thought that the Scots were English, more English than the English, and the English agreed ... Not that the English weren't English themselves, just that they were a little bit less English than the Scots'.[17] The popularity from the 1820s of English styles, especially neo-Tudor, perhaps indicated that many clients shared this complex hierarchy of esteem, and medieval Scottish buildings were often described in this way: for example, Sir James Hall of Dunglass considered (Romanesque) Kelso Abbey to have arches 'of the old Saxon form and character'.[18] Yet meanwhile, the new Scotch style was continuing to develop.

The 1822 Royal Visit

The landmark event in the emergence of nineteenth-century unionist nationalism was the visit of George IV to Scotland in 1822 – the first visit by a reigning monarch since 1651. For this the Tory-dominated establishment charged Scott with the task of orchestrating a royal pageant.[19]

As a pioneering presentation of 'ancient loyal Highlandism' to the British monarchy, it was usefully preceded in 1819 by a visit by Prince Leopold, the Prince Regent's son-in-law. His trip tested Scottish opinion and his Highland expedition included Braemar, where (anticipating Scott in 1822), the poet James Hogg, 'The Ettrick Shepherd', played a key organizational role. A tartan-clad 'Highland army' was marshalled and pipers played the Jacobite 'The Prince's Welcome', as if Leopold had become Bonnie Prince Charlie, 'loved and honoured by the unconquered people of the mountains of Caledonia'. Leopold returned home via Abbotsford, and Scott recalled how he 'really thought of getting some shooting-place in Scotland and promised me a longer visit on his return'. The provision of such a 'royal shooting-place' would only materialize a generation later, at the instigation of Albert and Victoria, as we will see in Chapter 8.[20]

The venue for the king's 1822 visit was Edinburgh, the symbolic historic capital. The king arrived at Leith, claimed as the time-honoured royal landing place. On 15 August he entered Edinburgh in Highland dress, passing triumphal arches and signs stressing national loyalty and his legitimacy as 'Descendant of the Heroic Bruce'. At the head of Leith Walk, at the symbolically named Union Street, the ceremonies commenced with a barrier, a theatrical request to admit the king and delivery to him of keys. From there, he travelled to Holyroodhouse via Picardy Place, St Andrew Square, Regent Road and Abbeyhill.[21] The Barons of Exchequer had recommended in 1821 that Holyroodhouse be prepared for the visit. Roads around Edinburgh were repaired or built, the town was tidied, some buildings were demolished, including those on Holyroodhouse's south side, where also a new entrance was made. A 'handsome portico' was added to the palace main entrance; Kensington gravel was laid in the inner courtyard and new gas lamps installed. The interior was overhauled by William Trotter, and partitions were removed to create a presence chamber.[22]

People enthusiastically dressed up, and there was tartan everywhere: the costumes devised by Scott included Highland dress and, for himself, the 'Windsor uniform'. The Honours were carried between the Castle and Holyroodhouse in theatrical processions, the grandest being a 'Riding of Parliament' (echoing a pre-1707 parliamentary ceremony), climaxing when the King ascended the Castle's Half-Moon Battery and waved his hat to the crowd (Figure 7.1). Balls and banquets were held in Parliament House (where toasts included 'The British Constitution', and the music, 'Scots wha hae') and at the specially adapted Assembly Rooms. He also attended a military review on Portobello sands (where there were reportedly 50,000 spectators), and on Sunday 26th he reluctantly attended the High Kirk,[23] thereby fulfilling Presbyterians' expectations.

The decision was taken that the king should stay with Scott's friend and 'clan chief', the Duke of Buccleuch, at Dalkeith Palace, which was 'fitted up in a most magnificent and costly manner', with new driveways built to bypass Dalkeith town and connect with Melville Castle. Holyroodhouse was given day duties, for formal ceremony; hundreds of people from Scotland's elites were presented there to the king, and a bodyguard, the Royal Company of Archers, 'Noblemen and Gentlemen' and others (including Scott and Burn) were tasked 'to line ... [Holyrood's] ... gallery and anti-chambers'.[24] Tower of London yeomen and London policemen reinforced the sense of Britishness, while the Honours had a 'Celtic' guard to stress Highlandism. The king gave a special order that 'Queen Mary's apartments' be preserved,[25] and at his visit's end, he left for a final party at Hopetoun House (at which artist Henry Raeburn was knighted), and sailed from Port Edgar.

The theme of the visit combined martial and loyal Scotland with Highlandism, complete with miniature clan 'armies', tartan,[26] and newly composed historicizing ceremonies – a formidable apparatus that underlined Hanoverian might in Scotland. The object was to assert royal legitimacy, to validate social hierarchy, the authority of the crown and establishment, and indirectly to undermine Radicalism. Here onlookers served as 'extras': 'The ... St Andrew's Cross ... is to be universally worn by way of cockade ... at an expence quite inconsiderable, it is hoped every loyal person, of whatever station, will sport the *St Andrew* upon this happy occasion.'[27] The 'white cockade', a rose hat motif, had been chosen by Prince Charles in 1745 for his army. Scott repackaged these symbols for the Hanoverian regime. For authentic 'Highlandizing', he engaged Highland military historian Major General David Stewart of Garth (1772–1829),[28] whose grandfather had 'fallen' at Culloden.[29] George IV was to be regarded like Bruce, but greater, being 'Monarch of the United Empire'.[30] The Celtic Society highlighted 'painful recollection

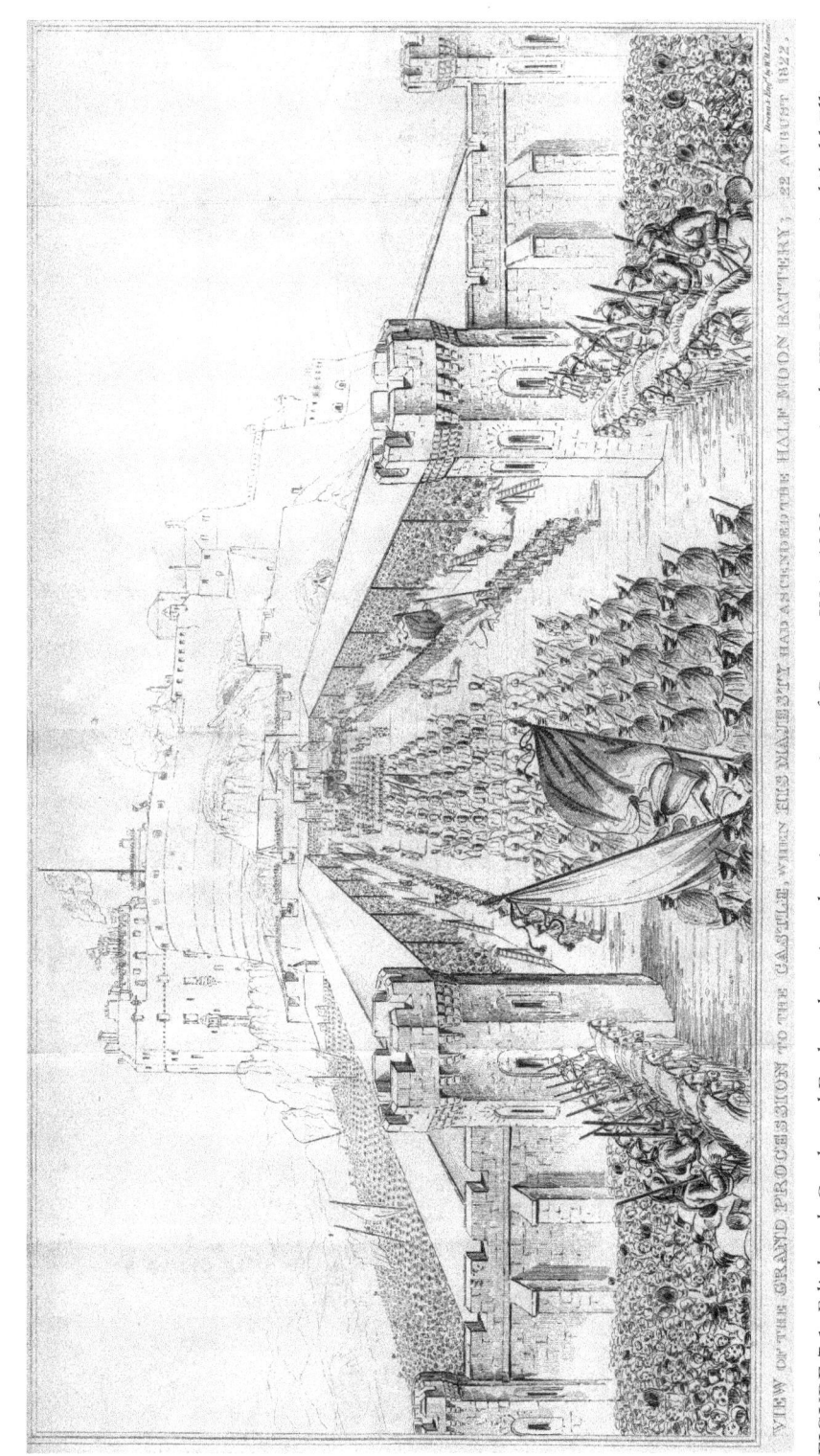

FIGURE 7.1 Edinburgh Castle and Esplanade – view showing reception of George IV in 1822; engraving by W. H. Lizars. Archibald Elliot may have designed the frontal temporary castellation shown here. © Historic Environment Scotland. https://canmore.org.uk/collection/1323021

of past sorrows and errors';[31] Highlanders' foremost offer was soldiery ('our swords and lives are at your Majesty's command').[32] Accounts of post-Culloden atrocities remained unpublished for another three generations.[33]

This was a comprehensive nation-rebuilding project, setting out to claim 'traditional Scotland' for the crown through the public spectacle of elites paying homage to their king. The theatricality of the event offended some of those elites, however: Lord Aberdeen protested that 'I cannot express the annoyance of being here';[34] 'The King . . . was in a Highland dress, which . . . although . . . a compliment to one part of the country, it is by no means so to the rest; and I suppose he is the first King of Scotland who ever wore it . . . "Oh that this solemn mockery were o'er"'.[35] Across the country, castle-builders now sought their own pipers to Highlandize their castles. Scott had 'John of Skye', veteran of the Leopold visit.[36] Angus MacKay, afterwards Queen's piper, produced a pipe music book in 1838, the frontispiece showing a piper and dancers in front of Crathes Castle.[37] Tartan's new unionist meaning was less universally accepted elsewhere. Emma Campbell of Islay recalled that she and her piper in 1827 or 1828 were 'turned out of Kensington Gardens' for wearing tartan – 'I remember the crowd and the stern Park-keeper who turned us away'.[38] Some establishment discomfort towards the Jacobite legacy continued: a celebratory inscription was added to the Culloden Pillar in the 1830s.

The royal visit's legacy embraced elements both of modernity and of 'Scottish tradition': in the first case, a new phase of Improvement projects in Edinburgh included the construction of the George IV Bridge, and names celebrating monarchy, loyalty and union.[39] In 1831, a statue of the king, commissioned not from a Scot but from English sculptor Francis Chantrey, was erected on an axis of Edinburgh's George Street. For this new, institutionalized 'traditional modern Scotland', Scotch Baronial architecture would provide in due course an eminently workable form of expression in the built environment.

Behind all of these interventions, whether traditional or modern, lay the urgent need to respond to the challenge of political Radicalism. Here a linchpin role was played by the staged process of parliamentary Reform, which increased the franchise while preserving all key privileges. The 'Great Reform Act' was passed in 1832 under Whig Prime Minister Earl Grey, and the equivalent Scottish Act followed the same year.[40] Reform stirred up fierce debates, focusing in some cases on the Scottish place in the union.[41] Pro-reformer Robert Ferguson of Raith MP for example, argued that Reform would put Scotland 'on a level with England . . . [and be] the real union of Scotland with England . . . [instead of the] . . . union of humility'.[42] The lawyers who piloted the Reform legislation in Scotland were both, significantly, castle-builders: Lord Cockburn, the Solicitor General, and Lord Jeffrey, the Lord Advocate. And perhaps significantly, in this restrainedly emancipatory context, Wallace's importance continued to be celebrated. In

Ayr, in 1831–4, a neo-Tudor steeple by Thomas Hamilton commemorated him, with a statue by James Thom.[43]

The architectural implications of the 1822 royal visit were pervasive and long-lasting, and combined a new sensitivity to the 'traditional' Scottish heritage, above all that of the royal palaces, and further efforts to evolve a new castellated Scotch architecture inspired by that heritage, especially for use in the country houses of the landed classes. In Edinburgh, calls grew to enhance the royal atmosphere of the area around Holyrood Palace, and to repair the building.[44] Robert Reid (1774–1856), appointed 'King's Architect and Surveyor in Scotland' in 1808, recommended repairs be supported 'for the honour of the Crown'. The antiquarian Charles Kirkpatrick Sharpe of Hoddam, a Burn client and friend of Scott, was horrified that they had 'erected a ... [Greek] ... cornice ... depriv[ing] the building of its resemblance to the old French palaces'.[45] At the other end of the Royal Mile, in 1829, the government returned Mons Meg to Scotland for display in Edinburgh Castle. In parallel with these romanticizing expressions of Scottish monarchist zeal, classical celebrations of national pride still continued, however. The National Monument project,[46] which had stalled following its 1816 commencement (see above) was begun anew with the laying of its foundation stone during George IV's visit. With the Whigs now in charge, the intention was that 'the building may be ornamented with groups of figures ... [illustrating] ... the history of Scotland, and particularly ... the memorable events of the late war'.[47] The object was to replicate the Parthenon, adapted to celebrate Scotland's heroes. £42,000 was needed, and with 'the assistance of England and the Colonies' it was achievable.[48] The 'real' Parthenon was threatened by decay and war, but would live on in facsimile, in the Northern Athens. The appeal was to British pride, but despite hope that the cost would be shared, the project remained unfinished.[49]

Meanwhile, this exploitation of royal castellated tradition, to help in the reframing of the monarchy, reflected a similar movement south of the border, above all in the rebuilding of Windsor Castle by (from 1828, Sir) Jeffrey Wyatville for George IV from 1824 (Abbotsford's completion date), continuing until Wyatville's death in 1840, following a likewise nationally historic nostalgic style.[50] At Windsor, England's most historic royal castle, Wyatville, working with a Strawberry Hill/Abbotsford-like committee, transformed the castle's profile by heightening the squat central Round Tower in a rather hybrid Norman-Gothic style – evoking royal antiquity – to give it a dominant presence; he also reconstructed the upper ward, recreating its south quarter as a regularized entrance front, gridded with projecting mostly-square towers and turrets, as would later be seen at the Houses of Parliament. More generally, it also reflected dramatic pan-British and English developments within the Gothic Revival during the second quarter of the nineteenth century, with Walter Scott in the vanguard: his *Ivanhoe* (1819), with English setting and heroes, nourished the Gothic Revival by popularizing neomedievalism and chivalry (like Windsor), as did works such as Kenelm Henry Digby's 1822 *The Broad Stone of Honour*, an elitist manifesto for neomedievalizing chivalry.

A variety of architectural expressions of this neomedievalism was possible. In England, promoting Gothic as a national style, A. W. N. Pugin condemned in 1836 what he regarded illogical cosmopolitanism: 'We have Swiss cottages . . . Italian villas . . . a Turkish kremlin . . . Greek temples . . . Egyptian auction rooms.'[51] The greatest opportunity to rectify that deficiency came in 1834, when London's Houses of Parliament suffered severe fire damage and a grand replacement complex was commissioned, which would fulfil the need for a truly national building as the hub of the world's greatest power. A classical design would be insufficiently 'national', and a competition in 1835 stipulated that the new building 'be either Gothic or Elizabethan', due to 'the Englishness of these styles'.[52] The new building by Charles Barry (and Pugin) exemplified nationalist historicism.[53] Pugin wanted ornament of 'purely national character': the main tower would be 'a monument of English art which has not been surpassed even in antiquity. This building is the morning star of the great revival of national architecture and art'.[54] In Germany a similar process was underway, but with slightly different stylistic outcomes, reflecting the growing efforts towards cultural and political unification. Some architects, such as Heinrich Hübsch in 1828, advocated that classicism should be replaced by a round-arched neo-Romanesque style as Germany's 'national' architecture.[55] Elsewhere, a castellated architecture similar to the English efforts was attempted, notably in the restoration of Stolzenfels Castle in the Rhineland from 1826. The Rhineland, like Scotland, was a symbolic place, associated with invasions, disputed boundaries, brave resistance, and Romantic ruined castles. At the 1814–15 Congress of Vienna it was assigned to Prussia, creating a nation-building task. In much the same way that George IV stressed his Scottishness in 1822, so a Berlin royal attempted to stress his Hohenzollern connections with the Rhineland and those of his wife's Wittelsbacher dynasty to help legitimize him. As in Scotland, architecture was necessary to the process, and an ancient castle represented ancient ownership or entitlement. The City of Koblenz gifted Stolzenfels – a castle ruin on the 'French side' – in 1823 to Crown Prince Friedrich Wilhelm, the future king of Prussia, which from 1826 he restored as a Romantic castellated palace.[56] Rather like Holyrood, Stolzenfels attempted to embed in tradition the expansive aspirations of a remote and somewhat arriviste monarchy.

Abbotsford: Curtain-raiser for Scotch Baronial

In Scotland, however, the pervasiveness of existing castles, both inhabited and ruined, ensured a far wider acceptance of neocastellated architecture among the landed classes in general, with Scottish architects, led by Burn, now increasingly taking the lead: by the late 1820s the involvement of leading

English architects in castle-building in Scotland was on the decline: Kinfauns (1820–22) and Erskine (1828) were Smirke's last Scottish houses. Scottish architects were quick not only to design in English styles, but also to evolve a new castellated Scotch synthesis. Not only architects were involved in this process, however, as it was arguably above all Walter Scott, in his own multiphase project for his own house at Abbotsford, who played the most unique and decisive role in the emergence of 'Scotch Baronial'.

Abbotsford is one of international Romanticism's highlights and, alongside Inveraray, Balmoral and the National Wallace Monument, one of the most important single works of the Second Castle Age[57] (Figure 7.2). A previously unremarkable house called 'Clartyhole'/'Clarty Hole' was aggrandized from 1811, the 1822–4 principal phase being developed by a Walpole-like committee. Scott wanted Abbotsford, his 'conundrum castle', both to startle, and to evoke the Scottish past, as Romantically as had his writings. The result bemused many: writer and artist Thomas Shepherd argued in 1829 that, 'disowned by all the "orders", Abbotsford is a heresy ...

FIGURE 7.2 *Abbotsford House, completed for Sir Walter Scott by William Atkinson, 1824 – extended to left of the porch by William Burn, 1853–7; view from south-east; photograph of c. 1880. © Historic Environment Scotland. https://canmore.org.uk/collection/1199043*

an order by itself; the first, and destined probably to be the last, of its race ... entirely a creature of the Poet's own fancy'.[58]

Scott recalled in 1817 he had 'often thought of buying ... [and] ... repairing the old tower' at his childhood haunt of Smailholm 'and making it his residence'; for it was there 'he first imbibed his passion for legendary tales, border traditions, and old national songs and ballads'.[59] However, Scott was building to enter the lairdly class, preferring new-manufactured historicizing architecture to an ancient tower which was not his through descent. He instead bought an existing farmhouse, Clarty Hole, where he initially (1811) commissioned William Stark to design 'an ornamental cottage in the style of the old English vicarage-house' for Abbotsford. Stark died in 1813, and this project for a 'whimsical, gay, odd cabin' was abandoned in favour of a staged enlargement of the existing farmhouse. However, the theme of 'old England' was to remain, most clearly in the form of Tudor arches, although now combined with 'old Scotland'. William Atkinson became Scott's main architect, charged with designing 'an old English hall such as a squire of yore dwelt in'.[60]

By 1816, Scott was obtaining architectural casts from Melrose Abbey for his interiors,[61] and in 1817, there 'were strewed various morsels from the ruins of Melrose Abbey, which were to be incorporated in his mansion'.[62] In 1817–18 a north-west extension was added, located towards a slope, making it possible to create a 'piano nobile' as viewed from the north while keeping the south-facing entrance and main floor at ground level. The new wing, which followed a rejected design by Blore for a Tudor-windowed but more tower house-like extension,[63] contained a big bay-windowed dining room, accessed via a new armoury, and a study.[64] The dining room north gable was crowstepped; and on the west flank, much as Blore had proposed, a slender tower with corner 'caphouse' was built, with external steps like those at Queen Margaret's Bower, Linlithgow, and a 'gothic balustrade' also copied from Melrose.[65]

The American writer, Washington Irving, visited Abbotsford in 1817, when work was incomplete and described it:

> It stood some short distance below the road, on the side of a hill sweeping down to the Tweed; and was as yet but a snug gentleman's cottage, with something rural and picturesque in its appearance. The whole front was overrun with evergreens, and immediately above the portal was a great pair of elk horns, branching out from beneath the foliage, and giving the cottage the look of a hunting lodge. The huge baronial pile, to which this modest mansion in a manner gave birth was just emerging into existence; part of the walls, surrounded by scaffolding, already had risen to the height of the cottage, and the courtyard in front was encumbered by masses of hewn stone.[66]

Inside,

> the drawing-room... served also for study and library. Against the wall on one side was a long writing-table, with drawers; surmounted by a small cabinet of polished wood, with folding doors richly studded with brass ornaments, within which Scott kept his most valuable papers. Above the cabinet, in a kind of niche, was a complete corslet of glittering steel, with a closed helmet, and flanked by gauntlets and battle-axes. Around were hung trophies and relics of various kinds: a cimeter of Tippoo Saib; a Highland broadsword from Flodden Field; a pair of Rippon spurs from Bannockburn; and above all, a gun which had belonged to Rob Roy, and bore his initials, R.M.G., an object of peculiar interest to me at the time, as it was understood Scott was actually engaged in printing a novel founded on the story of that famous outlaw. On each side of the cabinet were book-cases, well stored with works of romantic fiction in various languages, many of them rare and antiquated. This, however, was merely his cottage library, the principal part of his books being at Edinburgh. From this little cabinet of curiosities Scott drew forth a manuscript picked up on the field of Waterloo, containing copies of several songs popular at the time in France. The paper was dabbled with blood – 'the very life-blood, very possibly', said Scott, 'of some gay young officer, who had cherished these songs as a keepsake from some lady-love in Paris'.[67]

The main building phase began in 1822, the year of the royal visit, when Scott invited Lord Montague (the Duke of Buccleuch's uncle) 'to see what a romance of a house I am making which is neither to be a castle not abbey (God forbid) but an old Scottish manor-house'.[68] The new work comprised an agglomeration of Scottish and English features. On the south front, a Linlithgow-type porch was added towards the left, fronting a 'tower house'; on the right, an almost Germanic-looking angle turret by Blore.[69]

Scott thus alluded to specific royal palaces and pre-Reformation abbeys, but 'lairds' house' references were generic: for example, on the north façade a Fyvie arch was hinted at, but not used symmetrically. A version of the Scottish Renaissance corbelled-to-square stair turret was set off-centre on the entrance front, but was here almost the antithesis of First Castle Age 'originals', in which the top feature (a little room) was usually ashlar-built over rubble. At Abbotsford, it was the staircase element instead which was dressed ashlar; while the angles were almost like chamfers, rather than wall areas – possibly, if distantly, recalling Ferniehirst. Twinned windows projected over small corbels, like those Burn had already designed for Mey; 'spolia', crowsteps, spouts and much else derived from Scotland's castellated past; and diagonal-set chimneys possibly evoked Moray House. These ideas would help define Scotch Baronial. For example, the 'balanced' formula of setting an entrance tower to the left, and a turret to the right was adopted for Lauriston, Buchanan, Balmoral and Dunrobin.

Direct precedents were Sir John Soane's house in London, but more clearly, Strawberry Hill, which likewise had its own bespoke plan, historic references inside and out, plus a prodigious 'national museum' of contents.[70] For example, Strawberry Hill and Abbotsford each had both a large and a small library, an armoury, antique armour, a garden cloister; each was decorated with countless exotic gifts from admirers, and each was the product of a specialist 'committee'. Scott's consultees included antiquarian artist James Skene of Rubislaw,[71] as well as actor Daniel Terry who had architectural training, and architects Edward Blore and his principal designer, William Atkinson – who also helped shape the interiors, combining new carpets, curtains and fittings with a vast miscellany of old architectural fragments and pieces of furniture: the beginning of antique collecting in Scotland. The furnishing and interior decoration was organized for Scott by Edinburgh designer and decorator D. R. Hay, who recalled that 'Sir Walter desired that it should all be done in imitation of oak, not like woodwork newly fitted up, but to resemble the old oak carvings as much as possible . . . to appear somewhat weatherbeaten and faded, as if it had stood untouched for years'[72] (Figure 7.3).

FIGURE 7.3 *Abbotsford House – entrance hall and armoury; photograph of c. 1880.* © *Historic Environment Scotland. https://canmore.org.uk/collection/702476*

With its highly open face to the road and the river, Abbotsford projected a very different character from that of the increasingly private country houses of the landed elite: it was explicitly intended for public display and consumption, and soon began to attract a significant number of tourist visitors. Where Scott's works had promoted Scotland as an international tourist attraction, Abbotsford now itself became part of that tourist circuit, alongside Melrose Abbey; in 1844, Fox Talbot photographed the house for a book, 'Sun Pictures in Scotland' – only the second photographic book ever published – devoted to subjects associated with Scott and his novels. By the mid-1850s, when it was significantly extended by William Burn for Scott's descendants, James and Charlotte Hope-Scott, the house was receiving over 4,000 visitors a year, and by the mid-1870s over 2,000 Americans alone were visiting annually.[73]

The specifically architectural impact of Abbotsford was widely felt abroad, for example, in the building projects of Polish nobles and intellectuals lamenting the 'forsaken power of Poland'.[74] The writer and critic Michal Grabowski built a 'Scottish' turreted castle at Aleksandrowka; and at Zgorzany in 1834–9, architect Francis Maria Lanci was commissioned by the Skrzynski family to build a castle, described in 1875: 'Amid the greenery and shade of an English park, there arises a rough-hewn building of six towers, built in a square in the style of old Scots castles, appearing as if reproduced directly from a novel of Walter Scott.' Also from Poland came garden writer and architectural patron Princess Izabela Czartoryska, who toured Scotland in 1790. When, once back home, she created her garden at Pulawy, she had obtained for it 'stones from the castles of Mary Stuart, Holyrood, Fotheringay, recently made famous by Walter Scott', while her Gothic House included Scottish views inside, as well as a blade of grass from 'Fingal's tomb'.[75]

William Burn and the 'Scotch' Country House

Abbotsford's designers were significantly influenced by the work of William Burn, who was developing similar ideas in these same years around 1820, and moving decisively away from castellated classicism. Loudon, writing in 1842, contrasted the two, arguing that Abbotsford was merely 'curious': 'Sir Walter's taste was antiquarian rather than artistic . . . The house is a curious piece of patchwork.'[76] By contrast, as Robert Burn's son, William knew his own father's castellated work before training (1808–11) with Smirke, 'the favoured architect of the Tory establishment',[77] and in whose office he would encounter the thinking behind English castellation (such as the Inveraray/Adam-inspired Lowther). He secured a Tory clientele which increasingly favoured castellated 'Scotch' architecture to signal its Scottish national identity and underline its ancient continuing legitimacy. Burn, co-devisor of

Baronial, was also promoter of Edinburgh's Conservative Club in 1834–5 and confidant of that 'leading Tory', the Duke of Buccleuch,[78] for whom Burn designed the English Renaissance-style conservatory at Dalkeith and proposed reconstructing Dalkeith Palace as an Elizabethan mansion (1831). Burn's house-planning innovations stressed the upholding of the social hierarchy, making his architecture part of the conservative fightback against Radicalism. Scott, 'the chief ornament of . . . [the Tory] . . . party',[79] was open about his politics, and in 1819 was progressing plans for a Tory newspaper, *The Beacon*.[80] Burn, however, was discrete to the point of near invisibility, shunning any public profile, a policy that his clientele valued. Like Scott, however, Burn was intensely interested in old Scottish buildings.[81] Burn's obituarist, professor of architecture T. L. Donaldson, recalled that

> It is impossible to avoid noticing . . . [Burn's] . . . deep and loyal interest, which he took in the antiquities of his native country . . . These instances of his country's architecture were familiar to Mr Burn, who seems to have studied them with particular attention, and they appear to have formed the turning point of his taste and practice, and were by him often adopted with great success.[82]

One of the most significant 'turning points' in Burn's architectural development was his enlargement in 1820–22 of Luffness House, for Lieutenant General Sir Alexander Hope, son of the Earl of Hopetoun, who was appointed lieutenant-governor of Edinburgh Castle in 1819.[83] On the house's west side,[84] Burn created a crowstepped triple-gabled wing, the inner gable steeper and higher (implying greater antiquity) and corbelled to square. The design was dated January 1820.[85] 'Original' Tudor and Jacobean houses had mullioned and transomed windows, and parapeted bay windows set beneath curvilinear gables. Burn varied and recombined these ideas in a new way that pointed to significant elements of the future Scotch Baronial, including new features that enhanced modern domestic comfort – notably asymmetrical arrays of one or two-storeyed square or canted bay windows, frequently in asymmetrical combinations, with gables that were instead crowstepped, and ball finials like cannonballs. Bay windows had Scottish precedent only at Pinkie (where Burn later worked), and his diamond-set chimney stalks could have derived from Moray House. Burn now established all these as standard Scotch elements. Bay-windows admitted more light, reflecting changing tastes. Among his other commissions of the period, Dupplin (1828) and St Fort (1829) were among the most skilfully designed neo-Jacobean houses of the 1820s in Britain,[86] while Carstairs (1820), for the Tory MP Sir Henry Monteith MP, sometime Lord Provost of Glasgow, supporter of the execution of the 1820 'Martyrs' and of slavery,[87] was Tudor.[88] Burn's designs frequently included a semicircular miniature pediment on horizontal courses, possibly referencing the tower or courtyard string course of Heriot's, or Linlithgow's north quarter parapet, but equally likely to have an English source. This would also become a stereotyped detail of Scotch Baronial.

A further design challenge of the 'modern Scotch' house was that of floor levels. Scotland's old houses had their principal rooms on the first floor, but neo-Tudor demanded ground floor access. For cases where old houses were to be retained, Burn devised two main responses: either a stair was placed immediately inside, or the external ground level could be raised. In some, cantilevered platforms or terraces enabled the occupants to circulate outside at will. To accentuate his houses' asymmetry, Burn extensively exploited and normalized the traditional castellated L-plan façade, and even where no wing broke forward, he frequently heightened the wall at one end into a gable; likewise, he normalized the combination of projecting square and canted bays. Some of Burn's houses had two or more L-plan facades, as at Bourhouse (Bowerhouse) (c. 1835), designed for a prominent army officer by Burn's assistant-cum-protégé David Bryce, whom we will meet again shortly.[89] Bourhouse has also an engaged octagonal turret-cum-bay window at its entrance, with a pointed faceted roof and dormerheads – all anticipating the urban Baronial of Cockburn Street in Edinburgh (1859–64). The gate-lodge has curved-to-square bays.[90]

Overall, a gradual evolution is traceable in Burn's country-house work, from the Smirke-like castellation of the 1810s to neo-Tudor in the 1820s, thereafter becoming incrementally more Scotch, especially from the mid-1830s. Riccarton House was remodelled in 1823–7 for the advocate and future Whig MP, Sir William Gibson Craig, the result being an asymmetrical, ancient-looking tower-and-wing mansion. The tower was made convincingly to resemble a tower-house, and while the detailing was neo-Tudor, the dormer heads cut above the eaves as did Scots prototypes. At Pinkie, in 1825, Burn added a twin-crowstepped wing, bringing the entrance to ground level, a stair inside, and on one angle, a two-stage turret resembling those on the bigger tower-house alongside. Lauriston Castle was reconstructed by Burn in 1827. Several options were considered, including an 1825 proposal to demolish the tower, but as it had been the home of John Law, France's controversial early eighteenth-century finance minister, Scott argued successfully for its retention. A platformed terrace was added, with a stair to the garden. The detailing was Tudor, except for crowsteps and console overlays on otherwise Tudor-looking dormer heads. This model was repeated by Burn elsewhere – for instance at Newbattle and Kilconquhar – thereby injecting clear Scottish references to his neo-Tudor composition. Then, in 1828, lawyer James Balfour engaged Burn to add new public rooms to Pilrig, an L-plan house of 1638.[91] The new work had matching crowstepped gables; although Pilrig had one seemingly pre-existing curvilinear gable meaning Jacobean gables were an option. Burn further developed his own style at Tyninghame, which he enlarged (1829) (Figure 7.4). The turrets were given steep French-looking

FIGURE 7.4 *Tyninghame House – rebuilt by William Burn, 1829 (cantilevered terraces since removed); view from south-west; photograph by James Valentine, 1888.* © *Historic Environment Scotland. https://canmore.org.uk/collection/1212874*

roofs and the crowsteps were enriched in a Heriot's manner. A Pinkie-like bay was added, and Lauriston-like cantilevered terraces.

At Faskally and Milton Lockhart Burn designed wholly new houses, and at each he explored the possibilities of Baronial revivalism. They resembled sedate neo-Tudor mansions, but Burn added Scotch ornament such as extruded circular stair turrets. Faskally (designed 1829) was built for Archibald Butter. The public rooms and entrance were placed at ground level, and there was a combination of mullioned and transomed windows in projecting square or canted bays, all following the Tudor model. The gables were crowstepped, and turrets were tucked into some angles representing turnpikes. Milton Lockhart (1829–36)[92] was commissioned by soldier and politician William Lockhart, half-brother of Scott's Tory son-in-law and future biographer, John Gibson Lockhart.[93] In January 1829, a party which included Walter Scott and the sculptor John Greenshields walked the estate, 'to look out a situation for a new house'.[94] Lockhart decided the final location.[95] One contemporary argued that 'the details are taken from ancient Scottish buildings',[96] and in Loudon's view it was in 'Burn's peculiar combination of the old Scotch, or Belgian [i.e., "Flemish"], style and the Tudor Gothic'.[97]

Castles reconstructed, rather than built new, by Burn in the same years included Hoddam, for Charles Kirkpatrick Sharpe (1826), and Dalhousie (1826–8) for the Ninth Earl of Dalhousie – both huge castles, modified in a more Smirke-like character. In 1830, Scott visited his onetime school friend's Dalhousie Castle, and approvingly reported that while 'the old Castle . . . was mangled by a fellow called, I believe, Douglas, who destroyed, as far as in him lay, its military and baronial character . . . the architect, Burn, is now restoring and repairing it in the old taste'.[98] The client was a British military hero and colonial administrator, by then commander in chief in India. His re-Baronialized castle celebrated the martial heritage of Scotland's imperial leaders. In the 1830s, Burn produced two Baronial schemes for Kilconquhar Castle, for the soldier and diplomat, Sir Henry Lindsay Bethune, knighted in 1835 for services to the British government in Persia.[99] Both schemes retained the tower essentially unmodified, but the second version (1839) was more Scotch, its west front being dominated by a full-height corbelled-to-square bay.[100] In 1835, Burn enlarged Stenhouse by duplicating its L-plan, creating a near-symmetrical castle[101] for the slave owner and Eighth Baronet, Sir Michael Bruce.[102] It had been a seventeenth-century idea to duplicate the old, but here, the castellation was also celebrated and replicated as well. Similarly, Castle Menzies was extended in 1836–40 for 'Chief Sir Neil the Menzies', agricultural Improver and advocate, the '60th in descent, 23rd Baron and the 6th Baronet of Menzies'.[103] Burn's new west wing had bartizans and dormerheads cutting the eaves. Moray House-type balconies were intended, as was upper-level corbelling, but all was omitted in execution.[104]

Arguably the first example of Burn's more florid, sculptural mid-century manner was the polygonal, neo-Renaissance conservatory of Dalkeith Palace (1832–4) mentioned above; we will return in the next chapter to his subsequent work of this kind, increasingly shaped and then dominated by his assistant David Bryce.

W. H. Playfair: 'Liberal Scotch'

By the 1830s, between them, Burn and Scott had set out the main framework for the future Scotch Baronial style – in somewhat different ways. Burn's clients did not want imitations of Abbotsford any more than Scott wanted to copy any specific Scottish Renaissance castle. But despite the prominence of Scott and Burn in its development, the emergent Scotch style was not in any sense the exclusive property of the Tory landed faction within unionist Scotland. Its equal potential suitability for the building projects of Whig clients and institutions was underlined by its enthusiastic adoption by William Henry Playfair (1790–1857), trained partly in London and a protégé of neo-Classicist William Stark. Playfair became exceptionally skilled in British revivalist styles: alert both to Burn's innovations and the aims of the 1827 Edinburgh Improvement Act, Playfair would quarry the resource potential of George Heriot's Hospital in particular. The latter was by then widely regarded as an Inigo Jones design – a belief for which there was no evidence, but which doubtless reflected an assumption that a building of such quality could not be by a Scottish designer.

Playfair's first known Scotch design was, indeed, a new gatehouse for Heriot's on Lauriston Place (1828), where he reproduced the main building's detailing.[105] He also constructed terraces with square-section balustrades of the type he was to continue using in his Scotch designs.[106] In the 1830s, he followed these with four castle projects, several of which – including The Grange, Prestongrange, and Craigcrook – involved adaptation of a pre-existing castle. His vocabulary was largely derived from that of Burn, although with variations in detail: for example, Playfair's designs tended to include steep-gabled narrow jambs, and sometimes basket-arched entrance doors of c. 1700 type. The Grange, near Edinburgh, was reconstructed in 1830–31 for Scott's pro-Reform friend, the writer and soldier Sir Thomas Dick Lauder of Fountainhall (1784–1848). Lauder was a keen promoter of 'Scotch tradition' and encouraged the Sobieski Stuart brothers to publish their work on tartans.[107] This was Playfair's only castle that was not based on Heriot's. His extensions retained the house's L-plan and continued the existing theme of circular turrets, crowsteps and harled asymmetry. An unusual innovation here was the idea of corbelling circular turrets outwards at their top storey (typically, corbelled-out turrets were square), as at Bothwell Castle, a town-house in the burgh of Haddington; and so perhaps connecting to the cult of Mary Queen of Scots – Mary having married the Earl of Bothwell in 1567, whose house that had been. It became a popular feature; and Barry used it, for example, at Dunrobin. The garden was terraced on the south front, and gateways for the main entrance as well as to the courtyard were designed like barmkin gateways.

Prestongrange was a tower-house with a long east wing. Playfair enlarged it in a Scotch style twice: in 1830, for Sir James Grant Suttie,[108] and again in 1850, for his son, Sir George Grant Suttie. The 1830 work included deepening the eastern part of the wing by adding a Baronial entrance block to its north whose windows were unaligned between floors, suggesting preclassical; there was a mixture of towers and turrets – the doorway in a semioctagonal projecting tower referencing those on the Heriot's flanks. The 1850 work concentrated on the house's west end, and included a new 'tower-house'. Playfair's work at Craigcrook was commissioned by the anti-slavery lawyer, reformer and writer, Francis, Lord Jeffrey, Whig MP and Dean of the Faculty of Advocates, who had leased the house from 1815.[109] Jeffrey co-founded and edited the *Edinburgh Review*, which inspired Scott's rival Tory *Quarterly Review*. Playfair's 1835 interventions at Craigcrook focused on the north, being designed for viewing obliquely, from the north-east approach. The jamb of the pre-existing L-plan, on the right, was made, inexpensively, to look like a tower-house; and tucked closely alongside was a corbelled-to-square tower containing the entrance in one of the canted angles. The overdoor pediment derived from Heriot's. In 1808, Jeffrey had said of *Marmion* that 'to write a modern romance of chivalry seems to be such a phantasy as to build a modern abbey or an English pagoda'.[110] Here, contradicting himself, he now created a Romantic Scotch Baronial home made from an ancient castle.[111]

Another prominent Whig lawyer, Henry (later Lord) Cockburn, commissioned Playfair in the 1830s to remodel Bonaly, south of Edinburgh, to where he had moved in 1811 (the same year his fellow-lawyer Scott bought Abbotsford). Here he cleared an existing village settlement, keeping the farmhouse for himself,[112] which in 1815 he playfully called 'Bonaly Castle', his 'ancient & many-roomed chateau'.[113] Cockburn, a writer, pioneer architectural conservationist and judge,[114] had decided that Bonaly needed to be enlarged to host his Friday Club, becoming 'a mansion not only commodious but elegant, and whose lofty tower is often pointed out to the passing traveller as the most interesting object in the landscape, – interesting not from its picturesqueness alone, but also from the uses to which it is put'.[115] Bonaly, whose enlargement Playfair began in 1836, was made into a rubble tower-house with an off-centre stair turret and a forestair, the corners rounded in the manner of Cranshaws, a tower only around six miles from Cockburn Castle (dismantled in 1829),[116] thereby alluding to the family's Berwickshire origins ('I have destroyed a village and erected a tower, and reached the dignity of a twenty-acred laird'.[117]) (Figure 7.5). The old house became a wing, the service court a barmkin with a 1642 pediment, sourced from elsewhere, over its gateway. Bonaly's design was the opposite approach to Burn's low-slung mansions, which were generally entered at ground level in accordance with Tudor practice: an 1826 design of this kind, possibly by Burn, for a new mansion had been rejected.[118] Cockburn had visited Abbotsford in 1828,[119] but preferred his own style of Scotch revivalism. At Meadowbank House, however, Playfair worked from 1835 for an anti-Reform judge and Tory MP Alexander Maconochie, Lord Meadowbank (1777–1861).[120] A friend of Scott, he had publicly revealed him in 1827 (with Scott's consent) to be the author of *Waverley*.[121] Playfair's work echoed Burn's: having a crowstepped gable set over one side of the main front and a Burn-like round-arched bipartite window in a crowstepped projection, though Playfair's corbelled square turret seems more inventive.

In a succession of 1830s designs, Playfair extensively exploited the architectural vocabulary of George Heriot's Hospital. At Floors Castle, 1837–45, this source was supplemented by English details such as the ranks of chimney stalks, reminiscent of the older parts of Oxbridge colleges (Figure 7.6). The existing old building had square corner pavilions which

FIGURE 7.5 *Bonaly Tower by William Playfair, 1836, left-hand wing by Sydney Mitchell, 1888 – view from east; undated photograph.* © Historic Environment Scotland. *https://canmore.org.uk/collection/548561*

Playfair now dressed as Heriot's towers, and the wings comprised miniature Heriot's quadrangles with dumpy square corner towers. The new ballroom resembled the chapel that Playfair was designing at just this time for an urban project, Donaldson's Hospital School. Playfair considered Tudor revival appropriate for Scotland, on the widely accepted grounds that

FIGURE 7.6 *Floors Castle by William Playfair, 1837–45 – view from north-west; photograph of 2003. © Historic Environment Scotland. htttps://canmore.org.uk/ collection/1025761*

England's heritage was also a pan-British heritage – the same principle as was applied on a grander scale in the new Houses of Parliament project in London. Playfair had already used a stripped Tudor/Jacobean in 1829–30 at the Advocates Library. Now he was appointed to design Donaldson's Hospital.[122] The style – like Westminster – was to be Elizabethan (Figure 7.7). It was built in 1842–52, but its design dated from the 1830s. Playfair's 1835 scheme echoed Rickman's work at St John's College, Cambridge (completed 1831), as well as George Heriot's, in features including corner towers and stair turrets.[123] In 1839, Playfair said he was working on 'a Building, which in the correctness of its parts shall be worthy of comparison with the remains of Old English Architecture'. And in 1850 he wrote of the chapel being 'like a Baronial Hall fit to receive Henry VIIIth, Anna Bullen [Boleyn] and Wolsey'.[124] This great public building was given the task of underlining British unity by adopting England's paradigms and applying them in Scotland's capital. That Henry VIII had wanted to annex Scotland by military means in the 1540s was to be forgotten – he was now to be regarded fondly and romantically by Scots, and as a noble part of their heritage.

FIGURE 7.7 *Donaldson's Hospital by William Playfair – designed c. 1835; built 1842–52; view from south-east; undated photograph.* © *Historic Environment Scotland. https://canmore.org.uk/collection/1267204*

Proto-Baronialists in the East, West and North-East

Among other Edinburgh designers, as we saw, James Gillespie Graham's earlier works were classical, before moving on towards various permutations of the Gothic and national. One English admirer of his Gothic was J. P. Neale, who in 1828 argued that 'the alterations at Lee ... which give it a castellated appearance, were commenced by Sir Charles Lockhart, Bart., from ... designs of Mr. Gillespie Graham, an architect who has the merit of introducing the Gothic style into this country, in a greater degree of purity and perfection than had previously been exhibited'. Similarly, Neale praised Wishaw, 'by Mr Gillespie': 'The style of the architecture is the castellated, and the whole is a very successful alteration of an ancient building.'[125] In the late 1820s, Gillespie Graham studied English buildings in some detail, writing in 1827 from London that 'I have been at Cobham, Holland House, etc. and by the time I reach Auld Reekie [Edinburgh] I hope to have a sufficient knowledge of the Elizabethan style of buildings'.[126]

Gillespie Graham's Murthly, for Sir John Stewart, was intended as a neo-Jacobean palace and – had it been completed – would have rendered Murthly Castle obsolete.[127] In 1829, when already commissioned for Murthly, Gillespie Graham met the seventeen-year-old A. W. N. Pugin, whom he employed to make designs, and whom he sent to Hatfield 'to make Sketches'.[128] He recorded that he had 'visited and studied at Hatfield and several other Houses of the Reign of James the 1st. Murthly being a Model of Burleigh Hatfield etc. made me most anxious to have a grip of the true character of that style of Building'.[129] Murthly comprised a four-square symmetrical block with ogee-domed thin corner turrets and a central lantern tower. Pugin composed some interior designs for it, all in a Jacobean style except for the Louis XIV drawing room. Scott – who by this time had completed Abbotsford House – viewed the drawings in 1830, when they were on display in Edinburgh: he 'went to look at the drawings for repairing Murthly ... now building by Gillespie Graham, and which he has planned after the fashion of James VI's reign, a kind of bastard Grecian – very fanciful and pretty though'.[130] Interestingly, Scott seems to have thought the building evoked a Scottish historical timeframe (for instance, in its Heriot's-like buckle quoins), a conclusion which might have dismayed the architect, whose wish to draw on English sources is clear. There were at least two iterations of the Murthly project. In the first, it was intended to resemble Blickling Hall, but its front would be larger, with a complex entrance stair, and the centre lantern tower too would be grander, recalling Taymouth or Inveraray.[131] As executed, the house was more compact with gabled, twin-turreted ends, evoking Hatfield, and possibly Holyrood. According to MacAuley, the client, a Stewart, saw himself as 'intimately connected with kings', proposing his new house might therefore 'be called a Palace'.[132] In contrast with the Burn fondness for the more horizontally disposed Tudor arrangement, Murthly replicated the tight symmetry of the English Renaissance prototypes. But Graham also made it more Scottish, by incorporating low ground floor windows and a *piano nobile*, and (like Playfair's Donaldson's) by giving it Heriot's-like buckle quoins, a detail as unknown in England as the Tudor arch was in Scotland.

In the west of Scotland, David Hamilton's Castle Toward (1820) for Glasgow merchant Kirkman Finlay, echoed John Nash's work, as did Castle House in Dunoon (1823–4) for politician James Ewing. The client at Dunlop House (1832–4) was Sir John Dunlop, soldier and Liberal MP. It was a western version of Flemish, recalling Glasgow's tolbooth or its college, and with a right-hand turret resembling Abbotsford. But the Heriot's obsession was rare outside Edinburgh. Dunlop's 1643 parish church was rebuilt in 1835,[133] stereotypically Tudor Gothic, except for the fact that the jamb had Glasgow College-type sculpture incorporated.[134] Hamilton's client at Lennox Castle (1837–41) claimed descent from a Saxon who reached Scotland in 1069, and its neo-Romanesque style ('old Norman')[135] evoked that heritage[136] (Figure 7.8). *Ivanhoe* had recalled 'the tall, turretted, and

FIGURE 7.8 *Lennox Castle by David Hamilton, 1837–41 – view from north-east; photograph of 1959.* © Historic Environment Scotland. https://canmore.org.uk/collection/712276

castellated buildings in which the Norman nobility resided ... the universal style of architecture throughout England'.[137]

In the north-east, the most prestigious commissions were largely divided between Aberdeen's Archibald Simpson and John Smith. Simpson's 1830s castles mostly employed English Jacobean styling. Regardless of his high reputation as a classicist, his contribution to the development of Scotch Baronial was perhaps modest. Castle Newe (1831) was clearly acceptable as an image of an ancient clan castle, as it provided the frontispiece in 1859 for a book on the Romantic Gaelic Aberdeenshire Highlands, a background for Jacobite-looking retainers.[138] In 1830–8, Smith was busy at Castle Fraser, where he added crowstepped lodges to close the barmkin.[139] At Candacraig (1835) the combination of Scottish and English revivalism to create a Scotch style was recognized by contemporaries: 'The house of Candacraig is a mixture of the Elizabethan and Scotch manor-house.'[140] Smith's biggest house was probably Forglen (1839–42), built for former MP Sir Robert Abercromby. It echoed Abbotsford while anticipating the second Balmoral, having its porch towards the left, a diversity of ball-finialled projecting bay windows and an off-centre tower, but its style still Tudor rather than Scotch.[141] It also evoked local castles, having a composite tiered armorial in one turret containing reset armorials and 1577–8 datestones.

Towards an 'Urban Scotch'

Although the beginnings of the Scotch style were deeply intertwined with country-house patronage, the same formula now, significantly, began to spread to other, urban building types. Burn's Madras College (1830–2) in St Andrews, for instance, resembled a cross between a Jacobean country house and Heriot's. Its north-facing two-storey main block has a rank of bay windows beneath curvilinear gables, resembling Blickling Hall; while the quadrangular layout and open cloisters with pilastered bay divisions all recall Heriot's, and the spiral-twisted chimney flues hint at the precedent of Winton. We saw above that Robert Adam had reintroduced the use of castellation as a mark of civic authority. This idea got ever-firmer hold during the early nineteenth century, for example, with Burn's 1830s Inverness Castle. Other examples included Dufftown's Clock Tower, a freestanding tower-house within a newly planned town of the 1820s, and built in 1836–9 as a prison. It was given three diminishing stages topped by a castellated parapet and corbelled corner bartizans.[142]

Edinburgh was the headquarters of Scotch revivalism, and the city's multistage Improvement projects and redevelopments, from 1827 onwards, provided ample opportunity for experimentation in a hybrid Scots-Jacobean which was initially referred to as the 'Flemish style' in allusion to Scotland's historic trading partner and the supposed source of decoration such as that used at Heriot's. The style was adopted in 1826 by the town council for new Old Town elevations;[143] the 1827 Edinburgh Improvement Act specified 'Old Scots or Flemish'[144] – in other words, the style of George Heriot's Hospital.[145] Pioneers included Playfair, John Henderson, Alexander Black and George Smith, while in 1830 Thomas Hamilton proposed, unsuccessfully, new castellated buildings overlooking The Mound.[146] Flemish or Jacobean designs by George Smith included Melbourne Place (1837): maintaining the connection between Scotland's capital and British rulers, as it was named in honour of Prime Minister Lord Melbourne. It was Flemish, and a Jacobean gable with a balcony was intended.[147] Alexander Black built a series of 'daughter' Heriot's schools, including one alongside (1838) the main building, and branches in Cowgate (dated 1838), Old Assembly Close (1839), Borthwick's Close (c. 1840) and Broughton Street (1853), all ornamented like Heriot's.[148]

Within urban ecclesiastical architecture, however, castellation was seen as generally inappropriate, and tended to be confined to steeple-tops. Most churches now were Gothic, the default style for signalling a church in preference to the classical 'boxes' of the previous century; with a stereotyped formula comprising rectangular nave with an entrance steeple on one gable; the exemplar being Burn's St John's, Edinburgh (1816–18).[149] Usually, neither clients nor architects tended to engage deeply with the scholarship of English Gothic revivalism, and a simple Tudor-arched Gothic was popular – John Smith's north-eastern churches typically followed this formula. George Smith's St John's, Victoria Street (1838–40) is consequently all the more distinctive: Gifford observed that it looked 'less like a church than three bays of a Jacobean country house'.[150] It fitted quite well into the 'Improvement Flemish' context of post-1827 Edinburgh, but the idea did not become more generally popular – as was emphasized when in 1839 Gillespie Graham (with Pugin) designed the Victoria Hall (the Church of Scotland's General Assembly Hall), a tall, spired, somewhat church-like structure commandingly situated at the head of Edinburgh's Lawnmarket, whose ground stone was laid in 1842. In one sense, this was a consolation prize, as in 1835 he had expected to be commissioned to restore Holyrood Abbey Kirk as the General Assembly meeting place. King William had been persuaded to back the project and in 1836 Pugin produced designs,[151] but when William died in 1837, the project halted.[152]

The continuing preference for Gothic extended into the field of national monuments following the death of Walter Scott in 1832, when a succession of commemorative designs was duly produced and debated. In 1835, for example, a report by the Scott monument committee argued that

> the Gothic style is peculiarly appropriate to this country . . . exclusively and intimately associated with the events, eras, and characters, which occupied the genius of the man whose memory it is desired to honour . . . That Sir WALTER'S own predilections in favour of Gothic structures are well known to have been strong, having often expressed his wonder that, in raising monuments to the memory of illustrious Britons, we should confine ourselves to copying the styles of Rome, Greece, and Egypt.[153]

Burn, too, advised 'that if architecture of any kind was to be combined with the statue of Sir WALTER SCOTT, it must, in consistency with the genius of that great man, be in the Gothic style'. Clearly, a revivalist style such as Tudor was considered unsuitable in this instance. Scott's fondness for Melrose Abbey was well known, and at this juncture, the 'Scotch Baronial' was insufficiently well established and well defined to serve such an elevated purpose. In the event, George Meikle Kemp's tall, spired design, applauded by Burn, was chosen, being 'in strict conformity with the purity in taste and style of Melrose Abbey, from which it is, in all its details, derived'. It was 'gratifying . . . [as surely] . . . it would have been to Sir WALTER SCOTT himself, that the Designs . . . are the production of native artists, who owe their present success solely to their own genius and personal merits'[154] (Figure 7.9). Although the Scott Monument remained incomplete for several years, fund-raising was reenergized in 1844;[155] by 1846, the monument was complete, and a supporters' meeting enthused that the finished monument would be 'such a material fabric as may endure while "Scotland stands where now she does" – as long as she possesses a place and a name among the nations (Loud cheering)'.[156]

FIGURE 7.9 *Sir Walter Scott Monument, Edinburgh, designed by George Meikle Kemp, c. 1840 – view from north-west; photograph of c. 1910. https://canmore. org.uk/collection/1207974*

Scholarly Source Publications and Romantic Tournaments

Abbotsford, and the work of Burn, had answered Britton's claim that Scotland lacked historic national architecture, and that it was absurd to conceive of a separate Scottish architectural tradition; but there was still no authoritative equivalent to his publications. Walter Scott and J. M.

W. Turner collaborated on *The Provincial Antiquities and Picturesque Scenery of Scotland* (c. 1822–5), which included Romantic, rather than archaeological or academic images, for example depicting Linlithgow. Shortly thereafter, a more accurately detailed publication was made by Charles Joseph Hullmandel (1789–1850), a pioneering London-based lithographer of German descent,[157] who had studied with scientist Michael Faraday to help devise new techniques.[158] Hullmandel produced the first volumes of carefully detailed drawings of old Scottish buildings: *Castellated Mansions of Scotland* (1830) and *Specimens of old Castellated Houses in Aberdeenshire* (1838). The north-east bias of these books, and their drawings by the Aberdeen artist, garden designer and antiquarian, James Giles, all indicated Lord Aberdeen's encouragement.[159] Hullmandel had moved within a north-eastern community of artists and architects, and progressive clients: the latter would soon include Victoria and Albert. Lord Aberdeen had himself intended to publish a book on the subject, with the input not just of Giles but also of a talented documentary historian such as Joseph Robertson or John Hill Burton (both being Aberdonian); but the project collapsed following publication by Andrew Leith Hay (1785–1862) of his rival enterprise, *The Castellated Architecture of Aberdeenshire* in 1849. Its text was a rather downbeat narrative of Scotland's past.

In 1836, Loudon again published a project in an identifiably Scottish style of domestic architecture: a 'villa in the Old Scotch Style' (1831) at Springfield, designed by William Reid for David Scales Cleland. This had curvilinear twinned gables from the established revivalist canon, but Scotch pedimented dormer heads and ogee-domed corbelled bartizans. Loudon explained that

> every one who has seen the house of a Scotch laird, erected during the seventeenth century, will allow that this is a good imitation of the old Scotch manner . . . It is . . . proper to observe that the object of the Architect may be, to produce such an imitation as may actually be mistaken for the thing imitated . . . Mr Cleland may wish his villa to be taken for a real old Scotch house.

Loudon had no objection to anyone wanting their new house to look deceptively old, but encouraged originality and progress: 'Any builder can copy a style, but it requires an Architect to compose in it.'[160] Another example published by Loudon was *A Mansion, in the style of a Scotch Baronial House of the Sixteenth Century, with the accommodation and Arrangements suitable to a Villa of the Nineteenth Century*. The design was by David Cousin, who explained that 'I have endeavoured to adhere closely to examples of the style characterized by turrets, gables, steep roofs, high chimneys, bartisans &c . . . the style of the Scottish manor house'. Cousin had consulted only two publications in preparing this design, neither of them architectural in character, and neither containing any architectural details which could serve as models: Adam de Cardonell's *Picturesque Antiquities of Scotland* (1788) and Robert Forsyth's *Beauties of Scotland* (1805). While Giles's later drawings were carefully archaeological in nature, there was still no sense of a 'source book' for Scotch Baronial being planned, such as was now increasingly available for English Gothic. Cousin's formula drew from his analysis of old castles, and in particular from his insight that typically they comprised a nucleus tower with additions; but he claimed no authority in historical scholarship, being 'not antiquary enough'.[161]

Overall, however, the emergent Scotch Baronial discourse was still very free-ranging and Romantic in character – as exemplified in the neomedievalizing Tournament hosted in 1839 at Eglinton Castle by Archibald Montgomerie, Thirteenth Earl of Eglinton, a Tory politician later associated with the National Association for the Vindication of Scottish Rights, and thus an exemplification of Victorian unionist nationalism.[162] The 'Eglinton Tournament' was planned in the Gothic showroom of London dealer and decorator Samuel Pratt.[163] Gothic specialist architect Lewis Nockalls Cottingham was involved,[164] and the 'knights' practiced in London.[165] About 100,000 people attended the event.[166] The patriotic dressing-up of 1822 and 'ancient' rituals were repeated in a slightly different form, and spectators wore bonnets and plaids, representing 'the nation's peasantry'.[167] Social hierarchy, and the manliness and good taste of the wealthy, were all celebrated. Diversity within the Union was celebrated in 'international' sport. Campbell of Glenlyon, as for the 1822 celebrations, brought a clan 'army', although 'the tourney was of Gothic, not of Celtic origin . . . We should suppose that Eglinton Tournament will have been the first at which . . . tartan and . . . kilt were . . . conspicuous. There is nothing in the Highland dress which renders it appropriate for such a scene.'[168] Eglinton Castle served as a neomedieval stronghold. Everything was neomedieval and British, the temporary architecture Gothic.[169] Authentic armour was used; Lord Craven's had (reputedly) been worn by a participant at the Battle of Crecy.[170] The object was to showcase medieval society's hierarchical structure as an ideal for the present, to counterbalance the threat of Radicalism and democracy.[171] The castle provided an ideal backdrop. Eglinton hoped 'that tournaments would become fashionable amongst the nobility and gentry'.[172] The Marquis of Waterford even considered hosting one at Ford Castle,[173] near the battlefield of Flodden – a location of dubious resonance for even the most enthusiastic unionist.

Conclusion

The royal visit of 1822 had responded effectively to the political threat of Radicalism, by casting Scotland as a land that was highly esteemed in some symbolic ways, while still of secondary status in others.[174] Teutonist perspectives made English architecture symbolically valuable, as a supposed common heritage; yet an explicitly Scotch style, a new, unionist-nationalist style headed by the Tories, Scott and Burn, was all the time gestating. Abbotsford was influential, and Burn was polite about it to Scott.[175] But no one followed it closely, so it remained something of an outlier, whose spirit rather than form was emulated. Burn's work, however, and that of Playfair, was directly inspirational, gradually overtaking and submerging the English styles, and from it came the mainstream Scotch Baronial of the next phase of the Second Castle Age, led by David Bryce – as we will see in the next chapter.

8

1840–1870: Billings and Bryce – Mid-Century Baronial

The spots chosen as the most suitable for fortifications in the old days of family warfare, though generally selected by men who never looked at scenery, and cared for nothing but eating, drinking and fighting, have often supplied exquisite pieces of scenery, adapted entirely to our modern taste.[1]

– R. W. BILLINGS, 1852

The Scotch style (of the Elizabethan period), which has spread over Scotland and the North of England from the headquarters in Edinburgh ... [with its] pepper-box corners, battlemented parapets, and corbie-steps of the dreary middle ages of the Northern kingdom.[2]

– ROBERT KERR, 'LONDON SCOTTISH' ARCHITECT AND WRITER, 1864

Feudalistic in character, and necessarily ... crude in conception, [Scotch Baronial] has by the talent of able modern exponents been brought up to date through the happy transfusion into it of the style of the French chateaux, with which it is nearly akin.[3]

– G. S. AITKEN, 1890

Introduction

During the mid-nineteenth century, as the global power of the British imperial partnership experienced its most triumphant expansion, Scottish society responded with an optimistic mixture of commitment to the promotion of colonial-based capitalism, and confidence that its concomitant social evils could be conquered. Responding to this climate, the nation's architects and clients maintained, on the whole, their affiliation to monumental classicism, but at the same time as this, the specifically 'national' architectural images adumbrated by Scott were expanded into a Scotch Baronial style of imperial ebullience: the climactic phase of the Second Castle Age. The new waves of capitalist-driven social and economic transformation and urbanization were mainly still overwhelmingly dependent on laissez-faire efforts but were also attracting the first interventions by the state in social provision, mostly through local boards and committees, usually of a hybrid public/private character. Yet the landed class still managed to retain a prominent place in this aggressively modernizing, post-feudal society. In the countryside, there was at first little erosion of the old order, and the role of landowners remained prominent, but now with a greater impact on architecture under their old public title of 'Commissioners of Supply'.

In the area of national identity, by the time of the accession of Queen Victoria to the throne, the re-embedding of Scotland into the British system was almost complete, and the empire now seemed a compelling focus of Scottish national pride: the 'Queen of England', was also the tartan-draped Highland Queen beloved by Scots. Symbols of Scottishness were fashionable throughout Britain, and Scots felt increasingly satisfied by the wealth and power that stemmed from their partnership with England. But this created a new problem of rising expectations, and stimulated an upsurge in Scottish nationalism, here demanding not increased devolution of power within the union, but increased esteem for the Scottish contribution to the union and empire – as evinced for example in the 1853 foundation of the National Association for the Vindication of Scottish Rights [NAVSR].

How did mid-nineteenth-century buildings express the bewildering changes and challenges of the period? In high architecture, the dominant capitalist modernity of the age was expressed not through new materials but through a new, dense, cosmopolitan eclecticism, fed by an unprecedentedly prolific availability of sources – a combination of journals and books (as a miscellaneous and international stylistic source), and archaeological research into specifically national subjects on the lines set out by Scott and Kemp. In no previous age were such exact and extensive attempts made to reflect the social significance of Scotland's buildings in their outward appearance. Within the country houses of the landed elite, the new Scottish assertiveness allowed the lairds' continuing prestige to be expressed in ways that increasingly diverged from English architecture: whereas south of the border, castle-building was becoming distinctly unfashionable,[4] Scotland now entered into its high period of castle revivalism – a phase of full-blown Scotch Baronial led no longer by Burn, but his protégé, David Bryce.[5]

Scotch Baronial: For and Against

Mid-nineteenth-century Scotch Baronial, architecturally speaking, formed part of an international North European movement of intensification of the Picturesque. Universal 'Italian' styles were rejected in favour of more accurate national styles: for instance, in France, by a neo-Renaissance based on the Loire chateaux. For such a movement, new, national types of source publications were necessary – a need met in Scotland by a range of scholarly antiquarian inventories, which ensured that Scotland increasingly had a well-documented architectural history available to draw on. First and foremost among these was the four-volume *Baronial and Ecclesiastical Antiquities of Scotland,* published by architect Robert W. Billings in 1852.[6] Although based on accurate drawings, the finished illustrations presented dramatically shaded (and sometimes imaginatively embellished) perspectives of castles and churches. As with Adam, the subjects, even if symmetrical on plan, were presented in an irregular and asymmetrical manner, emphasizing mass and monumentality, characteristics which were to help shape the mature Scotch Baronial. Billings's survey work was assisted by advocate and historian John Hill Burton and local ministers;[7] subsidised by Burn,[8] he also befriended David Bryce, for whom he made some exhibition drawings. Burn's intervention came possibly because Bryce and his brother John had failed to publish their 1830s work on 'Sketches of Scotch and Old English Ornament'.[9] Home in London, Billings wrote regretfully of the demolition or ruination of old castellated buildings:

> We, therefore, warn Scotland of the everlasting disgrace which the neglect of her Stone Records is bringing, whether they be of ancient date or modern . . . Surely the mention of these matters should lead to a movement for results differing from the ruinous course still proceeding? Surely there should be patriotism enough in Scotland to effect something for preservation.[10]

The most popular strand of national architectural antiquarianism in those years focused not upon remote, ruined castles but upon Edinburgh Castle, and the intensification of its value as a 'national monument' – as we will see later. In 1859, military architect/engineer Francis Dollman prepared an ambitious, though unexecuted, scheme for Baronializing the castle. Dollman had studied in A. W. N. Pugin's father's classes, and, in 1861–3, published a beautifully engraved study of historic British architecture. Scotland featured prominently and respectfully – for example, in describing the view from Stirling Castle, it included what he called 'the nationally-cherished Bannockburn'.[11] The engravings differed from Billings's in being more two-dimensional and technical, with details and mouldings. The subject, Dollman explained, was 'treated not merely pictorially, but practically . . . that it should be not only useful to the Architectural profession, but also prove a valuable addition to the library of the Antiquary and the Archaeologist'.[12] The work was envisaged as an accurate aid to architectural interventions, such as that which he himself had proposed at Edinburgh; another engraving depicted the Great Hall at Stirling Castle (by then converted crudely to a multistoreyed barracks) in a hypothetical post-restoration condition.

By the middle decades of the century, the confidence and power of Scottish–British imperial culture, and the effective completion of improvement at home had both subtly altered the significance of the national, squeezing out the doubts felt by Scott and the romantics about the relation between Scottish nationality and the forces of modernity: now both could be expressed together. However, Scottish nineteenth-century architecture remained generally faithful to classicism in all its forms, with no attempt to elevate neomedievalism into a new mainstream suitable for any secular urban building use (as with the Gothic Revival in England). Thus, Scotch architecture played something of a minority role, closely associated with the success of the landed classes in perpetuating their role as a significant political and cultural power centre within the new, bourgeois-dominated society of unionist nationalism. Its key set-pieces continued to be country houses, built now for the ruling classes of Imperial Scotland, especially to the designs of Bryce, who combined Scottish and French elements in an eclectic, notionally 'Auld Alliance' synthesis of different branches of national Northern European Renaissance sources.

Paradoxically, in contrast to the regionally varied expressions of classicism across Scotland, the 'national' Baronial style was relatively homogeneous across the whole country, from the Northern Isles to Galloway (and even English Berwick). Indeed, the Scotch Baronial country house, despite its close association with the supposedly outmoded remnants of feudal society, was as much a product of cosmopolitan modernity as of national characteristics, as was acknowledged slightly later by G. S. Aitken: 'Feudalistic in character, and necessarily . . . crude in conception, it has by the talent of able modern exponents been brought up to date through the happy transfusion into it of the style of the French chateaux, with which it is nearly akin'; it had been 'refined in detail and translated into forms more appropriate to our modern ideas of domestic architecture'.[13] The Baronial patrons and designers looked on the old and new societies as diametrically opposed, but without the idealization of the former seen in the English Gothic Revival. Scots here saw their history in a negative light, characterized by failure and internecine conflict, whereas their English counterparts found a nationalistic pride in theirs. As Billings put it, 'The spots chosen as the most suitable for fortifications in the old days of family warfare, though generally selected by men who never looked at scenery, and cared for nothing but eating, drinking and fighting, have often supplied exquisite pieces of scenery, adapted entirely to our modern taste.'[14] Nor did nineteenth-century Baronial mansions follow Scott's admiration for old texture, nor spolia; there was an emphasis on precise, freestone finish, and plate glass windows.

There was vigorous debate among contemporary architects about the tension between the 'old' and 'new' connotations of Scotch Baronial. John Starforth published designs including a Baronial villa, but argued that although

> few ... [styles] ... have received a greater share of public favour in Scotland than the so-called Scotch or "Baronial" ... many of its great characteristic features are lost in consequence of the style being applied to peace and comfort instead of war and security, with which it had its origin; it produces a highly picturesque and pleasing effect; but to what extent such a modernizing of a style is proper for the advancement of architecture.[15]

Having trained with John Smith, architectural 'London Scot' Robert Kerr took up a more openly antagonistic line against Scotch Baronial, with its 'small turrets on the angles of the building, sometimes carried up from the ground, and sometimes built out on corbelling; crowstepped gables; battlemented parapets; small windows generally; the introduction almost always of a main tower; and over the whole, in one form or another, a severe, heavy, crude, castellated character ... an uncivilised style'.[16] To Kerr, Baronial signalled a past unworthy of celebration: there could be no point in 'the introduction of the old Scotch turrets for the mere sake of imitating the obsolete forms of a barbarous style'.[17] It would have been unthinkable to speak in such terms of England's (or France's) historic architecture, which as we saw had been eagerly replicated by Scots as a cultural triumph, which the union had entitled them to share. Only in the next phase of the Second Castle Age, at the end of the century, would a new movement, Traditionalism, begin to look on Scottish Renaissance castles with the same liking for 'old texture' as Scott, combined with a new strain of utopian social idealism.

Who were the patrons of this style of picturesque, national modernity? As we saw in previous chapters, landowners' attempts to appropriate the new Ossianic images of Scotland had become ever more closely linked with architectural images of castellated lineage. Mid-nineteenth-century Baronial works would be commissioned both by the established aristocracy, such as the Duke of Atholl (patron of Bryce's 1869–76 alterations to Blair Castle) and by the newly rich, such as chemical manufacturer Charles Tennant (patron of Bryce's The Glen, 1855–60) or opium trader Alexander Matheson (patron of Alexander Ross's Ardross, 1880–1). For businessmen who set out to build out of income rather than capital, the characteristic Baronial project of accretional additions to an existing house was highly suitable. In all these respects, we see distinct echoes of the castellated originals of the sixteenth- and seventeenth-century First Castle Age, and (although the nineteenth century did not know it) of their patrons – even if the wider context had changed radically with the onrush of Improvement and imperialism.

The 'Victorian' Castle

This distinct element of continuity in the patronage of castellated architecture was further accentuated by the strong legitimizing role played by the monarchy, and by the ever-increasing emphasis on Jacobite and Highland symbolism. During the mid-nineteenth century, the concept of Scotch Romanticism set out and elaborated by Sir Walter Scott was hugely reinforced through its enthusiastic appropriation by the monarchy – initially through a continuation and extension into the Highlands of the 'new tradition' of symbolically laden visitations in the 1840s, and then, in the 1850s, through the construction by Queen Victoria and Prince Albert of a 'Highland home' in a mature castellated style. From that point, the status of Scotch Baronial as the established architectural expression of landed authority was unchallenged, and it was able to significantly extend its reach into other neighbouring building types.

Prime Minister Melbourne reported to Queen Victoria that the Eglinton Tournament had been 'a great absurdity'.[18] But as 1822 had shown, historical pageants and their architectural stage settings also served a serious purpose, by enabling 'history' to be managed, stressing hierarchy, birthright, aristocracy and monarchy. A nebulous background role in the further elaboration of the ethos of 'royal Scotch' pageantry in the early nineteenth century was also played by the two mysterious 'Sobieski Stuart' brothers – artists and self-publicists – who had insinuated themselves into rich Highland society by around 1819, as princely descendants of the royal Stuarts, and had significantly helped in the revival of the Highland dress before the 1822 royal visit.[19] During the 1820s and 1830s, they had moved from one aristocratic Highland house to another, culminating after 1839,[20] when Lord Lovat housed them in a specially built, crowstepped house on the isle of Eilean Aigas in the Beauly River, possibly designed by William Burn.[21] They had 'fitted it up in imitation of the style in which Highland chieftains were wont to decorate their rooms in times of yore'.[22] In the late 1840s, however, their make-believe world was exposed, and they eventually moved to London.[23] The brothers' most notable publication, encouraged by Eglinton Tournament veteran and pageant enthusiast Dick Lauder,[24] was *Vestiarium Scoticum* (1842),[25] which provided castle builders with the necessary costume for use in their castles.

In 1842, the pace of royal pageantry quickened significantly, beginning with a ball at Buckingham Palace where Victoria and Albert dressed as the merciful Queen Philippa and warrior king Edward III, he being the epitome of English chivalry and manhood. In August of that year, Victoria announced she was *'very anxious* to visit Scotland', and a tour itinerary was duly set up, the prime mover being someone we have already met: George Gordon, 4th Earl of Aberdeen, laird of Haddo, a leading politician (notably as prime minister 1852–5), antiquarian and scholar.[26] Aberdeen held strong Jacobite sympathies, and on his Grand Tour in 1803 had sought out Prince Charles Edward Stuart's widow, the Countess of Albany, in Rome.[27] Connected to Lord Breadalbane's family by marriage, he orchestrated the royal tour to Taymouth in 1842,[28] and later introduced the artist James Giles to the Balmoral project. Aberdeen had as we saw supported Giles from around 1830, and commissioned him to record the historic castles of Aberdeenshire with archaeologically accurate paintings.[29] As at Prince Leopold's Highland holiday of 1819 (which had included visiting Taymouth),[30] and King George's visit in 1822, tartan-clad pageantry was central to the 1842 royal visit; and as in 1822, Holyroodhouse was used for the inaugural theatricals. From Berwick onwards, boats and sightseers came to meet the royal vessel; one dressed as if from a pageant 'for the entertainment of royal personages in ancient times',[31] others playing 'Scotch reels', and at Dunbar Castle, 'the union-jack of England fluttered in the breeze'.[32] The visit was a holiday, and thus the royals avoided the foundation stone laying ceremony for the new Church of Scotland General Assembly Hall ('the Victoria Hall as the building is henceforward to be called'),[33] waving at the ceremony instead as they passed to and from the Castle.[34] This was the beginning of a tour to the Highlands: at Dunkeld, for instance, Glenlyon turned out 700–800 tartan-uniformed Highlanders,[35] and Clan Menzies acted out 'ancient' hierarchical and lineal social ranking with a private clan army of 200 men officered by landowners, under their chief.[36] They marched to Taymouth, bagpipes playing the 'March of Clan Menzies'.[37]

However, the most complex display of Highlandism was at Taymouth Castle, which was fitted out with elaborately neomedieval pageantry to receive the royal guests.[38] As it happened, Taymouth was in the closing stages of an elaborate enlargement of 1837–42, with a new tower-wing by Gillespie Graham, with sumptuous interiors by Pugin;[39] these included a Gothic-windowed 'Baronial Hall', and a library in the area that would be used as the royal apartment[40] (Figure 8.1). The library ceiling possibly echoed Crosby Hall, of which Pugin's father had published drawings.[41] Interior work was by the London firm of Crace (one of Pugin's closest collaborators,[42] who subcontracted work to Trotter of Edinburgh), with much 'Gothic ornament', armour, and neomedieval weaponry.[43] In the 'Baronial Hall', Crace executed ninety ceiling compartments 'illustrating the Descent of the House of Breadalbane through the Blood Royal of Scotland & England The Lords of the Isles & the Lords of Lorne'.[44] The 'Sobieski Stuarts' had made a great impression on Pugin, who 'grew up with Walter Scott's novels',[45] and whose own father had also bemoaned a lost aristocratic past, lost in the French Revolution, claiming to be *'le Comte de Pugin'*.[46]

FIGURE 8.1 *Taymouth Castle – Banner Hall by James Gillespie Graham and A. W. N. Pugin, c. 1840; photograph dated 1997.* © *Historic Environment Scotland. https://canmore.org.uk/collection/1101727*

Having finished work at Taymouth, in 1842, Pugin visited Lord Lovat, who wanted to restore Beauly Priory as a neo-Catholic centre, and, while there, called on the 'princes' at Eilean Aigas. Pugin was attracted both by them and by their home, 'on a most romantic island surrounded by waterfalls & rocks in a vast glen between the mountains', adding that the elder brother 'has fitted up a gothic room'.[47] Pugin had as we saw contributed to Scotland's programme of anti-classical national architecture, soon to be exemplified by Balmoral, and this correspondingly excited his burgeoning preoccupation with the revival of Gothic as England's national style.[48]

Preparations for the Taymouth visit and ceremonial had been frantic, with agents trawling Edinburgh and elsewhere for the necessary paraphernalia. John MacKenzie wrote to Breadalbane: 'I have been promised six Lochaber Axes, which are all I can hear of in town. That number however will be sufficient for the Sentries to be mounted at the castle.'[49] The sudden need for tartan could not be met; the Bannockburn tartan manufacturers had to refuse an order from Lord Willoughby.[50] As in the case of the Eglinton tournament, the crowd at Taymouth was required to take the role of 'extras', by dressing as peasantry – the men in kilt and plaid, women ideally in white gown and tartan scarf.[51] The main day's event delighted the royal couple; tartan, military displays, dancing, piping; people dressed as shepherds and foresters, all exotic to the visitors.[52] A new aspect was the presence of the press, who sought and were provided with reporting facilities, allowing Highlandism to become far better known.[53] The royal couple viewed the pageantry from a platform on the main block's east side, which led from the great drawing room; the latter's corner turret, only a generation old, was called the Stuart Tower, highlighting Victoria's Scottish Jacobite credentials. The party ended with a voyage across Loch Tay. The little fleet rowed to Auchmore with two pipers at the bow of the royal vessel, which Crace had refashioned, the crew in sailors' gear,[54] and people singing Gaelic songs, all to the royal couple's delight.[55]

Victoria's impression confirmed the pageant's success – it 'seemed like the reception in olden feudal times, of the Sovereign by a chieftain. It was truly princely & romantic'.[56] Victoria reported the Taymouth visit to her mother: 'We have heard nothing but Bagpipes since we have been in the *beautiful* Highlands, & I am become so fond of it, that I mean to have a *Piper*.'[57] In 1843 Victoria engaged Angus MacKay to the new-made position of Queen's piper.[58] Immediately on his return to Windsor, Albert wrote to the Duchess of Saxe-Gotha, praising the beauty and people of the Highlands: 'Scotland has made a most favourable impression upon us both ... There is, moreover, no country where historical traditions are preserved with such fidelity, or to the same extent. Every spot is connected with some interesting historical fact, and with most of these Sir Walter Scott's accurate descriptions have made us familiar.'[59] For Albert's biographer Theodore Martin, the 1842 visit to Scotland had implicit anti-Radical political overtones, as it 'had been attended with the happiest results. While cementing the attachment of a large section of the people to the Sovereign, it had shown the truly insignificant proportions of the party, who, under the name of Chartism, were clamouring for revolutionary change'.[60] The imagery and impact of the holiday sent out a subliminal architectural royal message too; the royal couple would now find less interest in visiting neoclassical mansions. They liked neomedieval castles, and this aligned with the wish among elites to have Scott-inspired neocastellated homes for themselves – buildings which were both Scottish and therefore British. The couple's delight in the Romantic imagery was recreated for their next visits to Scotland, leading them to a decision to acquire a holiday home in the Highlands.

In the wake of the 1842 visit, efforts began to reorientate Holyroodhouse as a permanent focus of the new Scotch monarchical cult. These attempts were fronted by Lord Breadalbane, who, in 1844 planned to historicize his own Holyroodhouse apartment with a demountable carved oak neo-Elizabethan interior, complete with an 'Elizabethan Hall' and screen,[61] obtained from Samuel Pratt, the Eglinton supplier of 1839.[62] Whether this project was realized or not, this highlighted a problem with the Scotch Baronial. Authentic ancient Scottish interiors had not survived well. It was easier to reference England, by creating an 'Elizabethan' interior within the Stuarts' Holyroodhouse. The mounting pressure to evict Holyroodhouse's tenants had led the Duke of Hamilton to relocate from the north-west tower to the north quarter in 1852; in 1854, the 'Historical Apartments' in that tower, associated with Mary Queen of Scots, were opened to the public. The rights of the Earl of Haddington as hereditary park keeper were bought out in 1843, and in 1855–7 St Anthony's Loch was created, and lodges built – all signalling royal interest and presence. The royal apartment in the south and east quarters was brought into royal service, but its disposition was ignored, the spaces made to serve contemporary attitudes, including a newly created 'throne room'. A new royal apartment was created in 1871, but barely used.[63]

'Our Highland Queen': The Building of Balmoral

The symbolic role of Holyroodhouse was altogether eclipsed by the next stage in Queen Victoria's Highland involvement, when the queen acquired a Highland holiday estate, Balmoral, in 1848. Albert wanted a property which was personally his – unlike the state-owned palaces – while the political value of a Scottish royal presence was also clear. Here, again, the couple's friend, Lord Aberdeen, played a key role. Balmoral House had been rebuilt for his brother, Sir Robert Gordon, in 1834–9 by architect John Smith, in a simplified Scotch style derived from that of William Burn, with curvilinear gables and crowsteps. Gordon was a Romanticist, having Gordon tartan carpets in his house, and a personal prizewinning piper.[64] After his death in 1847, Aberdeen inherited the lease of Balmoral, and duly passed it on to the royals. On 8 August 1848, Victoria and Albert reached Balmoral. She documented her first impressions, praising the house as a 'pretty little castle in the old Scottish style' . . . 'It was so calm & so solitary . . . that it did one good & seemed to breathe freedom & peace making one forget the world & its sad turmoil.'[65] This fondness only grew in intensity; from Windsor, for example, she wrote about her 'homesickness for my beloved Highlands, the air – the life, the liberty'.[66] Balmoral reminded Albert of the Thüringer Wald.[67] He was likewise enthralled by the scenery, privacy and solitude; he had loved hunting, particularly since visiting Taymouth (when he had exclaimed that he had 'never spent a few hours more pleasantly in all his life').[68] The old castle, however, was too small, lacked privacy, faced the wrong way, and was rather plain in style. They took ownership in 1851, considered enlarging it, but decided instead to demolish it and build a new castle at the site.

The new Balmoral would be more emphatically 'Scottish', not least in its explicit use of the Scotch Baronial style, and in its explicit dedication to the elite pastime of hunting. Prince Albert himself had been born and brought up in one of the earliest neo-Gothic castles in Germany, Rosenau Castle, near Coburg (rebuilt 1808–17), and he and Victoria had in 1845 visited the castellated Rhineland showpiece of Stolzenfels (on which see Chapter 7). At Balmoral, Prince Albert as client played a central role in the design process but, for authenticity, he engaged local architects John (who soon died) and William Smith to provide the technical aspects of design and supervise the building work. Inscriptions state that the project was the responsibility of Prince Albert; as Victoria confirmed, 'all the creation of my dear Albert'.[69] The hunting allusions of a St Hubertus sculpture and a 'Jäger's [huntsman's] Room', and family crests emphasized this. Perhaps because of this close involvement by the patron, the new Balmoral did not excite widespread approval among architects, and was described in uncomplimentary terms by John Smith's former trainee, Robert Kerr.[70] But Balmoral was one of the defining moments in the Scotch Baronial and in Scotland's relations with the establishment: no clearer evidence exists than Balmoral to demonstrate that the Second Castle Age was a 'British nationalist' movement. Balmoral, the seat of 'Our Highland Queen' – the name of a strathspey composed by James Scott Skinner[71] – evidenced both the new royal commitment to 'Romantic Scotland', and the central role of the Highlands in that strategy – although, ironically, the architectural style upon which Baronial was based was really a Lowland style.

The new Balmoral was built in 1853–6 (Figure 8.2). It comprised two blocks – main, and service – each with central courtyard, and linked by a massive eighty-feet-high square tower with tourelles – possibly referencing fortified German city gateways such as those of Coburg, Albert's 'home town' (Albert had wanted its low windows to resemble gunholes); the tower's prominence was enhanced by placing it alongside the low-level connecting wing. The 'back entrance' was in the tower, beyond which was the Jäger's room. The main house was quadrangular, having outward-facing rooms and an inner perimeter of passages lit by an enclosed courtyard, all resembling Toddington, or Longleat. The main south front recalled Abbotsford, having

FIGURE 8.2 *Balmoral Castle by William Smith for Prince Albert and Queen Victoria, 1853–6 – view from south; undated photograph.* © *Historic Environment Scotland. https://canmore.org.uk/file/image/1201441*

a Linlithgow-type porch at the left fronting a tower, corbelled-out and gabled flat window bays, with a balancing turret on the right hand corner (which serviced the prime minister's room). That 'public' front contained visitors' rooms within its repetitive three-storey range, while the left hand tower cleverly carried the composition round to the two-storey west and north wings, where the private royal rooms were. Internally, most of the rooms were of a plain, rather classical style. However, a Tudor-arched ballroom, flamboyantly decorated with stags' heads – an afterthought, replacing an iron ballroom of 1851 – was tucked into the private northeast inner corner, and there the royals could participate in 'Highland life' by dancing with estate workers – something unthinkable in their normal lives, and showing they were on holiday in an exotic environment among loyal supporters.

The north-east-born architect Robert Kerr contrasted in 1864 the 'medievalism' of Balmoral's style with its planning, which displayed an 'obvious desire to provide that regular disposition of throughfare lines which is so important a means of convenience, and . . . that simple rectangularity of partition which belongs to good plain modern rooms'.[72] To Kerr, Balmoral was an 'Elizabethan Manor-house'[73] in its 'diagonal' plan, recalling recent neo-Tudor houses in the way its service court connected with the main house at one corner only.[74] Overall, its Burn-like combination of rationalistic planning and loosely picturesque elevations also recalled the old John Smith house, as well as Burn houses such as Auchmacoy, 1831, and Smith's Forglen, 1839. The west front, in particular, resembled Burn's Scotch work, and it faced westwards along the Dee valley, recalling the view from Albert's bedroom window at Rosenau, his childhood home. Iconography alluded to Albert's own family (on the south faces), UK union (the thistle and rose; arms with the English quarterings; statues of Saints Andrew and George), and St Hubertus, patron saint of hunters. Contrasting with these 'ancient' references, Albert required a modern fireproof construction after Windsor Castle was burned in 1853, and he installed a fire extinguishing system fed from a hillside water tank.

The Balmoral project formed part of a network of romantic royal castle projects across Europe, several influential examples having been built only a few years beforehand. For example, in 1838, King Ferdinand II of Portugal acquired an old Hieronymite monastery at Sintra and, with the help of German engineer Baron Wilhelm Ludwig von Eschwege, began to convert it into the fantastic hilltop palace of La Pena, the climax of early nineteenth-century Romanticism in Portugal, with its fusion of Manueline and Moorish architecture; he added an array of new rooms after 1843, and crowned the complex with a profusion of exotic turrets and towers.[75] Likewise, both Victoria and Albert had long delighted in castles. Each had grown up reading Scott's novels; Albert, himself brought up in 'Romantic' Rosenau, came from a family which delighted in neomedievalism, and Balmoral was partly a consequence of their own Romanticism. Then, in turn, other monarchs visited Balmoral and took their experience of Scotch castellation back home with them. Royal sanction of Baronial by 'the Queen of England' conferred on Scottish castles a new, internationally prestigious aura. It is difficult to assess how far Ludwig II of Bavaria's decision to build Neuschwanstein (from 1868) was inspired by Balmoral, or by Scott; or how far Viollet-le-Duc's ambitious castle projects – such as Emperor Napoleon III's (crowstepped) Pierrefonds, reconstructed from 1857 – were encouraged by it. But Balmoral was the certain source of the design of Alatskivi, in Estonia, built from 1876 by Baron Arved George de Nolcken;[76] Alatskivi has the distinctive Abbotsford-derived features of tower-house and porch, juxtaposed with a square-based polygonal turret opposite.

Within Scotland, the impact of projects for Queen Victoria was more immediate. In 1842, for example, the Conservative prime minister, Robert Peel, had dissuaded the royal couple from visiting Dunrobin, the castle of the Whig-supporting Duke and Duchess of Sutherland, on her Highland visit.[77] After the duchess, a friend of the queen, witnessed the Taymouth pageant, the Sutherlands set out to make Dunrobin into an improved Taymouth, and engaged Charles Barry in 1844 to design a semipolygonal complex with three broadly south-facing segments, featuring Burn-like tourelle roofs, Heriot's references, and a corbelled-to-square stair: a central

FIGURE 8.3 *Dunrobin Castle – north entrance front as remodelled by Charles Barry and William Leslie after 1844; undated photograph taken prior to fire of 1915.* © Historic Environment Scotland. https://canmore.org.uk/file/image/686521

oriel denoted the 'Queen's Bedroom' (eventually used by Victoria on a visit in 1872) (Figure 8.3). The entrance was set within a tower-house resembling the Victoria Tower at the Houses of Parliament, although also sporting a vigorous French roof, while to its right was a Big Ben-like clock tower, both recast by R. S. Lorimer in 1915 after a fire.[78]

From Burn to Bryce: The Emergence of the High Baronial Country House

The new, mature Scotch Baronial – the climactic phase of the Second Castle Age – was not chiefly the responsibility of Billings, although he built several projects in an angularly hard-edged style, including a warehouse at 115–137 Ingram Street, Glasgow (1854–6); the reconstruction of Dalzell House, Motherwell (from 1859) and of Castle Wemyss (from 1860) in a serrated, almost Pilkington-like manner; and additions to the King's Old Building within Stirling Castle (1857). Instead, the pivotal figure in this confident mid-nineteenth-century architectural expression of continuing landed prestige was David Bryce, heir to Burn's vast Scottish country-house practice.

William Burn had moved to London in 1844, becoming one of the English elite's most sought-after architects. His English and Irish output was mostly English revival or Classical, but he frequently squeezed in

Scottish references, notably buckle quoins at, for instance, the Second Earl of Harrowby's neo-Jacobean Sandon Hall (1852–5). Burn's most Scotch English building was Fonthill Abbey (1856–9), for the Second Marquess of Westminster. The intention in 1850 was for an enormous mansion, with a colossal Scotch entrance tower on its flank, rather foreshadowing that of Balmoral.[79] The executed design was scaled-down, but crow-stepped with bartizans. From 1838 to 1854, Burn and Bryce worked together at Harlaxton Manor, one of the most monumental set-pieces of early Victorian eclecticism in England, completing the mansion begun in 1837 by the John Paterson-trained Anthony Salvin. Burn and Bryce added neo-Jacobean, Baroque and other elements to the neo-Elizabethan concept of Salvin and his client, Gregory Gregory – notably the stables (probably by Burn) and orangery; gateways, forecourt and terraces (probably largely by Bryce).[80] Bryce appears to have been responsible for the interiors; above all, the Great Hall, and the South German Baroque Cedar Staircase, early illustrations of Bryce's enthusiasm for a flamboyantly plastic approach that would energize mid-century Scotch Baronial with a new sculptural vigour, and which had already been hinted at in the Dalkeith conservatory of 1832–4. Much of Harlaxton's detailing, despite its notionally Renaissance or Baroque style, would reappear in Bryce's Scotch domestic interiors and garden structures, including studded pilasters (at Castlemilk), tapered balusters or pilasters/square columns (Torosay) and key-blocked arches (Ballikinrain), while Burn's own now-extended experience of English historic styles possibly helped encourage his move to London in 1844.

In Scotland, Bryce steadily became more and more predominant in the country-house field. Having first joined Burn as an assistant around 1825, he became his partner from 1841 until 1850,[81] but soon he was designing houses himself, sometimes using his home address in Castle Street as distinct from the practice address at 131 George Street: Burn's own house, and latterly Bryce's. His politics were less explicitly articulated than Burn's, but he too became favoured by the wealthy landowning elite. Bryce's first house design was possibly Newton Hall (1829), a Burn-like design with L-plan fronts.[82] Cassilis House was extended 1830–2 for the Earl of Cassilis, possibly in a Bryce scheme designed while working in Burn's office.[83] An L-plan entrance front was added, with steps both externally and internally to the *piano nobile*; another extension had projecting square and canted bays. By 1849, Burn and Bryce were working as open rivals at Ladykirk House, Burn claiming his scheme would 'be more easily executed and at much less expense than Mr Bryce's'.[84]

Architecturally, Bryce's early grounding with Burn was predominantly classical in orientation, and many of his best known works are impressively Loire-school or baroque, while some of his baronial compositions retained strong elements of classical symmetry (such as the garden front of Craigends, 1857). The subtler nuances of the transition between the two were discernible in a succession of late 1830s/40s houses, including

House of Falkland, 1839–44.[85] The client was Onesiphorus Tyndall-Bruce, and the style was a hybrid English Jacobean and Scotch. The design was also reminiscent of Burn's contemporary Stoke Rochford, of 1841–3, and resembled Harlaxton in its florid Renaissance/Baroque interiors. Tellingly, correspondence of 1841 suggests that Bryce radically aggrandized the initial plasterwork designs without Burn's knowledge, and that the older architect had only reluctantly acquiesced in their increased exuberance.[86] By 1850, the Burn–Bryce partnership had been dissolved, and Bryce wrote to Tyndall-Bruce expressing his hope the latter would continue to employ him;[87] his sole name appears in the subsequent records, taking decisions or communicating directly with the client's agent.[88] Redcastle, a big tower-house with an L-plan front, a onetime MacKenzie property, became the property of Sir William Fettes – whose Franco-Scotch posthumous set-piece at Fettes College in Edinburgh we will return to later[89] – and then of former slave-owner Colonel Hugh Duncan Baillie MP, the Lord Lieutenant of Ross-shire, who commissioned a new scheme for it in 1840, from Burn,[90] using the compensation money he had received following the Slavery Abolition Act (1833).[91] Burn and Bryce Baronialized it, adding a Taymouth-like cloister which doubled as a terrace, and Pinkie bartizans.

As we saw in the previous chapter, Burn was often faced with the problem of seeking neo-Tudor-like ground-level main floors for conversions to piano nobile-structures whose established floor levels were too expensive to change. This (as we saw at Lauriston and Tyninghame) led him to introduce as one option technically daring first floor stone terraces, so the piano nobile rooms could access the exterior directly. By a further extension, these evolved into balconies, as seen in later Bryce houses such as Craigends. In the area of architectural detail, buildings the Burn practice had worked on provided specific and authentic details for revival on houses whose form was decidedly of their own time. For instance, at Stenhouse (1836), Burn and Bryce had revived the formula of a stilted crowstepped gable set between identical bartizans, often later used by Bryce – as was the 1570s window-surround detailing of Castle Menzies, with its elaborately variegated shafts and pilasters (repeated, e.g., at Seacliffe and Hartrigge).

Bryce's spell as chief clerk and (1841–50) partner to Burn had comprehensively trained him in the planning and practical building of country houses. Some of his own early designs continued Burn's low and rather sprawling Baronial style: for example, Tollcross (1848) or Ormiston Hall (1851). But by the early 1840s Bryce was already moving towards a more dynamic and heavily modelled Scotch Baronial. The key transitional design was that for Seacliffe House (1841). Here Bryce transformed an original plan by Burn into a more sculptural grouping, augmenting it with turrets and bay windows. The next decisive stage was reached at Balfour Castle, Shapinsay, Orkney (1846–50), where Colonel David Balfour, heir to a fortune made in India, commissioned Bryce to massively enlarge a 'neat little villa',[92] superimposing on it a battlemented and crowstepped block of public rooms. This design included for the first time one of the most characteristic of Bryce's 'trademarks' – a canted bay window corbelled out to a straight gable above. At Balfour, only the dining and drawing rooms were garden-facing, the rooms being arranged in an L-plan and the library accessed from the head of the entrance corridor.

Bryce's main series of country houses exemplified the capacity of the nineteenth century's eclectic modernity to adapt familiar old motifs to new uses and combinations, and to combine them with completely new features such as gas lighting and plate glass windows. Bryce's earlier Baronial works had drawn chiefly on historic models from places where he and Burn had worked. But Billings's engravings transformed his Baronial designs, as he quarried them for what became almost trademark elements such as Fyvie centrepieces and Castle Fraser round towers.[93] To these were added new combinations of these 'old' elements, notably the projecting bay corbelled to square below the gable (as at Hartrigge, 1852), which converted English-looking bay windows into a more Scottish form.

Within Bryce's country-house oeuvre, three basic plan-types predominated. The first was a mainstream of large Baronial complexes, grounded ultimately in the Burn tradition, and laid out in a fairly irregular manner with some symmetrical elements. The second was a new trend of large houses with more distinctly symmetrical planning (perhaps with garden front end gables), including elements from the early French Renaissance; and the third was a succession of small, compact houses. These varied plan-permutations, with their extensive service facilities and their careful segregation of functions, and their plans very frequently based on accretions to an existing core, arguably represent both a strong manifestation of elite Victorian modernity, and at the same time a continuation and culmination of planning developmental tendencies stretching back to the Scottish Renaissance – although that period's most prestigious plan-type, the courtyard palace, was no longer so relevant or popular in the nineteenth-century age of segregation and privacy.

In the development of the first, mainstream Baronial category, Bryce embraced and remained loyal to some of the general formulae evolved by Burn, as was clear in his L-plan facades and much-mullioned projecting bays, while pushing fashion far beyond Burn's cautious, and somewhat English-looking designs of the 1820s, with explicit replication of some of Renaissance Scotland's more flamboyant set-pieces. Playfair's pride in having introduced a historic English style into Scotland's capital at Donaldson's Hospital was now replaced by an insistence on the importance of celebrating Scotland's past. In these Bryce houses, the focus is normally a massive tower, or high, castellated range. This might be a 'real', old tower which Bryce was adding to, or a part of a new composition, on the model established by Gillespie Graham's tower at Brodick (1844), or Playfair's at Stonefield (1836). The tower section is normally part of an asymmetrical entrance front, while the garden-front may instead be symmetrical; if new, the tower normally is based on one of the major seventeenth-century castellated set-pieces, such as the round tower of Huntly or Castle Fraser, the arched towers of Fyvie, or the tall oriel-gabled tower of Maybole. At both Hartrigge (rebuilt 1854) and The Glen (1855–60), the dominant feature is a Maybole-pattern tower; The Glen features in addition a Meggernie-like 'tower-house' block, recessed from the symmetrical garden facade. In his house planning, Bryce favoured the Burn formula of a corridor plan.[94] Where scale precluded that option, then the rooms would often be set in an L-plan disposition, or a spiral, as at Carradale. He combined that with the idea of important spaces having projecting or canted bays, and so on these outer rooms Bryce added bay windows, either corbelled (sometimes, like Pittendreich, twice-corbelled) or chamfered to square. In some larger houses, there was enough space to add a conservatory at the south-west corner, entered from the drawing room (e.g. Seacliffe Castle).

In the late 1850s and 1860s, Bryce's mainstream of irregularly planned Scotch Baronial country houses reached its climax in a series of very large commissions. The first and most flamboyant of these was Craigends (1857–9), built for Alexander Cunninghame. Here, Bryce deftly balanced an overall rich eclecticism with an appropriate emphasis on the key elements of the building. The entrance facade had a massive, Fyvie-type entrance tower at one end, far more highly compressed than the Seton Tower original, built of smooth freestone rather than harled rubble, and bristling with additional details such as a balcony, a square balustraded tower behind, cast-iron ornamentation, and mullioned plate-glass windows. Balancing this at the far end of the entrance facade was a Maybole-type tower, here playing a subsidiary role; the garden front was symmetrical, and flanked by two gables. At the slightly later Ballikinrain (from 1864) for Sir Archibald Orr Ewing, another giant Huntly/Fraser corbelled-out round tower provides a fulcrum linking asymmetrical garden and entrance facades; the garden front features a busy conglomeration of gables and bay windows, while the stable block has a Fettes-like clock-tower. At Castlemilk (also from 1864), for Sir Robert Jardine of Hong Kong, a Fraser-style round tower was the focal feature, here with a porte-cochere and juxtaposed with a plain, flat-fronted main block: a blatant, stark suggestion of Baronial accretion. More severe designs among these principal Bryce works included Glenapp (1870), and the re-Baronialized Blair Castle (1869–76), expunging the classical 1740s scheme with a restrained sprinkling of turrets, heightened walls, new Fyvie arch, and new entrance hall lined with the weaponry of the Duke of Atholl's private army[95] (Figure 8.4). Fyvie itself was extended by Bryce's nephew, John Bryce: in 1890 he designed the new Leith Tower, with Huntly-type oriels.

In smaller houses, where sometimes a pre-existing structure restricted options, the plan was necessarily compacted, following Burn's precedent, but even here, bay windows, usually corbelled-to-square, were typically applied to the drawing and dining rooms. Sometimes, rubble masonry was used, as at Shambellie (1856), with cheaper small-paned sash windows

FIGURE 8.4 *Blair Atholl Castle – perspective drawing by David Bryce, 1869, proposing its conversion from a classical to a Scotch Baronial house.* © Historic Environment Scotland. *https://canmore.org.uk/collection/1093086*

and relatively few turrets and excrescences; Keiss (1859–62) was harled to conform to an earlier core. At Stronvar (1850), also rubble-built, a simple tripartite-plan laird's house was incorporated at the back; here Bryce used the old Burn idea of setting an internal stair beyond the entrance door to access the piano nobile. Inside, a central top-lit stairhall gave access to the various main spaces radiating off it. The same applied at Leny (1845–6), but here, more distinctively, the entrance was in a turret set in the inner angle between the old house and the new – and on a splayed orientation, as at Playfair's Craigcrook. Here, though, there was no pre-existing piano nobile to accommodate, and so the entrance could be at ground level – but the landscape was contoured to give the impression of a traditional, elevated piano nobile in views from the distant approach and the garden front.

Alongside this mainstream of development, the period from the mid-1850s also saw the emergence of a new Franco-Scotch Baronialism of high-roofed, spired castles, which evoked the closeness of the two countries' architectures in the early Renaissance years: Billings had claimed that Scottish Renaissance castles had been influenced by 'the airy turrets and fantastic tracery of France'.[96] Although the previous idea of 'the Auld Alliance' between France and Scotland had fallen from favour during the eighteenth and nineteenth centuries, the architectural links between Scottish and French Renaissance architecture were clear. The new Franco-Scotch style was rather more muscularly eclectic in character. As in neo-Renaissance nineteenth-century chateaux in France, these projects were usually symmetrical in plan and elevation, resulting in a return to the Adam principle of symmetrical plans and asymmetrical silhouettes. The symmetrical tendencies of the Scottish Renaissance originals were obviously a stimulus: already, in 1840–41, Bryce and Burn had embellished the spiky, towered skyline of Thirlestane with further turrets and flanking wings, and a frontal ogee-roofed central tower, creating a much more boldly pyramidal composition.

At Kinnaird (Angus),[97] Bryce in 1853–9 recast a castellated James Playfair house of 1785–93 in a Blois-like manner, with Scottish details; the central building was refaced and given dramatically tall roofs, and the south front, facing a symmetrical garden, was converted into the main facade. The client was James Carnegie, sixth Earl of Southesk, writer, poet, and antiquary, who, aged twenty-two, 'retired' from a military career in 1849 to succeed as laird. Southesk's family had lost its title for its role in the 1715 Rising, but in 1855 he successfully secured its restoration, and in 1869, on Gladstone's recommendation, he was made a knight of the Thistle, becoming Baron Balinhard of Farnell: he was also a leading Fellow of the Society of Antiquaries of Scotland.[98] As a descendant of a family which had challenged the new monarchy militarily but which now exemplified the Scotch establishment, esteeming the national past and building in a style hinting at Scotland's ancient anti-English alliance, Southesk exemplified the many-sided character of mid-Victorian unionist nationalism. Over a decade later, Bryce's enlargement of Cortachy Castle in 1870 for the Fifth Earl of Airlie was likewise focused on a new, symmetrical entrance facade, whose high roofs gave it an almost overpowering mass; the old house was tucked away to one side. The climax of this tendency, and the most triumphant Scottish contribution to Second Empire monumental eclecticism as a whole, was not, however, a country house, but a large private school in the capital, Fettes College (1864–70) – as we will see later.

Baronial Beyond Bryce

Bryce's Baronial country houses exerted a pervasive national influence during the heyday of the Second Castle Age, especially through the work of his pupils: David Walker lists twenty-five.[99] Off to Glasgow would go John T. Rochead and Thomas Turnbull; to Aberdeen, Marshall MacKenzie and J. B. Pirie; to Perth, Andrew Heiton; while others like Charles Kinnear and W. H. Beattie would set up practice in Edinburgh. Others who trained with Bryce included Campbell Walker, Wardrop, Morham and J. M. Henry. As a result, Scotch Baronial became a body of architecture which, like Bryce's own domestic oeuvre, spanned the whole country, without regard for geographical distinctions. While the latter was unusual for the mid-nineteenth century, the era of landed supremacy in the seventeenth and eighteenth centuries had, after all, preceded the urban explosion and the entrenchment of the East–West cultural polarity. Baronial houses by these former pupils included Rochead's Levenford House, Dumbarton (1853), the hard-edged, simplified Vogrie House, by Heiton (1875), or Wardrop's chateau-like enlargement of Callendar House (1869–77). Other large-scale Baronial castles included Ross & Macbeth's Skibo Castle in Sutherland (1900, for Andrew Carnegie, incorporating an 1880 house by Clarke & Bell); and J. Gillespie Graham's Ayton (1846–51), a massively towered castle built for William Mitchell-Innes of the Royal Bank of Scotland, whose wealth he inherited from, reportedly, Scotland's richest commoner.[100]

Although Scotch Baronial was clearly a movement that had originated in Edinburgh, it increasingly found popularity in the West of Scotland, where the clients might just as often be Liberal-leaning industrialists setting themselves up as lairds. As was the case with Burn and Bryce, many of these were enriched by the markets of empire, or were pro-establishment politicians. Among the architects most engaged with Scotch Baronial were the former David Hamilton apprentices, Charles Wilson and Rochead, as well as Hamilton's son-in-law, James Smith, and John Burnet the elder. The shipbuilder, Robert Napier, built the massive West Shandon (1851–8, by Rochead; published by Kerr),[101] which followed the Abbotsford model of placing a tower on the left of the main front, with a smaller but balancing tower on the right; in its plan, it followed the Burn 'corridor plan' model, with the main rooms facing the garden, and also like Abbotsford, its tower had a lofty caphouse. It further showed the influence of the Houses of Parliament, the main tower resembling the Victoria Tower, and the smaller tower Big Ben (following Dunrobin), the detailing otherwise a combination of Playfair and Bryce. Rochead's Levenford House (1853) was more explicitly Scotch than West Shandon, and a more idiosyncratic design than Bryce's formulae; while his Blairvadach for Sir James Anderson, Lord Provost of Glasgow 1848–51, had two front towers, one an overscaled version of Winton's.[102] Elsewhere in the west, Auchendennan (1864–6) has a Castle Fraser tower, while nearby Arden House, 1868, for Glasgow's Lord Provost, Sir James Lumsden, also designed by John Burnet the elder, has a forest of spiky roofline features, all composed around a 'tower-house'.[103]

A new phenomenon that reached maturity in the high Baronial years was an amplified presence for the gate lodge. Some were gatehouses, rather than lodges with gateways, sometimes with a barmkin-like archway over the driveway, signalling that a castle lay beyond. Dunecht has twinned tower-houses as gate lodges. Ballindalloch's gatehouse (1850–53), by Thomas Mackenzie and James Matthews, was a tower-house, with 'barmkin' gateway. At Castle Grant, the East Lodge (1864) was scaled and decorated almost like a tower-house with high walls and a massive castellated archway of 1864 alongside, and a similarly castellated railway bridge (1863) by Joseph Mitchell opposite.[104]

The mid-nineteenth century's requirement for more accurate national historical styles posed a problem for interior design in Scotch Baronial houses. The Adam formula of castellated exterior and classical interior no longer seemed appropriate, yet as we saw, there existed no accurate records of original Scottish interiors. Even if there had been records, the 'originals', with their tapestries, stools and chests, and small windows, would have appeared too sparse and gloomy for mid- nineteenth-century taste. In response, a new, eclectic Baronial interior style emerged, enlivened by details developed at Harlaxton and elsewhere. The architectural shell was treated in a massive, somewhat primitive manner, with unpainted stone fireplaces and pitch pine timberwork, and plastered or rubble walls crowned by seventeenth-century-style compartmented plaster ceilings. Early seventeenth-century silhouette balusters and three-sided door-heads were also used, along with tapered pilasters, and English precedents were also liberally plundered. Ornamental richness on the walls was created not just by heraldic decoration, as in the Renaissance originals, but also by a new and diverse range of conventionalized symbols of landed power and Scottish national identity, including tartan, weaponry and stuffed animals' heads. These Baronial chivalric displays were combined with fittings and services of explicit modernity, such as gas-lighting, sprung upholstery, and water-closets.

The National Wallace Monument and Baronial Public Architecture

During the mid-nineteenth century, the Scotch Baronial style began to spread from its country-house, landed-class redoubt to public buildings and non-aristocratic urban contexts, again largely at the hands of pupils of Bryce. The first and most obvious of these contexts was that of the burgeoning demand for projects for national monuments, where its confident massiveness seemed to reflect a rather incongruous combination of pride in the culture of imperial partnership, with growing disgruntlement over the allegedly inadequate London recognition of Scotland's place in the union. For a few years from 1853, this discontent gave rise to the NAVSR,[105] a Tory-backed protest movement against alleged favouritism by the Liberal government towards Ireland, chaired by the Earl of Eglinton and Winton, of Tournament fame.[106] Its object, of course, was not to challenge the union in any way, but rather to reinforce it, by achieving a true 'union of equals'. Eventually, the NAVSR petered out in 1856, whereupon some of its activists, such as historian William Burns,[107] launched a project for building a national shrine to Wallace, a project that would eventually result in the most grandiose single work of Scotch Baronial architecture, and one of the climactic set-pieces of the Second Castle Age: the National Wallace Monument, on

Stirling's Abbey Craig, dominating the campaign territory of the Wars of Independence, designed by J. T. Rochead, in 1859, and inaugurated in 1869 (Figure 8.5). In contrast to the previous uncertainty on the part of Scott and others about the propriety of Wallace commemorations, now several Wallace memorials already existed – but these were local or modest efforts, such as the Lanark statue of 1822.[108] In March 1856, 'in consequence of an article which had appeared in the *North British Review* impugning the purity of Wallace's motives, Mr Colin Rae-Brown published an address to Scotsmen ... urging the desirability of ... a National Monument to Wallace on Glasgow Green. The editor's desk was speedily inundated with letters warmly approving of the proposal'.[109] The focus of the initiative shifted immediately to Stirling, where the project was inaugurated on Bannockburn Day 1856 with a local holiday and rally, attended by 20,000 people.[110] The subsequent process of its creation, however, was tortuous, as its promoters represented all current permutations of Scottish patriotism, some favouring greater Scottish political autonomy than others: their continuous disagreements extended the construction period to eight years rather than the three initially estimated by Rochead.[111]

Architecturally, the building was a flamboyant set-piece of Scotch Baronial in its most mature and expressively plastic form. In 1860, the fund-raising committee described the monument as 'a Scottish Medieval Tower, 220 feet high, and 36 feet square, surmounted by a picturesque representation of the Crown Royal of Scotland, 50 feet high'.[112] The tower was constructed of rock-faced rubble, with extruded stair turret and heavily indented chamfering; it was topped by the imperial emblem of a crown spire, and contained a series of four grand chambers (some vaulted) above one another: one of these was conceived as a 'hall of heroes', as at Buchan's Dryburgh a half-century earlier (Buchan's plan was a 'Temple of Caledonian Fame'). In contrast to both the tower-house tradition and contemporary Scotch Baronial houses, the tower was faced inside and out not in smooth ashlar but in dramatically Sublime rubble – anticipating by several decades the preference for rock-faced stonework that became associated with 'traditional, national' monumental buildings around 1900, not just in Scotland but in other countries such as Germany or Finland. The completion of this giant monument to Scottish imperial, assimilative nationalism was, appropriately, greeted with telegrams of support from Italy's Garibaldi and Hungary's Kossuth. Across Europe, the predominant form taken by national monuments was still that of giant statues, among which probably the closest to Stirling, ideologically speaking, was the Niederwalddenkmal at Rüdesheim am Rhein, built from 1871 to celebrate reunification, by architect Karl Weisbach and sculptor Johannes Schilling, and explicitly anti-French in orientation and dedication (although in the context of Germany, the closest equivalent to England in this case was arguably Prussia rather than France).

In the context of mid-century Scotland, a more relevant German connection was that of Prince Albert, whose death in 1861 triggered an

FIGURE 8.5 *National Wallace Monument, Abbey Craig, Stirling, by John T. Rochead, 1859–69; drawing of c. 1859.* © *Historic Environment Scotland.* https://canmore.org.uk/collection/957513

empire-wide outburst of public grief. Scotland seized the opportunity to demonstrate loyalty and love of the monarchy, through yet another national memorial. The main Albert Memorial was in London. Victoria hesitated over G. G. Scott's design before its selection: 'too much an imitation of W. Scott's and too like a market cross'.[113] In Edinburgh, an 1865 competition for a 'Scottish National Memorial to the Prince Consort' generated a wide diversity of potential solutions, some of them 'buildings' – with the Baronial prominently represented – and others essentially statues, of a mainly classical character.[114] Bryce proposed the planting of a colossal, Balmoral-inspired tower, 165 feet high, within Edinburgh Castle, that would have soared over Princes Street and rivalled the National Wallace Monument in Baronial monumentality[115] (Figure 8.6). The design also demonstrated a close knowledge of Scotland's castles – for example, by replicating a Rosyth Castle-like window. But Victoria wanted a completely freestanding structure, as in the case of Scott's London memorial, and so this design was rejected. Peddie & Kinnear's design for a freestanding Prince Consort memorial, also Baronial, included an imperial crown.[116] In 1865 the intention had been to place the memorial on the Queen's Drive in Holyrood Park,[117] but it was finally relocated instead to Charlotte Square, and the eventual winning design was a piece of classical statuary, by sculptor John Steell, whom Victoria knighted at the monument's inauguration in 1876. In Perth, likewise, another classical statue, by William Brodie, was erected in 1864,

FIGURE 8.6 *Albert Memorial, Edinburgh – unexecuted project by David Bryce for Balmoral-type tower within Edinburgh Castle, c. 1864.* © *Royal Incorporation of Architects in Scotland. https://canmore.org.uk/collection/1126049*

portraying Albert in the dress 'of the Old Scottish Court',[118] as a Scottish Stuart courtier with chivalric orders of both Scotland and England: if Wallace could be a medieval Briton, then Albert could equally become a seventeenth-century Scot.

The Prince Consort proposals were only one episode in a succession of unrealized projects from the late 1850s onwards to convert Edinburgh Castle from a military barracks into a national monument – the first being Francis Dollman's above-mentioned and unexecuted scheme of 1859, put forward in association with Colonel Richard Moody of the Royal Engineers, to recast the New Barracks, Munition House and Ordnance Stores in a craggily romantic, chateau-like style[119] (Figure 8.7). As we will see in the next two chapters, the actual remodelling of the Castle from the 1880s by Hippolyte Blanc was more modest in scale, and only in the 1920s was a symbolic national monument, of a quite different purpose and character, completed there by R. S. Lorimer and John F. Matthew.

The ethos of competitive national pride expressed in all these initiatives was, naturally, easy to adapt to the local or municipal arena, especially in building types of civic authority and justice administration – the legal system being, of course, a cherished area of elite Scottish cultural autonomy. Scotch Baronial, with its strong flavour of landed tradition, was especially favoured for public buildings in rural towns or cities with a strong link to a rural hinterland. Glasgow had naturally chosen an eclectic classical style for its giant new Municipal Buildings of 1883–8, while Edinburgh's equivalent functions remained within the classical building constructed in the 1750s, which was simply enlarged. The prime example of this urban–rural hybridity was the monumental County and Municipal Buildings complex in Aberdeen's Castle Street, built in 1868–74 at a cost of £50,000 to the designs of Peddie & Kinnear, and incorporating the castellated, stumpy-towered Tolbooth of 1615 at its east end, rather like a tower-house embedded in a grand Baronial country house (Figure 8.8). The building was naturally constructed entirely in granite, and its sixty-metre-high, bartizaned main tower, for several decades by far the most prominent landmark in the city, echoed, in hugely amplified form, the old Schoolhill mansions illustrated by Billings, as well as the Baronial imagery of Balmoral and 'Royal Deeside'. Although hailed at its construction as a renewal of the 'hearth-stone of the burgh', and more generally known in recent years as the 'Town House', the building's government role within the strongly Liberal-sympathizing city, as the headquarters of the town council and the local commissioners of police (a local administrative department amalgamated with the town council in 1871), was balanced with its other functions as a sheriff courthouse for the city and county of Aberdeen, and as a rural county administration building.[120]

Following this resounding precedent, the urban, institutional use of Baronial architecture became commonplace. The most obvious context seemed to be that of municipal buildings, with their established

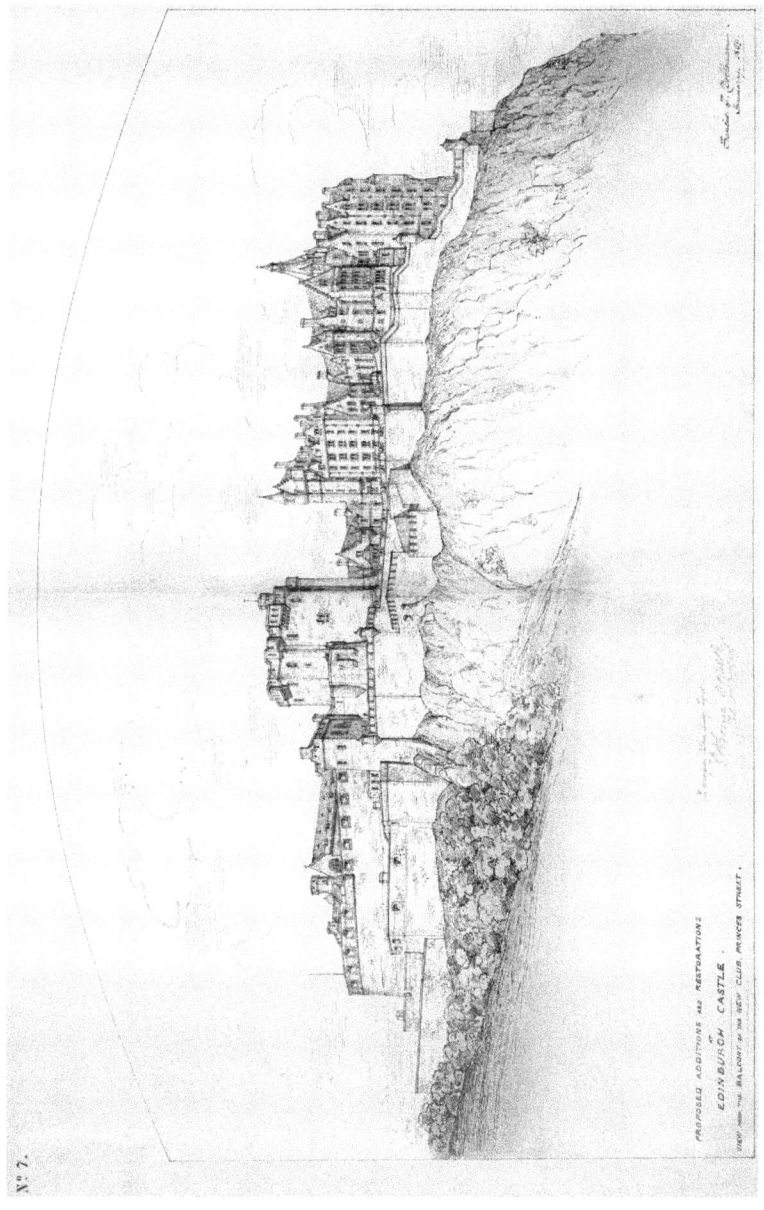

FIGURE 8.7 *Edinburgh Castle – unexecuted project by F. T. Dollman, 1859, entitled 'PROPOSED ADDITIONS and RESTORATIONS of EDINBURGH CASTLE/ View from the BALCONY of the NEW CLUB, PRINCES STREET'.* © Historic Environment Scotland. https://canmore.org.uk/collection/628874

FIGURE 8.8 *Aberdeen County and Municipal Buildings by Peddie & Kinnear, built 1868–74; architects' drawing.* © Historic Environment Scotland. https://canmore.org.uk/collection/756201

requirement for lofty towers as authority symbols, and a standard formula duly developed, featuring bartizaned steeples and grand vaulted interiors. A very early example, financed by local aristocrat and Liberal MP, Captain Alexander Mitchell-Innes, and thus neatly straddling the boundary between 'landed' and 'civic', was the town hall in the Borders village of Stow. Built in 1854–7, this unexpectedly grandiose small building is crammed with a wealth of overscaled components and gravity-defying corbelling, and a basket-arched open central loggia/porch connecting a fat corbelled-out turret to a gable with unequal-sized turrets in the Bryce manner, the outer one perched in an apparently precarious manner (Figure 8.9). Early pointers among towns of various sizes were Charles Wilson's Rutherglen (1862, with idiosyncratically shaved-off tower), followed by J. C. Walker at Dunfermline (1875) and Hawick (1883), and Bryce's Lockerbie (planned 1873, built from 1884). Local law courts, traditionally classical, often now seemed an equally appropriate context for Baronial, especially in view of the national construction programme authorized by the Sheriff Court Houses (Scotland) Act 1860 – a programme overseen largely by landowning Commissioners of Supply, who may have seen Baronial as a natural style to signify establishment authority. David Rhind designed sheriff courthouses at Dumfries (1863–6) and Selkirk (1868–70), both mighty rock-faced Baronial

FIGURE 8.9 *Stow Town Hall – built 1854–7, financed by local aristocrat and Liberal MP, Captain Alexander Mitchell-Innes; architect unidentified. Photograph by M. Glendinning, 2017.*

structures: Dumfries's courthouse took the form of a tower-house with Winton-style parapet, while Selkirk boasted a Castle Fraser tower. Peddie & Kinnear's Greenock Sheriff Courthouse, 1864–7, was a miniature Fettes-like composition with symmetrical central tower, and Brown & Wardrop's Stirling (1874–6) was a symmetrical, smaller-scale version of an original 1864 design.

The use of Scotch Baronial in other institutions and commercial buildings was more episodic. It was applied to the design of symmetrical, pavilion-plan hospitals by John Burnet Senior at Glasgow's Western Infirmary (1871–4, with turreted centrepiece based on the gables of Glamis Castle), and, on a much grander scale, by Bryce at Edinburgh Royal Infirmary (1872–9).[121] Bryce had previously prepared a succession of classical designs for the Infirmary's Committee of Management since 1849, but now, expectations changed abruptly, and ancient Scottish architecture became seen as appropriate to signal Scotland's cutting-edge medical modernity. Because of the emphasis upon fresh air and ventilation – Florence Nightingale was consulted on the plans – the new building was placed at the city's edge, beside the Meadows, where further development was prohibited and fresh air guaranteed. The hospital comprised two detached blocks with Holyrood-like towers for their wings. Some angles were chamfered in an inverted V-shape to a square, in the distinctive manner of Gogar's turret, while crowstepped gables punctuated the flanks, and the windows had high-level transoms to help manage the ventilation. The northern block, fronting Lauriston Place, was more architecturally monumental, featuring a steepled entrance block.[122]

In the educational field, the opposite edge of Edinburgh, to the north-west, became the location for the most grandiose set-piece of the Franco-Scotch style: Fettes College, an elite boys' private school built in 1864–70 to the designs of Bryce, who was engaged as architect in 1852 in place of Playfair, who had been the original choice (Figure 8.10). Sir William Fettes, a businessman, army contractor during the Napoleonic Wars, and twice Lord Provost of Edinburgh, had himself owned castellated houses at Redcastle and Gogarbank, where he died in 1836. His endowment envisaged a Heriot-like focus on orphans or destitute children, but the school as opened had a more elite orientation.[123] Built 'in the early French style',[124] this symmetrical, high-roofed composition of bartizans, towers and spires soars upwards, with a cavernous Fyvie-pattern entrance tower providing a massively plastic centrepiece. Its main front also resembled Kinnaird, having a similarly jagged skyline and square-towered ends. In the standard pattern of Heriot's schools, the ground floor features an arcaded shelter, treated as a loggia in Blois style, while a chapel is central at the rear as at Donaldson's and Heriot's – but here, with a further block beyond, to the north.[125] The convincing excellence of Bryce's detailing here suggests that he may have studied French architecture at first hand, precisely as Gillespie Graham had studied English models. Bryce's own perspective presented the building asymmetrically, but the college's main, axial avenue to the south – perhaps seen as another French touch – added yet another grand, spired vista to Romantic Edinburgh. The slightly later Morgan Hospital, Dundee (by Kinnear, 1866) clearly echoed Fettes, while the vast pile of J. Macleod's Christian Institute in Glasgow (1878, extended 1895–8 by Clarke & Bell and R. A. Bryden) more eclectically combined Baronial massing with some neo-Romanesque detail.

Within commercial architecture the hold of classicism remained much more secure, with significant Baronial exceptions: an early example of Bryce's Franco-Scotch manner was the Royal Exchange, Dundee (1854–5), like a miniature version of Aberdeen Town House in its squat corner tower and spikily dormered seven-bay main facade, while Rochead's exactly contemporary City of Glasgow bank offices in Trongate boasted a profusion of gables and other busy detailing: the *Building Chronicle* praised the 'grace, ease and picturesque fashion of outline, which gives so much interest and beauty to this peculiar cast of architecture'.[126] At a more utilitarian level,

FIGURE 8.10 *Fettes College, Edinburgh, by David Bryce, 1864–70 – view from south-east; photograph dated 1994.* © *Historic Environment Scotland. https:// canmore.org.uk/collection/793539*

the arrival of railways also notably coincided with the ascendency of Scotch Baronial, which allowed the use of cheap rock-faced rubble to be presented as an aesthetic choice. Viaducts and tunnel entrances became opportunities to display Baronial virtuosity in appropriate locations, such as the Killiecrankie viaduct and tunnel entrances on Joseph Mitchell's Highland Railway main line (1861–3) – echoing earlier English castellated examples such as the north portal of Clayton Tunnel, near Brighton (1838–41), or contemporary tunnels on the *Mittelrhein* lines in Germany.

Scotch City Improvement in Edinburgh

Within the urban context of Edinburgh, Scotch Baronial also began to find an increasing popularity within the background architecture of urban renewal in the Old Town within the framework of the City Improvement programme. In contrast to Glasgow, where classical models were generally favoured in the city's far more radical demolition zone, Edinburgh had a long-established history of contextual urban renewal. We saw in the last chapter the way in which, during the second quarter of the century, eclectic compromises mingling 'Flemish'/Heriot's sources, as well as features drawn from English architecture, were all seen as sufficiently 'national' in character to merit inclusion in Old Town interventions. From the mid-century, however, the Old Town began to be rebuilt in a far more explicitly Scottish revivalist style. The Outlook Tower, for example, was made into a new castellated tower-house in 1853 when converted from seventeenth-century tenements to become Short's Observatory.[127] The Old Town 'Flemish' was occasionally re-employed after the 1830s; it was used by Bryce, for example, for the 'Edinburgh Courant' (1871–2) office on St Giles Street, although his neighbouring 'Daily Review' office (1872–3) has fat bartizans and twinned crowstepped gables in a carefully massed face overlooking the New Town.[128] Other late examples of 'Old Town Flemish' were situated on George IV Bridge's west side, along with the prominent set-piece of the India Buildings, Victoria Street, by Cousin (1864–6), designed as if it were an agglomeration of separate buildings curving and sloping downhill.[129]

In parallel with these non-domestic buildings, Scotch Baronial increasingly also began to be applied to urban housing in the Old Town – and slightly beyond. In 1860, a report on the city's housing problem by a committee of artisans had defended the tenement pattern and advocated the 'benevolent and profitable' reconditioning of Old Town tenements 'with the idea of preserving the ancient and national character of the domiciles'.[130] The association between old burgh houses and 'national identity' would become increasingly strong after that, as we will see in the next chapter. Edinburgh in this period saw a vigorous Old Town redevelopment drive, based on a new City Improvement Act (passed 1867). Here the romantic and scenographic principles already established in the Old Town by Thomas Hamilton and Burn remained prominent, and led to the devising of an inner-urban street architecture based on Scotch Baronial. Billings had drawn attention to the 'peculiarities and merits' of old burghs' 'street architecture . . . private dwellings ornamented by that light, graceful, angular turret which was adapted from the French chateau architecture'.[131] An initial Baronial improvement project had already been promoted privately in the city, at one remove from the mainstream City Improvement programmes, through the 1853 Edinburgh Railway Station Access Act, which authorized the laying out of a curved street from the High Street down to the new station.[132] The new Cockburn Street was laid out in 1856 and developed in 1859–64 by speculative builders to the designs of Peddie & Kinnear (Figure 8.11). Although the new street's steeply curving route carved through a dense mass of 'medieval' fabric and thus contributed to the modern cutting-up of the Old Town into small chunks, its prospectus instead presented it as an exercise in heritage enhancement, pledging that 'it may not detract from the picturesque aspect of the Old Town, but rather serve to fix and perpetuate its peculiar and striking character'.[133] The resulting scheme provided a new, dramatic architectural gateway to the Old Town, loaded with turrets and crowstepped gables: overall, Cockburn Street, in its sheer length and variety, was one of the most variegated compendia of Baronial motifs attempted to that date. Typically of the picturesque design principles of Baronial, its lower (northern) entrance blocks were strongly asymmetrical and very different in character: no. 1 Cockburn Street featured a medallion head of Lord Cockburn, while opposite, at no. 2, projects a polygonal turret in the manner of Bryce's Bowerhouse, with pedimented dormer heads above each face, a tall pointed roof rising behind.

The Scotch Baronial agenda was then, in turn, applied to fully fledged City Improvement projects following the passing of the 1867 Act, whose prime mover was William Chambers, Lord Provost in 1865–9. Chambers was an indefatigable champion of social and civic improvement, promoting schemes under which the most densely overcrowded and deteriorated chunks of Old Town fabric would be selectively redeveloped with 'superior' tenements with a porter monitoring the entrance, in Parisian style, and intended for occupation by artisans, rather than the 'residuum' that currently lived in them, who would be expelled from the area. He published his ideas in 1855, contesting the preference for low-rise cottage solutions favoured by many and arguing that artisan tenements were an ideal urban housing pattern for the skilled working class, as 'there can be no proper comparison between the substantial Scotch structures and the slight brick edifices' typical of England and Wales.[134] Concerning Edinburgh, Chambers noted optimistically that 'latterly . . . some buildings have been erected in the more picturesque style of the sixteenth and seventeenth centuries; and everything connected with architecture in Scotland may well be said to be undergoing a rapid improvement'.[135] What was vital, he believed, was to combine this modernization with the safeguarding of 'tradition'. Chambers, whose own Scotch Baronial country house, Borthwick Hall, was designed by architect John Henderson (1852–5),[136] set out as Lord Provost to put his ideas into practice. The 1867 Act proposed the formation or widening of several streets on either side of High Street, with 'elevations . . . of plain but marked character, in harmony with those fine specimens of national architecture in many of the neglected and overcrowded areas'.[137] Following the passage of the 1867 Act, reconstruction and street-widening began in 1869 of the Old Town's worst slum pockets, at St Mary's Street and Blackfriars Wynd; the new tenements, mostly designed by the City Improvement Trust's architects, David Cousin and John Lessels, at St Mary's Street (from 1869) and Blackfriars Street (from 1870) echoed the Cockburn Street formula of busy picturesqueness, complete with crowsteps, splayed corners, 'Maybole' motifs, and a polygonal corbelled turret perhaps evoking Cardinal Beaton's House which had once stood nearby. Other architects such as Robert Morham and David Clunas designed individual blocks within the overall framework; the general architectural character was Baronial of a rather plainer kind than Cockburn Street.

FIGURE 8.11 *Cockburn Street, Edinburgh*: 'The New Communication between the Old Town and the Railway Termini Messrs Peddie & Kinnear Architects. Drawn, Printed & Published by Messrs Caldwell & Comp. 24 George St, Edin[burgh]'; engraving of c. 1860. © Historic Environment Scotland. https://canmore.org.uk/collection/793542

Overall, this formula of small-scale, context-responsive redevelopment in many ways presaged the 'conservative surgery' philosophy of Patrick Geddes at the turn of century – as we will see in Chapter 9. But Edinburgh's new, urban Baronial also began to spread into some of the city's suburban extensions and southern redevelopments from the 1860s, including the 1870s rebuilding of the triangle of Forrest Road, Teviot Place and Bristo Place, with inscription panels commemorating, for example, the '1513 Site of Town Wall'.[138] A special focus of activity was south of the Meadows and Links, including the villa area of the Grange, and the middle-class tenemental areas of Marchmont and Warrender. Here the urge for more vigorous architectural modelling was expressed not only through the ubiquitous use of canted bay windows, but also – doubtless evoking the romantic image of the capital – an explicit use of Baronial features, varying from details such as stop-chamfered or roll-moulded window-arrises to elaborate crowstepped gables. In the development of the Warrender estate, a 1869 feuing plan by Bryce laid down guidelines that were carried out with some gusto by architects such as Thomas Marwick and Edward Calvert. In the long ranges of streets such as Warrender Park Crescent or Road (both built from 1876), the traditional terrace repetition of Scottish and British housing – a somewhat classical approach that had dominated the development of the New Town earlier in the century – was combined with a proliferation of Baronial decoration, with towering, rock-faced bay-windowed facades, and crowsteps.[139]

Mid-Century Medievalism

In some respects, Scotch Baronial filled a similar, although more restricted, role in Scotland to that of secular Gothic Revival buildings in mid-Victorian England, such as Manchester Town Hall or St Pancras Station. In Scotland, with notable exceptions such as Sir G. G. Scott's Albert Institute in Dundee (1864–7) and Glasgow University (1864–70), neo-Gothic was largely confined to church building, which in the mid-century was dominated by the activity of the three Presbyterian groupings – the Established Church, the Free Church, and the United Presbyterians – although the revival of Catholicism and Episcopalianism would eventually diminish that dominance. The Free Church had seceded from the Church of Scotland in May 1843 following an intractable dispute over the powers of the government and the courts over the General Assembly – a cause that combined elements of theology and national *dignitas*, but without any suggestion of overt questioning of the union as such. Despite the mildly anti-establishment overtones of the Disruption, overall the Presbyterian kirk tended to regard social hierarchy, colonialism, and the union as all stemming from God's will. In 1850, the Reverend John Cumming preached at Crathie before 'the greatest Sovereign of the greatest nation upon earth'. He celebrated union, empire, and the rectification of past Scottish–English tensions. Differences between Scotland and England were now trivial: 'The forms of the English and Scottish Churches differ – their doctrines are the same. The greatest divines of each admit that they are sisters . . . we shall have salvation and happiness, whether we worship at Crathie or at Canterbury.'[140] The uncompromising Presbyterian ideologies which had inspired seventeenth-century warfare had now been significantly diluted.

For all three main Presbyterian denominations, the main concern, faced with the need to respond not just to the rapid expansion of the industrial cities in general but also to the consequences of the Disruption in particular, was quantity: the mid-1840s saw a frenzy of building activity by the Free Church, most often (outside classical Glasgow) in a rather basic Gothic style that focused on provision of large preaching boxes behind spiky facades. However, the Free Church also commissioned Playfair to design one very ambitious neo-Gothic project in the Edinburgh Old Town: a theological college and assembly hall on a very prominent site at the head of the Mound, dominating views from the New Town. Designed in a Tudor style, with a collegiate quadrangle-plan almost 'Oxbridge' in character,[141] the new Free Church College was embedded within the New Town's axial geometry, its twin-towered 'gatehouse' centrepiece being set – cleverly or mischievously – to enframe the steeple of the established Kirk's newly completed headquarters, Gillespie Graham's Victoria Hall (1839–44). The neighbouring tenements to the east were taken over as offices, each being redesigned by David Cousin 1858–65 and given Heriot's-like doorways; an assembly hall by Bryce was added next door to the college in 1858–9.[142] An equivalent college in Glasgow, by Charles Wilson, was designed in a north Italian Renaissance style with lofty campanile towers. The secular use of medieval styles was limited by the same code of appropriateness that, in Edinburgh, frowned on Grecian churches. David Thomson, for instance, claimed that the 'boldness and originality' of the round-arched Renaissance style used by Wilson at the Glasgow Free Church College was, compared to medievalism, 'more true to our modern requirements and more expressive of our aspirations in philosophy and art'.[143] Thus in Scotland, just as in the sixteenth and seventeenth centuries, a combination of external cultural circumstances and architectural preferences had once again created a significant space within secular architecture for castellated buildings large and small.

Scotch Abroad

The high profile of buildings such as the National Wallace Monument ensured that Scotland's Second Castle Age rapidly made a significant international impact. Scottish books and ideas were exported throughout the globe, and through this medium Scotch Baronial could be adopted by choice. Evidence of outside interest was the personal library of New York inventor and non-Scot Richard M. Hoe, which contained numerous Scottish books; the more predictable authors (Burns, Carlyle, Scott), but also engineer Robertson Buchanan, John Starforth, and Loudon.[144] As early as 1836, Loudon had envisioned Scotch Baronial having export potential, particularly for nostalgic expatriates: 'As the residence of a Scotsman, in a foreign country, it might raise up many associations connected with his native land ... [It could recall] pleasing emotions ... for an American family, in the twentieth century, may order a design for a villa, in the style that prevailed in the particular locality of the parent country.'[145]

Architects who emigrated from Britain during the mid-century included the well-known Alexander Kirkland and less well-known figures such as John Shaw, who moved to Canada in 1855.[146] New Zealand drew in numerous Scots. John Campbell became Chief Colonial Architect there,[147] and he employed James Nicoll, from Dundee.[148] To New Zealand and Australia went David Ross,[149] from Huntly, who became one of Dunedin's most significant architects. His Scotch designs included Charleville (1885), an Auckland villa; and the castellated pylons of Sidney's Long Gully Bridge (1892).[150] Thomas Bedford Cameron[151] worked at Ballarat, Dunedin, and Auckland, where his St James' Presbyterian Church (1864–5) was given a Scots-looking tower. While Dunedin's city and street names are a homage to Edinburgh, its historic architecture rather more closely resembles Victorian Glasgow than contemporary Baronial Edinburgh.

In the United States, more blatantly Scotch buildings included Bannerman Castle on Pollepel Island on the Hudson River, New York – a giant private arsenal store, intended to house up to thirty million cartridges and other explosives, and designed and built by Dundee-born munitions dealer Frank Bannerman in 1901. Incorporating a further castle residence for Bannerman immediately adjacent, and broadcasting its purpose through a giant external inscription, 'BANNERMAN'S ISLAND ARSENAL', it outdid even the most elaborate mid-nineteenth-century Baronial country houses in Scotland in its mountainous confection of bartizans, turrets and crenellations.[152] Robert Henderson Robertson, a leading New York architect of Scots parentage and designer of the corner-turreted Park Row Building, briefly the world's tallest building, designed Blantyre Castle in Massachusetts (1903) for Robert Paterson,[153] splay-planned, with turrets framing the bow-windowed axial gable. Henderson also designed Richmond Hill, Irvington (pre-1896); Tudor, but with a Scotch turret.[154] Canada's château style combined French and Scotch references, and was often exemplified by railway hotel architecture: the Château Frontenac in Quebec (1893) has a French name, but its monster tower (added in 1924) clearly derives more from Scotland than from France.[155]

Nearer to home, Protestant Ireland clung to its Scottish heritage, and in the later nineteenth century some elites chose Scotch Baronial to signal Presbyterian Britishness: Stormont Castle, Dundonald, County Down, was built in 1858 by Belfast architect Thomas Turner, and Ballymena Castle, 1865–87 by Lanyon and Lynn, also of Belfast, was for Sir Robert Adair of Ballymena and Flixton. The shift towards use of Baronial for urban institutions was also reflected in the derivatives of Edinburgh's Royal Infirmary design, including Seacliff Asylum in Dunedin (1874–84), which varied the Edinburgh formula because as an asylum it served a different purpose; some blocks were two rooms deep, the exteriors consequently twin-gabled, and there were three steeples; while some of the parapet corbelling was monumentally massive. The architect was Robert Lawson, from Newburgh, who had trained with Heiton, Gillespie Graham and Lessels, before becoming one of New Zealand's most celebrated architects, famous for Dunedin's First Church (designed 1862, with a Victoria Halls steeple), and designer too of Larnach Castle (1871).[156] In almost all these overseas echoes of Baronial, we have now moved chronologically into the late nineteenth and early twentieth centuries. By that stage, 'at home', as the next chapter will show, the values of the Second Castle Age had begun to significantly shift away from the decoration-encrusted castellated eclecticism exemplified by Scotch Baronial.

Conclusion

The period covered in this chapter witnessed a new British imperial triumphalism and empire-derived status and wealth. This was a period, too, when Scottish and English architecture once again markedly diverged. While English interest in castle-building now sharply declined, David Bryce emerged as the leading Scotch Baronial architect largely owing to his castle designs. Bryce also trained a new generation of architects who could further develop the style themselves, for a superlatively wealthy clientele anxious to live in new Scottish castles, both at home and, on occasion, even in the colonies. And now at last, through the work of Billings, who knew Bryce well, there was a published scholarly repertoire available to serve castle-builders as models: Fyvie arches, Maybole oriels and Castle Fraser towers became stereotypes. All this was reinforced by the personal impetus given to the development of Scotch Baronial and Highlandism by Queen Victoria and Prince Albert, when they 'discovered' and fell in love with Scotland at Taymouth in 1842. Through their personal preferences, and especially through Albert's architectural decisions about their Balmoral holiday home, Scotch Baronial, the architectural style derived from Scotland's own rhetorically martial history, became the style that denoted the establishment. Paradoxically, Baronial was also simultaneously a style of choice for those wishing to straightforwardly celebrate the Wars of Independence, as evidenced by the National Wallace Monument. And alongside all this, of course, a richly eclectic classical architecture still flourished in Scotland's cities, as exemplified in the work of Glasgow's Alexander 'Greek' Thomson.

But some Scottish architects, such as Robert Kerr, were by now growing impatient or embarrassed about Baronial, not least for its exuberantly 'modern' eclecticism. And as we will see in the next chapter, the period around the turn of century would see significant modifications and refinements to the castellated architecture of the country's landed elites, celebrating late imperialist Scottish society through the new, more elemental monumentality of 'Scotch Traditionalism'.

9

1870–1914: Scotch Traditionalism

Our ancestors put their hands to a mighty work, and it prospered. They welded two great nations into one common empire, and moulded local jealousies into a common patriotism. On such an achievement we must gaze with awe and astonishment, the means were so adverse and the result so surprising.[1]

– LORD ROSEBERY, 1871

The ideal life in the ideal, old, traditional 'un-hurrying' Scotland.[2]

– R. S. LORIMER, 1897

It is the native architecture of our own country and that of our forefathers ... just as much Scotch as we are ourselves – as indigenous to our country as our wild flowers, our family names, our customs or our political constitution.[3]

– C. R. MACKINTOSH, 'SCOTCH BARONIAL ARCHITECTURE', LECTURE TO GAA, 1891

Introduction

By the late nineteenth century, nationalisms across Europe and the Americas had largely caught up with the pioneering efforts in Scotland. Now, with the beginning of the race among the Great Powers to carve up the remaining uncolonized territories, a more sombre and threatening tone crept in. Within Scotland, the relatively consensual climate that had supported nineteenth-century unionist nationalism was becoming less stable, with a growing polarization between bellicose imperialism and demands for Irish-style 'home rule'. To help bridge this gap – even before the crofters' 'Land War' over security of tenure got underway in the 1880s, Victoria now spent extended periods in Highland seclusion, a Scottish presence which helped bind the union tighter while further promoting the cult of 'tartanry'; the continuing irony being that many castle-building landlords such as John Ramsay, who built Kildalton House in 1870, had been responsible for implementing the Highland Clearances. Architecturally, this was on the one hand an age when the piling up of eclectic historical decoration reached its climax, with the specifics of styles like Scotch Baronial becoming submerged in ever more elaborate and hybrid 'National Renaissances'. On the other hand, there was also a growing demand for a simpler, more restrained, crafts-influenced national architecture, an architecture whose aesthetics were strongly shaped by the international national-romantic liking for massive, rock-faced or rendered styles, but which also featured a heightened ethical commitment and a collective, urban scope – as exemplified in the reshaping of the Edinburgh Old Town and the concepts of Patrick Geddes. Both these trends fuelled the emergence of a last, vigorous phase of the Second Castle Age, a phase finally cut short by the First World War.

Political Background: Home Rule and Imperialism

By the 1880s, under the influence of the Home Rule debates in Ireland, a similar arrangement for Scotland was being debated openly. The post of Scottish Secretary was (re-)created in 1885, and a Scottish office was established in London. The journal *Scottish Review*, inaugurated 1882,[4] provided a forum for discussing Scotland's political future and the Scottish Home Rule Association was established in 1886, seeking to promote a Scottish legislature and to make Scotland's voice better heard in Westminster. In general, the landed classes trenchantly opposed this development, with only a few exceptions, such as the Third Marquess of Bute.[5] The rhetoric of nationality shifted gradually from National Association for the Vindication of Scottish Rights (NAVSR)-style demands for proper recognition to calls for self-government. In 1885, Thomas Drummond Wanliss[6] protested that 'to . . . ascribe all the honour, the glory, and the greatness of the Empire alone to England, and to Englishmen, is not to unite the British people, but to sow disunion and disaffection',[7] and in the same year Charles Waddie, writing under the pseudonym of 'Thistledown', went so far as to argue for 'national self-government' and 'a national parliament'.[8] The upsurge in self-rule demands was paralleled paradoxically by a swelling wave of imperialist rhetoric: 'Imperialism is in the air', exclaimed diarist Beatrice Webb at the Diamond Jubilee of 1897, with 'all classes drunk with sightseeing and hysterical loyalty'.[9] And military historian W. H. Fitchett wrote in 1900 that 'a fighting impulse is native to Scottish blood, whether Lowland or Highland'.[10] Scotland's pride in empire was at its zenith, even as protests bubbled over issues of nomenclature. In 1898, 106,647 people petitioned the Queen over the official use of 'England' in contexts where 'Britain' was appropriate.[11] *The Thistle: A Scottish Patriotic Magazine*, inaugurated in 1908,[12] took issue with the numbering of the king's official name, protesting that 'to call the British Monarch "Edward VII" is to make it seem as if the British Throne were merely English', in defiance of 'the National Honour of Scotland'.[13]

In May 1914, a Scottish Home Rule Bill was advanced by Sir James MacPherson, who argued that 'no person can urge that . . . we are seeking separation from the Imperial Parliament . . . In this Bill Scotland claims her privilege and her right . . . and to take her share in controlling the destinies of this Empire in a supreme Parliament in London.'[14] Yet in some ways, a more powerful expression of diversity and identity was the burgeoning activity of municipal government, especially after 1895, when the Town Councils of the four cities were designated city corporations, responsible for all local government and police functions in their areas: while Edinburgh was the centre of national institutions, the unchallenged focus of municipal endeavour was Glasgow Corporation. At both a national and municipal level, there was a growing suspicion of unfettered laissez-faire capitalism and a willingness to contemplate collective solutions. The building type which highlighted most sharply the redefinition of the nation in more collective terms, was the national or international exhibition. Imperial Scotland saw five such events before 1914: two in Edinburgh (1886, 1908) and three in Glasgow (1888, 1901 and 1911).

Scotch Traditionalism

The years from around 1880 in Scotland, as elsewhere in Europe, witnessed a growing rejection of picturesque complexity and mass-produced ornament, and an increase in calls for greater orderliness – a variegated ideal expressed in terms such as 'artistic', 'refinement' and (most frequently) 'simplicity'. Highly decorated, eclectic buildings sharply declined in status – a development that directly affected the public reception of the Second Castle Age, whose patronage base was now extending to the rapidly expanding middle-class and the suburban villa-builders. Especially in Edinburgh and Eastern Scotland, 'Scotch Baronial' mutated into 'Scotch traditionalism', a movement whose chief advocates, headed first by R. Rowand Anderson and then by Robert Lorimer, rejected florid stylistic eclecticism in favour of a more intuitive or ethically based individualism, still focusing on essentially castellated forms of expression but inspired directly by what they believed to be the lost golden age of the Scottish Renaissance, and trenchantly rejecting Scotch Baronial as a direct model. Here, as in the first decades of the century, Scottish architects set on a rejuvenation of 'national' architecture paradoxically looked once again towards developments in England – only here for a more complex kind of inspiration than the copying of Tudor or Gothic styles. Now they drew on a longstanding English architectural tradition of moral criticism of utilitarian modernity, led by Pugin, Ruskin and the Domestic Revival and Arts and Crafts movements, and on that basis they championed the 'traditional' against the modern, the hand-made against the mass-produced, the natural against the artificial, the old town or the country against the industrial city.[15] The established hierarchy of building status was up-ended, and attention was lavished not on the monumental public building but on 'the home'. In Scotland, the latter category was defined to embrace not only the middle-class 'artistic villa' and artisan cottage, but also the collective housing and 'community' of the 'traditional' burgh. The overall inspiration, in the words of Robert Lorimer, in 1897, was 'the ideal life in the ideal old, traditional "un-hurrying" Scotland'.[16]

An early pointer to this new English inspiration was the rebuilding of Macharioch House, Kintyre, for the Marquess of Lorne, following his 1871 marriage to Princess Louise. It fell to Islay to identify the appropriate tartan, in 1874, concluding that 'it is good for trade to believe in Clan Tartans. Why should I take any step to disturb Scotch manufactures?'[17] Architecturally, although the newlyweds wanted a Scotch house, they engaged an English Domestic Revival architect, George Devey, who set about enlarging Macharioch in a hybrid manner in 1873–7, inserting Tudor-type mullioned windows in the existing tower and adding a gabled wing a little like a Cotswold manor house – but all harled with stone dressings, and almost devoid of the florid projections normal within the Brycean Baronial; the detached gatehouse was also harled and had an exaggeratedly tall spire.[18] Despite the slightly incongruous effect in this instance, the combination of castellated massing with a more austere, harled exterior would begin in the 1880s–90s to appeal to Scottish designers tired of the floridity of mid-century Baronial, and would provide a key building block of traditionalism.

This architectural movement of Scotch traditionalism, with its appeals to a ruggedly castellated architecture grounded in a deeper coherence of national community, would endure, in various forms, until the 1950s. It drew its inspiration from the same, Scottish Renaissance, buildings as had the nineteenth-century movement – Baronial – that it most vehemently criticised. From 1887 onwards, study of Scottish Renaissance architecture was assisted by the publication of David MacGibbon and Thomas Ross's five-volume inventory of that period's secular architecture, followed by three volumes on churches; the 1880s also saw influential measured drawings published by the Edinburgh Architectural Association, led by Rowand Anderson. By now, the study of old buildings was becoming gradually interconnected with initiatives for their preservation: Kinross's restoration of the chapel range and gatehouse at Falkland for the Third Marquis of Bute (1887) was backed up by primary research into the Lord Treasurer's and Master of Works' Accounts. Non-coercive state intervention in preservation (at first only of prehistoric remains) began with the 1882 Ancient Monuments Act. Now, it had become important to document old buildings more voluminously and more precisely, with a range of scholars being consulted to inform the process. For example, historian-architect (and future archaeologist) Peter Macgregor Chalmers contributed his researches to MacGibbon and Ross's publications before going on to publish on his own account, as the study of Scotland's historic architecture became a higher-status area of academic study.

The first champion of traditionalism, R. R. Anderson – who would play the role of mentor to talented younger architects such as Sydney Mitchell and Robert Lorimer – attacked the mid-century Baronial of Bryce in uncompromising terms, in two papers of 1889 and 1901, for combining garish modernity (in its large plate-glass windows) and vulgar picturesqueness ('sham castles').[19] The rejection of Baronial was powerfully aided by the fact that it was now being used for very commercial building types, including even large hotels such as the turreted Trossachs Hotel (by G. P. Kennedy, 1848, and later) or Pitlochry's enormous Atholl Palace Hotel, by the younger Andrew Heiton of Perth (1875), in a spired Franco-Holyrood style, set on a hilltop site and, like a hilltop castle, visible for miles to the approaching traveller from the south.[20] By contrast with this, Anderson followed Billings in arguing that the houses of the fifteenth, sixteenth and seventeenth centuries were not designed for any conscious visual effect: instead, 'everything is built for the purpose of keeping out intruders'. But the results of this were praised for a new reason – that of social morality. In polarized terms, the Scottish Renaissance was acclaimed as 'true' rather than 'false' art, displaying 'natural dignity, not artificial picturesqueness', and 'functional truth'. And for this reason, it was 'thoroughly national in character'.[21]

The new rhetoric was abundantly displayed in the pages of James Nicoll's *Domestic Architecture in Scotland* (1908).[22] His introductory essay noted that in the case of sash windows, 'the older form, with its small divisions, seems admirably in keeping with our national style'.[23] However, he warned against drawing too literally on recent English precedent, as although 'we have to a large extent got rid of the shams, inanities, and affectations of the Victorian era, we may have too much of the "simple" dwelling and be in danger of Anglicizing our buildings till we have forgotten our national style'. All in all, he believed, 'as an appropriate and natural expression of . . . [Scotland] . . . and its conditions, nothing more fitting than the Scottish national style could be conceived, whether it be the turreted and corbelled mansion of opulence, or the simple step-gabled dwelling of moderate size'.[24] And thus 'the national style, essentially a domestic one, should be worked out logically and consistently as the main building force throughout the country ... always asserting its right to predominance ... always bearing the visible and unmistakable signs of its ancient lineage'.[25]

The robust opposition to Scotch Baronial in Anderson's rhetoric, was less clear in his architectural designs. His most influential domestic project was built as early as 1879: his own villa in Colinton, 'Allermuir'. Its basic elements were, in fact, derived directly from smaller-scale, cheaper Baronial houses of the mid-century, with sash-and-case windows and rubble walling, and their absence of ornamental excrescences: for instance, Bryce's Stronvar (1850) and Shambellie (1856). In more recent designs such as Wardrop's Kinnordy (1879), the later Scottish Renaissance of seventeenth-century houses such as Pinkie had been openly evoked. Anderson now proceeded to apply this plainer variant of Baronial to the design of an avant-garde 'artistic' villa. Built of pinkish, rock-faced rubble, the impression conveyed by Allermuir was one of heavy sobriety, shorn of skyline trimmings and sharp edges, not explicitly 'castellated' yet clearly grounded in the castellated tradition. There was a miniature Pinkie-like bay window, set asymmetrically below a large crowstepped gable. Internally, the 'comfort' of the 'artistic' house resulted not only from the avoidance of even and bright daylighting, and from the studiedly plain, bulky panelling and woodwork, but also from the collecting of antiques, including preindustrial, archaic-looking furniture and other items. Despite previous efforts such as William Leiper's own plain gabled house in Helensburgh (Terpersie, 1871), or his Coll-Earn, Auchterarder (1869), Allermuir immediately became the most influential exemplar of the artistic villa in the new Scottish Renaissance style, and a growing number of key architects in the East embraced the ideal of the 'artistic' bourgeois house.

By the turn of the century, the most articulate and successful exponent of the new Scotch traditionalism was Robert S. Lorimer. He had previously worked as an assistant to Anderson (in 1885–9), and recalled his advice concerning Scotch design:

'Go and analyse the old Scotch buildings' [he used to say] study them as a medical student has to study anatomy, study the plan, see how the exterior is the natural expression of the interior, see how the later type of plan is a development of the earlier, look at the character of the masonry, measure the mouldings and plot them full size, and if you study the old buildings in this fashion it is conceivable you may one day become an architect.[26]

Lorimer's own career, and patrons, exemplified the growing wealth of the professional middle classes and their aspiration to the values of the landed strata of society. Lorimer's childhood home had been Kellie Castle, and now he both restored and built castles, his restorations beginning with Earlshall in 1890–4 and culminating with Balmanno in 1916; Kellie Castle had already been cautiously restored in 1878 by Lorimer's father, to the designs of John

Currie of Elie.[27] It was Lorimer above all who piloted the development of the Baronial style into a new interpretation of Scotch, reflecting the material sensitivity of the Arts & Crafts and the Domestic Revival of architects such as Shaw and Nesfield in England. He followed Anderson in use of textured or rocky facades, multipaned windows and tall slated roofs, and ornament such as elongated ogee domes derived from early seventeenth-century prototypes. Like Anderson, he rejected the grand old Scottish classical tradition, disparaging the New Town and referring to himself as a 'Gothic' man. Being a Goth in this case involved rejecting 'classic' regularity for a philosophy of 'no repeats',[28] while celebrating what were thought to be the social values of the Scottish Renaissance golden age. The aristocratic connotations of this ideal would serve both to ennoble designs for bourgeois clients, and maintain an appropriate decorum in houses for lairds. Lorimer eulogized Balcaskie in particular as 'the ideal of what a Scotch gentleman's home ought to be . . . dignified and yet liveable'.[29]

Scotch Monumentality: Harl and Rubble

While the first phase of the movement in house architecture pioneered by Anderson insisted on a demure reticence, there was a parallel trend, especially in the West of Scotland, which treated the Scottish Renaissance in a rougher or more assertively monumental castellated manner, in the design of both houses and public buildings. The years when this movement reached its climax coincided with the most impassioned Scottish commitment to a bellicose imperialism. The first signs of this new, more monumental traditionalism came with the return to favour of harling from the 1880s. Up to the late nineteenth century, the use of harling on domestic buildings had been a sign of low status. But by the time of James Nicoll's *Domestic Architecture in Scotland* of 1908, it had been reframed as a guarantee of 'more individuality and more sanity in our modern houses', in contrast to the 'stodgy respectability' of late nineteenth-century villas built in local freestone. The beginning of this revival in the status of harling, as with traditionalism as a whole, was bound up with English Arts and Crafts influence – as was highlighted especially at Fortingall Village and Glenlyon House, rebuilt at the end of the century for Sir Donald Currie of Garth and Glenlyon,[30] ship-owner, philanthropist, politician and diplomat in South Africa. Currie, who bought Glenlyon in 1885,[31] was a key 'gatekeeper' to the South African colonies: his 'Castle Line' steamships connected colony with metropolis in a new way, serving economic and military imperatives, settler transport and tourism,[32] and were named after Scottish castles (*Dunnottar Castle*, etc.); the company flag was a modified saltire. He engaged the London Scottish architect James MacLaren to create a little Highland Perthshire utopia at Fortingall. Although MacLaren died in 1890, the work was continued by his former assistants, W. Dunn and R. Watson – all in a harled, somewhat primitivist style mingling Scotch Traditionalist and English Arts and Crafts elements. First of all, the late seventeenth-century Glenlyon House was reconstructed from 1891 in a crowstepped dormer-headed style, with a conical-roofed entrance turret, small multipaned windows, and a Mackintosh-like oriel.[33] At Fortingall village, the hotel boasted Scotch crowsteps, as did the church, rebuilt in 1901–2 with nave and chancel differentiated as if pre-Reformation.[34] Currie also financed the part restoration of Dunkeld Cathedral in 1908, leaving the choir and tower still as ruins.[35]

The other monumentalizing interpretation of the castellated Scottish Renaissance involved the use of rough, especially rock-faced rubble. Like harling, this had been a utilitarian method during the mid-nineteenth century, associated especially with industrial and rural structures. But the 1880s extended its scope also to prestigious public buildings and country houses. Rubble building allowed Traditionalists to become involved in the designing of stone-built monumental projects, particularly those associated with Scottish imperial themes, while remaining true to their image of archaic roughness. In this area, too, the influence of both Maclaren and the US architect H. H. Richardson was felt: Maclaren's Stirling High School (1887–8) perched a heavy rubble tower and low wing on a sharply sloping site. The first association between rock-faced plasticity and imperial Scottish symbolism had been several decades earlier, in the National Wallace Monument. But that was a largely isolated set-piece, albeit one that was steadily adorned with further patriotic fittings over the decades: a Wallace statue by D. W. Stevenson was installed in 1887, and 'Wallace's sword' in 1888;[36] a 'Hall of Heroes' (intended as yet another 'national Walhalla'[37]) was inaugurated in 1886 with a bust of Burns, gifted by Andrew Carnegie. The colossal Wallace statue bequeathed by John Steill to Aberdeen (made by W. G. Stevenson and unveiled in 1888) also featured a huge rocky plinth.[38]

It was, indeed, only in the late 1880s, when the wide acceptance of British 'manifest destiny' further inflated the established concept of Scotland as an 'imperial partner', that the imperialist associations of 'Scotch rubble' consistently emerged. Its first architectural manifestation in this period was the most startling: an 1889 proposal for the building at Dalmeny of an inflated copy of Linlithgow Palace, complete with heightened towers (Figure 9.1). The architect for this unrealized scheme was Sydney Mitchell, and the client was the Fifth Earl of Rosebery, Conservative Prime Minister in 1894–5 and one of the most ardent Imperialist spokesmen during the Boer War, as well as a passionate unionist.[39] Marriage into the Rothschild banking family had left Rosebery the owner of estates in the Lothians and England, including the neo-Elizabethan Mentmore Towers. In his view, Scots and English had successfully 'welded two great nations into one common empire, and moulded local jealousies into a common patriotism'.[40] In a later booklet for schoolchildren he argued that 'you all know that Scotland became united

FIGURE 9.1 *Dalmeny House – unexecuted proposal by Sydney Mitchell & Wilson, 1889, for a replacement house modelled on Linlithgow Palace.* © *Dalmeny Estates. HES reference WLD/45/40.*

to England first by our King James VI . . . taking possession of England – which I am happy to think the Scottish have kept ever since'.[41] Alarmed the neglect of Scotland by London risked spawning an irresistible home rule movement, he instead successfully pressed in the early 1880s for creation of a post of Scottish Secretary, with the aim of channelling devolutionary pressure into administrative rather than legislative channels.

Like Lord Aberdeen a generation earlier, Rosebery was anxious to celebrate Scotland's, and his own, castellated heritage. And already, on his own estate, Barnbougle Castle, partially ruined a half-century earlier to make a garden ornament, had provided him with a golden opportunity to do so. In the years around 1880, Rosebery first reconstructed Barnbougle – 'my house by the sea' – as a library-cum-retreat[42] (Figure 9.2). His son-in-law, the Marquess of Crewe, later recalled that 'a vast hall or picture gallery was

FIGURE 9.2 *Barnbougle Castle by Wardrop and Reid – completed 1881; view from south-west; undated photograph.* © Historic Environment Scotland. https://canmore.org.uk/collection/1646102

the main feature, furnished with many bookcases, which overflowed into another large saloon adjoining. There were other smaller dwelling-rooms, but very little bedroom accommodation. Rosebery himself, however, in his widowed days, slept at the castle oftener than not, soothed by the rhythm of the dolorous sea.'[43] Restoration was already under consideration by 1873, and variant projects included small tower-houses.[44] The design completed by Wardrop and Reid in 1881 was plain and plausibly old-looking,[45] anticipating Lorimer's more austere Scotch traditionalism – unsurprisingly, as Lorimer had been a pupil of Hew Wardrop in 1884. The house has large, vertical, transomed and single-mullioned windows not unlike Rosyth Castle's on the opposite shore – a model replicated frequently by Lorimer and used by Blanc in his Edinburgh Great Hall restoration, 1887–91 (see below). In 1889, however, Rosebery's Scotch ambitions stepped up onto another plane altogether, when he commissioned Mitchell's project for the Linlithgow-style replacement of Dalmeny House.[46] The drawings demonstrate a close archaeological study of the Linlithgow ruins. The new building would be near identical to the palace, albeit with Stirling Great Hall bay windows, and would even share its orientation; although the steep contouring and setting could not be replicated, the Forth would substitute for Linlithgow Loch. Had the project ever been executed, this would have been the biggest and probably costliest Scotch revivalist house of all – although the Baronial it evoked was not that of the barons, but of the Stuart kings: the symbolism which had contributed to Linlithgow's destruction by a government army in 1746[47] was now seen as a virtue. Enthused with this monumental spirit, Mitchell & Wilson built a series of rubble palace-houses in those years, loaded with Stewart imperial imagery, including Sauchieburn (1889–90); Duntreath (1889–93, where Mitchell enlarged the existing Charles Wilson-designed mansion for Sir Archibald Edmonstone by adding a twin-turreted gatehouse set between unequal-sized tower-houses) and the five-storey block of Glenborrodale (1898–1902). An earlier and more domestic version, but with crowstepped gables, was Mitchell's reconstruction of Leithen Lodge, Innerleithen, in 1885–7.

Across the whole range of domestic architecture, the years around the turn of century saw an increasing attention to the theatrical potential of the Second Castle Age. In places, the difference from Bryce's Baronial was relatively limited, although without the latter's hard-edged, large-windowed modernity and add-on ornament, and often incorporating early classical interior features, such as ceilings evoking the late seventeenth-century plasterwork (by, as we saw, English court craftsmen) associated with Sir William Bruce. The towered rhetoric of Mitchell and Wilson was reflected in work such as Thoms & Wilkie's twin-towered Kinpurnie Castle (1911), and the rubble and harled block of Niven and Wigglesworth's Kincardine (1898), with its opulent Baroque porch. By 1908, Nicoll's *Domestic Architecture* set out a wide diversity of designs in what he referred to as the 'Scottish national style'.

Even Anderson and Lorimer were on occasion caught up in this new enthusiasm for massive rubble monumentality – in the former's case with a house set in one of the most Romantically picturesque locations conceivable, beneath the Pap of Glencoe, overlooking Loch Leven, and built in 1896–7 by Donald Smith, who in 1897 became Lord Strathcona and Mount Royal. Smith, originally stemming from Forres, had a career in Canada, becoming 'easily the wealthiest Canadian of his time'.[48] He was also a philanthropist, who promoted women's education and funded a new hospital in Forres (also Scotch in style, by John Rhind, 1889), as well as co-financing a new Scotch Baronial-style Royal Infirmary in Montreal (1887–93), closely based on Bryce's Edinburgh complex.[49] The 'Mount Royal' of his title referred to Canada, while 'Strathcona' evoked Glencoe, albeit rejecting the Gaelic name. The site was steeped in historic romance, being near the location of the Massacre of Glencoe and of the murdered MacIan's house: Smith commissioned Rowand Anderson to design a new Scotch Traditionalist house there. Glencoe House was built of rock-faced grey granite with stridently contrasting red ashlar highlights.[50] Strongly evoking the seventeenth-century castellated classicism of Heriot's, Pinkie and elsewhere, it featured a forest of crowstepped gables and wings, ornate pediments, and canted or square bays, some corbelled outwards above ground level.

In the case of Lorimer, a certain grandiosity also began to assert itself: in an unrealized rebuilding scheme for Newark Castle (1898), he boasted of 'my great vista'.[51] And in other projects, he developed a monumental manner of bare rubble walls, archaic classicizing detail and rounded, integral massing, which he referred to simply as his 'Scotch' style; the plans of these houses, with their first-floor principal apartments, were equally intended to evoke the Scottish Renaissance. For instance, a new Rowallan Castle, Lorimer's first completely new Scotch house, was built from 1901 for the Liberal Unionist MP, A. Cameron Corbett.[52] In 1905–7, Lorimer built Ardkinglas for Sir Andrew Noble. It was composed asymmetrically around a tower-house.[53] Across Loch Fyne, at Dundarave (1911), he restored a long-roofless tower, which he connected to a new wing by a rubble-columned loggia reminiscent of Chalmers' Celtic Revival church interiors (see below). The declared aim was that the new should harmonize with, but be distinguished from the old.[54] The climax of this series of houses was Formakin, in Renfrewshire, built in 1912–14 for a rich connoisseur and horticulturalist, the Paisley stockbroker John A. Holms. It combined an L-plan with the diagonal arrangement of Balmoral: Lorimer considered it 'the purest Scotch I've ever done'.[55] An austerely primitivist exterior, with bare apertures and thick-jointed rubble was combined with a meticulous constructional ethos, recalling Lorimer's larger tower-house restorations, and a climactic first-floor great chamber intended to display a set of fifteenth-century tapestries. Elsewhere, Lorimer projected his 'Imperial Scotch' mode more assertively in an unbuilt triumphal arch project (1911) for the King Edward Memorial in Edinburgh – some of whose characteristics, such as a Stirling Palace-type archway, would eventually re-emerge in the Scottish National War Memorial project after World War I (see Chapter 10).

As a rule, Scotch traditionalism in all its forms was concentrated in Edinburgh and Eastern Scotland, and was rarer in classical Glasgow and the West of Scotland – with some notable exceptions, such as the work of A. N. Paterson of Helensburgh, who argued in 1895 that the 'Scottish character' should be expressed in a 'national style', drawing in particular on the Renaissance period and 'our national Scottish development of that style'.[56] The design of his own house in Helensburgh, The Longcroft (1901), gave Paterson an ideal opportunity to explore this approach fully (Figure 9.3). The re-entrant angle turret of the L-plan villa was balustraded, copying Cessnock Castle. It combined crowstepped and curvilinear gables, and different dormer window types; there was a single bartizan enriching the guest bedroom, and a piano nobile as viewed from the garden front, with a balcony recalling Burn's prototypes. The Glasgow-born but London-based J. J. Stevenson, writing in 1880, attacked the 'wild' Baronialism of the Wallace Monument.[57] But the reaction of most architects in the West towards more artistic Scottish Renaissance houses assumed a more scenographic form – as exemplified in Leiper's towered villa, Dalmore (1873), which a later writer claimed in 1898 exemplified

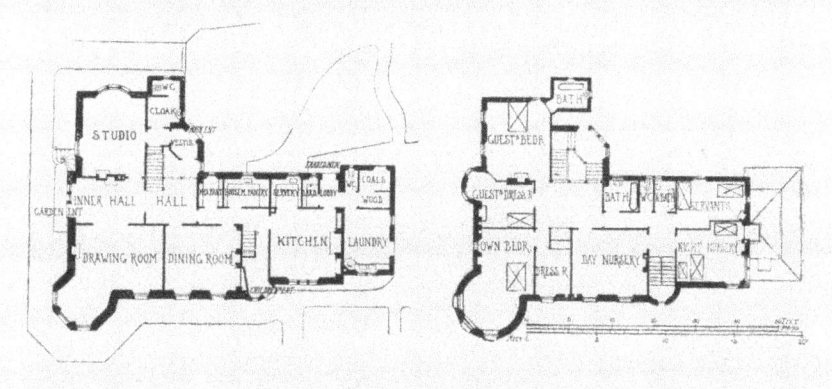

FIGURE 9.3 *The Long Croft, Helensburgh, by A. N. Paterson; drawing published 1903.* © *Historic Environment Scotland. https://canmore.org.uk/collection/1022451*

the work of the mature artist, able to seize and reproduce the spirit of the old work, its picturesque skyline, combined with the dignified simplicity of wall-spaces, while at the same time adapting it without loss of effect to modern requirements in matters of ample light and a liberal use of bow-windows, a very different thing to the lover of Scottish architecture from the affectation of crow-steps and meaningless turrets.[58]

Dalmore was still ashlar faced but Leiper's Auchenbothie (1898), near Kilmacolm, was white-harled and built round a courtyard, the entrance in a fat corner turret (and with a 1901 gate lodge by Mackintosh).[59]

The west of Scotland work of C. R. Mackintosh also introduced significant innovations in the interpretation of Scotch architecture, both in domestic and public buildings – for example, in taking rather further the shift towards a more obliquely geometrical massing, employing harling rather than facing stonework, and multipaned glazing rather than large plate-glass panes, coupled with more idiosyncratically modern design features. In Mackintosh's architecture, values related to mainstream traditionalism came perhaps into play, including an emphasis on the 'national', 'a feeling that has grown with our growth'. Architecture, Mackintosh argued in 1892, 'should be . . . less cosmopolitan and rather more national'. The only true model was the buildings of the First Castle Age.[60] In 1891, Mackintosh praised old castellated buildings, arguing that theirs was 'the native architecture of our own country and that of our forefathers . . . just as much Scotch as we are ourselves – as indigenous to our country as our wild flowers, our family names, our customs or our political constitution'.[61]

Mackintosh's admiration for this 'national' past was unmistakeably expressed in his built architecture. In his first works for Honeyman & Keppie, a Scotch Renaissance with Baroque elements was offset by touches of personal individuality, notably the tall, corbelled-out angle tower of the Glasgow Herald building (1893–4). The beginning of the mature phase of his architecture was heralded in 1896 by the award of the Glasgow Art School commission. Located on a steeply sloping site, its plan is an elongated letter 'E', with north-facing main facade and three wings falling to the rear, in a castle-like composition (seen from the south) which recalls the main front of Fyvie. Mackintosh's domestic architecture sought inspiration in the rendered geometry of preindustrial dwellings. Where his Viennese or German contemporaries looked towards 'folk' houses or Mediterranean vernacular, Mackintosh's designs were inspired by harled Scottish Renaissance domestic architecture, and on the recent work of MacLaren and Voysey. His personal interpretation of Scotch architecture was best exemplified by the Hill House, Helensburgh (1902), a long, relatively low block recalling precedents such as the south façade of Keith Marischal, but with Jugendstil-like blank-walled expanses and random-looking multipaned windows (Figure 9.4). The first view of the house, from the gate, is an L-plan garden façade. Hill House has itself an L-plan, formed of two wings connected at their angles. An entrance adjoins the inner angle of the 'L', near a projecting stair turret. Dormers cut through the eaves, while inside, the principal bedroom is partly barrel-vaulted in suggestion of a castle's stone vault. The external-facing angle where the two wing gables connect has a conical-roofed turret suggesting a splay-planned house or turreted internal angle as at Lickleyhead.[62] Windyhill (1899–1901), in Kilmacolm, equally recalled the two-storey flat-fronted and grid-windowed 'laird's house' formula. At Glasgow's Queen Margaret's

FIGURE 9.4 *Hill House, Helensburgh, by C. R. Mackintosh, 1902* – view from south; 1904 photograph by Henry Bedford Lemere. © Historic Environment Scotland. https://canmore.org.uk/collection/677386

College (1895), Mackintosh (with Keppie) produced an Art Nouveau L-plan castle, complete with polygonal stair turret in the inner angle, the frontal jamb near-unwindowed, parapeted like a tower-house.[63] The culmination of this aesthetic, outside as much as inside, was the *Haus eines Kunstfreundes* competition design: here, the near symmetry and horizontality seemed to draw on the seventeenth-century laird's house as a model.

From 1904 to 1914, under principal architect W. T. Oldrieve (a former Baldwin Brown pupil), Government buildings also became a redoubt of the new monumental variant of Scottish traditionalism. Oldrieve's post offices are often asymmetrical compositions, featuring crowstepped gables or towers (as at the Aberdeen GPO, 1907). Oban and Lerwick both date from 1908: the latter has a roughly U-plan façade, with projecting off-centre bay in ashlar (hinting at Burn's style).[64] In 1912, Oldrieve prepared abortive designs for government offices on Calton Hill in a towered palace style, while the military also adopted the theme for barrack projects – for instance, at the Cameron Barracks in Inverness (completed 1886, by the Royal Engineers' office in Edinburgh).[65] Similarly, police stations were now firmly within the Baronial ambit: that at Renfrew by A. N. Paterson (1910) comprises a square tower-house with low wing, while Thornhill (Dumfriesshire), by James Barbour and John M. Bowie (1909), reversed that arrangement, having a prominent two-storey house block with a tower on one side.[66] J. A. Campbell built the Institute for Women in Alexandria (1888–91) as a low, squat tower-house with a gabled, L-plan wing on one side and a stern-looking wall and gateway on the other, all sculpturally rock-faced, the gift of industrialist and estate owner William Ewing Gilmour.[67] In 1901, a new edition of Billings was published, with an introduction by Anderson, which repeated his contrast between the 'sham castles' of Baronial and the supposedly unselfconscious 'functional truth' of the Renaissance originals. The most ambitious Imperial Scottish Renaissance design for a social institution was a school for soldiers' children – Queen Victoria Memorial School, Dunblane (1907–8) – built to commemorate the monarch and Scottish soldiers killed in the Boer War. Designed by J. A. Campbell, it combined crowstepped gables with gridded fenestration on the main frontage; the chapel had a 'King's College' window and a squat, St Monans-like spire.

The years after 1910 also saw the climax of another grandiose fashion within the Second Castle Age, namely the restoration, or reconstruction, of fantasy castles in rock-faced rubble. Rosebery's earlier project at Barnbougle pointed to a reinvigoration of the fashion for reoccupation of ruins, a fashion that gained further force from the movement for rubble monumentality. A key landmark in this process was the remodelling of Edinburgh Castle from a Georgian barracks to a focus of Scottish imperialist symbolism: from the mid-1880s, many of its structures were subjected to a Baronializing reconstruction by Hippolyte Blanc. This programme was launched chiefly at the instigation of Francis, Tenth Lord Napier of Merchistoun and first Baron Ettrick, best known for chairing the Napier Commission which resulted in the Crofters' Act of 1886.[68] From 1883, Napier scolded what he called 'the English government' for having presided over a degradation of Scotland's ancient royal buildings, and he successfully secured government finance for Blanc's remodellings. The Great Hall (like St Giles's) was reopened and reunified, and the Argyll Tower and Regent Morton Gate were reshaped (1885–7) to resemble a tower-house. The Castle's north-west corner, facing visitors arriving from the west, was rebuilt in the 1890s, to look more Scotch, with a tall block which gave presence to a previously flimsy looking corner.

From now on the phase of castle re-creation began in earnest. Already in 1883 Andrew Kerr had reroofed Doune Castle for the Earl of Moray; in 1897–1902, R. W. Schultz had rebuilt the ruined Wester Kames Tower for the Third Marquis of Bute. Now two much larger schemes started, at Eilean Donan and Duart Castles, both deriving from clan Romanticism, each being commissioned by a clan descendant who was in fact a British army officer resident in England.[69] At Eilean Donan (Figure 9.5), destroyed by the British navy in 1719, Major John MacRae-Gilstrap embarked in 1913 on a

£250,000 programme, spanning two decades, to rebuild the ruined stump into a huge, block-like tower, in rubble inside and out, to the designs of Edinburgh architect George MacKie Watson (a former Anderson assistant); the MacRaes had been Constables of Eilean Donan Castle since 1511. Duart Castle, the ancient MacLean clan seat, was purchased in 1911 by the seventy-six-year-old Lieut. Col. Sir Fitzroy MacLean, who commissioned J. J. Burnet to rebuild it (completed by 1916). MacLean, a former President of the Highland Society of London, held a formal inaugural ceremony on 24 August 1912, and a gathering 'to witness the re-crowning of a Chief and the re-birth of a Clan'.[70] In each case, the rebuilt castle announced ancient clanship and status, binding its reoccupiers to their ancient territory and claimed entitlements. Similarly, in the Inverness area, Castle Stuart had been abandoned, then reinhabited, and then restored by Brown and Wardrop in

FIGURE 9.5 *Eilean Donan Castle – rebuilt from 1911 by George Mackie Watson; view from south-east; photograph dated 1995. © Historic Environment Scotland.* https://canmore.org.uk/collection/707300

1869.[71] Now its neighbour and contemporary, Dalcross, was restored in 1897–8 to designs by W. L. Carruthers.[72] In Perthshire, Ardblair, a multiphase courtyard castle with a 1668 datestone, was enlarged and remodelled by Sydney Mitchell and Wilson in 1894–1908 for Philip Laurence Kington Blair-Oliphant, to provide a renewed family 'seat' in Scotland: Blair-Oliphant was later killed in World War I.[73]

Other projects remained on paper only – such as an 1891 proposal to make good the 1746 ruination of Linlithgow. In that year, local magistrate James MacAlpine wrote to the Marquess of Lothian, then Secretary for Scotland: 'There is . . . a strong desire that something should be done by the Government to restore the Royal Palace of Linlithgow so as to make it suitable for a Royal residence or for some other Government purpose.' An official commented privately, 'Something *should* be done, but nothing *will* be done.'[74] Visits and reports followed, and the idea of a royal use was rejected. Government architect W. W. Robertson argued that the palace was now an established monument rather than a building fitted for reuse. In the event, it was decided to opt for the cheaper option of repair rather than restoration – disregarding conservation arguments from the Edinburgh Architectural Association, encouraged by Rowand Anderson, Thomas Ross and others, that restoration would be the best way to preserve the building.[75] Overall, the general opposition to government involvement in historic building conservation deterred any official restoration interventions in the manner of French 'monuments historiques'. These constraints were highlighted in a 1906 lecture to the Edinburgh Architectural Association by W. T. Oldrieve, optimistically entitled 'What HM Office of Works Is Doing for the Historical Buildings in Scotland'.[76] He was unsuccessful in proposing restoration of the fifteenth-century ruins of Rosyth Castle as 'the central feature of the proposed northern naval base', including 'a Reading room for Naval Officers' and 'a Naval Museum'.[77] The castle, Oldrieve emphasized, was associated with Mary Queen of Scots. He proposed minimal external change, but the tower would have gained a renewed superstructure and stone-slabbed roof; the proposal was turned down by the admiralty and the tower remains a ruin today.

More generally, the outbreak of World War I brought to an end the Imperial Scotch style, in its original form of 'manifest-destiny' confidence; as we will see in Chapter 10, a more restrained outlook succeeded it in the interwar years, as exemplified in Lorimer's Scottish National War Memorial project of the 1920s, with its emphasis on artistic *Gesamtkunstwerk* rather than muscular rhetoric as an expression of national pride.

The Scotch Old Town

In contrast to the rhetorical assertiveness of turn-of-century Imperial Scotch architecture, another contemporary strand within the Second

Castle Age pursued large scale and monumentality in a completely different way: through the 'artistic' reform of working-class housing, and of the city as a whole – in the belief that one source of golden-age Scottish harmony had been the collective values of burgh community. Here the doctrine of the ennoblement of the ordinary home, applied by Anderson, Lorimer and the others chiefly to bourgeois villas, was for the first time extended into the field of the collective urban fabric. Internationally, architectural heritage efforts in many European countries were increasingly concerning themselves with the 'Old Town', or '*Altstadt*', as a focus of 'traditional' townscape and community.[78] In Scotland, the unchallenged focus of this concept was the now-dilapidated Old Town of Edinburgh, celebrated in the writings of Scott and Robert Louis Stevenson. The very characteristics previously most reviled now began to inspire admiration: a 'very metropolis of squalor, yet likewise of Romance'. This new movement initially defined itself chiefly against the classicism of the 'regular and utilitarian modern New Town':[79] in 1889 the Marquis of Lorne attacked its 'facades which look as if they were all punched out of grey paper with one machine'.[80] However, there was already the beginning of a revival in the public esteem of the New Town too. Robert Louis Stevenson extended the growing artistic prestige of the Old Town to embrace the New: 'The two re-act in a picturesque sense, and the one is the making of the other'; in site and layout, 'how much description would apply commonly to either'. Instead, he proposed a new bogeyman: the 'monstrosity' of suburban villa development.[81]

This new sensitivity to historic context also began to influence new design. In 1907, the Tory politician and judge, Sir John Hay Athole Macdonald, argued that

> it is pleasing to know that an enthusiasm has arisen for preserving ancient picturesque features in the City, and bringing the work of necessary new building into congruity as far as possible ... There is no branch of architecture in which there is more need to study the congruous than where the new must take its place beside the old.[82]

As we saw in the previous chapter, this idea had already featured prominently in the mid-Victorian Scotch Baronial years, especially in the design of City Improvement projects.[83] For Old Town infills, however, the once self-evidently national Flemish style had now largely lost its appeal, and merged in with the Franco-Renaissance of George Washington Browne's Edinburgh Public Library (1887–90), looming above the Cowgate.[84]

Some turn-of-century neobaroque urban complexes also overlapped with the last urban phases of Scotch Baronial, through a forceful and pictorial eclecticism that included some castellated, towered aspects, as seen notably in the domineering structures built as gateway blocks flanking

Edinburgh's new North Bridge, opened in 1897.[85] The 'Scotsman' building on the west side, built 1899–1905 by Dunn and Findlay (the latter being *Scotsman* proprietor J. Ritchie Findlay's son), was composed as an array of individual towered structures, the tallest totalling thirteen storeys, including cavernous substructures.[86] Its corbel-turreted angles attempt to echo old Scottish castles, either directly or via the medium of the work of 'London Scottish' architect Richard Norman Shaw (especially New Scotland Yard of 1887–90); the interior of the 'Scotsman' building's Advertisement Office (c. 1900) featured sumptuous neo-seventeenth-century ceilings. At the southern end of the eastern range, a colossal tower-house for the Commercial Bank of Scotland by Sydney Mitchell & Wilson (1898–9) features overscaled detailing throughout, mainly classical, but at the wallhead, a mighty parapet supported on multi-corbelled brackets, and dormers with Newark Castle-type pediments.

But just as Anderson's traditionalist school of house designers was by the 1880s sharply reacting against the supposedly tasteless ornamentation of High Baronial, a similar process was underway in the same years in this architecture of urban ensembles. Partly in reaction against commercialized tenemental Baronial or Baronial-cum-Baroque, a 'Scotch Old Town' architecture, sharing many of the same ethical and aesthetic values as traditionalism, began to emerge, and from the 1890s this was elaborated by Patrick Geddes into a full-blown philosophy of artistic 'conservative surgery' that would condition all subsequent regeneration efforts in other historic urban areas, such as Stirling, Jedburgh – or in the Canongate in Edinburgh itself.

In the field of new architecture, this concept sprang into life almost fully formed in 1883–6, in the most remarkable of Sydney Mitchell's prolific works: Well Court, Edinburgh – a courtyard block of working-class tenements commissioned by J. R. Findlay in the heart of Edinburgh's picturesque industrial colony, the Dean Village.[87] Findlay had already commissioned Mitchell to remodel his house at 3 Rothesay Terrace – on a New Town escarpment directly overlooking the site – in the same year, with an eclectic mix of neo-Renaissance detailing and 'neo-Scotch' small-paned windows of a kind that Lorimer and Mackintosh were later to popularize. Well Court was a microcosm of advanced architectural ideas about housing reform: a sanitary slum redevelopment of 'artistic' character, not as scattered cottages but as a dense block arranged around a garden courtyard. Although its centrepiece was an emphatically Scotch community hall, with oriel turrets like the Earl's Palace in Kirkwall and a tall tower like Stirling Town House, its picturesque grouping and steep roofs, designed to be viewed at its most dramatic from Findlay's house across the Water of Leith, evoked the image of an old Germanic walled city rather than Old Edinburgh. It also synthesized, in a way that could be adapted in twentieth-century social housing design, centuries-old features of Scottish tenement architecture, such as paired windows. A rather similar, agglomeratively picturesque approach – appearing to combine several structures in one – was adopted later by Anderson in his Pearce Institute complex in Govan, near Glasgow (1903–5), which seemed to develop from Mitchell's Dean Village. It was a benefaction to the 'people of Govan' from Dinah Pearce, widow of the former owner of Fairfield's shipyard. Its east face was almost tenemental, while the hall on its west had large Lorimerian windows separated by Falkland-like buttresses, with a near-free-standing polygonal stair turret. The main south front had asymmetrical flanking gables, one curvilinear and the other crowstepped, enhanced with a profusion of historical references, such as an oriel and twinned empty niches derived from Linlithgow, a Moray House balcony, and Newark Castle dormer heads.

'Old Town' Scotch became more specific to Old Edinburgh in a display (also by Mitchell) at the 1886 Edinburgh International Exhibition. The notion of a replica old city to recall the national past, pioneered only thirteen years earlier at the Vienna world's fair, was here carried through with Mitchell's usual gusto. In 1885, he had already restored the real Mercat Cross in the High Street, at the instigation of the Liberal Prime Minister, W. E. Gladstone – an Eton and Oxford-educated Anglo-Scot – using fragments retrieved from Drum's garden.[88] The cross's design was Scotch Baronial.[89] According to an 1898 account,

> The turreted octagon was constructed after . . . [that] . . . of 1436; the old stone pillar, strengthened by a bar of bronze through the centre, was re-erected on its summit. The old medallions, which, in 1814, fell into the hands of Sir Walter Scott and were inserted in an ornamental garden wall at Abbotsford, were reproduced, bearing heraldic devices of the arms of the United Kingdom of Scotland, England, and Ireland, of the City of Edinburgh, of the Burgh of Canongate, of the Town of Leith, and of the University of Edinburgh.[90]

A similar mercat-cross pattern was used for the 1912 Wallace Memorial at Elderslie, authored by London Scots John G. T. Murray and J. Andrew Minty.[91] At the exhibition on the Meadows, Mitchell's 'Old Edinburgh' display was a microcosm of the High Street in earlier days, containing recreations – slightly miniaturized, and populated by authentically clad actors – of the vanished landmarks celebrated in Robert Louis Stevenson's novels. The spiny skyline of Mitchell's miniature *Altstadt* protruded incongruously from the rear section of Burnet's overall glazed roof.

The 1886 exhibition made a deep impression on the man who would actually begin the revitalization of Old Edinburgh: the pioneering city planner Patrick Geddes. Inspired partly by Scott and Stevenson's Romanticism, and by the building of Well Court (which he acclaimed in 1889 as the 'best modern addition' to the 'old city'), Geddes embarked on an ambitious strategy in the mid-1880s to revive the eighteenth-century 'Golden Age' of Edinburgh, seeing the Old Town as a diseased organism which could be regenerated, spiritually and academically, and through actual physical recuperation of its fabric.[92] Drawing on his love of property speculation, he began to buy decayed tenements and sites, and began a piecemeal programme of 'conservative surgery', intended to revitalize the Old Town as a university city. He condemned the City Improvement Acts' sweeping demolitions and remodelling as 'civic ruin': 'We shall not get art . . . by piling up colossal rabbit hutches.'[93] 'What we want is Centres of Life.'[94] Reconditioned old buildings were converted to workers' housing or University halls, ornamented with picturesque timber outshots, and interspersed with 'reclaimed' garden spaces. Geddes's most spectacular building achievement, and the most prominent 'Scotch Old Town' project in general, was the Ramsay Gardens university apartment development overlooking the Castle Esplanade, where he commissioned Henbest Capper (from 1892) and Sydney Mitchell (1893) to enlarge modest existing buildings into a lofty, turreted outcrop, adapting the dramatic style of Well Court in harling with stone dressings. In 1894, Geddes described Ramsay Garden as 'not indeed, happily, a New, but a renewed Old Town'.[95]

'The Renascence of Worship': A Scotch Ecclesiastical Architecture?

Scotch traditionalism's overtones of crafts wholeness overlapped significantly with turn-of-century religious architecture, where a new Presbyterian liturgical movement to heighten the devotional and ceremonial element of worship was under way.[96] In purely stylistic terms, too, the previously sharp division between secular Baronial and religious Gothic was beginning to become more fuzzy. For example, the Wallace monument reintroduced to ecclesiastical architecture the idea of a crown spire, extending the repertoire of Scotch Baronial, after a fashion, to churches: Bruce & Sturrock added a crown spire to St John's, Gourock, as early as 1877–8, and many others were built in the 1880s.[97] The London Scot, J. J. Stevenson, designed two churches with mightier spires: St Leonard's/Free St Leonard's Perth (1882–5, which echoes Stirling's Holy Rude)[98] and Kelvin Stevenson Memorial in Glasgow (1902), whose flanking steeple derived from King's College, and its west window from late Scottish Gothic prototypes (Figure 9.6). The biggest crown, however, was that of Coats Memorial Baptist Church, Paisley (1894), by Hippolyte Blanc.[99] By the 1890s, although crown spires were falling somewhat from favour, a number of churches now featured steeples in the even more literal form of small tower-houses, or at any rate castellation of some sort, following the ultimate precedent of St Machar's, Aberdeen or New Abbey. The foremost designer of these was John J. Burnet, with examples at Lossiemouth (St Geraldine's, 1899–1903),[100] Grangemouth (Dundas Church, 1894),[101] and Stenhouse and Carron (1900) – which

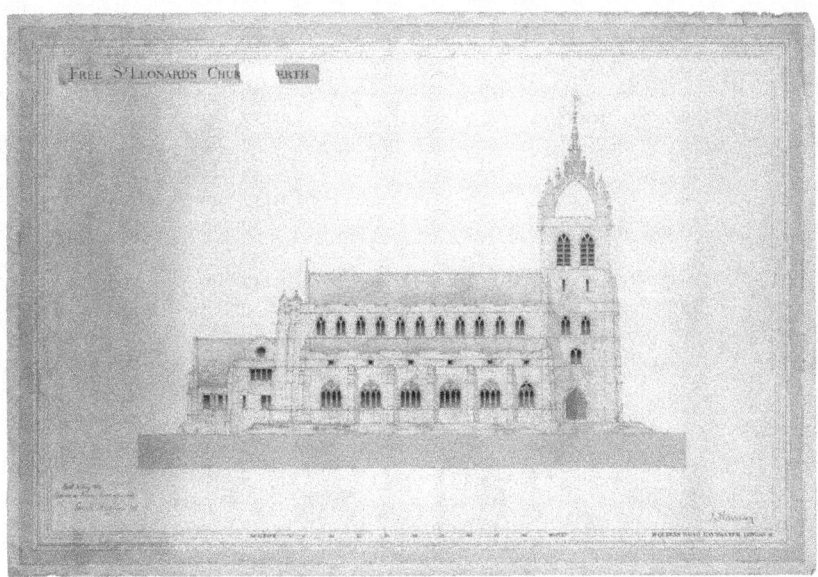

FIGURE 9.6 *St Leonard's/Free St Leonard's Church, Perth, drawing by J. J. Stevenson, 1882.* © Historic Environment Scotland. *https://canmore.org.uk/collection/1309245*

even has bartizans.[102] Subsequently, the idea of the 'church tower-house' was repeated in the work of Reginald Fairlie, notably at Our Lady of the Assumption, Troon (1909–11).

At these churches, Burnet also made ostentatious use of round-arched openings – a feature connected not just to the neo-Romanesque (both fifteenth century, as at St Machar's, and nineteenth century), but also to the contemporary Celtic Revival, which was itself, arguably, in some ways also an offshoot from the Baronial. The fashion for erecting wheeled Celtic memorial crosses came first, and was probably well underway when Billings published his drawing of St Martin's Cross in Iona. Then followed a restrained fashion for architectural Celticism. MacGibbon and Ross had already pointed to the use of round arches in transitional Celtic/Romanesque works,[103] and round-arched architecture started to become popular towards the century's end. An early exemplar was Anderson's Catholic Apostolic Church in Edinburgh (1872). The characteristic Irish-type round tower seen at Brechin and Abernethy provided a third model for Celtic Revivalists. This pattern was most prominently displayed in the 1912–13 monument, designed by J. Sandyford Kay, to the 1263 Battle of Largs (against the Vikings), but prior to that, it had also been adopted in a little grouping of churches by Chalmers – St Leonard's Dunfermline (1904), Dervaig (1905) and Canna (1913), all with round-arched neo-Celtic windows and the latter two featuring exaggeratedly rustic rubble. The Dunfermline tower doubtless alluded to the town's former role as the seat of the last representatives of the Gaelic royal dynasty.

As in the case of castles and palaces, restoration projects infused with national values, sometimes competing, became increasingly prominent in these decades, alongside completely new architecture. In Edinburgh, the internal arrangements of St Giles's Church in Edinburgh provided a barometer of the shifting balance of power between Presbyterianism and Episcopacy: subdivided after the Reformation, made unicameral in the 1630s at the instigation of Charles I; repartitioned in 1639 to defy him; and finally reunified yet again in 1871–83 in the wake of Burn's exterior regularization from 1829. The internal reunification stemmed from an 1867 proposal by Robert Chambers, who commissioned Robert Morham, then William Hay, as architects.[104] Queen Victoria headed the subscription list.[105] The project was intended to respectfully supplement Westminster Abbey by providing a Scottish national 'Walhalla', including a 'Poet's Corner', to accommodate Scottish heroes who failed to qualify for admission in London.[106] Here, with the growing appetite of the period for martial heroes, the duopoly of Wallace and Bruce no longer seemed sufficient or appropriate, and later centuries were trawled for noteworthy warrior nobles – the obvious candidates being the Royalist martyr James Graham, Marquess of Montrose, and the Presbyterian martyr Archibald Campbell, Marquess of Argyll, both executed outside St Giles's in 1650 and 1661 respectively. With the aim of celebrating the reconciliation of the two opposed traditions in Imperial Scotland, sumptuously classical recumbent monuments in an appropriately seventeenth-century style were commissioned for both. Queen Victoria announced the idea of a Montrose memorial in 1886;[107] it was executed by John and W. Birnie Rhind from designs by Rowand Anderson, 1887–9. Argyll's monument of 1894–5 was designed by Sydney Mitchell & Wilson, carved by Thomas Beveridge, the effigy sculpted by Charles McBride.[108]

The culmination of the national works at St Giles, and a microcosm of Scotch Traditionalist ideas and imagery in general, was Robert Lorimer's Thistle Chapel, built in 1909–11 as a permanent home for the ceremonial 'Ancient Order of the Knights of the Thistle', whose rituals celebrated the continuing prestige of the Scottish nobility within the British imperial monarchy (Figure 9.7). Thomas Ross had investigated the possibility of restoring Holyrood Abbey Kirk for the Order, but instead, a new chapel was tucked into St Giles's south-east corner. It was of tiny area but great height, and externally expressed as a restrainedly castellated, angle-turreted block. Its interior was unambiguously Gothic, with densely encrusted decoration: a continuous range of canopied stalls, carved by William and Alexander Clow with countless variations of detail, is surmounted by a soaring vault congested with ribs and bosses. All stonework was carried out by Joseph Hayes and his assistants, some from models by Louis Deuchars. Internally, the chapel contains the greatest number of heraldic symbols in any Scottish

FIGURE 9.7 *Thistle Chapel, St Giles, Edinburgh, by Robert Lorimer, 1909–11 – interior view; photograph by Henry Bedford Lemere, c. 1911.* © Historic Environment Scotland. *https://canmore.org.uk/collection/488799*

building – over 260 of them, made almost exclusively by Scottish artists and craftspeople – a forest of crowns, crests and symbols, all celebrating social hierarchy and elitism as the essence of Scotland's proud and ancient heritage. The chapel was inaugurated by the king in 1911, and Lorimer was knighted.[109] As we will see in Chapter 10, the chapel's integration of crafts designers into a monumental 'national Scotch' context would later be echoed in the very different context of Lorimer's Scottish National War Memorial (1924–7).

Although the St Giles project was actually a 'unification' rather than a 'restoration', the turn of century witnessed several more orthodox restorations of significant religious ruins – with strong interconnections with the sturdy ethos of Scotch traditionalism. Restored churches included the abbeys of Iona and Paisley, and the more modest Episcopal church in South Queensferry. Like Chalmers' pre-Gothic-style churches, these shared a concept of the distinctiveness of medieval Scottish church architecture, and were promoted by both the kirk and the Episcopal Church. A particularly significant project was the restoration of Dunblane Cathedral by Anderson in 1888–93. The nave roof was ornamented with representations of historic figures and monarchs, and a seventeenth-century-style pulpit was installed.[110] Some smaller Highland churches were also reroofed for use, including tiny Ensay, in 1910,[111] and in 1912, Eoropie, motivated by the incumbent Rev Henry Anderson Meaden, who was advised by architect J. S. Richardson, soon to be government Inspector of Ancient Monuments. It was, however, the ruin of Iona Abbey that commanded the highest Romantic prestige, as the ancient centre of Christianity in Scotland. Although the Episcopal church made an early bid for the ruin by holding an open-air service in it in 1848,[112] it stood on Argyll Estate lands, and the Eighth Duke ultimately gifted the abbey to the Church of Scotland in 1899. The nave was rebuilt from 1908 to designs of historian architect Dr Peter MacGregor Chalmers (1859–1922).[113] As the original great west window (presumably pointed) no longer existed, Chalmers instead designed a round-arched window arcade: Romanticism demanded a Celtic-looking resolution.

A comprehensive synthesis of both Gothic and Scotch elements under a national aegis was brought together by Anderson in 1885–9 at the Scottish National Portrait Gallery and National Museum – a project significantly grounded in the palatial Gothic eclecticism of the grand country house he was building for the Marquess of Bute at Mount Stuart (from 1878 onwards) (Figure 9.8). Largely financed through anonymous donations (totalling £50,000) from J. R. Findlay, the realization of the Gallery was the climax of a long campaign for the building of a national pantheon. Anderson, here acting in his capacity as architect to the Board of Manufactures (as the Government was shouldering half of the cost), conceived the building as a massive rectangular rubble block with corner spires, and contrasted the ornate central entrance bay with a vast expanse of bare upper walling. Findlay encouraged the Board to provide an extensive decorative scheme – an intention which accorded well with Anderson's concern to foster the building crafts. The scheme included nationally symbolic external and internal sculpture, and, in the central hall, a frieze of historical figures, as well as a cycle of historical murals by William Hole (painted from 1895), including the battles of Largs and Bannockburn (Figure 9.9). Evoking as it did the Doge's Palace, Anderson's design reconciled medievalism with

FIGURE 9.8 *Scottish National Portrait Gallery, Edinburgh, by Robert Rowand Anderson, 1885–9 – view from north-east; photograph by Henry Bedford Lemere, c. 1900.* © Historic Environment Scotland. https://canmore.org.uk/collection/684146

classical gravity and symmetry, and thus upheld the hierarchical primacy of the great public building. Such a combination of palazzo architecture and symbolic decoration was a well-established tradition within turn-of-century northern European public buildings of national status (as exemplified for instance at Martin Nyrop's near-contemporary Copenhagen Town Hall of 1892). The overall impression, with its giant bartizan-like turrets and

FIGURE 9.9 *Scottish National Portrait Gallery, Edinburgh – entrance door with sculptures including national heroes Sir William Wallace and King Robert I, 'the Bruce'; photograph dated 2012.* © *Historic Environment Scotland. https:// canmore.org.uk/collection/1268125*

rock-faced rubble masonry, seemed distinctly Scotch, and yet featured no specifically castellated motifs – a shift from a literal stylistic recipe to a more indirect evocation of national qualities that would only gather pace in the twentieth century.[114]

Conclusion

The turn-of-century architectural trend towards sobriety and dignity, and the ever-increasing emphasis on the national, seemed to run hand in hand. The result was that the Second Castle Age, and its values of national identity, mutated steadily away from the eclectically ornamented Baronialism of the Burn-Bryce generation, confined chiefly to country houses, towards a more diffuse architectural expression and a wider range of building types, epitomized both by the traditionalism of Anderson and the Old Town Scotch of Mitchell and Geddes – patterns which, however, all retained some links to the castellated tradition. In 1914, however, all this was put in suspense, as the arguments for greater respect or autonomy for Scotland, or for refreshing the union, were drowned out by the call for the nation to resume its traditional martial role.[115] The story of Scotch Baronial was abruptly interrupted as war took away patrons, architects, builders, and resources. And when the war was concluded, society had new expectations: the old elites would find themselves sharing power with others, and over the next half-century their houses might be lost to them, or become 'heritage', their liberty to treat them as they willed curtailed by society. During the half-century after 1918, the 'disciplining' of the built environment would assume a more and more concentrated form, as the Scottish nation's attention turned inwards rather than outwards. Architecture and building would increasingly become an arena for the action of the state, undertaking initiatives of modernization determined by 'social needs', 'standards' and 'planning' – a context within which the architectural expression of national identity would become a more and more complex matter, and the Second Castle Age would gradually but inexorably come to an end.

10

1914 Onwards: Scottish Architectural Identity in the Age of Modernism

A new sharp sense of the national past of Scotland, not as the board for an antiquary's game or a pageant of the romantic and picturesque, but as something real, and important to the present.[1]

– AGNES MURE MACKENZIE, 1941

The true Scots tradition – I do not mean tripe a la Bryce, overloaded with mullions, plate glass, stringcourses and useless turrets – but that sane line of work refounded and continuously practised by the late Sir Robert Lorimer.[2]

– LESLIE GRAHAM THOMSON, 1932

Scottish architects are European and cosmopolitan in outlook . . . and eager to lead the country in another cultural revival comparable to that which took place a hundred years ago.[3]

– CHARLES MCKEAN, 1992

Introduction

The devastating effects of World War I, and the gradual decline and disappearance of the British Empire over the following decades, severely challenged the confidence and pride of unionist nationalism, and in its wake, the ideal of an independent Scottish nation-state made its first tentative reappearance. Paradoxically, however, these were also the years when all forms of traditional and explicitly national architectural style were beginning to give way to the international trends of the modern movement: the last set-piece of the Second Castle Age was Lorimer's National War Memorial in Edinburgh Castle. After 1945, as the authority of modern architecture and planning became all-embracing, the ideals of Scottish tradition were increasingly siphoned away from new architecture altogether, into the field of architectural conservation – a field that now increasingly embraced the monuments of the mid-nineteenth century, including Scotch Baronial houses, alongside earlier, more conventional 'castellated heritage'. Later in the twentieth century, under postmodernism, demands began for a return to more explicit references to 'context', but the predicament this posed for contemporary architecture was highlighted in the Holyrood parliament – a building laden with heady expectations of 'cultural renewal' and yet, in its metaphoric, 'iconic' vocabulary, tied to an intrinsically transient, globalizing ethos.

Interwar Traditionalism: Reshaping 'National Community'

The early twentieth century saw a growing demand for far-reaching social reforms, resting partly on the new structures of mass democracy, but more immediately on a huge expansion of administrative devolution through Scottish Office boards and departments, motivated by the philosophy of 'planning'. Planned social intervention was paralleled by the growth of planned economic corporatism, to combat the 1930s slump. These changes had a marked material impact on architecture and its patronage. The swashbuckling individualism of the turn-of-century patrons seemed to have vanished without trace.[4] There was an increasing reluctance, among architects of all persuasions, to describe buildings in terms of particular 'styles'. Instead, a more abstract or metaphoric language, with terms such as 'mass' or 'sculpture', was used. There were still sharp divergences, which in some ways perpetuated the pre-war division between the Beaux-Arts classical and traditionalist schools. The traditionalists, as inheritors of the Second Castle Age, continued to elaborate their discourse of golden-age Scottish 'essence' with an increasingly impassioned rhetoric of nationality, focusing architecturally on the precedent of the Scottish Renaissance, with its combination of castellation and classicism: one architect argued that James V's architecture had featured 'the classic feeling appearing alongside a rough and bold flavour of Scottish character'.[5] After Lorimer's death in 1929, his disciples elevated him to the status of a patriotic standard-bearer: John Begg in 1932 hailed him as a saviour and rescuer of 'the Scottish tradition' as 'a living modern body', and Lorimer's pupil Leslie Grahame Thomson asserted that he had 'rejected the classic styles – perhaps unconsciously defending the northern ethos from the domination of an alien and southern philosophy in stone'.[6] Thomson defined Lorimer's architecture as 'sane modernism': 'the true Scots tradition – I do not mean tripe a la Bryce, overloaded with mullions, plate glass, stringcourses and useless turrets – but that sane line of work refounded and continuously practised by the late Sir Robert Lorimer'.[7]

The building of Lorimerian country houses had now largely finished – a rare exception being the young Basil Spence's Broughton Place of 1935–8, echoing Formakin in harled form, and with sculpture by Lorimer's son Hew (Figure 10.1). Instead, the most important individual work of early twentieth-century castellated Scotch traditionalism was a great public monument to imperial warfare: Lorimer's Scottish National War Memorial, built in 1924–7. Following much debate, it had been decided that this temple of martial sacrifice should take the form of a memorial hall, converted from an eighteenth-century barracks building within the castellated setting of Edinburgh Castle. Lorimer remodelled the barracks into a sumptuous

FIGURE 10.1 *Broughton Place by Basil Spence, 1935–8 – view from south-west; undated photograph from Basil Spence Archive. © Historic Environment Scotland.* https://canmore.org.uk/collection/1053959

nave-like space (the 'Hall of Honour') of somewhat sixteenth-century Scottish Renaissance character, with tall octagonal columns, round-headed windows and a Falkland Palace-like bay arrangement, including roundels (Figure 10.2). Attached at the centre was the 'Shrine', a neo-Romanesque apse with Gothic vaulting and separately articulated roofline, strikingly similar in character to the Thistle Chapel. Externally, the building was like a compendium of Scotch traditionalism, in its archaic rubble walling, simplified castellation and cavernous Stirling Palace-type main portal,

FIGURE 10.2 *Scottish National War Memorial – interior view of Hall of Honour; photograph of c. 1927.* © Historic Environment Scotland. https://canmore.org.uk/collection/702426

juxtaposed with the massive ecclesiastical traditionalism of the Shrine, a neo-Romanesque apse with taller roofline (Figure 10.3). Lorimer said that the memorial should 'look as if it was a hundred years old', with its 'bold and rather heavy type of detail'. Internally, *Gesamtkunstwerk* predominated: the non-denominational memorial, crowded with quasi-funerary monuments, provided an opportunity, normally denied to Presbyterians, for an interior laden with 'religious' symbolism, commemorating not just the war itself but also exemplary biblical characters and Scottish patriots as far back as Calgacus (a mythical hero of resistance against Roman invasion in 83–4 CE). Inside the Shrine, the bare Castle rock pushes through into the building, supporting a steel casket, guarded by angels, which contains the names of the one hundred thousand Scottish soldiers killed in the war. Above soars a suspended statue (designed by Alice Meredith Williams and carved by the Clow Brothers) of the Archangel Michael. The central panel of Douglas Strachan's encircling stained-glass windows, depicting Christ rising free from the cross, hints at the 'resurrection' of the warrior-martyrs.[8] The number of visitors, or 'pilgrims' as they were often called in the 1920s, was

FIGURE 10.3 *Scottish National War Memorial by Lorimer and Matthew, 1924–7 – view from south; photograph of c. 1927, including array of commemorative wreaths.* © *Historic Environment Scotland. https://canmore.org.uk/collection/1201763*

so great that the rough rock on the Shrine floor was worn smooth within a few years.

By the late 1930s, however, a new, state-based national identity was in course of construction, whose dynamic momentum was provided not by imperial and industrial expansion, but by disciplined social reconstruction at home. A new generation of traditionalists, rejecting the establishment patriotism of the Anderson generation, called for a different sort of 'community', looking to the future but rooted firmly in concepts of the national past. There was heady talk of 'rebirth', and an outpouring of popularized publications. In 1941, for instance, Agnes Mure Mackenzie wrote of 'a new vision, a new sense of Scotland' . . . 'the bare trees are flushing with rising sap' . . . 'we have Scotland's future history to shape'. In opposition to socialist class politics, there was an insistence on a classless national community – accentuated by conviction of the 'organic' cohesion of Scotland in comparison with England's 'caste-ridden society'.[9]

In architecture, these new ideas prompted the emergence of a new generation of aggressively modernizing traditionalists. Prominent was a new hostility to cosmopolitanism, and the drawing of a sharp contrast between avant-garde 'flashy, international' continental modernism and the concept of a 'wholesome' or 'national' Scottish modernism. For public buildings serving the new tasks of the modern planned economy, a severely monumental classicism initially prevailed, but sometimes substantially overlapping with traditionalism in use of crafts details or massive rubble monumentality – as exemplified in the state-sponsored grandeur of the power stations built in the highlands from 1946 by the north of Scotland Hydro-Electric Board, designed by architects including H. O. Tarbolton and James Shearer: the castle-like outcrop of Pitlochry (1947–53), integrated with a dam and bridge, was faced in granite, and prominently adorned with the Board's coat of arms and motto, *Neart nan Gleann* (*Power of the Glens*) (Figure 10.4). Shearer used locally quarried rubble for his stations, to achieve an 'appropriate sense of rugged strength' and 'massive simplicity'.[10]

The overwhelming focus of the new generation of traditionalists, like their predecessors, was still domestic architecture – although they drew a sharp distinction between the 'authentic' castellated tradition and the supposedly vulgar ornamentation of nineteenth-century Scotch Baronial, and favoured an elemental, harled simplicity, with massive, steep roofs.[11] Ian Lindsay, one of the most prominent of this new grouping of designers, noted in 1935 that, in old tower houses, 'turrets . . . are not crudely stuck on the corners but grow out, and form an organic part of the building . . . simplicity and functionalism is not modern.'[12] To some extent, Spence's Broughton Place exemplified this outlook. However, reflecting the collectivism of the times, as well as the ideas of Geddes, the focus of admiration now was less the freestanding landed castle than the picturesque, wholesome townscape of the small burgh, whose buildings, traditionalists believed, shared in the classless folk community: 'the big rubs shoulders with the small, and all stand in a

FIGURE 10.4 *Pitlochry Dam and Power Station by Sir Alexander Gibb and Partners; Generating Station by H. O. Tarbolton; built 1947–53; photograph of 2018 by M. Glendinning*

warm and friendly neighbourliness' – ideas that echoed continental 'blood and soil' nationalism in a mild form.[13]

Just as in the time of Mitchell and Geddes, the design of new housing inspired by the picturesque groups of the past naturally linked up with the aim of preserving those old groups, an area within which the landed classes were still able to maintain a prominent role, as defenders of 'tradition'. Geddes's advocacy of 'conservation of the historic heritage'[14] was developed into a full-scale burgh preservation programme by the newly founded (1931) National Trust for Scotland ('NTS'), supported by much rhetoric by propagandists, many of them lairds who in wealthier times might instead have occupied themselves in rebuilding their own castles: for example in 1937, Sir John Stirling-Maxwell hailed the 'smaller houses . . . in which the bulk of the Scots race has been reared' as 'precious records of the national life', while Scotland's premier interwar preserver, the Fourth Marquess of Bute, authored a polemical pamphlet on the same subject in 1936, *A Plea for Scotland's Architectural Heritage*, and financed the NTS to carry out a national survey of old burgh houses by the young architect, Ian Lindsay.[15]

After the war, although the growing public acceptance of state socialism diminished the ideological base of social traditionalism and the Second

Castle Age in general, the tradition of Geddesian conservative surgery continued in a range of set-piece burgh schemes, notably architect Robert Hurd's 1950s programme for the revitalization of the Canongate in Edinburgh as a focus of 'organically sound . . . healthy community life', and its 'repopulation . . . drawn from all classes'.[16] Hurd's most renowned scheme focused on a severely run-down area at the Canongate Tolbooth, in which he proposed selective redevelopment around retained architectural set-pieces. The programme comprised Tolbooth Area (1953–8), Morocco Land (1956–7), and Chessel's Court (1958–66): the project architect was Ian Begg (Figure 10.5). Redevelopment, said Hurd, must preserve enclosure: 'the couthy, intimate quality of the street'. Broken rooflines and levels would avoid repetitive fenestration: there would be bright colours, pantiled roofs, balconies, and arcading – 'an old feature treated with modern simplicity and restraint'. The new buildings would not be 'reproductions', but a '20th-century development of Scottish burgh architecture'.[17]

During the 1950s, the final disappearance of anything resembling castellated new architecture was matched by the evolution of preservation into a separate movement in its own right. Increasingly, Ian Lindsay became a leader of that grouping. He continued to organize improvement schemes in the old burghs, both through the new medium of NTS's 'Little Houses' programme, in burghs such as Culross and Dunkeld, and through local

FIGURE 10.5 *Chessel's Court, Canongate – redevelopment scheme by Robert Hurd and Ian Begg; drawing dated 1957.* © Historic Environment Scotland. https://canmore.org.uk/collection/989028

authority-promoted schemes such as Inveraray. In 1953, he explained that NTS aimed 'not to encumber the land with museums but to give the people of Scotland civilized decent homes of character and beauty'.[18] And as the government's Chief Investigator of Historic Buildings, he expanded the pre-war 'Bute lists' into a nationwide inventory by 1967 – as part of which the chronological scope of heritage now began, tentatively, to extend forwards to embrace Victorian architecture, including even Scotch Baronial. Significantly, in 1948 Lindsay's listing guidelines argued that 'we may not like revival "baronial", but future generations may'.[19]

From 'Vernacular' Modernism to 'National' Postmodernism

Where the new traditionalists answered the demand for disciplined reconstruction by invoking national community, other young architects pointed instead to the sweeping rationalistic and socialistic utopianism of the Continental Modern Movement as the best way to rebuild the nation – and in the aggressively modernizing welfare-state epoch after 1945, their approach became increasingly dominant. But even here there was a widespread feeling that one should reflect 'Scottish tradition', however obliquely, especially in the form of the 'vernacular' – a concept of place-specific, 'organic' modernism supported by many up-and-coming younger designers such as Robert Matthew, Basil Spence and Alan Reiach. The polemical book written by Reiach with Hurd, *Building Scotland* (1941), advocated a revival in new modernist architecture of the 'homely and spacious' values embodied in old houses: 'Tradition is the pool of a nation's continuous experience.'[20]

Architecturally, a marked shift towards more modern ideas in small-burgh infill schemes, expressed through a complex, Geddesian tapestry of old and new, began at Basil Spence's picturesque Dunbar fishermen's housing scheme (1949–52) (Figure 10.6), followed by his more rhetorical concrete and rubble group at 79–121 Canongate, Edinburgh (1966–8). The Glasgow-trained H. Anthony Wheeler, for example, emerged as a dominant force in the rich field of Fife burgh redevelopments. A long series of schemes in the 1950s and 1960s (latterly in partnership with Frank Sproson) culminated in the multistage Dysart redevelopment (from 1958), dotted picturesquely with miniature 'tower house' blocks.[21] The work of Robert Matthew in the five to ten years following his return to Edinburgh in 1953 attempted to apply the inspiration of Scottish vernacular to a wide range of other building types beyond housing – some of which were tower-like in form, but designed with a modernist informality remote from the hierarchical ornamentation of Scotch Baronial. His Queen's College Dundee tower (1958–61) added a vertical punctuation in a modern idiom to Perth Road, idiosyncratically faced in vast expanses of rubble and timber, while

FIGURE 10.6 *Dunbar, Fishermen's Housing, by Basil Spence, 1949–52; page of practice portfolio.* © *Historic Environment Scotland. https://canmore.org.uk/collection/1075943*

his George Square redevelopment for Edinburgh University included a fifteen-storey Arts Tower (1960–63) clad in black slate and polished ashlar, in response to its classical surroundings.[22]

In the early 1960s, the hegemony of modernism in Scotland seemed to be at its peak, with vast 'comprehensive developments', urban motorways and regional plans underway, and the ethos of rationally precise 'scientific' design unambiguously dominant. At this point, any overt pursuit of the national or of traditionalist ideas seemed, for the moment, deeply unfashionable, although these were the years when the national reshaping of the Scottish physical environment reached its height. Yet even in the grandest realizations of planned reconstruction, ideas of 'tradition' and 'vernacular' were not completely absent. The world-renowned 'cluster' design (from 1957) for Cumbernauld New Town, for instance, included dense housing layouts with traditional-looking steep roofs.[23] In sharp contrast to this ebullience, the post-1968 years saw a steady undermining of the mid-century Scottish consensus between capitalism and socialism in support of corporatist welfare state provision with a corresponding rejection of modern architecture and planning in any form. The strength of this reaction was epitomized in the way in which that central modernist sociopsychological ideal, 'community', was turned on its head. It was seen no longer as something created for users by design of new buildings, but as something to be protected against new development by the action of residents or users. The 1970s were the first and, perhaps, only decade in which the central driving force in Scottish architecture was not new buildings of any kind, but preserved old ones. This was the decade of reaction, the decade of ascendancy of the Conservation Movement. But one element within it was a reinvigoration of the traditionalist movement for conservation of ordinary homes, now focusing mainly on 'rehab' of nineteenth-century housing.[24]

With conservation as the lead tendency in 1970s architecture, one easy way for architects to distance themselves from mainstream modernism was to look back to the Vernacular architecture built in the 1950s and 1960s by architects such as Wheeler & Sproson: Colin McWilliam in 1974 hailed the 'simple vernacular' as 'the most deeply relevant tradition' in Scottish architecture.[25] These ideas were developed in numerous projects of the 1970s and 1980s, for example by Baxter Clark & Paul in east-coast towns such as Fraserburgh or Montrose. But alongside this consistent evolution, others, by the beginning of the 1980s, began to question the use of Vernacular in urban contexts. In 1982 one architectural commentator blasted the loss of urban 'monumentality' caused by 'Neukery . . . a transitory, neo-vernacular fishing-village imagery' which has 'now started to invade our major cities'.[26] Among many urban designers, the word 'Vernacular' now acquired strongly pejorative overtones.

In the 1980s, the initial phase of negative reaction against the modern movement was succeeded by the postmodernist movement, whose very name emphasized that it would be systematically opposed to old-style social modernism. It involved the detachment of higher architectural value from the fabric of the building, in the interests ultimately of profit, and a renewed focus on facades, styles and the inspiration of the past.[27] Architects were no longer interested in the regional synthesizing vision, only with 'The City' as a theatre of 'mixed use' display or money-making: each city or country had to brand itself for the global market.

The postmodernist movement in Scottish architecture was spearheaded by the Royal Incorporation of Architects in Scotland (RIAS) and its dynamic chief executive from 1979 to 1995, Charles McKean. Although many postmodernist themes, such as 'traditional mixed urban renewal', were in fact strongly international in character – as exemplified in the Berlin 'IBA' project of the 1970s – McKean packaged the movement in explicitly 'national' terms, reflecting the growth in Scottish cultural nationalism in reaction to the rule of Margaret Thatcher. In 1987 he proclaimed 'the stirring of a new Scots architecture. The first element that strikes is the colour, accompanied by picturesque shapes: no more grey monoliths. Massing, roofscape, craftsmanship and applied art seem set to make a comeback.'[28] But this renewed concern for the national took place in a radically changed cultural and political context. The decline in the prestige of the centralized state had undermined modernism, but also impeded any return to old-fashioned traditionalism, with its messianic calls for a 'national awakening'. No period was now privileged as a golden age or seen as a threatened essence. In place of the latter, McKean identified an open-ended series of 'revival cycles' since the eighteenth century – including, significantly, nineteenth-century Scotch Baronial – which had acted as a counterweight to internationalist tendencies in Scottish architecture. In 1987, he enthused that 'a new Scotland is in the making. Out of unemployment . . . out of strength comes sweetness . . . the stirrings of a new Scots architecture. The challenge is to produce an architecture at once richly Scottish *and* international.'[29]

Architecturally, there could be no question of reviving the old academic classical training, whose rules had provided a shortcut way to convey meaning in architecture. So the most relevant period of the past was inevitably the modern movement, especially that strand which emphasized the individual creative genius, and which could now be gradually, during the 1980s and early 1990s, turned into a signature architecture of competing, branded designers. The heritage that was exploited most relentlessly by Scottish postmodernists was the work of Mackintosh. Its appeal lay in its multifaceted character, reinforcing the artist-architect ideal with conservationism, civic pride, and kitsch commercialism. Initially pioneered by Gillespie, Kidd & Coia's Robinson College, Cambridge, 1974–80, this movement was by 1990 widely denounced by younger architects as 'Mockintosh' and for its 'myopic . . . slavish imitation'.[30] The only direct connection back to the days of Scotch traditionalism was a series of 'postmodern Baronial' projects by Ian Begg, Robert Hurd's former partner, designed with a scenographic panache quite different from Hurd's modestly scaled projects. The grandest of these projects was the Scandic Crown Hotel (1988–9), situated in one of the most prominent sites in the Edinburgh Old Town (Figure 10.7). This was treated as a picturesque composition in the Sydney Mitchell Old Edinburgh manner, with the addition of a massive Holyrood-style tower as a corner feature: like Matthew's Queen's College Dundee tower of 1958, rubble was here used to clad a reinforced-concrete, multistorey structure. Begg described the Scandic Crown as 'bold and gutsy . . . robust . . . a positive statement of renewal'.[31] Similar in appearance was the Cathedral Square Visitors' Centre, Glasgow (1990–93). The climax of the series was Begg's own house, Ravens' Craig, Plockton (1987–9), a five-storey tower of harled blockwork, rising from a massive ground-floor arched vault and crowned with an Old Edinburgh-style timber gable. The architect described the genesis of this 'huge statement in the landscape': 'The idea was to see if I could build something modern, meeting all building regulations, using modern materials, and yet get a feeling inside that this was a protecting structure, achieve that very strong sense of enclosure.' Begg's rhetoric also echoed the heady language of the 1930s: 'I've tried to make statements, not of where we are, but restatements

FIGURE 10.7 *Scandic Crown Hotel, Edinburgh, by Ian Begg, 1988 – view from north-west in the 1990s.* © Historic Environment Scotland. https://canmore.org.uk/collection/426694

of roots and memory, and more than that . . . of connecting points for people to see and realize, this is Scotland. We know this is Scotland and we can push on forward.'[32]

Moving from the RIAS into academia in the mid-1990s, McKean shifted his focus from the postmodern present to the Renaissance castellated past, applying to that heritage his concept of the 'European' identity of Scottish architecture, in a series of publications trumpeting the concept of the 'Scottish Chateau'[33] – an appropriate shift in focus, as the 1970s and 1980s were not only the years of conservation triumph in general but the culmination of a second wave of restorations of ruined castles. The years of dynastic conflict and 'improvement' had left thousands of castellated houses from the First Castle Age abandoned and in ruins: it was estimated in the 1960s that only 1,250 out of an all-time maximum of 3,000 castles had survived roofed and intact. Hundreds of these still remained in the 1980s, despite the grand rebuilding projects of the turn of century, such as that of Eilean Donan. By that stage, it was clear that the prestige of the Scottish lairds had outlasted the challenge of socialism, and they still dominated heritage organizations such as the NTS. With the 1979 advent of the Thatcher Conservative government, the cause of the 'baronial castle' in Scotland made a dramatic comeback. The flamboyant laird, castle-owner and Tory government minister Sir Nicholas Fairbairn grimly recalled the welfare-state 1960s–70s, when 'those who strove to save our heritage, grand or humble, were branded as outcasts and pariahs . . . determined to live in the grisly past, not appreciating the liberal worth of contemporary concrete brutalism. We were like the 600 at Thermopylae against the infidel hordes'.[34]

In the late 1970s and 1980s, the government architectural heritage authority, the Scottish Development Department's Historic Buildings inspectorate, under chief historic buildings inspector David Walker, sanctioned a veritable explosion of castle-rebuilding, fuelled by mounting prosperity as well as government grants (Figures 10.8 and 10.9). This work was mostly undertaken, however, not by lairds but by middle-class enthusiasts, such as Graham Carson, restorer of Rusco Tower: he decided in 1970 that 'I had to restore a tower house, now', and picked Rusco from a shortlist of eleven ruined castles suggested to him by the popular castle historian, Nigel Tranter. The restorations of these years varied from conservative repair of castles that had been disused for only a few decades, to Pierrefonds-like re-creations of buildings that had been in ruins for several centuries. An extreme example of the latter was the 1991 rebuilding of Forter Castle, Perthshire, a 1560 tower that had been roofless ever since it was burned in 1640 by the Earl of Argyll. The restoration campaign gradually petered out in the late 1980s owing to a drying-up in the supply of easily restorable towers and an escalation of costs in some prominent projects such as Fawside, near Edinburgh, a castle abandoned in the eighteenth century and restored between 1976 and 1982 with the aid of a £104,000 government grant.[35]

In parallel with these high-prestige building types, a new area of postmodern 'national identity' debate opened up over the issue of urban housing. By the late 1980s, Glasgow's community-based housing associations – 'the Medicis of Maryhill' (McKean) – had virtually completed the improvement of nineteenth-century tenements, and now shifted their attention to energetic new building on cleared sites.[36] Here, under the influence of 'rehab', there

FIGURE 10.8 *Hillslap Tower – view from north; photograph of c. 1940 showing Hillslap as a neglected ruin.* © *Historic Environment Scotland. https://canmore.org.uk/collection/1232888*

FIGURE 10.9 *Hillslap Tower – photograph of 2002, following restoration.* © *Historic Environment Scotland. https://canmore.org.uk/collection/1232911*

was a return to building tenements along street frontages. This neotenement style at first used bright red brick – a tendency which was avidly developed in the 1980s, when English brick companies sponsored numerous Scottish design awards in an attempt to make brick architecturally 'respectable'. But soon there were growing criticisms of the results: in 1991, Scottish brickmaker Charles Wemyss, after vainly trying to foster a Scottish brick style by commissioning an innovative range of Mackintosh-like house types from Roger Emmerson (1990), ruefully concluded that there seemed no way of throwing off 'the old adages of utilitarian, incompatible and English'.³⁷ By the late 1980s and early 1990s, many Glasgow projects showed concern for greater scale and dignity, and facing in stone or stone-like treatments. Emblematic of this mature postmodern urbanism in Scotland was Glasgow's Crown Street Project, whose 1992 plan, inspired by the Berlin IBA, emphasized an urbanist stress on tenements and street-grids, and on the collective 'bustle of city life', in a modern 'rethink of the tenement concept'.³⁸

'Built Out of Land': Iconic Modernism and the Scottish Parliament

As the 1990s wore on, the dominant discourse in Scottish society increasingly shifted to the political struggle for home rule. The inevitable architectural consequence was an upsurge in the rhetoric of 'Scottish pride'. But even more than under postmodernism, this rhetoric arguably masked even stronger global processes of capitalist image led commodification and branded, image-led homogenization (Figure 10.10). And within architecture, the expression of genuine cultural distinctiveness would now be an even more complicated task. Despite Begg's rhetoric, the Second Castle Age was long gone, and international architectural fashion had shifted from postmodernism to a revived modernist style. In many ways, the change from postmodernism to 'iconic modernism' was purely skin-deep. The dominance of images, signature architects and market-driven building types grew stronger, and all

FIGURE 10.10 *Edinburgh taxi advertising Holyroodhouse, 2017, proclaiming the palace's role as the 'home of Scottish royal history'; photograph of 2017 by A. MacKechnie*

that changed was the styling. This new approach relied on metaphoric or theatrical *architecture parlante* gestures as a way of conveying elevated or symbolic content.[39] But in the *inner* areas of cities, the continuing prestige of heritage dictated a balance between contextual respect and iconic modernist style. For example, Benson & Forsyth's Museum of Scotland in central Edinburgh (1991–8) combined an array of 'gestural' Corbusian modernist motifs with stone cladding and, even, the overtly castellated feature of a castle-like corner round tower.[40]

The problems and challenges now faced by any architectural celebrations of national identity, in the new century of globalization, were highlighted in the controversial project for a new Scottish parliament at Holyrood, initiated in 1998. In a designer competition otherwise dominated by domineering monumental structures of a somewhat commercialized character, the eventual winner, Catalan architect Enric Miralles, seemed strikingly different, and more sophisticated, in his approach. Politically, the choice of architect seemed uncannily appropriate, given the devolved status of Catalonia within Spain. Architecturally, in keeping with his own ethos of organic deconstructivism, Miralles envisaged Holyrood as an anti-monumental design dominated by natural shapes: his initial design proposed a scattering of shell-like structures, with roofs shaped like leaves or upturned boats (Figure 10.11). In this apparently anarchic context, the only

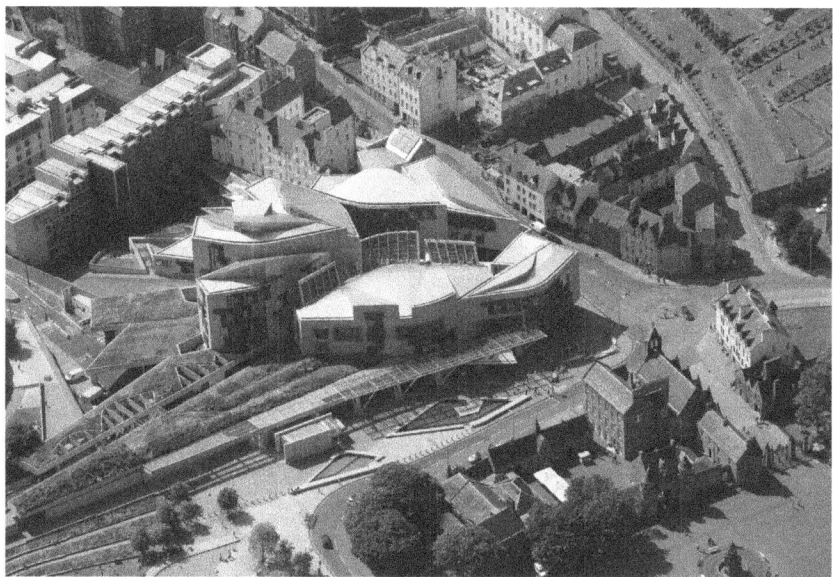

FIGURE 10.11 *Scottish parliament, Edinburgh, by Enric Miralles, after 1998; aerial view of 2014.* © *Historic Environment Scotland. https://canmore.org.uk/ collection/1433778*

way left of communicating architectural meaning and status was through metaphoric, poetic motifs. Miralles's disavowal of traditional monumental grandeur was accentuated by the avant-garde, manifesto-like style language of his presentations: his competition-winning presentation in Edinburgh repudiated the formal monumentality traditionally associated with parliaments and talked expansively of a modest incision in the landscape, of 'carving a gathering place in the land': 'The building should be land . . . built out of land . . . floating in the landscape'.[41]

Meaning in this new complex would be conveyed not by grand arches or towers, as would have happened in the Second Castle Age, but by randomly gathered metaphorical references – leaves, boat-hulls, sails, mountain crags. All these were only too familiar to anyone acquainted with iconic modernism's stock rhetoric, but seemed mouth-wateringly exotic to a Scottish audience hitherto used only to 'real' buildings with right angles and solid walls. The exalted, poetic style of Miralles's presentations to Scottish audiences helped whip up an atmosphere of reverence. Newspapers noted his 'radicalism . . . at odds with the system' . . . this was 'an architect whose creative juices thrive best in an atmosphere of chaos'. But the underlying reality of the hierarchy of brands revealed itself occasionally, in the language of Miralles's political patrons: Secretary of State Donald Dewar praised Miralles's competition entry as 'great advertising hoardings for his talent' and junior minister Henry McLeish predicted that his design would 'help brand Scotland'.[42]

The project took up a highly explicit urban design stance of iconic contextualism, chiefly through the restoration of a historic seventeenth-century mansion, Queensberry House, as the focus of the complex. However, that project, like Miralles's own reconstructions of Utrecht Town Hall (1997–2000) and Barcelona's Santa Caterina market (completed posthumously in 2005), was like an iconic echo of the Viollet and Ruskin ethos of radical restoration – namely, a radical hollowing-out and restyling. Queensberry House was transformed into a trophy fragment, an artificial objet trouvé.[43] Yet it was unclear, to say the least, whether Miralles's own design was any less rhetorical and image-driven, than mainstream classicism or modernism – especially as the design as executed (in 1999–2004) became more dense and even monumental, while trumping the most elaborately ornate of the stately parliament buildings of the nineteenth century in its prodigious architectural excess, heaping detail upon detail, leaving no space or surface untouched by motifs and metaphoric references. For example, an enigmatic role was played at Holyrood by the repetition of an upside-down L-motif on the main facades of the complex, which provoked much speculation about what Miralles had intended it to signify: was it an echo of Le Corbusier's Modulor, or of a 1784 painting of a Scottish skater in the National Galleries of Scotland?[44] Although widely acclaimed by the Scottish architectural and cultural elite, the completed building remained as closed to the public as any traditional monumental parliament, owing to its fortress-like plan as built. Its main 'gathering place' was, in the event, a pleasantly toplit 'garden court' in the centre of the ensemble, inaccessible from the street or to the public.

Conclusion

Overall, Miralles's forceful metaphoric method of communication seemed ideally attuned to today's incessant need to create a marketable, commodifiable image – in this case, of Scotland as a whole – rather like a pavilion in a world-fair or a theme park. This loss of certainty in the architecture of ruling authority forms only one facet of a more general architectural dilemma. Internationally, no ethos or approach can any longer command general credibility.[45] And for Scotland, it is a paradox that the proud talk of a national rebirth, and of the central role to be played by architecture in 'building a nation', coincides with an underlying reality of international homogenization and commercialization. In contrast to the strong integration between imagery and political-economic reality in both the First and Second Castle Ages, the story of 'national identity' in contemporary Scottish architecture – so far – ends on an uncertain rather than triumphal note.

NOTES

Chapter 1

1. Gavin Douglas, *The Shorter Poems of Gavin Douglas*, ed. Priscilla J. Bawcutt (Edinburgh: Scottish Text Society, 1967), 93.
2. Norman Macdougall, *James III: A Political Study* (Edinburgh: John Donald, 1982), 98.
3. Walter Bower, *Scotichronicon*, trans. D. E. R. Watt et al., 9 vols (Aberdeen: Aberdeen University Press, 1987–1998), vol. 8, 120–1.
4. Dauvit Broun, 'When Did Scotland Become Scotland?', *History Today*, 46(10) (October 1996), 16–21.
5. Roger Mason, 'Chivalry and Citizenship: Aspects of National Identity in Renaissance Scotland', in *People and Power in Scotland: Essays in Honour of T C Smout*, ed. Roger Mason and Norman Macdougall (Edinburgh: John Donald, 1992), 50–73.
6. Michael Bath, 'Anglici Caudati: Courtly Celebration and National Insult in the Stirling 1566 Royal Baptism', in *Le livre demeure: Studies in Book History in Honour of Alison Saunders*, ed. Alison Adams and Philip Ford (Geneva: Librairie Droz, 2011), 183–94.
7. This date is indicated by evidence from Glasgow University's Forteviot and Strathearn Environs and Royal Forteviot ('SERF') project. It could be argued that the stone tradition continued from prehistoric times.
8. Joseph Robertson (ed.), *Concilia Scotiae ecclesiae Scoticanae statuta tam provincialia quam synodalia quae supersunt, MCCXXV-MDLIX*, 2 vols (Edinburgh: Bannatyne Club, 1866), vol. 2, 11.
9. Allan Rutherford and John Malcolm, '"That Stalwart Toure": Bothwell Castle in the Thirteenth and Early Fourteenth Centuries', in *Scotland's Castle Culture*, ed. Audrey Dakin, Miles Glendinning and Aonghus MacKechnie (Edinburgh: Birlinn, 2011), 189–98.
10. David Hume of Godscroft's *History of the House of Douglas*, ed. David Reid, 2 vols (Edinburgh: Scottish Text Society, 1996), vol. 1, 78–89.
11. Joe Donnelly, 'An Open Economy: The Berwick Shipping Trade, 1311–1373', *SHR*, xcvi (April 2017), 1–31.
12. John Dunbar, *Scottish Royal Palaces: The Architecture of the Royal Residences during the Late Medieval and Early Renaissance Periods* (East Linton: Tuckwell Press, 1999), 75–6.
13. Ian Campbell, 'A Romanesque Revival and the Early Renaissance in Scotland', *Journal of the Society of Architectural Historians* (September 1995), 302–25.
14. James Moir (ed.), *Hectoris Boetii Murthlacensium et Aberdonensium Episcoporum Vitae* (Aberdeen: New Spalding Club, 1894), 95.

15 Maureen M. Meikle, 'The Invisible Divide: The Greater Lairds and the Nobility of Jacobean Scotland', *SHR*, lxxi (April–October 1992), 70–87.
16 Fiona Watson, 'The Expression of Power in a Medieval Kingdom: Thirteenth-Century Scottish Castles', in *Scottish Power Centres*, ed. Sally Foster et al. (Glasgow: Cruithne Press, 1993), 59–78.
17 NRS GD8/231, GD93/85.
18 Cosmo Innes, ed., *The Black Book of Taymouth* (Edinburgh: T. Constable, 1855), 35–6.
19 John Gifford, *The Buildings of Scotland: Perth and Kinross* (New Haven: Yale University Press, 2007), 262–7.
20 W. Douglas Simpson, *The Castle of Bergen and the Bishop's Palace at Kirkwall* (Edinburgh: Oliver and Boyd, 1961), 57.
21 Charles McKean argued the presence/absence of this corbelling connects to pro/anti-French political signalling: Charles McKean, 'A Cult of Mary Queen of Scots?', *Architectural Heritage*, 18 (March 2008), 55–72.
22 Castle Menzies's decoration in this style became a popular specific model from the 1830s, following William Burn's employment there.
23 Ebenezer Henderson, *The Annals of Dunfermline* (Glasgow: J. Tweed, 1879), 254.
24 https://canmore.org.uk/site/49351/dunfermline-anne-of-denmarks-building; https://canmore.org.uk/collection/251026 (accessed January 2018).
25 Ian Campbell and Aonghus MacKechnie, 'The "Great Temple of Solomon" at Stirling Castle', *Architectural History*, 54 (2011), 91–118.

Chapter 2

1 P. Hume Brown, ed., *Early Travellers in Scotland* (Edinburgh: David Douglas, 1891), 111, 139.
2 David Laing, ed., *Correspondence of Sir Robert Kerr, First Earl of Ancram and His Son, William, Third Earl of Lothian*, 2 vols (Edinburgh: Bannatyne Club, 1875), vol. I, 64.
3 *Ezechiel* 37:22, cited in Bruce Galloway and Brian Levack, *The Jacobean Union. Six Tracts of 1604* (Edinburgh: Scottish History Society, 1985), 48.
4 Introduction to Galloway, *Jacobean Union*, xx, xxv–xxvi.
5 Thomas I. Rae, 'The Historical Writing of William Drummond of Hawthornden', *SHR*, 54 (April 1975), 41.
6 Brown, *Early Travellers*, 111, 139.
7 *RPC* (1st series), vol. 11, 203.
8 Introduction to John Imrie and John Dunbar (eds), *Accounts of the Masters of Works*, vol. 2 (Edinburgh: HMSO, 1982), lviii–lix; Aonghus MacKechnie, 'Sir James Murray of Kilbaberton: King's Master of Works, 1607–1634', in *'The Mirror of Great Britain': National Identity in Seventeenth-Century British Architecture*, ed. Olivia Horsfall Turner (Reading: Spire Books, 2012), 15–49.
9 We owe this reference to Michael Pearce.
10 William Hamilton, *Descriptions of the Sheriffdoms of Lanark and Renfrew Compiled around MDCCX*, ed. John Dillon and John Fullarton (Glasgow: Maitland Club, 1831), 131, 141.

11 James Fraser, *Chronicles of the Frasers, the Wardlaw Manuscript Entitled 'Polichronicon seu Policratica temporum, or, the True Genealogy of the Frasers', 916–1674*, ed. William Mackay (Edinburgh: T & A Constable, 1905), 244–5.
12 Walter MacFarlane, *Geographical Collections Relating to Scotland: Edited from Macfarlane's Transcript in the Advocates' Library*, ed. Sir Arthur Mitchell, 3 vols (Edinburgh: Scottish History Society, 1906–8), vol. 3, 187.
13 Aonghus MacKechnie, 'Design Approaches in Early Post-Reformation Scots Houses', in *Scottish Country Houses 1600–1914*, ed. Ian Gow and Alistair Rowan (Edinburgh: Edinburgh University Press, 1995), 14–33.
14 Cosmo Innes, *The Book of the Thanes of Cawdor: A Series of Papers Selected from the Charter Room at Cawdor, 1236–1742* (Edinburgh: Spalding Club, 1859), 283–4.
15 Ibid.
16 *RPC* (2nd series), vol. 1, 328.
17 David Stevenson, *Alasdair MacColla and the Highland Problem in the 17th Century* (Edinburgh: John Donald, 1980), 34–61; Aonghus MacKechnie, 'Renaissance Scotland's Martial Houses', *History Scotland*, 10(5) (September–October 2010), 48–54; 10(6) (November–December 2010), 36–43; Aonghus MacKechnie, '"For Friendship and Conversation": Martial Scotland's Domestic Castles', *Architectural Heritage* (2015), 5–24.
18 Imrie and Dunbar, *Accounts*, 79.
19 Ann MacSween, 'Craigievar Castle: Changing Perceptions', in Dakin, *Castle Culture*, 297–306; Joseph Sharples, David W. Walker and Matthew Woodworth, *The Buildings of Scotland: Aberdeenshire: South and Aberdeen* (New Haven: Yale University Press, 2015), 431–7.
20 Ibid., 448–53.
21 Ibid., 537–44.
22 *RPC* (2nd series), vol. 6, 55.
23 Laing, *Correspondence*, vol. 1, 64.
24 John Gifford et al., *The Buildings of Scotland: Edinburgh* (Harmondsworth: Penguin, 1984), 590.
25 Mary Anne Everett Green, ed., *Calendar of State Papers Domestic: James I, 1611–18* (London: HMSO, 1858), 4.
26 George Seton, *A History of the Family of Seton During Eight Centuries*, 2 vols (Edinburgh: T&A Constable, 1896), vol. 2, 792–3.
27 From the 1610s, the astronomical and mathematical study pursued on roof platforms was translated into the construction of complex multi-dial sundials within castle gardens.
28 R. K. Hannay and G. P. H. Watson, 'The Building of the Parliament House', in *Book of the Old Edinburgh Club*, vol. 13 (Edinburgh: 1924), 1–78; *RPC* (2nd series), vol. 4, 448–9; Aonghus MacKechnie, 'The Crisis of Kingship', in *The Architecture of Scottish Government: From Kingship to Parliamentary Democracy*, ed. Miles Glendinning (Dundee: Dundee University Press, 2004), 94–134; Alan R. MacDonald, *The Burghs and Parliament in Scotland, c. 1550–1651* (Aldershot: Ashgate, 2007).
29 RCAHMS, *Tolbooths and Town-houses: Civic Architecture in Scotland to 1833* (Edinburgh: RCAHMS, 1996), 98–101.
30 NRS HR175/1, HR175/6; RHP7370-3.
31 Fraser, *Chronicles*, 287.

32 The place-name 'Fort Field' survived at Kingillie into the nineteenth century (ibid., 288).
33 Ibid., 288.
34 Ibid., 315.
35 John Nicoll, *A Diary of Public Transactions and Other Occurrences, Chiefly in Scotland, from January 1650 to June 1667* (Edinburgh: Bannatyne Club, 1836), 24–6.
36 C. H. Firth, ed., *Scotland and the Protectorate* (Edinburgh: Scottish History Society, 1899), 368–70.

Chapter 3

1 Rev. Robert S. Mylne, *The Master Masons to the Crown of Scotland* (Edinburgh: Scott & Ferguson, 1893), 172–4.
2 John Macky, *A Journey through Scotland* (London: J. Pemberton and J. Hooke, 1723), 135, 140.
3 *RPC* (3rd series), vol. 1, 451, 522.
4 *RPC* (2nd series), vol. 8, 465.
5 *RPC* (3rd series), vol. 1, 28.
6 NRS GD220/6/1744/5.
7 John R. Young, *The Scottish Parliament* (Edinburgh: John Donald, 1996), 328.
8 *RPC* (3rd series), vol. 1, 97.
9 John Gifford, 'Yester Chapel', in *Classicism in Scotland 1670–1748*, ed. K. Cruft et al. (Edinburgh: SAHGB, 1983), 24–5.
10 H. C. G. Matthew et al. (eds), *Oxford Dictionary of National Biography*, 60 vols (Oxford: Oxford University Press), vol. 36, 222.
11 C. Sanford Terry (ed.), *The Cromwellian Union: Papers Relating to the Negotiations for an Incorporating Union between England and Scotland, 1651–1652* (Edinburgh: T & A Constable, 1920), 189, 195.
12 R. S. Mylne, 'Masters of Work to the Crown of Scotland', in *PSAS*, 30 (Edinburgh, 1896), 60–61.
13 Mylne, *Master Masons*, 172–4.
14 Domhnall Uilleam Stiùbhart, 'Highland Rogues and the Roots of Highland Romanticism', in *Crossing the Highland Line*, ed. Christopher MacLachlan (Glasgow: Association for Scottish Literary Studies, 2009), 161–93; Aonghus MacKechnie, 'Birth-stool of Scottish Romanticism? Holyrood and Sir William Bruce, "Surveyor-general and Overseer of the King's Buildings in Scotland"', *Architectural Heritage*, 23 (2013), 133–62.
15 Jayne Elizabeth Lewis, *Mary Queen of Scots: Romance and Nation* (London: Routledge, 1998), 77, 81; John Evelyn, *The Diary of John Evelyn*, ed. William Bray, 2 vols (London: W. W. Gibbings, 1907), vol. 1, 305; vol. 2, 285.
16 John D. Staines, *The Tragic Histories of Mary Queen of Scots, 1560–1690: Rhetoric, Passions and Political Literature* (Farnham: Ashgate, 2009), 223.
17 Helen Smailes and Duncan Thomson, *The Queen's Image: A Celebration of Mary Queen of Scots* (Edinburgh: Scottish National Portrait Gallery, 1987), 59.
18 Konrad Ottenheim, 'Dutch Influences on William Bruce's Architecture', *Architectural Heritage*, 18 (2007), 135–49.
19 Daniel Defoe, *A Tour thro' the Whole Island of Great Britain, Divided into Circuits or Journies*, 3 vols (London: G. Strahan, 1724–7), vol. 3, letter xi.

20 Stiùbhart, 'Highland Rogues', 174, 184.
21 *ODNB*, vol. 36, 218–25.
22 Patrick, 'First Earl of Strathmore', in *A Book of Record – a Diary ... and Other Documents Relating to Glamis Castle, 1684–1689*, ed. A. H. Millar (Edinburgh: Scottish History Society, 1890), 1st series, vol. 9, 27.
23 Macky, *Journey*, 135, 140.
24 Gifford, *Edinburgh*, 538–43.
25 Firth, *Protectorate*, 150.
26 Dunbar and Davies (eds), 'Some Late seventeenth-Century Building Contracts', in *Miscellany*, vol. 11 (Edinburgh: Scottish History Society, 1990), 293; David MacGibbon and Thomas Ross, *Castellated and Domestic Architecture of Scotland*, 5 vols (Edinburgh: David Douglas, 1887–92), vol. 3, 620–1.
27 Iain Lom/John MacDonald, *Orain Iain Luim: Songs of John MacDonald, Bard of Keppoch*, ed. Annie M. MacKenzie (Edinburgh: The Scottish Academic Press for the Scottish Gaelic Texts Society, 1964), 158–9.
28 Historic Environment Scotland, 'Neidpath Castle', https://canmore.org.uk/site/51539/neidpath-castle (accessed 24 June 2017).
29 Kitty Cruft et al., *The Buildings of Scotland: Borders* (New Haven: Yale University Press, 2006), 576–81.
30 Historical Manuscripts Commission, *The Manuscripts of His Grace the Duke of Buccleuch and Queensberry*, 15th report (London: Historical Manuscripts Commission, 1897), appendix, part VIII, 540.
31 Dunbar, 'Contracts', 321–3.
32 NRS RD.2/66, pp. 54–6; RCAHMS, *Inventory of Midlothian and West Lothian* (Edinburgh: HMSO, 1929), 149–50.
33 Anon., *A Genealogical Deduction of the Family of Rose of Kilravock*, ed. Cosmo Innes (Edinburgh: Spalding Club, 1848), 370.
34 John Gifford and Frank Walker, *The Buildings of Scotland: Stirling and Central Scotland* (New Haven: Yale University Press, 2002), 185.
35 Charles Wemyss, 'Paternal Seat or Classical Villa? Patrick Smyth, James Smith and the Building of Methven 1678 to 1682', *Architectural History*, 46 (Edinburgh, 2003), 109–26.
36 Gifford, *Edinburgh*, 638–40.
37 Dunbar, 'Contracts', 295–9.
38 MacGibbon, *Architecture*, vol. 4, 64–6.
39 Daniel Wilson, *Memorials of Edinburgh in the Olden Time*, 2 vols (Edinburgh: Hugh Paton, 1848), vol. 1, 127.
40 NRS GD203/11/5/15.
41 NRS PA2/33, f. 36v-40.
42 *RPC* (3rd series), vol. xiv, 22, 86–7.

Chapter 4

1 NRS GD124/15/471.
2 John Lowrey, 'Bruce and His Circle at Craigiehall', in *Aspects of Scottish Classicism: The House & Its Formal Setting, 1690–1750*, ed. John Frew and David Jones (St Andrews: Blakely Milroy, 1989), 3.
3 Sir John Clerk, *Memoirs of the Life of Sir John Clerk of Penicuik*, ed. John M. Gray (Edinburgh: Scottish History Society, 1892), 253n2.

4 Howard M. Colvin and Maurice Craig (eds), *Architectural Drawings in the Library of Elton Hall by Sir John Vanbrugh and Sir Edward Lovett Pearce* (Oxford: Oxford University Press, 1964), xxxviii.
5 *RPC* (3rd series), vol. xiv, 22, 86–7.
6 NLS ms 7028, f.62.
7 NLS ms 7011, f.208.
8 NRS GD26/13/227.
9 NLS ms 7016, f.56.
10 NLS ms 7015, f.171.
11 NLS ms 7012, f.169.
12 Hon. William H. L. Melville (ed.), *Leven and Melville Papers* (Edinburgh: Bannatyne Club, 1843), 391.
13 Ibid., 393, 387.
14 NRS E28/580/12.
15 Melville, *Papers*, 386.
16 NRS GD124/15/303.
17 Melville, *Papers,* 611.
18 Ibid., 626.
19 Ibid., 463, 627.
20 NLS ms 7014, f.13.
21 NRS GD406/1/4670–1.
22 Lord Patrick Fraser, *Sketch of the Career of Duncan Forbes of Culloden, Lord President of the Court of Session, 1737–47* (Aberdeen: D Chalmers, 1875), 8.
23 Ibid., 11.
24 Introduction to Colen Campbell, *Vitruvius Britannicus: Or the British Architect*, 3 vols (London, 1715–25), vol. 1.
25 NRHE PBD/285/66.
26 Sir William Fraser, *The Melvilles, Earls of Melville and the Leslies, Earls of Leven*, 3 vols (Edinburgh: privately printed, 1890), vol. 3, 238–9.
27 RCAHMS, *Peebles-shire: An Inventory of the Ancient Monuments*, 2 vols (Edinburgh: RCAHMS, 1967), vol. 1, 311–26.
28 Margaret Stewart, *The Architectural, Landscape and Constitutional Plans of the Earl of Mar, 1700–32* (Dublin: Four Courts Press, 2016).
29 John Gifford, *The Buildings of Scotland: Fife* (Harmondsworth: Penguin, 1988), 298.
30 Colin MacWilliam, *The Buildings of Scotland: Lothian* (Harmondsworth: Penguin, 1978), 327–8.
31 NRS RD.4/71, pp. 603–5.
32 NLS ms 580, no. 404 (f.129).
33 Alexander Pennecuik, *Works of Alexander Pennecuik Esq., of New-Hall, MD* (Leith: A Allardice et al., 1815), 217.
34 William Adam, *Vitruvius Scoticus: Being a Collection of Plans, Elevations and Sections of Public Buildings, Noblemen's and Gentlemen's Houses in Scotland* (Edinburgh: Adam Black and J. & J. Robertson, n.d. [c. 1812]), plates 50–51.
35 http://nms.scran.ac.uk/database/record.php?usi=000-000-579-757-C (accessed January 2018).
36 Clerk, *Memoirs*, 115.
37 Ibid., 253n.2.
38 *ODNB*, vol. 32, 493–5.

39 Batty Langley, *Ancient Masonry, Both in the Theory and Practice, Demonstrating the Useful Rules of Arithmetic, Geometry, and Architecture, in the Proportions and Orders of the Most Eminent Masters of All Nations*, 2 vols (London, 1736), vol. 2, 321.
40 Ibid., vol. 2, 323.
41 Ibid., vol. 2, 276–8.
42 Batty Langley, *Ancient Architecture Restored, and Improved, by a Great Variety of Grand and Useful Designs, Entirely New in the Gothick Mode* (London: J Hugginson, 1742), 277–8; Batty and Thomas Langley, *Gothic Architecture, Improved by Rules and Proportions* (London: John Millan, 1747), 6.
43 Preface to Batty Langley, *The Builder's Director, or Bench-Mate: Being a Pocket Treasury of the Grecian, Roman, and Gothic Orders of Architecture* (London: H. Piers, 1747).
44 *ODNB*, vol. 32, 494.
45 Arthur Penrhyn Stanley, *Historical Memorials of Westminster Abbey*, 8th edn (London: John Murray, 1896), 231–2, 234.
46 Colvin and Craig, *Drawings*, xxxvii, 12, plate xxxvi(b).
47 *ODNB*, vol. 9, 726–33.
48 Ibid., vol. 9, 733.
49 Walter Biggar Blaikie (ed.), *Origins of the Forty-Five: And Other Papers Relating to That Rising* (Edinburgh: T & A Constable, 1916), xxiv, ff.
50 Fraser, *Forbes of Culloden*, 14.
51 Ian Lindsay and Mary Cosh, *Inveraray and the Dukes of Argyll* (Edinburgh: Edinburgh University Press, 1973), 56.
52 Langley, *Gothic Architecture, Improved*, 6; plates lvii–lxi.
53 Lindsay, *Inveraray*, 35ff.

Chapter 5

1 Margaret H. B. Sanderson, *Robert Adam and Scotland: Portrait of an Architect* (Edinburgh: HMSO, 1992), 88.
2 NRS GD248/589/3/2.
3 John Murray, *Holyrood-house: An Elegy. Addressed to the Nobility of Scotland. Ornamented with a Front View of the Royal Palace* (Edinburgh: [John Murray], 1781).
4 19 George II, chap. 39, sec. 17, 1746.
5 William Ferguson, *The Identity of the Scottish Nation: An Historical Quest* (Edinburgh: Edinburgh University Press, 1998), 227–8.
6 NRS GD224/628/5/8.
7 History of Parliament online: http://www.historyofparliamentonline.org/volume/1790-1820/member/dundas-henry-1742-1811 (accessed January 2018).
8 For example, James Beattie, *Scoticisms . . . Designed to Correct Improprieties of Speech and Writing. To Which Is Added, a Lecture on Elocution: By Dr. Blair* (Edinburgh: n.p., 1797).
9 Michael Lynch, *Scotland: A New History* (London: Pimlico, 1992), 334.

10 Kenneth Macdonald (ed.), *Antiquarian Notes . . . by Charles Fraser-Mackintosh* (Stirling: Eneas MacKay, 1913), 349.
11 Right Rev. Robert Forbes, *Journals of the Episcopal Visitations of the Right Rev. Robert Forbes . . . 1762 & 1770*, ed. J. B. Craven (London: Skeffington and Son, 1886), 11.
12 Preface to John Howie, *The Scots Worthies* (Edinburgh, 1902), xxiii, xxv.
13 John Frew, 'Gothic Is English: John Carter and the Revival of the Gothic as England's National Style', *Art Bulletin*, 64(2) (June 1982), 316.
14 Ibid., 315.
15 Jayne Elizabeth Lewis, *Mary Queen of Scots: Romance and Nation* (London: Routledge, 1998), 103, 110–11, 162.
16 Robert L. Mack, *Thomas Gray: A Life* (New Haven: Yale University Press, 2000), 544.
17 Horace Walpole, *The Castle of Otranto, A Story. Translated by William Marshal, Gent. from the Original Italian of Onuphrio Muralto* (London: Thomas Lownds, 1764).
18 Michael McCarthy, *The Origins of the Gothic Revival* (New Haven: Yale University Press, 1987), 63.
19 David Watkin, *The English Vision: The Picturesque in Architecture, Landscape and Garden Design* (London: John Murray, 1982), 93.
20 Margaret H. B. Sanderson, *Robert Adam and Scotland: Portrait of an Architect* (Edinburgh: HMSO, 1992), 88.
21 Roderick Graham, *Arbiter of Elegance: A Biography of Robert Adam* (Edinburgh: Birlinn, 2009), 149–50.
22 John Adam, 'Chapiteau Ecossais', http://collections.soane.org/OBJECT1441 (accessed January 2018).
23 John Fleming, *Robert Adam and His Circle in Edinburgh & Rome* (London: J. Murray, 1962), 305.
24 Inrtroduction to *Archaeologia Scotica: Or Transactions of the Society of Antiquaries of Scotland*, vol. 1 (Edinburgh: 1792), xxvi.
25 Allan I. Macinnes, *Clanship, Commerce and the House of Stuart, 1603–1788* (East Linton: Tuckwell Press, 1996), 220.
26 www.ceolsean.net/content/MacKay/Book08/Competitions.pdf (accessed January 2018).
27 James A. Stewart Jr., 'Lost Highland Manuscripts and the Jacobite Rebellion of 1745–6', in *Celtic Connections: Proceedings of the 10th International Congress of Celtic Studies*, ed. R. Black et al., vol. I (East Linton: Tuckwell Press, 1999), 287–308.
28 *ODNB*, vol. 35, 987–90.
29 NRS GD18/4890.
30 NRS GD80/936.
31 Bailey Saunders, *The Life and Letters of James MacPherson* (London: MacMillan, 1894), 283.
32 NRS GD44/28/30/1.
33 Christian Ludwig Stieglitz, *Plans et Dessins Tires de la Belle Architecture* (Paris, 1801).
34 NRS GD80/936.
35 Murray Pittock, *The Myth of the Jacobite Clans* (Edinburgh: Edinburgh University Press, 1995), 37.

36 MacDonald, *Antiquarian Notes*, 346.
37 Mary Miers, *The Western Seaboard* (Edinburgh: RIAS, 2008), 74.
38 NRS GD224/84/9/4a.
39 NRS GD224/655/2/61–3.
40 NRS GD174/722; Frank Arneil Walker, *The Buildings of Scotland: Argyll and Bute* (London: Penguin, 2000), 579–81.
41 NRS GD174/1287.
42 NRS GD224/257/10; Cruft, *Borders*, 356.
43 www.nationalgalleries.org/art-and-artists/3078/sir-alexander-macdonald-1744-1795-9th-baronet-sleat-and-1st-baron-macdonald-slate-about-1772 (accessed January 2018).
44 NRS RH4/90/11.
45 www.legislation.gov.uk/apgb/Geo2/20/43/introduction (accessed January 2018).
46 Gifford, *Perth*, 260.
47 Donald J. Withrington and Ian R. Grant (eds), *The Statistical Account of Scotland*, 20 vols (Wakefield, 1976), vol. 11, xi, 331.
48 MacDonald, *Antiquarian Notes*, 346.
49 NRS GD248/176/3/15.
50 Cruft, *Borders*, 597–601, plate 51.
51 David W. Walker and Matthew Woodworth, *The Buildings of Scotland: Aberdeenshire: North and Moray* (New Haven: Yale University Press, 2015), 217–29.
52 NRS GD248/588/15.
53 Sharples, *Aberdeenshire*, 538.
54 NRS GD44/Sec 49/bundle 16.
55 NRS GD44/43/29/36.
56 NRS GD44/43/82/20.
57 Sharples, *Aberdeenshire*, 544.
58 NRS GD44/43/134/5.
59 NRS GD18/4745.
60 NRS GD18/4848.
61 Adam, *Vitruvius Scoticus*, plate 74.
62 Ibid., plates 135–6; Ian Gow, *Scotland's Lost Houses* (London: Aurum, 2006), 43–51.
63 NRHE LAD/28/10.
64 David Brown, 'The Government of Scotland under Henry Dundas and William Pitt', *History*, 83(270) (April 1998), 265–79; Michael Fry, *The Dundas Despotism* (Edinburgh: Edinburgh University Press, 1992).
65 NRS RHP3154, RHP6699.
66 History of Parliament online: http://www.historyofparliamentonline.org/volume/1754-1790/member/dundas-henry-1742-1811 (accessed January 2018).
67 NRS RHP3154/42.
68 Robert and James Adam, *Works in Architecture of Robert and James Adam*, ed. Robert Oresko, 3 vols (New York: St Martin's Press, 1975), vol. 1, I.46.
69 Alistair Rowan, *Designs for Castles and Country Villas by Robert and James Adam* (Oxford: Phaidon, 1985), 17.

70   Howard Colvin et al. (eds), *Architectural Drawings from Lowther Castle* (Society of Architectural Historians of Great Britain, 1980), plates 24–7.
71   NRHE BWD/57/50–51.
72   NRHE BWD/57/3 & 13.
73   Cruft, *Borders*, 389–90.
74   Alistair Rowan, 'Wedderburn Castle', in *The Country Seat: Studies in the History of the British Country House Presented to Sir John Summerson on His Sixty-Fifth Birthday*, ed. Howard Colvin and John Harris (London: Allen Lane, 1970), 174–7.
75   NRS GD267/22/7/37.
76   History of Parliament online: https://www.historyofparliamentonline.org/volume/1754-1790/member/fraser-simon-1726-82 (accessed January 2018).
77   Rowan, *Castles*, 118–19.
78   NRHE WLD/45/24.
79   NRS GD27/7/323.
80   Rowan, *Castles*, 124–7.
81   NRS GD18/4965.
82   Ibid.
83   Michael Moss, *The 'Magnificent Castle' of Culzean and the Kennedy Family* (Edinburgh: Edinburgh University Press, 2002).
84   NRHE BWD/52/7–8.
85   Sir William Fraser,*The Annandale Family Book of the Johnstones, Earls and Marquises of Annandale*, 2 vols (Edinburgh: privately printed, 1894), vol. 1, cccxxxvi–cccxxxxix.
86   NRS GD353/144/4/5.
87   NRS GD248/589/3/.
88   NRS GD44/43/54.

Chapter 6

1   *Gentleman's Magazine*, xcix(ii) (1814), 631.
2   Anon., *A Sketch of a Tour in the Highlands of Scotland; through Perthshire, Argyleshire and Inverness-shire, in September and October, 1818: With Some Account of the Caledonian Canal* (London: Baldwin et al., 1819), 70.
3   Lady Frances Balfour, *The Life of George, Fourth Earl of Aberdeen*, 2 vols (London: Hodder and Stoughton, 1923), 1, 20.
4   Emma Vincent, 'The Responses of Scottish Churchmen to the French Revolution, 1789–1802', *SHR*, lxxiii (October 1994), 191.
5   Kathryn Chittick, *The Language of Whiggism: Liberty and Patriotism, 1802–1830* (London: Routledge, 2016), 113.
6   Alexander Carlyle, *National Depravity: The Cause of National Calamities, A Sermon, From Jeremiah vi. 8. Preached in the Church of Inveresk, Feb. 25. 1794; Being the Day Appointed by His Majesty for a General Fast* (Edinburgh: John Ogle, 1794), 33–4. The formula 'Honour the King' was well known from 1 Peter 2.17, but there it stands alongside what for Carlyle would have been the less palatable 'Honour all men. Love the Brotherhood.'

7. David Thomson, *Europe since Napoleon* (Harmondsworth: Penguin, 1966), 119.
8. *The Art-Union*, vol. 4 (1842), 157.
9. T. C. Smout, 'Problems of Nationalism, Identity and Improvement in Later Eighteenth-Century Scotland', in *Improvement and Enlightenment*, ed. T. M. Devine (Edinburgh: John Donald, 1989), 4.
10. Patrick Hogg, 'Robert Burns under the Microscope', *Herald*, 25 January 1996; Robert Crawford, *The Bard: Robert Burns, A Biography* (Princeton: Princeton University Press, 2009), 10.
11. James Simpson, *A Visit to Flanders, in July, 1815: Being Chiefly an Account of the Field of Waterloo* (New York: S. Campbell, 1816), 128, 131–2.
12. Ibid., 142.
13. Ibid., 133–4, 155.
14. John Gifford, 'The National Monument of Scotland', *Architectural Heritage*, xxv (2014), 43–83; James Aikman, *The Cenotaph: A Poem* (Edinburgh, 1821), ix. For 'national monuments', see Johnny Rodger, *The Hero Building – The Architecture of Scottish National Identity* (Farnham: Ashgate, 2015).
15. J. C. B. Cooksey, *Alexander Nasmyth HRSA 1758–1840: A Man of the Scottish Renaissance* (Whittingehame House: Paul Harris, 1991), 92–3, catalogue pp. 23, 36–7.
16. *The Scots Magazine*, 69 (Edinburgh, 1807), 874.
17. J. C. Loudon F.L.S., *Observations on Laying Out Farms, in the Scotch Style, Adapted to England* (London: John Harding, 1812), 72.
18. Andrew Hook, 'Scotland and Romanticism: The International Scene', in *The History of Scottish Literature*, general ed. Cairns Craig, 4 vols (Aberdeen: Aberdeen University Press, 1987), vol. 1, 319.
19. Preface to *Archaeologia Scotica*, vol. i, iii–iv.
20. *ODNB*, vol. 59, 110.
21. J. E. Cookson, 'The Napoleonic Wars, Military Scotland and Tory Highlandism in the Early Nineteenth Century', *SHR*, lxxviii (April 1999), 60.
22. Ibid., 73.
23. T. Devine, *Scottish Nation: 1700–2007* (London: Penguin, 2006), 234.
24. Introduction to Jenny Wormald, *Scotland Revisited* (London: Collins and Brown, 1991), 9.
25. Graeme Morton, 'The Social Memory of Jane Porter and her *Scottish Chiefs*', *SHR*, xci (October 2012), 311–35.
26. Graeme Morton, 'The Most Efficacious Patriot: The Heritage of William Wallace in Nineteenth- Century Scotland', *SHR*, lxxvii (October 1998), 224–51.
27. Morton, 'Jane Porter', 318.
28. Graeme Morton, *Unionist Nationalism: Governing Urban Scotland 1830–1860* (East Linton: Tuckwell Press, 1999), 144–5.
29. *Gentleman's Magazine*, xcix(ii) (1814), 631.
30. *Fraser's Magazine*, 10 (1834), 153.
31. Mr Thomas H. Shepherd, *Modern Athens! Displayed in a Series of Views: Edinburgh in the Nineteenth Century* (London: Jones, 1829), 50.
32. Robert Forsyth, *The Beauties of Scotland*, 5 vols (Edinburgh: T. Bonar and J. Brown, 1805), vol. 1, 9–10.

33 Henry Lord Cockburn, *Memorials of His Time* (Edinburgh: A & C Black, 1856), 300.
34 Michael Penman, 'Robert Bruce's Bones: Reputation, Politics and Identities in Nineteenth Century Scotland', *Institute for Research in Social Sciences*, 34 (2009), 7–73.
35 Penman, 'Bruce's Bones', 22–3.
36 *Blackwood's Magazine*, xxxiii (December 1819), 297–304; David Ditchburn and Catriona M. M. MacDonald, 'Bannockburn, World War I and the Referendum', *SHR*, xciii (October 2014), 164.
37 *Archaeologia Scotica*, ii (1822), 449.
38 Miles Glendinning et al., *A History of Scottish Architecture* (Edinburgh: Edinburgh University Press, 1996), 227.
39 Shepherd, *Modern Athens*, 58.
40 Margaret H. B. Sanderson, 'This Disagreeable Business: John Paterson against the Earl of Eglinton', in Gow, *Country Houses*, 192–205.
41 NRS RH15/119/48.
42 NRHE, AND/37/42; HCC 1991/32 (Inv 2/61).
43 James MacAuley, *The Gothic Revival 1745–1845* (Glasgow: Blackie, 1975), 190–1.
44 R. Jaques, *Falkirk and District* (Edinburgh: RIAS, 2001), 136.
45 NRS GD112/20.
46 Cooksey, *Nasmyth*, 32, 35, 84–5.
47 NRS GD112/20/4/5/1.
48 NRS GD112/20/1/13/1.
49 NRS GD112/20/4/5/1.
50 NRS GD112/20/4/5/8; GD112/20/1/23.
51 NRS GD112/20/1/15/8.
52 NRS GD112/20/4/12/49.
53 NRS GD112/20/4/12/58.
54 Simon Bradley, 'The Englishness of Gothic: Theories and Interpretations from William Gilpin to J H Parker', *Architectural History*, 45 (2002), 325–46.
55 Ibid., 346.
56 George Whittington, *A Historical Survey of the Ecclesiastical Antiquities of France* (London: J. Taylor, 1809).
57 John Britton, *The Architectural Antiquities of Great Britain*, 5 vols (London: Longman, 1807–26), vol. 3, 49.
58 Thomas Rickman, *An Attempt to Discriminate the Styles of English Architecture, from the Conquest to the Reformation*, 6th edn (Oxford: John Henry and James Parker, 1862), 434.
59 Colin Kidd, '*The Strange Death of Scottish History* Revisited: Constructions of the Past in Scotland, c.1790–1914', *SHR*, lxxvi (April 2007), 87.
60 Sir James Hall, *Essay on the Origin, History, and Principles of Gothic Architecture* (Edinburgh: Andrew Balfour, 1813).
61 *ODNB*, vol. 24, 620–21; Basil Hall, *Travels in India, Ceylon and Borneo* (London: Routedge Curzon, 2005), 1–2.
62 Hall, *Essay*, 147.
63 Ibid., 18–19.
64 Ibid., 34.
65 Ibid., 83, plate L, fig. 1.

66 Preface to Robert Lugar, *Plans and Views of Buildings Executed in England and Scotland, in The Castellated and Other Styles* (London: J. Taylor, 1811).
67 NRHE PTD/94/17.
68 Copies of the proposed south and east elevations are at NRHE PTD/94/16; David Walker, 'Scone Palace', Colvin and Harris, *The Country Seat*, 200–214.
69 Gifford, *Perth & Kinross*, 689–94.
70 Nick Haynes, *Perth & Kinross* (Edinburgh: RIAS, 2000), 167.
71 J. C. Loudon, *Treatise on Forming, Improving, and Managing Country Residences*, 2 vols (London: Longman, 1806), vol. 1, 117–18.
72 Ibid., 1, 109, 162–3.
73 Ibid., 1, 111.
74 GD170/2451.
75 Lugar, *Plans and Views*, 9.
76 Cruft, *Borders*, 239–44.
77 NRHE BWD/52/13; BWD/52/21.
78 J. P. Neale, *Views of the Seats of Noblemen and Gentlemen in England, Wales, Scotland and Ireland*. Second series, 5 vols (London Sherwood: Jones, 1824–29), vol. 1, unpaginated.
79 NRS GD52/349; Macauley, *Gothic Revival*, 339; Sharples, *Aberdeenshire*, 402–4.
80 J. P. Neale, *Views of the Seats of Noblemen and Gentlemen in England, Wales, Scotland and Ireland*. First series, 6 vols (London: W. H. Reid, 1818–23), vol. i, unpaginated.
81 NRS GD142/10/184-185x.
82 Referred to as Crawford Priory by 1808 (GD20/7/245).
83 Gifford, *Perth and Kinross*, 461.
84 Gifford, *Edinburgh*, 336.
85 Walker, *Argyll and Bute*, 242.
86 John Leyden, *Journal of a Tour in the Highlands and Western Islands of Scotland in 1800 by John Leyden*, ed. J. Sinton (Edinburgh: Blackwood, 1903), 77–8.
87 RCAHMS, *Argyll: An Inventory of the Monuments, Volume 7, Mid Argyll and Cowal* (Edinburgh: HMSO, 1992), 282.
88 [Jane Graham], *Lacunar Strevelinense: A Collection of Heads, Etched and Engraved after the Carved Works Which Formerly Decorated the Roof of the King's Room in Stirling Castle* (Edinburgh: William Blackwood, 1817), 1.
89 *RPC* (3rd series), vol. xv, 327.
90 NLS ms.1646 Z.02/19a.
91 Gifford and Walker, *Stirling*, 674.
92 *Lacunar Strevelinense*, 4.
93 Helen Douglas-Irvine, *The Royal Palaces of Scotland*, ed. Robert S. Rait (London: Constable, 1911), 44–5.
94 NRS GD152/209/1/4.
95 NRS GD152/218/5/20.
96 NRS GD248/464/9.
97 M. E. Chamberlain, *Lord Aberdeen – A Political Biography* (London: Longman, 1983), 75.
98 NLS Ms 353, folders 98–103.
99 NRS GD1/1398/6/7.

100 J. Stark, *Picture of Edinburgh* (Edinburgh: A. Constable, 1806), 109.
101 www.buildingsofireland.ie/Surveys/Buildings/BuildingoftheMonth/Archive/Name,3148,en.html
102 Judith Hill, 'Architecture in the Aftermath of Union: Building the Viceregal Chapel in Dublin Castle, 1801–15', *Architectural History*, 60 (2017), 183.
103 www.buildingsofireland.ie/niah/search.jsp?type=record&county=OF&regno=14916022
104 https://en.wikipedia.org/wiki/List_of_Irish_Volunteer_corps
105 www.dia.ie/architects/view/814/CHARLEVILLE-CHARLESWILLIAMBURY-1STEARLOF
106 www.dia.ie/works/view/220/building/CO.+WESTMEATH%2C+TULLYNALLY
107 www.buildingsofireland.ie/niah/search.jsp?type=record&county=SL&regno=32402620
108 J. E. Cookson, 'The Edinburgh and Glasgow Duke of Wellington Statues: Early Nineteenth-Century Unionist Nationalism as a Tory Project', *SHR*, lxxxiii (April 2004), 37.
109 Ibid., 30.
110 Cairns Craig, *Out of History: Narrative Paradigms in Scottish and British Culture* (Edinburgh: Polygon, 1996), 10.

Chapter 7

1 Introduction to James Hogg, *The Jacobite Relics of Scotland; Being the Songs, Airs, and Legends of the Adherents of the House of Stuart*, 2 vols (Edinburgh: William Blackwood, 1819–21), vol. 1, xi.
2 Sir Herbert Grierson, *The Letters of Sir Walter Scott*, 12 vols (London: Constable, 1932–7), vol. 4, 282, 333–4.
3 Preface to Henry Lord Cockburn, *Life of Lord Francis Jeffrey* (Edinburgh: Adam and Charles Black, 1872), 151.
4 Cockburn, *Lord Jeffrey*, 151; Craig, *Scottish Literature*, vol. 2, 319.
5 Leah Leneman, 'A New Role for a Lost Cause: Lowland Romanticism of the Jacobite Highlander', in *Perspectives in Scottish Social History: Essays in Honour of Rosalind Mitchison* (Aberdeen: Aberdeen University Press, 1988), 116.
6 Hogg, *Relics*, vol. 1, x.
7 Sir John Sinclair of Ulbster, *An Account of the Highland Society of London* (London: B. McMillan, 1813), 10–11.
8 Preface to Anon., *Jacobite Minstrelsy; with Notes Illustrative of the Text, and Containing Historical Details in Relation to the House of Stuart, from 1640 to 1784* (Glasgow: R. Griffin, 1829), v–vi.
9 Cookson, 'Napoleonic Wars', 69.
10 *Inverness Courier*, 12 November 1828.
11 NRS GD160/557.
12 William Hazlitt, *The Spirit of the Age: Or, Contemporary Portraits*, 2 vols (Paris: S. & R. Bentley, 1825), vol. 1, 38.
13 Colin Kidd, 'Race and the Scottish Nation: 1750–1900' (lecture to the Royal Society of Edinburgh, 13 January 2003).

14 Matthew Hammond, 'Ethnicity and the Writing of Medieval Scottish History', *SHR*, lxxx (April 2006), 3–4.
15 Hammond, 'Ethnicity', 1–27; Colin Kidd, 'Teutonist Ethnology and Scottish Nationalist Inhibition, 1780–1880', *SHR*, lxxiv (1995), 45–68.
16 Kidd, 'Race'.
17 Ibid.
18 Hall, *Essay*, 93.
19 John Prebble, *The King's Jaunt: George IV in Scotland, August 1822: 'One and Twenty Daft Days'* (London: Penguin, 1988); Cookson, 'Statues', 40.
20 *Blackwood's Edinburgh Magazine*, vol. 5 (1819), 720–36.
21 Anon., *A Narrative of the Visit of George IV to Scotland in August 1822. By an Eye-Witness of Most of the Scenes Which Were Then Exhibited* (Edinburgh: Macredie et al., 1822), 23–4; Robert Mudie, *Historical Account of His Majesty's Visit to Scotland* (Edinburgh: Oliver & Boyd, 1822), 33ff.
22 Mudie, *Visit*, 20ff.
23 Anon., *Hints Addressed to the inhabitants of Edinburgh and Others, in Prospect of His Majesty's Visit. By and Old Citizen* (Edinburgh: Macredie et al., 1822), 28.
24 *Hints*, 13.
25 Mudie, *Visit*, 250.
26 *Hints*, 52.
27 Ibid., 12.
28 *ODNB*, vol. 52, 653.
29 Col. David Stewart of Garth, *Sketches of the Character, Manners, and Present State of the Highlanders of Scotland*, 2 vols (Edinburgh, 1822); J. E. Cookson, 'The Napoleonic Wars, Military Scotland and Tory Highlandism in the Early Nineteenth Century', *SHR*, lxxviii (April 1999), 68.
30 *Narrative*, 54.
31 Anon., *Remarks on Colonel Stewart's Sketches of the Highlanders* (Edinburgh: Archibald Constable, 1823), 8n.
32 Ibid., 8.
33 Henry Paton (ed.), *The Lyon in Mourning*, 3 vols (Edinburgh: Scottish History Society, 1895–6); Leneman, 'Lost Cause', 115.
34 Lady Frances Balfour, *The Life of George Fourth Earl of Aberdeen*, 2 vols (London: Hodder & Stoughton, 1923), vol. 1, 206–7.
35 Ibid., 209.
36 J. G. Lockhart, *The Life of Sir Walter Scott*, 10 vols (Edinburgh, 1902–3), vol. 5, 340, 342; vol. 6, 122.
37 Preface to Angus MacKay, *A Collection of Ancient Piobaireachd or Highland Pipe Music* (Aberdeen: Logan, 1838).
38 NLS ms 50.3.9, p. 109.
39 Matthew Williams, 'Planning for the Picturesque: Thomas Hamilton's New Roads to the Old Town, 1817–1858', *Architectural Heritage*, xx (2009), 33–53.
40 W. Ferguson, 'The Reform Act (Scotland) of 1832: Intention and Effect', *SHR*, xlv (1966), 105–14.
41 Graeme Morton, 'Scotland is Britain: The Union and Unionist-Nationalism, 1807–1907', *Journal of Irish and Scottish Studies*, 1(2) (March 2008), 131–2.

42 Gordon Pentland, 'The Debate of Scottish Parliamentary Reform, 1830–32', *SHR*, lxxxv (April 2006), 122.
43 Rob Close and Anne Riches, *The Buildings of Scotland: Ayrshire and Arran* (New Haven: Yale University Press, 2012), 134.
44 Anon., *Improvements in Edinburgh During the Year 1823* (Edinburgh: n.p., 1824), 20–21.
45 Alexander Allardyce (ed.), *Letters From and To Charles Kirkpatrick Sharpe Esq*, 2 vols (Edinburgh: William Blackwood, 1888), vol. 2, 356, 360.
46 John Gifford, 'The National Monument of Scotland', *Architectural Heritage*, xxv (Edinburgh, 2014), 43–83.
47 NLS ms 352, p. 166.
48 NLS ms 15973, f.14.
49 Cookson, 'Napoleonic Wars', 74.
50 Joseph Nash, *Views of the Interior and Exterior of Windsor Castle* (London: Thomas McLean, 1852).
51 A. Welby Pugin, *Contrasts: Or a Parallel between the Noble Edifices of the Middle Ages, and Corresponding Buildings of the Present Day; Shewing the Present Decay of Taste* (London: A. Welby Pugin, 1836), 30–31.
52 H. M. Colvin, general ed., *The History of the King's Works*, 6 vols (London: HMSO, 1963–82), vol. 6, 576.
53 Simon Bradley and Nikolaus Pevsner, *The Buildings of England: London 6: Westminster* (New Haven: Yale University Press, 2003), 219.
54 Augustus Pugin, *An Apology for the Revival of Christian Architecture in England* (London: John Weale, 1843), 10.
55 Herrmann Wolfgang (ed.), *In What Style Should We Build? The German Debate on Architectural Style* (Santa Monica: Getty Center, 1992).
56 A. MacKechnie and F. Urban, 'Balmoral Castle: National Architecture in a European Context', *Architectural History*, 58 (January 2015), 159–96; Robert R. Taylor, *The Castles of the Rhine: Recreating the Middle Ages in Modern Germany* (Waterloo, Ontario: Wilfrid Laurier University Press, 1998), 134–48.
57 John Frew, 'Scott, Abbotsford and the Antiquaries', in *Abbotsford and Sir Walter Scott: The Image and the Influence*, ed. Iain Gordon Brown (Edinburgh: Society of Antiquaries of Scotland, 2003), 37–48; Cruft, *Borders*, 91–8.
58 Shepherd, *Modern Athens!*, 67.
59 Washington Irving, *Abbotsford and Newstead Abbey* (Philadelphia: Carey et al., 1835), 68.
60 Cruft, *Borders*, 92; Glendinning, *History*, 38.
61 Scott, *Letters*, vol. 4, 289–90.
62 Irving, *Abbotsford*, 43.
63 NRHE D62412.
64 NRHE RXD/6/8.
65 Scott, *Letters*, vol. 5, 61.
66 Irving, *Abbotsford*, 6.
67 Ibid., 35–6.
68 Scott, *Letters*, vol. 7, 111.
69 NRHE RXD/6/9.
70 Horace Walpole, *A Description of the Villa of Mr Horace Walpole . . . at Straw-berry-Hill near Twickenham* (1774).

71 R. J. Hill. 'Walter Scott and James Skene: A Creative Friendship', *Romantic Textualities: Literature and Print Culture, 1780–1840*, 21 (Winter 2013), 72–87.
72 Frew, 'Scott', 37; Cruft, *Borders*, 91–8; Glendinning, *History*, 240.
73 Glendinning, *History*, 240; Alastair Durie, 'Tourism in Victorian Scotland: The Case of Abbotsford', *Scottish Economic & Social History*, 12(1) (1992), 42–54.
74 Katia Kretkowska, 'Scotland in the Life of a Polish Country Sstate, 1790–1830', in *Scotland and Europe 1200–1850*, ed. T. C. Smout (Edinburgh: John Donald, 1986), 183.
75 Ibid., 180–83.
76 J. C. Loudon, *The Gardener's Magazine* (London, 1842), 440.
77 H. Colvin, *A Biographical Dictionary of British Architects 1600–1840*, 4th edn (New Haven: Yale University Press, 2008), 931.
78 NRS GD224/507/1; GD224/582/9/1.
79 *The Westminster Review* (April 1829), 261.
80 Kathryn Chittick, *The Language of Whiggism: Liberty and Patriotism, 1802–1830* (London: Routledge, 2010), 113.
81 David Walker, 'William Burn: The Country House in Transition', in *Seven Victorian Architects*, ed. Jane Fawcett (London: Thames & Hudson, 1976), 23.
82 Royal Incorporation of British Architects, *RIBA Transactions* (1869–70), 121–9.
83 NRS GD364/1/1295; *ODNB*, vol. 28, 6.
84 NRS RHP97911, RHP97915-23.
85 NRHE B61662P.
86 *ODNB*, vol. 8, 880.
87 Walker, 'Burn', 14–15.
88 Neale, *Seats*, second series, vol. 1, unpaginated.
89 *Alexander's East India and Colonial Magazine*, viii(49) (December 1834), 626.
90 McWilliam, *Lothian*, 122–3.
91 Barbara Balfour-Melville, *The Balfours of Pilrig: A History for the Family* (Edinburgh: William Brown, 1907), 197, 213–14.
92 NRS GD463/2/6.
93 Chittick, *Whiggism*, 116.
94 J. G. Lockhart, *Memoirs of the Life of Sir Walter Scott*, 10 vols (Edinburgh: T&A Constable, 1902–3), vol. 9, 248, vol. 10, 76.
95 NRS GD463/2/6.
96 *New Statistical Account*, vol. 6, 582 (report dated 1839).
97 J. C. Loudon, *The Gardener's Magazine*, 19 vols (London: Longman et al., 1826–44), vol. 8, 388–9; Lockhart, *Memoirs*, vol. 4, 268.
98 Sir Walter Scott, *The Journal of Sir Walter Scott 1825–32: From the Original Manuscript at Abbotsford* (Edinburgh: Douglas & Foulis, 1927), 507.
99 *The United Service Journal and Naval and Military Magazine* (1836), part II, 123–8, 279.
100 Burn drawings are in NRHE; Gifford, *Fife*, 261.
101 Michael Davis, *Scots Baronial Mansions & Castle Restorations in the West of Scotland* (Ardrishaig: Spindrift, 1996), 10.

102 'Sir Michael Bruce 8th Bart. of Stenhouse', *Legacies of British Slave-ownership*. www.ucl.ac.uk/lbs/person/view/1301240057 (accessed January 2018).
103 D. P. Menzies, *The 'Red and White' Book of the Menzies: Leabhair Dearg is Geal na Meinenich. The History of Clan Menzies and Its Chiefs* (Glasgow: Banks, 1894), plate xxxix.
104 NRHE E42292/P (PTD/3/12).
105 Shepherd, *Modern Athen*s!, 71.
106 Gifford, *Edinburgh*, 182.
107 *ODNB*, vol. 32, 677–8.
108 *Gentleman's Magazine* (August 1836), 206.
109 *The Anti-Slavery Reporter*, vol. 4 (London: Society for the Abolition of Slavery, January–December 1831), 25ff; *ODNB*, vol. 29, 876–81.
110 Ibid., vol. 29, 878.
111 Gifford, *Edinburgh*, 532–3.
112 David Shankie, *The Parish of Colinton: From an Early Period to the Present Day* (Edinburgh: John Wilson, 1902), 106.
113 NRS GD155/896.
114 *ODNB*, vol. 12, 337–40.
115 Lord Cockburn, *History & Laws of the Bonaly Friday Club* (Edinburgh: The Club, 1842), 7.
116 https://canmore.org.uk/site/58589/cockburn-tower (accessed January 2018).
117 Henry Cockburn, *Memorials of His Time* (New York: D. Appleton, 1856), 242.
118 Originals in RIAS, copies in NRHE EDD/16/17, PTD/93/18.
119 Cockburn, *Memorials*, 427.
120 www.historyofparliamentonline.org/volume/1790–1820/member/maconochie-alexander-1777–1861; https://canmore.org.uk/collection/1040317 (accessed January 2018).
121 *ODNB*, vol. 35, 972–4.
122 David Walker, 'The Donaldson's Hospital Competition and the Palace of Westminster', *Architectural History*, 27 (1984), 488.
123 Ibid., plate 4a.
124 Ibid., 493, 496.
125 Neale, *Seats*, second series, vol. 4, unpaginated. https://archive.org/details/viewsseatsnoble01moulgoog (accessed January 2018).
126 James Macaulay, 'James Gillespie Graham and A.W.N. Pugin – Some Perthshire Connections', *Architectural Heritage*, 8 (August 1997), 28.
127 Macaulay, 'Gillespie Graham', 136–47.
128 Ibid., 28.
129 Ibid.
130 Scott, *Journal*, 758.
131 Macaulay, 'Gillespie Graham', 28, plate 3.4.
132 Ibid., 28.
133 Close, *Ayrshire*, 311.
134 https://canmore.org.uk/site/42915/dunlop-parish-church?display=collection&GROUPCATEGORY=5&per_page=49
135 *New Statistical Account*, vol. 7, 244.

136 Diane Watters, 'David Hamilton's Lennox Castle', *Architectural Heritage*, 5 (1994), 51–65.
137 https://en.wikisource.org/wiki/Ivanhoe/Chapter_2
138 Glenmore Donald Shaw, *Highland Legends: Fugitive Pieces of Original Poetry: Translations from the Gaelic and Vice Versa*, 2nd edn (Edinburgh, 1859), frontispiece.
139 Harry Gordon Slade, 'Castle Fraser', *PSAS*, 109 (1977–8), 246, 260–61.
140 *New Statistical Account*, vol. 12, 546.
141 Walker, *Aberdeenshire*, 184.
142 Ibid., 549.
143 Joe Rock, *Thomas Hamilton Architect 1784–1858* (Edinburgh: Talbot Rice, 1984), 17.
144 David W. Walker, 'A Look at Edinburgh's Cockburn Street', *Urban Realm* (5 June 2008).
145 J. C. Loudon, *An Encyclopaedia of Cottage, Farm, and Villa Architecture* (London, 1836, 1853), 1162–3.
146 Thomas Hamilton, *Report Relative to the Proposed Improvements on the Earthen Mound* (1830).
147 Matthew H. Kaufman, 'An Engraving Entitled: "Melbourne Place and Victoria Terrace from George IV Bridge"', *Res Medica: Journal of the Royal Medical Society* (Summer 2003), 19–23.
148 www.scottisharchitects.org.uk/architect_full.php?id=100214 (accessed January 2018).
149 Diane Watters, *St John's Episcopal Church Edinburgh* (Edinburgh: RCAHMS, 2008).
150 Gifford, *Edinburgh*, 168.
151 Ibid., 129.
152 NRS GD112/20/5/10/1.
153 *Second Report of the Subcommittee for Erecting a Monument to Sir Walter Scott* (Edinburgh: The Committee, 1835), 11.
154 *Third Report of the Subcommittee for Erecting a Monument to Sir Walter Scott* (Edinburgh: The Committee, 1838), 7–12.
155 Graeme Morton, *Unionist Nationalism: Governing Urban Scotland 1830–1860* (East Linton: Tuckwell Press, 1999), 169; *Proceedings at the Public Meeting Regarding the Monument to Sir Walter Scott Held 5th February 1844* (Edinburgh: Constable, 1844), 10.
156 *Proceedings at the Public Meeting*, 6–11.
157 *ODNB*, vol. 28, 713–14; C. J. Hullmandel, *The Art of Drawing on Stone* (London: Longman, 1833).
158 https://archive.org/details/gentlemansmagaz331unkngoog
159 NLS ms20346.
160 Loudon, *Encyclopaedia*, 879–84.
161 Ibid., 888–9.
162 *ODNB*, vol. 38, 814–16.
163 Rosemary Hill, *God's Architect: Pugin and the Building of Romantic Britain* (London: Allen Lane, 2007), 212.
164 *Tait's Edinburgh Magazine* (November 1839), 712; Clive Bloom, *Gothic Histories: The Taste for Terror, 1764 to the Present* (London, 2010), 36.

165 *Examiner: A Weekly Paper on Politics, Literature, Music and the Fine Arts* (1839), 441.
166 *The Tournament at Eglinton Castle August 30th 1839* (London, 1840), 3.
167 *Tait's Edinburgh Magazine* (November 1839), 701.
168 *Examiner* (1839), 554.
169 Ibid., 555.
170 *Tait's Edinburgh Magazine* (November 1839), 708.
171 Peter Buchan, *The Eglinton Tournament, and Gentleman Unmasked; in a Conversation between the Shades of King James V. of Scotland, and Sir David Lindsay of the Mount, Lyon King-at-Arms* (London, 1840), 7–8.
172 *Examiner*, 1839, 555.
173 Ibid., 555.
174 Hogg, *Relics*, vol. 1, xi.
175 Scott, *Journal*, 817.

Chapter 8

1 R. W. Billings, *Baronial and Ecclesiastical Antiquities of Scotland . . . 1845–52*, 4 vols (Edinburgh: W. Blackwood, 1852), vol. 3, unpaginated (Kilravock).
2 Robert Kerr, *The Gentleman's House, or, How to Plan English Residences, from the Parsonage to the Palace*, 2nd edn (London: John Murray, 1865), 343, 450.
3 *Transactions of the National Association for the Advancement of Art and Its Application to Industry, Edinburgh Meeting* (London, 1890), 182.
4 Roger Dixon and Stefan Muthesius, *Victorian Architecture*, 2nd edn (London: Thames & Hudson, 1985), 44.
5 *Builder*, 27 May 1876, vol. xxxiv, 508.
6 Billings, *Baronial*; *ODNB*, vol. 5, 725–6.
7 Introduction to Billings, *Baronial*, vol. 1, 2.
8 The initial plan was that Burn's and Billings's names would both be on the books' title pages, but following a dispute, Burn withdrew from the venture and Billings had Burn's name removed by the engraver. See Introduction by Ian Gow to *The Baronial and Ecclesiastical Antiquities of Scotland Illustrated by Robert William Billings, Architect 1845–52* (Edinburgh: Birlinn, Ltd., 2008).
9 www.scottisharchitects.org.uk/architect_full.php?id=100014 (accessed January 2018).
10 Ibid., vol. 1, 5.
11 F. T. Dollman and J. R. Jobbins, *An Analysis of Ancient Domestic Architecture, Exhibiting Some of the Best Existing Examples in Great Britain, from Drawings and Measurements Taken on the Spot*, 2 vols (London: Jobbins, 1861–63), vol. 1, unpaginated.
12 Preface to Dollman and Jobbins, vol. 1.
13 *National Association for the Advancement of Art*, 182.
14 Billings, vol. 3 (Kilravock).
15 John Starforth, *Designs for Villa Residences with Descriptions* (Edinburgh: William Blackwood, 1866), 7, plates xiii–xix.

16 Kerr, *Gentleman's House*, 376–7.
17 Ibid., 450.
18 *Examiner: A Weekly Paper on Politics, Literature, Music and the Fine Arts* (1839), 555; Lord Esher's Typescripts in *Queen Victoria's Journal*, 2 September 1839. www.queenvictoriasjournals.org/search/displayItem.do?FormatType=fulltextimgsrc&QueryType=articles&ResultsID=2997118757982&filterSequence=0&PageNumber=1&ItemNumber=1&ItemID=qvj02565&volumeType=ESHER (accessed January 2018).
19 NLS ms 50.3.9, pp. 108–9.
20 NLS ms 50.3.9, p. 78; Andrew Wiseman, 'The Sobieski Stuarts and Eilean Aigas', *Scottish Islands Explorer* (May–June 2012), 37–9; Walker, *Aberdeenshire*, 484.
21 Lovat was a Burn client (obituary by T. L. Donaldson in *RIBA Transactions* [1869–70], 121–9).
22 *New Statistical Account*, vol. 14, 488.
23 Elizabeth Grant, *Memoirs of a Highland Lady*, ed. Lady Strachey (London: John Murray, 1911), 368–9; NLS ms 50.3.9, p. 107.
24 *Tait's Edinburgh Magazine*, 1839, vol. 6, 716; NRS GD41/623.
25 NLS ms 50.3.9, pp. 75–107.
26 NAS GD 112/39/416/5; Alex Tyrrell, 'The Queen's "Little Trip": The Royal Visit to Scotland in 1842', *SHR*, lxxxii (April 2003), 50.
27 Sir James Balfour Paul (ed.), *The Scots Peerage: Founded on Wood's Edition of Sir Robert Douglas's Peerage of Scotland*, 9 vols (Edinburgh: D. Douglas, 1904–14), vol. 1, 94–6.
28 NAS GD 112/39/416/5.
29 W. Douglas Simpson (ed.), *Drawings of Aberdeenshire Castles by James Giles R.S.A.* (Aberdeen: Spalding Club, 1936).
30 Michael E. Vance, *Imperial Immigrants: The Scottish Settlers in the Upper Ottawa Valley, 1815–1840* (Toronto: Dundurn, 2012), 86.
31 Sir Thomas Dick Lauder, *Memorial of the Royal Progress in Scotland* (Edinburgh: Adam and Charles Black, 1843), 39.
32 James Miller, *The Lamp of Lothian, or, The History of Haddington . . . from the Earliest Records to the Present Period* (Haddington: J. Allen, 1844), 368.
33 Lauder, *Memorial*, 115.
34 Ibid., 269ff.
35 NRS GD 68/2/144; GD 112/50/1/11.
36 Menzies, *Clan Menzies*, 423–4.
37 Ibid.
38 Chamberlain, *Lord Aberdeen*, 264–5.
39 Hill, *God's Architect*, 188–9.
40 Gifford, *Perth & Kinross*, 722–7 and plates 85–6; James Macaulay, 'James Gillespie Graham and A.W.N. Pugin – Some Perthshire Connections', *Architectural Heritage*, 8 (August 1997), 30–31.
41 A. Pugin with E. J. Willson, *Specimens of Gothic Architecture Selected from Various Ancient Edifices in England*, 2 vols (London: M. A. Nattali, 1821), vol. 1, plates xlii–xliv.
42 Hill, *God's Architect*, 315.
43 Gifford, *Perth & Kinross*, 724.
44 NRS GD 112/20/Box 1/46/5.

45 Rosemary Hill, 'Pugin and Scotland', *Architectural Heritage, viii: Caledonia Gothica: Pugin and the Gothic Revival in Scotland* (1997), 10.
46 Hill, *God's Architect*, 9–11.
47 Ibid., 274–5; Hill, 'Pugin and Scotland', 17.
48 Hill, *God's Architect*, 273.
49 NRS GD 112/50/2/8.
50 NRS GD 112/50/1/7.
51 NRS GD 112/50/5.
52 NRS GD 112/50/3/8.
53 NRS GD 112/50/1/14.
54 NRS GD 112/50/3/9.
55 *Queen Victoria's Journals*, 10 September 1842. www.queenvictoriasjournals.org/search/displayItem.do?FormatType=fulltextimgsrc&QueryType=articles&ResultsID=2882064480481&filterSequence=0&PageNumber=1&ItemNumber=3&ItemID=qvj03636&volumeType=PSBEA (accessed January 2018).
56 *Queen Victoria's Journals*, 7 September 1842.
57 Letter dated 11 September 1842 (Windsor archives, RA Z287/13).
58 *ODNB*, vol. 35, 500–501; Neville T. McKay, 'A History of the Office of Piper to the Sovereign', *Folk Music Journal*, 7(2) (1996), 188–204.
59 Theodore Martin, *Life of His Royal Highness the Prince Consort*, 5 vols (London: Smith Elder, 1875–80), vol. 1, 47.
60 Ibid.
61 NRS GD 112/20/5/10/4.
62 NRS GD 112/20/5/10/2–3.
63 Gifford, *Edinburgh*, 129.
64 Pipe Major Robert Meldrum in *Oban Times*, 4 January 1941.
65 *Queen Victoria's Journals*, 8 September, 1848. www.queenvictoriasjournals.org/search/displayItemFromId.do?FormatType=fulltextimgsrc&QueryType=articles&ResultsID=2731785811802&filterSequence=0&PageNumber=1&ItemID=qvj05770&v olumeType=PSBEA (accessed January 2018).
66 Christopher Hibbert, *Queen Victoria in Her Letters and Journals* (London: John Murray, 1984), 147.
67 Ronald Clark, *Balmoral, Queen Victoria's Highland Home* (London: Thames and Hudson, 1981), 25.
68 *The Examiner*, 1809 (1 October 1842), 629. https://books.google.co.uk/books?id=29RMAAAAcAAJ&pg=PA434&lpg=PA434&dq=dismissal+of+colonel+dundas+1842&source=bl&ots=G2vWfZB8X1&sig=3CRONcTnOVgh4fHOFWdqCq3- 1G0&hl=en&sa=X&ved=0CDUQ6AEwBmoVChMI1pqx1caUxwIVzFcUCh2sSgXP#v=onepage&q=tay mouth&f=false (accessed January 2018).
69 Hibbert, *Victoria*, 146; MacKechnie, 'Balmoral', 159–96.
70 Kerr, *Gentleman's House*, 376ff.
71 www.abdn.ac.uk/scottskinner/display.php?ID=JSS0038 (accessed January 2018).
72 Kerr, *Gentleman's House*, 57.
73 Ibid., 57.
74 Ibid., 51.
75 Antonio Pereira, Nuno Oliveira and Ana Oliveira Martins, *Park and Palace of Pena, Parques-Sintra- Monte da Lua* (Sintra, 2016), 15–20.
76 www.wikiwand.com/en/Talk:Alatskivi_Castle (accessed January 2018).

77 NAS GD 112/39/416/5; Tyrrell, 'Little Trip', 47–73.
78 Gifford, *Highland and Islands*, 570–77.
79 Hunterian Collection, Glasgow, GLAHA 42038.
80 Jill Allibone, *Anthony Salvin: Pioneer of Gothic Revival Architecture* (Cambridge: Lutterworth, 1987), 48–52; N. Pevsner, J. Harris and N. Antram, *The Buildings of England: Lincolnshire* (London: Penguin, 1989), 362–7; G. Rowlands, *Harlaxton Manor* (1984), 157.
81 *ODNB*, vol. 8, 400–402.
82 Gifford, *Fife*, 338 and plate 79.
83 Presumed to be the otherwise meaningless 'Currattis' in Bryce's obituary.
84 NRS GD 413/23/3; GD 152/57/1/22.
85 Gifford, *Fife*, 221–5.
86 NRS GD 152/58/2/2-3x.
87 NRS GD 152/53/6/28; GD 152/58/2/2-3.
88 NRS GD 152/58/5/34-35x; GD 152/53/4/26/18.
89 Gifford, *Highland and Islands*, 446–7.
90 https://canmore.org.uk/site/12662/redcastle https://en.wikipedia.org/wiki/Hugh_Duncan_Baillie http://www.histparl.ac.uk/volume/1820-1832/member/baillie-hugh-1777-1866 (accessed January 2018).
91 www.ucl.ac.uk/lbs/person/view/29829 (accessed January 2018).
92 Gifford, *Highland and Islands*, 360.
93 Valerie Fiddes and Alistair Rowan, *Mr David Bryce* (Edinburgh: University of Edinburgh, 1976), 20.
94 A plan classification is argued for in Fiddes, *Bryce*, 87–91.
95 John Gifford, 'From Blair Castle to Atholl House to Blair Castle', in Dakin, *Castle Culture,* 240–54.
96 Billings, vol. 4 (Udny).
97 *The Builder*, 26 April 1856; Fiddes, *Bryce*, 125 and plates 41–4, 73–4.
98 *ODNB*, vol. 10, 193–4.
99 www.scottisharchitects.org.uk/architect_full.php?id=100014 (accessed January 2018).
100 Cruft, *Borders*, 110–12; *Gentleman's Magazine* (1840), 222. http://heritagearchives.rbs.com/people/list/gilbert-innes.html (accessed January 2018).
101 Kerr, *Gentleman's House*, 58–9, plate xx.
102 Frank A. Walker and Fiona Sinclair, *North Clyde Estuary* (Edinburgh: RIAS, 1992), 96.
103 Ibid., 51–2.
104 Gifford, *Highland and Islands*, 84.
105 Morton, *Unionist Nationalism,* 132–54.
106 Ibid., 147–8.
107 Kidd, 'Race'.
108 *Descriptive Catalogue of Statuary from the Chisel of Mr Robert Forrest*, 3rd edn (Edinburgh: Thomas Allan, 1835), 19.
109 *Some Records of the Origin and Progress of the National Wallace Monument Movement. Initiated at Glasgow in March, 1856* (Glasgow: privately printed, 1880), 5.
110 Morton, *Unionist Nationalism,* 177.
111 James Coleman, 'Unionist Nationalism in Stone', in *The Wallace Book*, ed. Edward Cowan (Edinburgh: Birlinn, 2012); Helen Smailes, 'A Pride of

Lions: Nöel-Paton and the National Wallace Monument', *Architectural Heritage*, xxv (2014); 85–106; Colin Kidd, 'The English Cult of Wallace and the Blending of Nineteenth Century Britain', in Cowan, *Wallace Book*, 136–50.
112 *Some Records*, 16.
113 Roger Fulford (ed.), *Dearest Mama. Letters between Queen Victoria and the Crown Princess of Prussia, 1861–1864* (London: Evans Brothers, 1968), 177.
114 NRS GD 224/666/3; GD 224/1040/42; *Catalogue of Designs for the Scottish National Memorial to H R H The Prince Consort* (Edinburgh: December 1864).
115 A close-up version of the design is displayed in the Argyll Tower, Edinburgh Castle.
116 NRHE SC 684876.
117 NRS RHP94324.
118 *Illustrated London News*, xlv (July–December 1864), 9 July 1864, 256.
119 *Builder*, 25 April 1858, xvi.
120 RCAHMS, *Aberdeen on Record* (Edinburgh: Stationery Office, 1997), 11, 36–8.
121 Fiddes, *Bryce*, 99–100.
122 Gifford, *Edinburgh*, 259–60.
123 *ODNB*, vol. 19, 455.
124 *Illustrated London News*, xlv (July–December 1864), 9 July 1864, 46.
125 Fiddes, *Bryce*, 94 and plates 49–50.
126 *Building Chronicle*, 9 November 1854.
127 Gifford, *Edinburgh*, 192.
128 Ibid., 233.
129 Ibid., 237.
130 A. MacPherson (ed.), *Report of a Committee of the Working Classes of Edinburgh* (Edinburgh, 1860).
131 Billings, *Baronial*, vol. 1 (Aberdeen).
132 F. A. Walker, 'National Romanticism and the Architecture of the City', in *Perspectives of the Scottish City*, ed. George Gordon (Aberdeen: Aberdeen University Press, 1985), 149.
133 *Prospectus of the Edinburgh High Street & Railway Station Access, and Sanitary Improvement Company* (n.p., n.d.).
134 William Chambers, *Improved Dwelling-Houses for the Humbler and Other Classes: Based on the Scottish Dwelling-House System* (London: W. and R. Chambers, 1855), 6.
135 Ibid., 8.
136 www.scottisharchitects.org.uk/building_full.php?id=206155 (accessed January 2018).
137 Walker, 'National Romanticism', 151.
138 Gifford, *Edinburgh*, 178–9.
139 Ibid., 499.
140 John Cumming, *Salvation: A Sermon, Preached in the Parish Church of Crathie, Balmoral, before Her Majesty the Queen, Sunday, September 22, 1850* (London: Arthur Hall, Virtue, 1850).
141 Gifford, *Edinburgh*, 84–5.

142 Ibid., 179, 196; M. Glendinning (ed.), *The Architecture of Scottish Government* (Dundee: Dundee University Press, 2004), 211–22.
143 David Thomson, *The Works of the late Charles Wilson*, Glasgow Philosophical Society, paper 13 (March 1882), 9.
144 Richard M. Hoe, *Catalogue of the Library of Richard M Hoe* (New York: privately printed, 1878).
145 Loudon, *Encyclopaedia*, 884–90.
146 http://scottisharchitects.org.uk/architect_full.php?id=203213
147 http://scottisharchitects.org.uk/architect_full.php?id=203451
148 http://scottisharchitects.org.uk/architect_full.php?id=202790
149 http://scottisharchitects.org.uk/architect_full.php?id=203010
150 https://builtindunedin.com/2013/01/05/david-ross/
151 https://builtindunedin.com/page/5/
152 http://bannermancastle.org/island-history.html
153 http://lenoxhistory.org/tag/blantyre/
154 www.hudsonvalleyruins.org/yasinsac/irvington/richmondhill.html
155 https://en.wikipedia.org/wiki/Ch%C3%A2teau_Frontenac
156 www.scottisharchitects.org.uk/architect_full.php?id=200587 (all accessed January 2018).

Chapter 9

1 Lord Rosebery, *The Union of England and Scotland: An Inaugural Address Delivered at the Opening of the Session of the Edinburgh Philosophical Institution, 1871–72* (Edinburgh: Edmonstone and Douglas, 1871), 30–31.
2 Peter Savage, *Lorimer and the Edinburgh Craft Designers* (Edinburgh: Paul Harris, 1980), 20.
3 Charles Rennie Mackintosh, *Charles Rennie Mackintosh: The Architectural Papers*, ed. Pamela Robertson (Wedlebury: Hunterian Museum, 1990), 50–51.
4 cat.nls.uk/vwebv/holdingsInfo?searchId=2228&recCount=25&recPointer=5&bibId=2752925 (accessed January 2018).
5 James Joseph Coleman, 'The Double-Life of the Scottish Past: Discourses of Commemoration in Nineteenth-Century Scotland' (PhD diss., University of Glasgow, 2005), 111.
6 cat.nls.uk/vwebv/search?searchType=7&searchId=1635&maxResultsPerPage=25&recCount=25&rec Pointer=0&resultPointer=0&headingId=7273636 (accessed January 2018); Catriona MacDonald, 'Andrew Lang and Scottish Historiography: Taking on Tradition', *SHR*, xciv (October 2015), 207.
7 T. D. Wanliss, *The Bars to British Unity, or, A Plea for National Sentiment* (Edinburgh: Paterson, 1885), viii.
8 Charles Waddie, *An Inquiry into the Principles of National and Local Self-Government. By Thistledown* (Edinburgh, 1885), 3, 10.
9 Beatrice Webb, 'Diary of Beatrice Webb', typescript vols 13–16, p. 500. http://digital.library.lse.ac.uk/objects/lse:wip502kaf/read/single#page/500/mode/2up (accessed January 2018).
10 W. H. Fitchett, *Wellington's Men* (London: Smith Elder, 1900), 238.

11 Graeme Morton, 'Scotland Is Britain: The Union and Unionist-Nationalism, 1807–1907', *Journal of Irish and Scottish Studies*, 1(2); *Unions: Past-Present-Future* (Aberdeen, 2008), 127–8.
12 https://archive.org/details/thistlescottishp01edin (accessed January 2018).
13 *The Thistle*, 15 (October 1909), 2–3, 232.
14 http://hansard.millbanksystems.com/commons/1914/may/15/government-of-scotland-bill#S5CV0062P0_19140515_HOC_91 (accessed January 2018).
15 R. S. Lorimer, 1894, cited in Savage, *Lorimer*, 113.
16 Ibid., 20.
17 NLS ms 50.3.9, p. 76.
18 Jill Allibone, *George Devey Architect, 1820–1886* (Cambridge: Lutterworth, 1991), 167.
19 *British Architect*, 6 December 1907; *National Association for the Advancement of Art* (1889), 363.
20 Gifford, *Perth & Kinross*, 675.
21 *National Association for the Advancement of Art*, 149–55; foreword to Billings, *Baronial*, vol. 1 (1901 edition).
22 James Nicoll (ed.), *Domestic Architecture in Scotland: Illustrations of Scottish Domestic Work of Recent Years* (Aberdeen: Daily Journal Offices, 1908).
23 Ibid., xv.
24 Ibid., xviii.
25 Ibid., xviii–xix.
26 Harriet Richardson, 'Lorimer's Castle Restorations', in *Architectural Heritage, iii, The Age of Mackintosh* (Edinburgh, 1992), 69.
27 Savage, *Lorimer*, 20 and 92; *British Architect*, 20 April 1900.
28 Savage, *Lorimer*, 65, 83; Lindsay MacBeth, 'The Nuremberg Twist and the Amsterdam Swing', in *Scotland and Europe: Architecture and Design 1850–1940*, ed. J. Frew and D. Jones (St Andrews: University of St Andrews, 1991), 41–51.
29 *Architectural Review* (November 1899); Savage, *Lorimer*, 51.
30 NRS GD1/1419/4.
31 Gifford, *Perth and Kinross*, 373–5; NRS GD57/1/306.
32 Britta Ansen, 'On One of Donald Currie's Ships' (2014). www.slideshare.net/BrittaAnson/anson-colloquium-jan-28–2014 (accessed January 2018).
33 Gifford, *Perth & Kinross*, 404–5.
34 Ibid., 373.
35 Ian Gordon Lindsay, *The Cathedrals of Scotland* (London: W. and R. Chambers, 1926), 85.
36 James Joseph Coleman, 'The Double-Life of the Scottish Past: Discourses of Commemoration in Nineteenth-Century Scotland' (PhD thesis, University of Glasgow, December 2005), 107.
37 Coleman, 'Discourses', 105–9.
38 https://canmore.org.uk/site/125427/aberdeen-rosemount-viaduct-wallace-statue (accessed January 2018).
39 *ODNB*, vol. 45, 370–83. https://en.wikisource.org/wiki/1911_Encyclop%C3%A6dia_Britannica/Rosebery,_Archibald_Philip_Primrose,_5th_Earl_of (accessed January 2018).
40 Lord Rosebery, *The Union of England and Scotland: An Inaugural Address Delivered at the Opening of the Session of the Edinburgh Philosophical Institution, 1871–72* (Edinburgh: Edmonston and Douglas, 1871), 30–31.

41 Lord Rosebery, *Address on the 'Union Jack'* (Edinburgh, 1911), unpaginated.
42 Robert Marquis of Crewe, *Lord Rosebery* (London: J. Muray, 1931), 545.
43 Ibid., 545n.
44 NRHE MLD/190/6-8 & /9-11.
45 Colin McWilliam, *The Buildings of Scotland: Lothian* (Harmondsworth: Penguin, 1978), 93.
46 NRHE WLD/45/ 27-40.
47 Hugo Arnot, *The History of Edinburgh, from the Earliest Accounts, to the Year 1780* (Edinburgh: Thomas Turnbull, 1816), 235.
48 *ODNB*, vol. 51, 80-82.
49 Walker, *Aberdeenshire*, 635.
50 Gifford, *Highland and Islands*, 245.
51 Savage, *Lorimer*, 22.
52 Ibid., 56ff.
53 Ibid., 94ff.
54 Richardson, 'Lorimer's Restorations', 71.
55 Savage, *Lorimer*, 115.
56 Anne Riches, 'The Architect's House and the Search for a "National Style"', in Gow, *Scottish Country Houses*, 325.
57 J. J. Stevenson, *House Architecture*, 2 vols (London: MacMillan, 1880), vol. 1, 377.
58 *Builders' Journal*, 12 January 1898, 487.
59 William S. Murphy, *Captains of Industry* (Glasgow: William Murphy, 1901), 217-21; W. Hamish Fraser and Irene Maver (eds), *Glasgow 1830-1912* (Manchester: Manchester University Press, 1996), 412.
60 Robertson, *Mackintosh*, 196.
61 Ibid., 50-51.
62 MacGibbon, *Castellated and Domestic*, vol. 2, 133.
63 Charles McKean et al., *Central Glasgow* (Edinburgh: RIAS, 1989), 196.
64 www.scottisharchitects.org.uk/architect_full.php?id=200735 (accessed January 2018).
65 Gifford, *Highland and Islands*, 192-3.
66 Gifford, *Dumfries and Galloway*, 543.
67 John Gifford and Frank Arneil Walker, *The Buildings of Scotland: Stirling and Central Scotland* (New Haven: Yale University Press, 2002), 122-4.
68 Robert Morris, 'Edinburgh Castle and the Remaking of Medieval Edinburgh', in Dakin, Castle Culture, 266-78.
69 Iain Anderson, 'Duart and Eilean Donan Castles', in Dakin, *Castle Culture*, 280-96.
70 John MacCormick, *The Island of Mull* (Glasgow: A. Maclaren, 1923), 117-18.
71 Gifford, *Highland and Islands*, 156-7.
72 Ibid., 161-2.
73 *Harrow Memorials of the Great War: April 11th, 1917, to April 10th 1918*, vol. 5 (Harrow School: Philip Lee Warner, 1920), unpaginated. www.archive.org/stream/harrowmemorialso05warn/harrowmemorialso05warn_djvu.txt (accessed January 2018).
74 NRS HH1/1131.
75 Ibid.

76 W. T. Oldrieve, 'What HM Office of Works Is Doing for the Historical Buildings in Scotland', *Journal of the RIBA*, xiii(17) (London, 1906), 463.
77 Ibid., 475, fig. 16.
78 Miles Glendinning, *The Conservation Movement* (Abingdon: Routledge, 2013), 168–79.
79 *Scottish Geographical Magazine* (September/October 1919).
80 National Association for the Advancement of Art, *Transactions* (1890), 20.
81 R. L. Stevenson, *Edinburgh – Picturesque Notes* (London: Seeley, 1903), 13, 70, 78.
82 John Hay Athole Macdonald, *Incongruity and Disfigurement in Edinburgh and Elsewhere: an Address Delivered to the Edinburgh Architectural Association, 4th November 1907* (Edinburgh: Edinburgh Architectural Association, 1907), 10.
83 Gifford, *Edinburgh*, 229–30.
84 Ibid., 178–9.
85 Ibid., 231–2.
86 *The Centenary of the Scotsman 1817–1917* (Edinburgh: J. Ritchie, 1917), 34–5.
87 Gifford, *Edinburgh*, 393–7.
88 Ruth Clayton Windscheffel, 'Gladstone and Scott: Family, Identity and Nation', *SHR*, lxxxvi (April 2007), 69–95.
89 NRS RHP141886.
90 Rev. William Wood Seymour, *The Cross in Tradition, History, and Art* (New York: G. P. Putnam, 1898), 313–14.
91 Frank Arneil Walker, *The South Clyde Estuary* (Edinburgh: RIAS, 1986), 52. www.scottisharchitects.org.uk/building_full.php?id=211236 (accessed January 2018).
92 *Evergreen* (Spring 1895); *National Association for the Advancement of Art*, 307.
93 *National Association for the Advancement of Art*, 301.
94 Ibid., 307.
95 Margo Johnston, 'Ramsay Garden, Edinburgh', *Architectural Heritage*, xvi (1989), 3–19.
96 Andrew Landale Drummond, *The Church Architecture of Protestantism* (Edinburgh: T&T Clark, 1934), 88.
97 Walker, *Argyll and Bute*, 475; Cruft, *Borders*, 616.
98 Gifford, *Perth & Kinross*, 586–7; Haynes, *Perth & Kinross*, 27–8.
99 Walker, *South Clyde Estuary*, 16.
100 Walker, *Aberdeenshire*, 693, plate 48.
101 Jacques, *Falkirk*, 119.
102 Ibid., 58.
103 David MacGibbon and Thomas Ross, *The Ecclesiastical Architecture of Scotland*, 3 vols (Edinburgh: David Douglas, 1896–7), vol. 1, 79; 174ff.
104 William Chambers, *Story of St. Giles' Cathedral Church, Edinburgh* (Edinburgh: W&R Chambers, 1879), 25.
105 Ibid., 26–8.
106 Ibid., lxvii.
107 Rosalind K. Marshall, *St Giles': The Dramatic Story of a Great Church and Its People* (Edinburgh: St Andrew Press, 2009), 144.

108 Gifford, *Edinburgh*, 106, 114–15; Marshall, *St Giles'*, 117ff.
109 *The Thistle Chapel within St Giles' Cathedral* (Edinburgh: Order of the Thistle, 2009).
110 W. B. Bruce, *Dunblane Cathedral* (Glasgow: Robert Maclehose [c. 1895]), 9–10.
111 Gifford, *Highland and Islands*, 612.
112 Rt. Rev Kenneth MacKenzie, Lord Bishop of Argyll and the Isles, 'Some Churches of a West Highland Diocese', *Transactions of the Scottish Ecclesiological Society* (1920), 51–7.
113 www.scottisharchitects.org.uk/building_full.php?id=201152 (accessed January 2018).
114 Gifford, *Edinburgh*, 283–4; R. Anderson, *Examples of the Municipal, Commercial and Street Architecture of France and Italy from the 12th to the 15th Century/ Measured and Drawn by R. Anderson* (London: W MacKenzie, 1870–75); Helen Smailes, *A Portrait Gallery for Scotland* (Edinburgh: SNPG, 1985); Duncan Thomson, *A History of the Scottish National Portrait Gallery* (Edinburgh: SNPG, 2011), plates 17 and 21.
115 Hew Strachan, 'Scotland's Military Identity', *SHR*, lxxxv (October 2006), 328.

Chapter 10

1 Agnes Mure Mackenzie, *Scotland in Modern Times* (London: W & R Chambers, 1941), 376.
2 *QRIAS*, 38 (1932).
3 *RIAS Review of Scottish Architecture* (1992).
4 Glendinning, *History*, 385.
5 Henry R. Kerr, *Edinburgh Architectural Association Transactions*, 10 (1933); Sir J. Stirling-Maxwell, *Shrines and Homes of Scotland* (London: Alexander Maclehose, 1937), 205; *QRIAS*, 38 (1932).
6 *QRIAS*, 31 (1929).
7 *QRIAS*, 38 (1932).
8 *QRIAS*, 51 (1935); Juliette MacDonald, 'Let Us Now Praise Famous Men', *Journal of Design History*, 14(2) (2001), 117–28.
9 Mackenzie, *Scotland in Modern Times*, 1, 3, 386, 380, 383; interview by M. Glendinning with R Cant, 1991.
10 The Scotsman, *New Scotland* (1958); *The Builder*, 30 November 1956; 31 October 1952; 4 May 1956.
11 See, for example, J. Steel Maitland, *QRIAS* (August 1952); R. Hurd, *QRIAS* (July 1939), 11–17; R. Hurd, in London Scots Self-Government Committee, *New Scotland* (1942).
12 *QRIAS*, 49 (1935).
13 *QRIAS*, 44 (1933); 52 (1936); 62 (1939); 65 (1946).
14 *Scottish Geographical Magazine* (September/October 1919).
15 Stirling-Maxwell, *Shrines and Homes*, 210; Lord Bute, *A Plea for Scotland's Architectural Heritage* (Edinburgh: NTS, 1936).

16 London Scots Self-Government Committee, *New Scotland* (1942); Town Planning Institute, *Report of St Andrews Summer School* (1941); *The Builder*, 15 February 1952.
17 National Trust for Scotland, *Newsletter* 14, April 1956, p. 11; *Edinburgh Architectural Association Yearbook*, 3 (1959); *The Builder*, 1 August 1952, 7 December 1951, 20 June 1952 and 15 February 1952.
18 *QRIAS* (February 1953); *The Builder*, 12 December 1952.
19 Department of Health for Scotland, *Notes for Guidance of Investigators* (1948) (text by I. G. Lindsay).
20 A. Reiach and R. Hurd, *Building Scotland: A Cautionary Guide* (Edinburgh: Saltire Society, 1941).
21 Royal Fine Art Commission for Scotland, 'Minds Meeting' seminar, 1993: lecture by Sir Anthony Wheeler; *Scottish Field*, April 1967.
22 *Prospect*, February 1956.
23 Royal Fine Art Commission, 'Minds Meeting', seminar by Bill Gillespie, 17 August 1995.
24 *Edinburgh Architectural Association Yearbook* (1968), 101–2; *Building*, 25 August 1967.
25 *The Architect* (May 1974).
26 *Scottish Review* (August 1982). The term derives from Fife's East Neuk, famed for its 'vernacular' villages.
27 See, e.g., Paulo Portoghesi, *Postmodern* (New York: Rizzoli, 1983).
28 Letter from C. McKean to M. Glendinning, 1995; RIAS, *Scottish Architecture in the Nineteen-Eighties* (1987); *Scottish Review* (August 1982).
29 C. McKean, 'Local Roots and the Revival Cycle', *Royal Society of Arts Journal* (January 1987); *Scotsman*, 19 April 1993, 11; RIAS, *Scottish Architecture*, 1; Glendinning, *History*, 491.
30 Ibid., 485–8.
31 *Prospect* (Summer 1988 and Spring 1990).
32 *Scotsman*, 11 April 1994.
33 See, e.g., Charles McKean, *The Scottish Chateau* (Stroud: Sutton, 2001); 'Finnart's Platt', *Architectural Heritage*, 2 (1991), 3–17; 'Hamilton of Finnart', *History Today*, 43(1) (January 1993); 'The Scottishness of Scottish Architecture', in *Scotland: A Concise Cultural History*, ed. P. H. Scott (Edinburgh: Mainstream, 1993).
34 D. Walker, 'The Adaptation and Restoration of Tower Houses', in *Restoring Scotland's Castles*, ed. R. Clow (Glasgow: John Smith, 2000), 1–29; D. McCrone and A. Morris, *Scottish Elites*, ed. T. M. Devine (Edinburgh: John Donald, 1994), 171; N. Fairbairn, *Scottish Field*, September 1985, 39.
35 The story of this unique movement of individual, private restorations was traced in two unpublished government reports of 1982–5: David Walker, 'The Restoration of Ruined Castles', January 1982, Scottish Development Department paper, revised 1985 (courtesy of D. Walker); see also R. Fawcett, 'The Portfolio of Monuments within the Estate: The Inspectorate View', Scottish Development Department paper, 1991; Bruce Walker, *Scots Magazine* (February 1982); E. W. Proudfoot (ed.), *Ancient Monuments, Historic Buildings and Planning*, CBA Scotland Occasional Papers No. 1 (1984); Clow, *Castles*, 161–92; Walker, 'Restoration of Ruined Castles'; R. Fawcett and A.

Rutherford, *Renewed Life for Scotland's Castles* (York: Council for British Archaeology, 2011); H. Fenwick, *Scots Magazine* (July 1979).
36 McKean letter to M. Glendinning, 1995.
37 *Prospect*, 42 (1990).
38 Royal Fine Art Commission for Scotland, 1994 Festival exhibition: caption.
39 Miles Glendinning and Aonghus MacKechnie, *Scottish Architecture* (London: Thames and Hudson, 2004), 211.
40 Glendinning, *Scottish Architecture*, 211–12.
41 F. Massad and A. G. Yeste, *Enric Miralles, Metamorfosi del Paesaggio* (Turin: Test & Immagine, 2004); see also Miralles display panels, June 1998 exhibition, Museum of Scotland.
42 *Evening News*, 29 February 2000; M. Glendinning, *Architecture's Evil Empire* (London: Reaktion, 2010), 130.
43 *El Croquis* (January 2009), 39.
44 G. Murray, *Prospect* (September/October 2000).
45 Glendinning, *Architecture's Evil Empire*, 127–33.

INDEX

Note: *Italic* page numbers refer to figures.

Abbey Craig: *see* National Wallace Monument
Abbotsford House 140–5, *141*, *144*, 155, 183
Abercromby, Sir Robert 156
Aberdeen 114, 129, 138, 160, 172, 211
Aberdeen, County and Municipal Buildings ('Town House') *190*, 192
Acheson House 39
Adair, Sir Robert 200
Adam, James 96–7, 102, *103*, 104, *107*
Adam, John 96, 102, *103*
Adam, Robert 3, 94, 96–8, 100, 102, 104, 106, *107*, 108, 109, *109*, 110, 111, 120, *121*, 157
Adam, William 70, 79, *80*, 81, 96
Airthrey Castle 120
Aitken, G. S. 166
Albany Street Chapel 128
Albert Institute in Dundee 197
Albert Memorial 187, *187*
Albert, Prince Consort 168, 173, *174*, 175, 185, 187, 188
Alexander III 13
Alexander, Sir Anthony 29
Alexander, John 52
Alexander, Sir William 29, 39
Alloa House 75
'alteration of the government' 66–7
Amisfield Tower 37
Amsterdam Town Hall 47
Ancient Monuments Act, 1882 207
Anderson, Sir Robert Rowand 3, 205–7, 209, 213, 220, 222, 226, 228, *229*
Anderson, Sir James 183
Anglo-Norman castle 106
Anna, Queen 21–3
Annandale, Earl of 30

Aray Bridge 102, 112
Archangel Michael statue 237
architecture of theatre 54–9
Ardblair castle 220
Arden House 183
Argyll, 2nd Duke of 83–4
Argyll, 3rd Duke of 70, 84–6, 100, 102, 112
Argyll, 9th Earl of 65
Argyll, Marquis of 45, 226
Argyll Lodging 65–6
Argyll Tower (Edinburgh Castle) 218
Armadale Castle 127
Arthur, King 10
Arts Tower (Edinburgh) 242
Atholl Palace Hotel 207
Atkinson, William 126, 127, *141*, 142, 143–4
Auchans ('Mannor House') 78
Auchenbothie 216
Auchendennan 183
Auchmacoy 175
Auckland 199
Auld Alliance 181
Ayton 183

Baberton House (formerly Kilbaberton) 64
Baillie, Hugh Duncan 178
Balcaskie House 60, *65*, 79
Balfour Castle 178
Balfour, Arthur 134
Balfour, David 178
Balfour, James 147
Ballarat 199
Ballencrieff 32
Ballikinrain 180
Ballindalloch gatehouse 183

Balloch Castle 126, 127
Ballymena Castle 200
Balmanno 208
Balmoral Castle 143, 169, 172–6, *174*, 188
Bannerman Castle 199
Bannockburn Day 1856 185
Bannockburn, Battle of 10, 16, 119
Banqueting House 27, 41
Barbour, James 218
Barcelona, Santa Caterina Market 251
barmkin 19
Barnbougle Castle 108, 211, *212*, 218
Barnton castle 120
Baronial and Ecclesiastical Antiquities of Scotland (Billings) 165
Baron's Hall (Taymouth) 123
Barry, Charles 140, 150, 175, *176*
Battle of Bothwell Bridge 51
Baxter, John 100, *101*, 110
Bayne, James 61
The Beacon 146
Bear Gates 75
Beattie, James 94
Beattie, W. H. 182
Beauly Castle 108
Beauly Priory 170
Beauly River 168
Beauties of Scotland (Forsyth) 161
Begg, Ian 240, *240*
Begg, John 234
Ben Alvie, Kinrara 117
Bernasconi, Francis 123
Bethune, Sir Henry Lindsay 149
Beveridge, Thomas 226
Big Ben 176, 183
Billings, Robert W. 40, 163–201
Black, Alexander 157
Blair Castle (Blair Atholl) 46, 180, *181*
Blair-Oliphant, Philip Laurence Kington 220
Blairvadach 183
Blanc, Hippolyte 188, 218, 224
Blantyre Castle (Massachussets) 199
Blickling Hall 155, 157
Blore, Edward 125, 143–4
Boece, Hector 10, 15
Bog-of-Gight 46
Bolsover Little Castle 29

Boleyn ('Bullen'), Anna 153
Bonaly Castle 151
Bonaly Tower *152*
Book of Kings 23
Borthwick Hall 195
Boru, Brian 130
Bothwell Bridge, Battle of 51
Bothwell Castle (Haddington) 150
Bothwell Castle (Lanarkshire) 11, *13*
Bothwell, Earl of 21, 150
Bourhouse 147
Bower, Walter 10
Bowie, John M. 218
Boyd, John 43
Boyd, Thomas 61
Boyle, David 76
Branxholm Tower 98
Brisbane House 79
British classicism 73–9
British Parliament House 97
Britton, John 123
The Broad Stone of Honour (Digby) 140
Brodick Castle 179
Brodie, William 187
Broughton Place 235, *235*, 238
Brown, Michael 5
Bruce, Edward 29
Bruce, Sir Michael 149
Bruce, Sir William 51, 63, *64*, 74, 213
Bryce, David 2, 3, 99, 121, 147, 149, 162, 165, 176–82, *181*, 182–4, *187*, *193*, 208
Buccleuch, Duke of 136, 146
Buchanan Castle 143
Buchanan, Robertson 199
Buckingham Palace 168
Building Chronicle 192
The Buildings of Scotland 4, 241
Bullen (Boleyn) Anna 153
Bunchrew House 30
Burn, Robert 108, 111, 114, 115, *116*, 145
Burn, William 3, 117, 126, 131, 134, 140, *141*, 145–9, 168, 172, 176–82
Burnet, J. J. 183, 191, 219, 224
Burns, William 184
Burton, John Hill 160, 165
Butter, Archibald 148

: INDEX

Caerlaverock Castle 11, *12*
Callendar House 183
Calton Hill 115, 217
Calvert, Edward 197
Cameron Barracks 217
Cameron, Thomas Bedford 199
Campbell, Alexander 120
Campbell, Colen 73, 74
Campbell, Colin 32
Campbell, Dougal 86, 87, 97
Campbell, Sir Duncan 19
Campbell, Emma 138
Campbell, Ian 5
Campbell, J. A. 218
Campbell, John 79, 81, 84, 199
Candacraig 156
Canna 225
Canongate Kirk 71
Canongate Tolbooth 240
Cant, Ronald 4
Capper, Henbest 224
Cardonell, Adam de 161
Carlyle, Alexander 114
Carmichael, John 45
Carnasserie 66
Carnegie, Andrew 183, 210
Carnegie, James 182
Carnegie, Sir David 122
Carruthers, W. L. 220
Carsewell, John 21
Carson, Graham 246
Carstairs 146
Carter, John 95
Cassilis House 177
castellated architecture 9–10
   castles and palaces 10–18
   from 'court style' to classicism 20–3
   Gothic Revival 120–8
   post-reformation dispersion of 18–20
The Castellated Architecture of
   Aberdeenshire (Leith Hay) 160
Castellated Mansions of Scotland
   (Hullmandel) 160
Castle Esplanade (Edinburgh) 224
Castle Forbes 127
Castle Fraser 31, 33, 35, 36, 156, 179, 180, 183, 191, 200
Castle Gogar 38
Castle Grant 79, 99, 183

Castle Huntly 99, *99*
Castle Menzies 19, 31, 149, 178
Castle Newe 156
The Castle of Otranto (Walpole) 96
Castle Street 177, 188
Castle Stuart 30, 31, 219
Castle Toward 155
Castle Wemyss 176
Castlemilk 180
Catholicism 197
Cawdor Castle 32, 62
Celtic Revival 225
Cessnock Castle 214
Chalmers, Peter MacGregor 207, 228
Chambers, Robert 226
Chambers, William 195
Chantrey, Francis 138
Chapel Royal 22–4, 81, 130, 131
Charles, 8th Lord Kinnaird 127
Charles I 16, 25, 27, 43, 45
Charles II 45, 47, 50–2, 62, 66
Charles Edward Stuart, Prince 95, 136
Charleville Castle 130, 199
Charleville, Earl of 130
Charlotte Square 187
Chartism 171
Château Frontenac 199
Chessel's Court 240, *240*
Chronica Gentis Scotorum
   (Fordun) 10
City Improvement programme
   (Edinburgh) 193–7
Clan Menzies 169
Clartyhole/ Clarty Hole 141, 142
Claypotts 20
Clayton Tunnel 193
Cleland, David Scales 160
Clerk, Sir John, of Penicuik 81
Clow, Alexander 226
Clow, William 226
Clunas, David 195
Cluny Crichton 63
Coats Memorial Baptist Church 224
Cockburn Castle 151
Cockburn, Henry, Lord 138, 151
Cockburn Street (Edinburgh) 194–5, *196*
Coll-Earn, Auchterarder 208

Commissioners of Supply 164
Cookson, J. E. 117
Copley, John Singleton 120
Corbett, A. Cameron 214
Cortachy Castle 182
Cottingham, Lewis Nockalls 161
County Down 199
court architecture, under regnal union 25–6
  descent into chaos 44–6
  episcopacy 43–4
  houses and civic projects 38–43
  political context 26–7
  royal architecture 27–30
courtier castles 54–9
Cousin, David 160, 195, 198
Covenanting movement 51
Craig, Sir William Gibson 147
Craigcrook 150, 181
Craigends 180
Craighall Castle 77, 77
Craigievar Castle 33, 34
Craigmillar Castle 57, 64
Craigston 35
Crathes Castle 138
Craven, Lord 161
Crawford Priory 127
Crichton Castle 21
Crichton House 62
Crofters' Act of 1886 218
Cromwell, Oliver 45, 66
Crosby Hall 169
Crown Street Project 249
Cruden, Stewart 5
Culloden Pillar 94, 138
Culross Abbey House 29, 35
Culzean Castle 109, 110
Cumming, John 197
Cunningham, Sir David, of Robertland 23, 27
Cunninghame, Alexander 180
Currie, Sir Donald, of Garth and Glenlyon 209
Currie, John, of Elie 208–9
Czartoryska, Izabela 145

Daily Review 194
Dalcross Castle 30, 220
Dalhousie Castle 149
Dalkeith Palace 70, 74, 136, 146, 149
Dalmeny House 126, *211*, 212
Dalmore 214, 216
Dalquharran 108
Dalrymple, Sir John 96
Dalzell House 176
Darnaway Castle 122, *123*
Dauphin 18
David I 10
David II 11–12
David's Tower (Edinburgh Castle) 11, 12, 23
Davis, Michael 5
Dean Village 222, 223
Dervaig 225
Deuchars, Louis 226
Devey, George 206
Dick, Sir James 63
Dictionary of Scottish Architects 5
Digby, Kenelm Henry 140
Dollman, Francis T. 165, 166, 188, *189*
Domestic Architecture in Scotland (Nicoll) 207, 209, 213
Donaldson, T. L. 146
Donaldson's Hospital 153, *154*, 179
Douglas Castle 102, *103*
Douglas, Sir James, of Kelhead 77
Douglas, John 75
Douglas, William 57
Doune Castle 218
Downton Castle 96
Drum Castle 35
Drumlanrig Castle 57, *59*
Drummond Castle 66
Dryburgh 185
Duart Castle 46, 72, 218, 219
Dublin Castle 130
Dufftown, Clock Tower 157
Dumfries 190
Dunbar Castle 169
Dunbar fishermen's housing scheme 241, *242*
Dunbar House (Berwick) 29, 38
Dunbar, John 4
Dunblane Cathedral 228
Dundas, Henry 102, 113, 129
Dundonald 199
Dunedin 199, 200
Dunfermline Palace 21, 27, 190, 225

Dunkeld Cathedral 210
Dunlop House 155
Dunlop, Sir John 155
Dunn, W. 209
Dunnikier House 77
Dunnottar 46
Dunrobin Castle 143, 150, 175, *176*
Duns Castle 110;
  Pavilion Lodge 110–11
Dunstaffnage 66
Dunsterfield, George 54
Duntreath 213
Duntrune Castle 129
Duntulm Castle 98
Dupplin 146

Earlshall 208
ecclesiastical architecture 224–30
Edinburgh Castle 12, 21, 27, 29, 33, 38, 47, 112, 118, 128, 136, *137*, 139, 146, 147, 157, 165, 187, *187*, 188, *189*, 193–7
Edinburgh Courant 194
Edinburgh Improvement Act 150, 157, 194, 224
Edinburgh Railway Station Access Act, 1853 194
Edinburgh Review 150
Edinburgh Royal Infirmary 191
Edward, Alexander 75
Edward III 168
Edward VII 205
Eglinton Castle 120, 161
Eglinton Tournament 161, 168
Eilean Donan Castle 218, 219, *219*, 246
Eizat, Alexander 51
Elcho Castle 20, *21*, 31
Elizabeth I, Queen 18, 130
Elizabethan Hall 172
Elliot, James 122
Ellon Castle 110
Elphinstone, John 42
Emmerson, Roger 248
episcopacy 43–4, 226
Episcopal Church 228
Episcopalianism 197
Erik Rosenkrantz Tower (Bergen) 19
Erskine House 126, 141
Erskine, John 75

Eschwege, Baron Wilhelm Ludwig von 175
Esplanade (Edinburgh) *137*
Ewing, James 155
Ewing, Sir Archibald Orr 180

Fairbairn, Sir Nicholas 246
Falkland Palace 27, 51, 236
Faraday, Michael 160
Faskally 148
Fentoun, Thomas Viscount 33
Ferdinand II, King 175
Ferguson, Robert 138
Fetteresso Church 128
Fettes College 182, 192, *193*
Fettes, Sir William 178, 192
Findlay, J. R. 222, 228
Finlarig 46
Finlay, Kirkman 155
Fitchett, W. H. 204
Flemish style 157
Floors Castle 151, *153*
Fonthill Abbey 177
Forbes, Lord 127
Forbes, Duncan 73
Forbes, Robert 95
Forbes, William (Craigievar) 33
Forbes, William, of Leslie 62
Ford Castle 161
Ford House 63
Forglen 156, 175
Forsyth, Robert 118, 161
Fort George 97
Fort William 73
Forter Castle 246
Fortingall Village 209
Fotheringay 145
Francois I 16
Francois II 18
Fraser, John 45
Fraser, Sir Simon 30
Frederick, King 22
Free Church 197, 198
French Revolution 113–15, 169
Fyvie Castle 21, 22, 100, 180
Fyvie-style arch 27, 30, 35, 36

Gallery House 64
Gate lodges 183

Geddes, Patrick 197, 204, 222, 223
George, 3rd Earl of Winton 39
George Heriot's Hospital 40, *41*, 47, 57, 150, 151, 157
George III 117
George IV 117, 120, 135, 136, *137*, 139, 140
George IV Bridge 138, 194
Gibb, Sir Alexander *239*
Gibbs, James 70, 73, 74, 79, 83
Gifford, John 4
Giles, James 160, 169
Gilmour, Sir John 57
Gilmour, William Ewing 218
Gladstone, W. E. 223
Glamis Castle 57, *58*
Glasgow 76–7
Glasgow College 43, 51, 61–2, 188, 191
Glasgow Corporation 205
Glasgow Green 185
Glasgow Herald building 216
Glasgow Tolbooth (1626) 16
Glasgow University 197
Glenapp 180
Glenborrodale 213
Glencoe House 213
Glengarry Castle 99
Glenlyon House 209, 210
The Glen 180
Goethe, Johann Wolfgang von 97
Gordon Castle 100, *101*
Gordon, George 169
Gordon, Sir Robert 172
Gospoole, John 38
Gothic Revival 120–8, 139, 197
Gothic, rise of 79–83
Gothic style 154
government architecture 70–3
Grabowski, Michal 145
Graham, James Gillespie 120, 127, 154, 155, 158, 169, *170*, 179, 183, 192, 198, 226
Graham, John, of Claverhouse 70
Grange 150
Grangemouth 224
Gray, Anne 99
Gray, Thomas 96
Great Hall (Stirling) 16, 129, 166; (Edinburgh) 218

Great Reform Act (1832) 138
Greenock Sheriff Courthouse 191
Greenshields, John 148
Grey, Earl 138

Half-Moon Battery (Edinburgh Castle) 12, 136
Hall, Sir James, of Dunglass 124, 135
Halmyre, Walter Murray of 72
Ham House 84
Hamilton Palace 74
Hamilton, David 127, 155, *156*, 183
Hamilton, Malcolm 36
Hamilton, Thomas 139, 157, 194
Hardwick Hall 96
Harlaxton Manor 177
harling 209–20
Hartrigge 180
Hastie, Robert 77
Hatton Castle 62
Hatton Lodging: *see* Queensberry House
Hawick Tower 98, 190
Hay, Andrew Leith 160
Hay, D. R. 143–4
Hay, Robert 110
Hay, William 127, 226
Hayes, Joseph 226
Heiton, Andrew 182, 183, 207
Helensburgh 208
Henderson, John 157, 195
Henry Frederick, Prince, 23
Henry, J. M. 98, 182
Henry VIII 130, 153
Herder, Johann Gottfried 82
Heriot, George 38, 57
Highland Railway main line 193
Highland Society of London 134
Highlandism 1, 134, 136, 169, 171
Hill House 216, *217*
Hill, John 73
Hillslap Tower *247*, *248*
The Historic Architecture of Scotland (Dunbar) 4
Hoe, Richard M. 199
Hogg, James 118, 135
Hole, William 228
Holland House 154
Holy Roman Empire 16

Holyrood Abbey Kirk 27, 28, 52, 119–20, 158, 226
Holyrood Park 187
Holyroodhouse, Palace of 12, 18, 27, 51–52, 71, 72, 112, 135, 136, 139, 145
  rebuilding of 50–4, 52, *53*
Home Rule 204–5
Home, Sir George 29
Home, Patrick, of Billie 106
Honeyman, John 216
Hope, Sir Alexander 146
Hope-Scott, Charlotte 145
Hopetoun House 136
Hopetoun, Earl of 146
Houlbert, John 54
House of Falkland 178
Houses of Parliament 183
Howard, Deborah 5
Howie, John 95
Hübsch, Heinrich 140
Hullmandel, Charles Joseph 160
Hume Castle 106
Hume, David 94
Huntly Castle *32*, 35, 100, 180
Huntly, Marquis of 117
Hurd, Robert 240, *240*
Hydro-Electric Board 238

Iconic Modernism 249–52
iconography 175
Imperial Parliament 205
Imperial Scotch 214
imperial symbolism 13, 16
Imperialism 204–5
Inglis, Robert 61
Institute for Women in Alexandria 218
interwar traditionalism 234–41
Inventory series (RCAHMS) 4
Inveraray 97, 102
Inveraray Castle 61, 83–9, *84*, *87*, *88*, 106
Invergarry Castle 60, 99
Inverness Castle 127, 157
Iona Abbey 228
Ireland 130–1
Irvine, Alexander 35
Irving, Washington 142
Ivanhoe (Scott) 139, 155

Jacobite Minstrelsy (1829) 134
Jacobite Relics of Scotland (Hogg) 134
Jacobitism 94
James I 16, 23
James II 12
James III 14–16
James IV 16, 17, *17*
James V 12, 16–18, 27, 52, 54, 234
James VI 18, 21–3, 25–7, 30, 43, 46, 113, 145, 155, 211
James VII 47, 50, 51, 66
Jardine, Sir Robert 180
Jeffrey 138, 150, 151
John of Fordun 10
Johnston, Francis 130
Jones, Inigo 41, 74, 150

Kay, J. Sandyford 225
Keiss 181
Keith Marischal 216
Kelburn Castle 76, *76*
Kellie Castle *20*, 33, 208
Kelly, Thomas 26
Kelso Abbey 135
Kelvin Stevenson Memorial 224
Kemp, George Meikle 158, *159*
Kennedy, John 71
Kensington Gardens 138
Kent, William 83
Keppie, John 216
Kerr, Andrew 218
Kerr, Robert 167, 173, 174, 201
Kilbaberton House (now Baberton) 64
Kilconquhar Castle 149
Kildalton House 204
Kilmaron Castle 120
Kilravock Castle 62
Kinfauns Castle *128*, 141
King Edward Memorial 214
King's College, Aberdeen 15, *15*
King's Manor, York 27
Kinnaird 122, 182
Kinnear, Charles 182
Kinneil House 61
Kinnordy 208
Kinpurnie Castle 213
Kinross House 52, 63–5, *64*
Kirkland, Alexander 199
Kirkpatrick, Charles 139

Kirkpatrick, Sir Thomas 62
Klenze, Leo von 115
Knight, Richard Payne 96

Ladykirk House 177
Laing, Alexander 122, *123*
Lamb's House (Leith) 39
Lanark, statue of William Wallace 185
Lanci, Francis Maria 145
Langholm Castle 98
Langley, Batty 82–3
Lanyon and Lynn 200
Larnach Castle 200
Lauder, Sir Thomas Dick, of Fountainhall 150, 168
Lauriston Castle 143, 147, 150, 192
Lawson, Robert 200
Le Corbusier 251
Leiper, William 208, 216
Leithen Lodge 213
Lennox Castle 155, *156*
Leny 181
Leopold, Prince 135, 169
Leslie Castle *60*, 62–3
Leslie, George 71
Leslie, John 55
Leslie, William *176*
Lessels, John 195
Leven, Earl of 74
Levenford House 183
Lewis, Sir Frederick 120
Lickleyhead 33
Lindsay, Ian 238–40
Linlithgow Palace 16, *28*, 40, 57, 129, 210, 220
Little Houses programme 240
Lizars, W. H. *137*
Loch Fyne 214
Loch Leven 213
Loch Lomond 126
Lochbuie House 98
Lockerbie 190
Lockhart, James 77
Lockhart, John Gibson 148
Lockhart, Sir Charles 154
Lockhart, William 148
London, Houses of Parliament 140
Longford, Earl of 131
Longcroft 214, *215*

Lorimer, R. S. *20*, 188, 205, 207–9, 213, 214, 222, 226, 227, 235, 237, *237*
    Scottish National War Memorial 234
Lorne, Marquis of 206, 221
Lossiemouth 224
Loudon, J. C. 199
Louis XIV 155
Louise, Princess 206
Ludwig II of Bavaria 175
Ludwig, King 115
Luffness House 146
Lugar, Robert 126
Lumsden, Sir James 183
Lynch, Michael 5
Lynn (Lanyon and Lynn) 200

MacAlpine, James 220
MacAuley 155
MacColla, Alasdair 45
MacDonald, Alan 5
MacDonald, Lord 127
MacDonald, Sir Alexander 98
Macdonald, Sir John Hay Athole 221
MacDonell of Glengarry 60
MacGibbon, David 206
MacIan of Glencoe 73
McGill, Alexander 73, 75, 78, 85
MacGregor, Rob Roy 143
MacKay, Angus 138, 171
McKean, Charles 4, 243–5
Mackenzie, Agnes Mure 238
MacKenzie, Alexander 108
MacKenzie, John 171, 178
MacKenzie, Marshall 182
MacKenzie, Sir George 78
Mackenzie, Thomas 183
Mackintosh, C. R. 216–17, *217*, 222
MacLaren, James 209, 216
    Stirling High School 210
MacLean, Sir Fitzroy 219
McLeish, Henry 251
Maconochie, Alexander 151
MacPherson, James 97–8, 205
MacRae-Gilstrap, John 218
McWilliam, Colin 4, 243
Macharioch House 206
Madeline, daughter of Francois I 16
Madras College (St Andrews) 157
Mair, John 18

INDEX 293

Maitland, John 51, 55
Malcolm, Neil 128
Manchester Town Hall 197
Manueline architecture 175
Marie de Guise 16
Markree Castle 131
Marmion (Scott) 151
Mar, Regent Earl of 20
Mar, Sixth and Eleventh Earl of 75
Mar's Wark 23–4
Marten, Moses 16
martial independence 9–24
Martin, Theodore 171
Marwick, Thomas 197
Mary I 18, 50–4, 96, 112, 130, 145, 150, 172
Mason, Roger 5
Matheson, Alexander 167
Matthew, John F. 188
Matthew, Robert 241
Matthews, James 183
Mauldslie Castle 120, *121*
Maybole 19, 200
Meaden, Henry Anderson 228
Meadowbank House 151
medievalism 174
Melbourne, Lord 157, 168
Melbourne Place 157
Melrose Abbey 142, 145, 158
Melville, Lord 72
Melville Castle 102, *104*, *105*, 112, 123, 130, 136
Melville House 70, 74
Menzies, James 19
Methven 63
Michael Chapel 81, *82*
Michelangelo 21
Midhope Castle 77, *78*
Milton Lockhart 148
Minty, J. Andrew 223
Miralles, Enric *250*, 250–1
Mitchell, Joseph 183, 193
Mitchell, Sydney 3, 207, 210, 213, 220, 222, 224, 226
Mitchell-Innes, Alexander 190
Mitchell-Innes, William 183
Modulor 251
Monck, George 46, 60
Monea Castle 36

Mons Meg 12, 94, 139
Montague, Lord 143
Monteith, Sir Henry 146
Montgomerie, Archibald 161
Montrose, Marquis of 45
Monzie Castle 120, *122*
Moody, Richard 188
Moorish architecture 175
Moray House 39, 62, 146, 223
Morgan Hospital 192
Morham, Robert 182, 195, 226
Morice, David 112
Morocco Land 240
Morris, Roger 86, *88*
Moy Castle 98
Mure, William 108
Murray, Sir Archibald, of Blackbarony 71, 72, 78
Murray, David 126
Murray, Earl of 30
Murray, James 29, 38, 39, 41, 44
Murray, John G. T. 223
Murray, Sir Gideon 32
Murthly Castle 155
Mylne, John 54, 55, 63
Mylne, Robert 51, 63, 73

Nairne, Lord 74
Napier Commission 218
Napier, Francis, Lord 218
Napier, Robert 183
Napoleon 97, 115, 120
Nash, John 155
Nasmyth, Alexander 111, 115
National Association for the Vindication of Scottish Rights (NAVSR) 164, 204
National Monument project (Calton Hill) 139
National Museum 228
National Trust for Scotland (NTS) 239
National Wallace Monument 118, 184–93, 185, *186*, 187, 198
Neale, J. P. 154
Neidpath Castle 59, 61, *61*
Nelson Monument (Edinburgh) 115, *116*, 117
neo-Gothic 197
neo-Palladianism 74, 81

neo-Romanesque 81
Newark Castle 214, 222, 223
Newton Hall 177
Nichol, John 61
Nicholson, George 32
Nicholson, Robert 32
Nicoll, James 199, 207, 209, 213
Nicolson, Robert 62
Nightingale, Florence 191
Noble, Sir Andrew 214
North British Review 185
Nyrop, Martin 229

Old Town 193–7, 220–4
Oldrieve, W. T. 217, 220
Ormiston Hall 178
Ossian 97–100
Outlook Tower 194
Oxenfoord Castle 96

Palazzo Senatorio 66
Palladianism 79, 134
Pallas Armata (Kelly) 27
Panmure House 63
Park Row Building (New York) 199
Parliament Close 66
Parliament House (Edinburgh) 41, 42, 47
parliamentary union 73–9
Paterson, A. N. 214, *215*, 218
Paterson, George 99
Paterson, John 94, 99, *99*, 108, 120, *122*, *124*, 128
Paterson, Robert 199
Patrick, Earl of Strathmore 57
Pearce, Dinah 223
Pearce Institute 223
Peddie & Kinnear 187, 188, *190*, 191, 194
Peel, Robert 175
Perth 182
Petticrew, John 51
Philip II 30
Philip 'the Good,' 12
Philippa, Queen 168
Picturesque Antiquities of Scotland (de Cardonell) 161
Pinkie 147, 208, 213
Pirie, J. B. 182

Pitlochry Dam and Power Station 238, *239*
Pitreavie Castle 38, *39*
Place Royale 66
Playfair, James *99*, 100, 102, *104*, *105*, 122, 128
Playfair, W. H. 149–53, *152–4*, 157, 179, 183
Port Edgar 136
Porta Pia 21
Porter, Jane 118
Pratt, Samuel 161, 172
pre-Gothic-style churches 228
Presbyterian kirk 197
Presbyterianism 49, 226
Preston Tower 38
Prestonfield House 63, 64
Prestongrange 150
Privy Council 26, 49–50, 55, 57
proto-Romanticism 52
The Provincial Antiquities and Picturesque Scenery of Scotland (Scott & Turner) 160
Pugin, A. W. N. 140, 155, 165, *170*

Quarterly Review 150
Queen Margaret's College 216–17
Queen Mary's Houses 52
Queen Victoria Memorial School, Dunblane 218
Queen's House (Greenwich) 41
Queensberry Aisle 81
Queensberry House 65, 73, 74, 251
Queensberry, Duke of 57, 61

Radical War 113–15
Radicalism 136, 146, 161
Rae-Brown, Colin 185
Raehills House 111, *111*
Ramsay Gardens 224
Ramsay, John 204
Rawlinson, Ralph 33
Redcastle 178
Regent Morton Gate 21, 218
Regent, Prince 135
regnal union, court architecture under 25–6
  descent into chaos 44–6
  episcopacy 43–4

houses and civic projects 38–43
political context 26–7
royal architecture 27–30
Reiach, Alan 241
Reid, Charles (Wardrop and Reid) 212, *212*
Reid, Robert 139
Reid, William 160
Restoration 50–4
reuse 128–30
Rhind, David 190
Rhind, John 226
Rhind, W. Birnie 226
Riccarton House 147
Richardson, H. H. 210
Richardson, J. S. 228
Richmond Hill 199
River Tweed 30
Rizzio, David 52, 104
Robert I 10, 12, 119, *230*
Robertson, Joseph 160
Robertson, Robert Henderson 199
Robertson, W. W. 220
Rochead, J. T. 182, 183, 185, *186*
Rochester 106
Romanticism 1, 2, 54, 94–7
Rose, Hugh 62
Rosebery, 5th Earl of 108, 211, 212, 218
Rosenau Castle 173
Roslin Chapel 123
Ross Priory 127
Ross, David 199
Ross, James 112
Ross, Thomas 206, 220, 226
Rossie Priory 127
Rosyth Castle 187, 212, 220
Rowallan Castle 214
Roy, Nicholas 16
Roy, Rob 143
Royal Deeside 188
Royal Exchange, Dundee 192
Royal Incorporation of Architects in Scotland (RIAS) 243
Royal Infirmary design (Edinburgh) 200
Royal Mile 139
royal visit (1822) 135–40; (1842) 168ff.
Royston 78

rubble 209–20
Rubens 27
Rusco Tower 246
Rutherglen 190

Saltoun Parish Church 128
Salvin, Anthony 177
Samson's Hall 39
Sandon Hall 177
Santa Caterina Market, Barcelona 251
Sauchieburn 213
Saunders, George 126
Scalloway 46
Scandic Crown Hotel 244, *245*
Schaw, William 22, 35
Schilling, Johannes 185
Schultz, R. W. 218
Scotch Baronial style 133, 145–9, 165–8, 173, 187, 193, 198–200, 205–20
Scotichronicon (Bower) 9, 10, 26
Scotophobia 94–7
Scott, Sir Francis, of Thirlestane 72
Scott, Sir G. G. 187, 197
Scott, Sir James 36
Scott, Sir Walter 1, 3, 51, 95, 114–20, 133, 139, 141, *141*, 145, 148, 158, 159–60, 168, 171, 223
Scottish Baronial Castles 1250–1450 (Brown) 5
(Scottish) Calvinist Reformation 44
The Scottish Chiefs (Porter) 118
Scottish Enlightenment 94
Scottish National Portrait Gallery 228, *229*, *230*
Scottish National War Memorial 235, *236*, *237*
Scottish parliament (Holyrood) 249–52, *250*
Scottish Renaissance 2
Seacliff Asylum 200
Seacliffe House 178
Selkirk 190
Seton, Alexander 21
Seton House 108, *109*
Seton, John 30
Seton Palace 39
Seton Tower 180
Shambellie 180, 208
Sharpe, Charles Kirkpatrick 149

Shaw, John 199
Shaw, Richard Norman 222
Shearer, James 238
Sheriff Court Houses (Scotland) Act 1860 190
Sidney, Long Gully Bridge 199
Simpson, Archibald 127, 156
Simpson, William Douglas 5
Sinclair Castle 46
Sir Walter Scott Monument 158, *159*
Skae, David 128
Skelmorlie 31
Skene, James, of Rubislaw 143–4
Skibo Castle 183
Skinner, James Scott 173
Skipness 66
Slade, Harry Gordon 5
Slavery Abolition Act 178
Slighting of castles 128–30
Smirke, Robert *128*
Smith, Donald 213
Smith, George 157
Smith, James 57, 62, 71–3, 75, 78, 81, 85, 183
Smith, John 35, 127, 156, 158, 167, 172, 173, 175
Smith, William 173, *174*
Soane, Sir John 143
Sobieski Stuarts 169
Solomon's Temple 23
Specimens of Old Castellated Houses in Aberdeenshire (Hullmandel) 160
Spence, Basil 235, *235*, 241
Spottiswood, Archbishop John 44
Springfield 160
St Anthony's Loch 172
St Eustache 16
St Fort 146
St Giles project 228
St Giles Street 194
St Giles's Church 226
St Hubertus sculpture 173
St James' Presbyterian Church (Auckland) 199
St Leonard's/Free St Leonard's Church, Perth 224, *225*
St Machar's Cathedral 12, *14*
St Mary's Dundee 16
St Mary's Haddington 16

St Michael's church, Linlithgow 16
St Nicholas Church 125
St Pancras Station 197
St Patrick 130
Starforth, John 167, 199
Stark, William 142, 149
Steell, John 187
Steill, John 210
Stevens, Alexander 111, *111*
Stevenson, D. W. 210
Stevenson, J. J. 214, 224
Stevenson, Robert Louis 221, 223
Stewart Castle 112, 155
Stewart, Charles 74, 117
Stewart, Dame Jean 30
Stewart, David, of Garth 136
Stewart, Margaret 75
Stewart, Sir John 155
Stieglitz, Christian Ludwig 98
Stirling Castle 16, *17*, 27, 76, 166, 176, *186*
Stirling Chapel Royal 5, 46
Stirling Great Hall 16, 212, 129, 166
Stirling Town House 74, 222
Stirling-Maxwell, Sir John 239
Stobs Castle 120
Stolzenfels Castle 140
stone castle-building 11
Stonefield 179
Stormont Castle 199
Stow Town Hall *191*
Strachan, John 20
Strawberry Hill 96, 122, 143–4
Stronvar 181, 208
Stuart, Charles Edward 169
Suttie, Sir George Grant 150
Suttie, Sir James Grant 150

Tabraham, Chris 5
Talbot, Fox 145
Tarbert 66
Tarbolton, H. O. 238, *239*
Taymouth Castle 79, *80*, 123, *124*, *125*, 169, *170*;
 Stuart Tower 171
Temple of Liberty (Stowe) 83
Tennant, Charles 167
Terry, Daniel 143–4
Test Act (1681) 66

Teutonism 134
Thatcher, Margaret 243
The Thistle: A Scottish Patriotic Magazine 205
theatre architecture 54–9
Third Marquis of Bute (1887) 207, 218
Thirlestane Castle 55, *56*
Thistle Chapel 226, *227*, 236
Thom, James 139
Thomson, Alexander 'Greek,' 200
Thomson, David 198
Thomson, Leslie Grahame 235
Thornhill 218
Tippoo Saib 143
Tollcross House 178
Tolquhon 23
Tower Style 126
Trafalgar Day 115, *116*
Tranter, Nigel 5, 246
Traquair House 74, 75, *75*
Triumphal arches 16
Trossachs Hotel 207
Trotter, William 136
Tullynally 130
Turnbull, Thomas 182
Turner, J. M. W. 159–60
Turner, Thomas 200
Tyndall-Bruce, Onesiphorus 178
Tyninghame House 147, *148*

'Unio unionum,' 43
Union of the Crowns (1603) 1, 2
unionist nationalism 1, 5

Vanbrugh, Sir John 85
Vernacular architecture 243
Vernacular modernism 241–9
Vestiarium Scoticum (John Sobieski Stuart) 168
Victoria Hall 158, 198, 200
Victoria, Queen 1, 164, 168, *174*, 175, 226
Victoria Street 158
Victoria Tower 176, 183
Villa d'Este 30
Villers-Côtterets 16

Vitruvius Britannicus (Campbell) 74, 79
Vitruvius Scoticus (Adam) 79
Vogrie House 183

Waddie, Charles 204
Waitt, Richard 79
Walker, Campbell 182
Walker, David 5, 182, 246
Walker, J. C. 190
Wallace Memorial 223
Wallace, Sir William 10, 118, *119*, *230*
Wallace, William 40
Wallyford 64, 65
Walpole, Horace 96
Wanliss, Thomas Drummond 204
Wardlaw, Sir Henry 38
Wardrop, Hew 182, 183, 208, 212
Wardrop and Reid 212, *212*
Waterford, Marquis of 161
Watson, Fiona 5
Watson, George MacKie 219, *219*
Watson, R. 209
Waverley (Scott) 133, 151
Wedderburn 106, *107*
Weisbach, Karl 185
Well Court 222
Wemyss, Charles 248
West Shandon 183
Wester Kames Tower 218
Western Infirmary (Glasgow) 191
Westminster Parliament 79
Westminster Abbey 226
Wheeler, H. Anthony 241
Whittington, George 123
Wilhelm, Friedrich 140
William, King 70, 158
Williams, Alice Meredith 237
Willoughby, Lord 171
Wilson, Charles 183, 190, 198, 213
Wilson, Sydney 213, 222, 226
Windsor Castle 139, 175
Windyhill 216
Winton House 38, *40*
Woolmet 62
Wren, Sir Christopher 81
Wyatville, Jeffrey 139